Canada, 1900–1945

UNIVERSITY OF TORONTO PRESS   Toronto   Buffalo   London

ROBERT BOTHWELL, IAN DRUMMOND, JOHN ENGLISH

Canada, 1900–1945

© University of Toronto Press 1987
Toronto Buffalo London
Reprinted in paperback 1990, 1998, 2003
Printed in Canada

ISBN 0-8020-5690-3 (cloth)
ISBN 0-8020-6801-4 (pbk)

∞

Printed on acid-free paper

Canadian Cataloguing in Publication Data

Bothwell, Robert, 1944–
    Canada, 1900–1945

    Bibliography: p.
    Includes index.
    ISBN 0-8020-5690-3
    ISBN 0-8020-6801-4 pbk.

    1. Canada – History – 1914–1945.   2. Canada –
    History – 1867–1914.   3. Canada – Politics and
    government – 20th century.   4. Canada – Economic
    conditions – 1918–1945.*   5. Canada – Economic
    conditions – 1867–1918.*   I. Drummond, Ian M.,
    1933–   .   II. English, John, 1945–   .
    III. Title.

    FC540.B68 1987   971.06   C87-093264-0
    F1034.B68 1987

To J.W. Pickersgill

Contents

PREFACE   ix

1 Canadians in their Setting   1

2 A Nation and its Parts   25

3 Politics and Political Culture   37

✳ **4** The Great Boom of 1900–13   55

5 Drink, Labour, Public Ownership, and Corruption, 1900–14   85

✳ **6** Canada, the World, and the Empire   107

✳ **7** The Politics of War   119

8 Canada's Army   139

9 The War at Home   153

10 Slump and Boom and Slump Again, 1913–22   169

11 Literacy, Literature, and Education   187

12 The Politics of the 1920s   199

13 The Economy in the 1920s   211

14 Defining Canada and her New Empire, 1917–31   229

15 The Social and Economic Impact of the Depression   245

16 Politics and Policy in the Great Depression   259

17 The Making of Modern Times: Culture and Communications, 1919–39   279

18 The Dominion and the Dictators   295

19 The Politics of War, 1939–45   317

20 Fighting the War   337

21 The War Economy, 1939–45   349

22 The Second World War at Home   375

23 Planning for Reconstruction   389

APPENDIX   399

BIBLIOGRAPHY   401

INDEX   411

Preface

Canada, 1900–1945 is the companion volume to *Canada since 1945: Power, Politics, and Provincialism*. Together, these books provide an economic and social background and a narrative to Canadian history in the twentieth century. In stressing the links among economics, society, and politics, these books may seem to depart from some current themes in modern Canadian historiography. We are writing not only for our colleagues but also for our students and a more general audience. History, in our opinion, fails if it does not reach a large and literate public.

The new social history and the new economic history are not ignored in our book, but to thrust the latest specialized research upon the general audience and our students is professionally self-indulgent and, for most of these readers, exasperating. As Professor Gerald Feldman has recently commented, 'Of course we are all born, live in household and communities, do various things, and die. On what grounds should our students be urged to see themselves as "historical actors" on this account, and to what end should they extend their personal acquaintances in the manner of the "new history"?' We also believe that it is more important for our students and readers to transcend 'everyday life' and recognize how much that life is determined 'by the state and concrete developments in state, economy, and society.' This belief animates our book.

In writing this book we have accumulated many debts. First, we would like to thank Gail Heideman who many times typed and retyped this manuscript. Her patience with us was remarkable; our debt to her is enormous. Virgil Duff encouraged us to write this volume and offered us support at every stage. Rosemary Shipton was, as usual, a splendid editor and a good friend. Irene Knell, Carol Kieswetter, Bruce Uttley, and Dave Bartholomew helped greatly with different stages of the manuscript. Gerard Campbell and Monica Dunn compiled the index and Don Evans devised the cover illustrations. Susanne McAdam and Peter Scaggs similarly handled the mysteries of the computer in publishing. We owe all of the above great thanks, but they should receive none of the blame for any deficiencies in this book.

Canadians in their Setting

When the new century dawned, there was so much that was Canada but so few who were Canadians. The land spread broadly across the North American continent, reaching far beyond the relatively narrow strip along the lakes, the St Lawrence, and the Atlantic coast which had constituted Canada at Confederation. Canadians, however, were sparsely placed upon this enormous land: only 5.4 million of them occupied over three million square miles. Their style of life was very different from that in 1867. The country remained rural, but much less so than before. As a result, Canadians in 1900 were less like each other than they had been. Some dwelt in the fabled Victorian homes, adorned with gables and splendid, well-tended gardens; homes filled with delicate children, pampered cats, and low-paid servants who served capons on Royal Crown Derby as adults in the family sipped Château Margaux in Waterford crystal. Others lived in sod huts, on prairie ground which yielded its fruits grudgingly, and still others lived in slums in Canada's industrial towns and cities.

This variety of experience among Canadians in 1900 makes generalization difficult. Historians and popularizers, following in the fashions of their own times, have tended to focus their attention narrowly, at one moment on the intricate ritual of Victorian high life with its materialistic frenzy, at another on the long working hours and damp bedrooms of the industrial working class. Both settings are easily discovered and, because the images of the rich and poor are so clearly etched in history and literature, they tend to blur the image of how others who were neither plutocrats nor impoverished spent their lives. The 'ordinary Canadian' of 1900 is as mythical a figure as today.

A general study cannot pretend to sketch more than an outline of the diverse experiences of Canadians as the twentieth century began. Nevertheless, the Canadian census of 1901, the increasing range of contemporary research on Canadian 'problems' carried out by churches, government agencies, social commentators, and the burgeoning historical literature dealing with Canada in the late nineteenth and early twentieth century permit us to be more detailed and accurate in our description than is true for historians of most periods.[1] It is appropriate that we begin this sketch of Canadians with the farmer.

A RURAL NATION

Most Canadians in 1900 lived close to the land, but their relationship with the land had changed considerably since Confederation. The self-sufficient farmer of early frontier days had become the specialized producer for broader markets as well as the largest consumer of the increasing variety of goods manufactured in Canada's growing cities. Even in these cities, however, the odours, noises, and mentality of rural life were present. Only two electoral constituencies in Canada did not contain a farm, and Canada's largest cities, Montreal and Toronto, abounded with cows, chickens, and, of course, horses, for in January 1900 not even Sam McLaughlin, the father of the Canadian automobile, had seen a horseless carriage.

Canada, then, was very much a nation where countryside overwhelmed cityscape, with only 34.9 per cent of its population living in urban areas.[2] Over one-third of the workforce was engaged on the farms, and almost 45 per cent were in the primary sector of the economy. The percentage of workers in 1901 in the manufacturing and construction sectors was only 27.9 per cent, actually a lower proportion than in 1881. The growth had occurred in the tertiary sector, a reflection of the greater complexity of the society, not least in the area of food production. By 1900 agriculture had become much more sophisticated, specialized, and successful, and most Canadians could not imagine a future when Canada would not be an agricultural country. The publicity which flooded Europe luring young immigrants to Canada's shores presented the image of a land of sturdy yeomen, prosperous and free. Rural life was said to be a finer life, one fostering good health, moral behaviour, and human charity, items which were lacking in the cities where Mammon and immorality thrived. Even so celebrated an observer of Canada as J.S. Woodsworth idealized rural society. The problem with the modern busi-

---

1 Statistics which follow are drawn from the 1901 census unless otherwise indicated. Where appropriate, F.C. Leacy, ed., *Historical Statistics of Canada* (2nd edition, Ottawa 1983), is followed. We have also used William Marr and Donald Paterson, *Canada: An Economic History* (Toronto 1980).
2 Before 1951 the census defined an urban resident as anyone residing in an incorporated city, town, or village, regardless of size.

nessman, he declared, was that he had moved too far from the communal ties and restraints of rural life, where the young boy 'swam in the village millpond, cut his name in the desks of the little red school-house, and generally lived the all-round democratic life of a farmer's boy.'[3]

A charming vision of equality and simplicity, to be sure, but one of Canada's major problems in 1900 was the existence of too many farmers' boys and girls, especially in central Canada where 71.3 per cent of Canadians lived. Although some publicists in Ontario and Quebec waxed eloquent about the extraordinary agricultural prospects of the 'clay belt' of northern Ontario and northern Quebec, the prospects were really not very bright. Farms along the St Lawrence system were already inconveniently small. In Ontario the 1901 census reported that, on average, a farmer tilled about forty acres. The result was a steady flow of young people from the farm to the city. Even more troubling was the knowledge that many chose not Canadian but American cities. In 1900 there were 1,179,922 Canadian-born living in the United States, a figure equal to 22 per cent of Canada's population. What talents and energies had been lost can only be imagined. Small wonder that the Canadian west, with its abundant free land, was becoming the grand hope for Canada's new century.

On the prairies it was already clear that the future would lie with agriculture – mainly with wheat. Ranching and grazing would develop too, but again there were problems because the local demand was small and the larger markets were thousands of miles away. Admittedly, the progress of settlement had been discouraging since the completion of the CPR. The wheatfields of Manitoba had been opened up through the settlement of émigré Ontarians, but even there, the frontier of wheat production had not been pushed very far to the northwest. And in present-day Saskatchewan and Alberta (then part of the North-West Territories) there had as yet been little settlement.

The weight of Canadian agricultural efforts, like the weight of population, was still concentrated in central Canada. In 1901 half (52.2 per cent) the value of agricultural capital was in Ontario and another quarter (25.9 per cent) in Quebec. In 1900 the two central provinces produced three-quarters (77.7 per cent) of all Canada's agricultural output. The agriculture of central Canada was long-established. Ontario and Quebec farmers had shown an enviable potential for adaptation, having transferred much of their wheat acreage to other uses as new and more attractive possibilities emerged. The cities of the region provided large and growing markets for

3 Quoted in S.D. Clark, *The Social Development of Canada* (Toronto 1942), 452. For contrasting views based on an early 1914 social survey of the Turtle Mountain District of Manitoba see ibid., 448.

meat, dairy products, vegetables, and fruit. There was even a tiny grape and wine industry on the Niagara frontier. The oat-propelled transport system of the farms and cities required plenty of fodder for horses. There were even export markets for Ontario cheddar cheese and butter, which were sent to Britain in enormous quantities, and Ontario pigs, their breeds improved, were turned into bacon for British breakfast tables. Local demand absorbed, indirectly, enormous quantities of grain for brewing and distilling.

In fact, Ontario agriculture and, to a lesser extent, farming in Quebec and the Maritimes, had undergone a successful transformation after Confederation. Central Canadian agriculture in 1867 had been a mixed farming régime with a perceptible concentration on cereal production, but, for various reasons – soil exhaustion, declining and fluctuating prices for the old grain crops, emergence of attractive new markets for other products, and technological progress – Ontario and Quebec had shifted some distance away from wheat production into dairy and livestock. This trend, along with a variety of developments on the prairies – better wheats, more knowledge about dry farming, and much lower transportation costs – meant that wheat production became less significant in central Canada. With fewer workers than would have been needed in 1871, central Canadian farms could now produce more. Not that farms or farmers in central Canada were declining in number: far from it. Between 1871 and 1901 the number of farms in Ontario and Quebec increased by 30 per cent, and the number of farmers and other agricultural workers increased by 29 per cent.[4] At the same time, the average cultivated acreage per farm was rising in central Canada, and mechanization had proceeded apace. Horse-powered farm machinery, which was already widespread in Ontario by 1871, became much more common throughout central Canada, while steam power made a small contribution to ploughing and a larger contribution to threshing; tractors were still unknown, and few farms possessed electricity or any form of mechanical power. Nevertheless, a simple invention, the centrifugal cream separator, had reduced the labour of dairying, shortening the hours which many farm wives gave to the task, just as, in the fields, horse-powered mechanization reduced the drudgery for husbands and sons. At the same time, however, the more intensive cultivation of livestock demanded new sorts of work, and more

4 *Census of Canada, 1870-1*, volume 2, table XIII, and volume 3, table XXI; *Census of Canada, 1901*, volume 2, table XXI; *Census of Canada, 1941*, volume 8, table II. The 1901 data include 'lots' of less than five acres, because such very small holdings were counted as farms in 1871. Even when these lots are deducted, the data still show a sharp increase in the number of 'farms' as defined in either census year. As for occupations, the 1871 data include all members of the 'agricultural class,' and those for 1901 include all 'agricultural occupations' according to the 1941 definitions. There is no doubt that the figures are broadly comparable.

regular and intensive work, from the farm families of Ontario and Quebec.

Many contemporary observers and some later historians wrongly believed that the countryside of central Canada was being depopulated. To some extent these commentators were misled because certain branches of rural industry were declining, or shifting from the country and the small town to the city; they also thought that labour-saving developments in agricultural work must necessarily displace farm labour. Few of them troubled, then or later, to examine the census occupational data or the local patterns of population shifts. One of Canada's early academic social scientists, the political economist O.D. Skelton, described the sources of change as he understood them: 'The inclusion of one farm task after another – weaving, toolmaking, soap-making, slaughtering – in the scope of the urban factory; the improvement of farm methods and farm machinery, making it possible to do the work still left to the farm with fewer hands; the encouragement given the city, as contrasted with the country, by tariff favours; the increasing array of financial and commercial middlemen required as communities became less self-sufficient and more dependent on world-wide exchanges.'[5] Today's historians and economists would mention the same factors when explaining the changing balance between country and town, but in the context that the cities could grow larger without the farm population growing smaller.

In central Canada, farmers were shifting from wheat production towards livestock, dairy products, and the fodder crops on which the livestock lived. Increasingly the population of central Canada would eat western wheat, while absorbing ever larger amounts of local fruit, vegetables, meat, and dairy products. For bacon and cheese, furthermore, export markets had become quite important, although that importance would not continue long into the new century. These developments depended crucially on technological progress – the cream separator, the meatier hog, the refrigerated railway car, and transatlantic steamer. Thus, by the mid-1890s Canada earned more by exporting livestock and dairy products than by selling grain, and, on the other side of the Atlantic, Britain was spending more on overseas meat than on raw cotton. So far as exports were concerned, the great days of the Ontario wheat economy were long in the past, and the prairie wheat boom had only just begun.

Dietary habits were changing in both Britain and Canada, increasing the consumption of meat, butter, and milk. Ordinary people were becoming better off, and technological advances – faster and cheaper transport, refrigeration, pasteurization, dramatic improvement in urban food distribution – made animal products cheaper and safer. The domestic kitchen was

5 O.D. Skelton, 'General Economic History, 1867-1912,' in Adam Shortt and A.G. Doughty, eds., *Canada and Its Provinces,* volume 9 (Toronto 1914), 196

changing too. By 1900 gas and electric cooking was widespread, at least in the cities. Domestic refrigeration still relied upon ice, chiselled from wintry lakes and packed in sawdust for summer use. But canned goods were common, and tinned food often provided a welcome element of variety, even for the poorest.

The changes were not always healthy. Many babies perished in the late nineteenth century as mothers fed them cows' milk from unsterilized bottles rather than their own milk. The tin cans of foodstuffs which proliferated on the shelves of the grocery stores brought a few cases of botulism; more seriously, the fruits and vegetables they contained and preserved were drained of many nutrients. White bread, which had become much cheaper in relation to brown bread because the new technique of 'roller milling' could more expeditiously produce pure white flour, was less nutritious than the bread it displaced. Removing the bran and wheat germ, the millers also took out much of the iron and almost all of the vitamins and 'fibre.' The poor, for whom bread remained a staple, presumably suffered the most. But white bread was fashionable, in part because the prosperous had always eaten it, and no one knew enough about nutrition to worry about the distressing side effects.[6]

Thus city and country relied on one another. Even on the lonely outreaches of the western prairie, farmers were dependent on the external world not only for markets but for supplies and services: tinned food, the ubiquitous railway, telegraph, mail-order catalogue, farm-implement dealer, and, by 1900, a cheap and efficient post provided links that earlier pioneer communities had not possessed. These links provided the tentacles upon which both a national feeling and a national economy could grow.

TRANSPORTATION AND COMMUNICATION

The links had grown quickly in the nineteenth century. In the middle of the century Thomas Keefer, a young engineer, wrote a book called *The Philosophy of Railways* in which he prophesied for his fellow British North Americans that the railway would bring far more than its steel tracks. It would engender a new spirit 'which is not confined to dress and equipage, but is

---

6 On this question see J.C. Drummond, *The Englishman's Food* (London 1957), 297. These changes in diet may have been responsible for serious problems in infant size and infant mortality which appeared in the late nineteenth century in Montreal, and, perhaps, other Canadian cities. On infant size see Patricia and Peter Ward, 'Infant Birth Weight and Nutrition in Industrializing Montreal,' *American Historical Review* 89 (1984): 324-45. It is sometimes suggested that roller milling created a special demand for prairie wheat, but this is not true as the technique could handle any and all sorts of wheat.

rapidly extended to agriculture, roads, and instructive societies.' With a 'restless, rushing assiduity' which waited for no convenient season, the steam miracle would impel the isolated countrymen unconsciously but irresistibly 'to a more intimate union with their fellow men.' By 1900 that more intimate union had come, almost entirely through rail and canal, and Keefer, now Canada's most noted civil engineer, continued to cheer on the 'civilizing' influence. Railways remained at the heart of politics and inspired the wildest flights of the Canadian imagination.

There were few alternatives to rail, and many parts of Canada where railways did not run. Except in central Canada, the railway network was still sketchy, although in most parts of the eastern and western extremities of the country there was little alternative to rail. Nor were there any long-distance pipelines. Motor cars and trucks were few in number, and there was nothing corresponding to a road system; indeed, Ontario's first paved road was fourteen years in the future. In British Columbia the fjords and inlets provided almost all the coastal transport. In central Canada, for part of every year, the Great Lakes and the St Lawrence provided a splendid water-based transport system – a system which moved not only heavy goods such as crude oil, grain, coal, and iron ore, but also passengers: there were regular liners plying the route from Toronto to Montreal, and other liners operated between Georgian Bay and the head of Lake Superior. Much effort had gone into the improvement of the water system, through canal-building at the Soo, Welland, and the St Lawrence between Kingston and Montreal. The season, however, was short. Furthermore, the sizes of the various canal locks were not standardized. The result often was transshipment, with concomitant delay and loss. Ports had been improved to speed and cheapen the import-export trade. In summer, ships came to Montreal; in winter, Canada's Atlantic trade used Saint John, Halifax, and even the city of Portland, Maine, which had a direct rail connection to Montreal. Waterborne transport mattered a lot, but rail transport mattered much more. In the heartland of the dominion, between Sarnia and Rivière-du-Loup, there was a dense network of rail lines, the product of subsidy and competition in the period 1840-1900. Beyond this area, however, the rail lines were few and thin. Westward, the Canadian Pacific stretched out to Vancouver. In Manitoba and the North West Territories there were a few local enterprises and branch lines, to such outposts as Saskatoon and Edmonton. To the north there was nothing – no lines to Hudson Bay or Prince Rupert, no National Transcontinental line through northern Ontario and Quebec. To the Maritimes ran the government-owned Intercolonial, snaking its way through a morass of patronage as far from the American border as it could get. There was also a CPR 'air line' which ran through Maine to Saint John. But much of the country, with the resources it contained, was simply out of reach. The railway was, for many Canadians, a distant dream.

COMMUNICATIONS

Electric communications were in their infancy. Broadcasting had not been invented, and radio was used only for marine signalling. The promise, however, was already there: in 1899 Marconi made radio connections between Britain and France, and in 1901 between Newfoundland and Ireland. At first, radio could not transmit voices; it was little more than a wireless substitute for the telegraph. Naturally, the telegraph itself was widespread in the dominion. The railways relied on it, so that wherever the rails went, the overhead wires went also. Furthermore, in certain directions the telegraph lines went far ahead of the railways – for example, overland to the Yukon gold fields. Submarine cables carried telegraph signals to Britain, Europe, Australia, and the Far East. Messages as well as money could be transmitted by 'telegraphic transfers.' But telegraphy was cumbersome and not inexpensive, depending as it did on a network of skilled operators, receivers, and deliverers of messages. A variant of the telegraph, the ticker tape, connected the North American stock exchanges with one another and with brokers' offices in such cities as Montreal and Toronto. The telephone was beginning to be used in the same way. Since 1880 the Bell Telephone Company of Canada had been constructing its network of long-distance lines. By 1900 southern Ontario and southern Quebec had been wired up. Bell itself provided the long lines and operated the local system in the larger cities and towns, while in many rural areas independent companies, which might or might not be connected to the Bell system, provided service. In the more remote cities of eastern and western Canada telephones existed, but no trans-Canada linkage, and many local telephone systems were not connected to anything or anyone, although roundabout routings through the United States could sometimes be pieced together. Direct distance dialling was impossible; indeed, dial telephones were very rare.

Thus, by 1900 telephone wires were densely threaded along the streets of Canada's cities, intermingling their overhead networks with the rapidly expanding systems of electric delivery. In the 1880s and 1890s electricity had revealed itself as a great boom industry of the future. Horsecar transit systems were converted into electric streetcar lines. Steam generating plants were constructed and the first large hydroelectric stations began to function. By 1900, for instance, although Toronto still depended on thermal electricity, Hamilton and Vancouver were served by hydro power. Some small towns, such as Orillia, opted for publicly owned hydro plants, but, in the larger towns and cities, electricity and electric streetcars were private property. The battles for 'franchises' – permission to operate the systems – could be furious and sometimes corrupt. Where the utilities were unpopular, as in Montreal, the promoters might be forced to put their wires in underground conduits. Where back alleys were available, as in Vancouver, the overhead wires might follow them, avoiding the public roadways. The general tendency, however, was to put the wires where installation was cheapest – on poles along the streets.

Not in rural areas, however. Although rural telephone systems could and did become widespread, because they were powered by magnetos or by batteries, electricity was still a rarity on Canada's farms and in the small villages of the countryside, where kerosene ruled supreme. Admittedly there was a new challenge to this 'coal oil' – acetylene gas, which could be produced in small inexpensive retorts on demand, by applying water to calcium carbide. In 1900 this system was thought to have a bright future: cheap electricity meant cheap carbide, and few people expected that the central generating stations would ever send their power over the countryside.

In cities, electric light competed with manufactured gas, or 'coal gas,' which was extracted from coal in enormous ovens. In parts of southwestern Ontario, furthermore, there was natural gas, and this was used not only in rural areas but in such cities as Hamilton – though not in Toronto.

Railways, canals, telegraphs, telephones, electricity – for lighting, industry, and transport – and, not least, the motorcar, whose number was still few but whose promise seemed great, were the wonders of the age, and their discoveries and builders were much honoured in their time. Knighthoods fell upon them, and so did material rewards. Their homes were models of what modern technology could bring with their telephones, gramophones, central heating, electric stoves and illumination, indoor plumbing, and bric-à-brac accumulated from the many corners of the empire. By 1900 some of these wonders were becoming available to the middle class, although for most workers they remained elusive. Knowledge of these conveniences, however, was widespread because of the great improvements in photography in the later nineteenth century, the growth of advertising and literacy, and the expansion of the press.

Photography moved from the studio and into the streets and countryside in the 1890s with the development of the box camera in 1888 and celluloid film in 1890. By 1900 Eaton's catalogues were advertising box cameras for $5 and 'pocket kodak' films of twelve exposures for twenty-five cents. Snapshots of prairie homesteads, of Sunday outings, and of the new baby now flowed through the mail and became a visual record of individual Canadian lives. By the turn of the century, photographs had begun appearing regularly

TABLE 1
Literacy and Illiteracy

	Per cent of population five years and over		
	Can read and write	Can read only	Cannot read or write
Canada	82.88	2.74	14.38
British Columbia	74.56	0.60	24.84
Ontario	89.78	1.47	8.75
Quebec	77.92	4.37	17.71
Nova Scotia	81.29	4.46	14.25

Source: *Census of Canada 1901*

in newspapers and were a part of a major transformation that took place in the newspapers in the late nineteenth century.

Very simply, there were many more daily newspapers in 1900 than there were in 1880, and they were no longer four pages with few illustrations, straight columns, and little flair. Now, they were twelve pages with blaring headlines and lavish illustrations, abundant and enthusiastic advertisements, and on Saturday they were often accompanied by a colourful supplement. The new popular press relied on widespread basic literacy, cheaper paper, and a public thirst to know about the latest scandal, murder, or mystery. 'What,' the Hamilton *Herald* had asked, 'is a newspaper published for if not to produce a sensation to make an impression upon its readers and the public?'[7] The question was a rhetorical one for the Canadian self-made and self-declared press barons such as Hugh Graham of the *Montreal Star,* Joe Atkinson of the *Toronto Star,* and Trefflé Berthiaume of *La Presse,* whose reporters became sleuths sniffing out the perverse, trivial, and glamorous. These large metropolitan dailies extended their web over the city and into the surrounding countryside. Entertainment took precedence over education, and the stories required little more than basic literacy, a level which most Canadians had obtained by 1901 (see Table 1).

For all readers, the flood of newspapers carried the interests of the readers far beyond the local confines of the small town weekly or daily which now seemed restrained and parochial. 'News' became what it remains today, immediate, cosmopolitan, personalized, and often sensational. Newspapers were less tied to political parties, but, as Graham's *Star* showed in its rau-

---

7   Quoted in Paul Rutherford, *The Making of the Canadian Media* (Toronto 1978), 56

cous 1899 campaign to have Canadians go to war for the empire in South Africa, the political influence of newspapers was greater than ever.

Popular journalism – the 'yellow press' – repelled many Canadians, including the preachers, teachers, and local community leaders who feared this craving for sensation which could also be seen in the music hall, barroom, and new mass sports. Newer, more specialized publications developed to appeal to these arcane interests. Professional groups developed their own publications, in medicine, law, and religion. For the educated, periodicals such as *Queen's Quarterly* surveyed from an august height the political and intellectual currents of the day. Along with the increasing differentiation within local civic cultures there developed a growing specialization which linked Canadians across the country who shared these interests.[8]

In the nineteenth century, men at the top of the occupational structure in American cities were less likely than lower-status workers to move elsewhere. Their local interests were intensive, their ties with one another dense and varied. In the twentieth century the affluent strata of urban society have often become the most transient, and many of those who remain settled in one locality withdraw from active participation in local institutions as their careers and horizons move outward to wider but also more specialized connections. This process was incomplete in 1900, but it had most certainly begun and its consequences were deeply felt.

While isolation and localism were breaking down, knowledge was becoming more specialized and less general. In the field of natural science, for example, the Victorian naturalists who combed and catalogued for the local natural history society gave way to the biologist and anatomist who worked in the university or in the governmnt bureaucracy.[9] Similarly, in fields as different as history and engineering, the amateur was superseded by the professional. Writers often often harked back to what seemed a simpler time where differences were fewer and definitions were easier, yet almost no one believed such times could or should return. There had to be new solutions for new times.

8 The American historian John Higham's description of the differences in this respect between the nineteenth and twentieth century also applies to Canada. See 'Herbert Baxter Adams and the Study of Local History,' *American Historical Review* 89 (Dec. 1984): 1223.
9 See Carl Berger, *Science, God, and Nature in Victorian Canada* (Toronto 1983), 76-7.

ORDERING DISORDER

Nearly all Canadians were of European stock, and they brought to the new world the Christian sense that social order and spiritual belief were symbiotically related. Religious practices and institutions pervaded Canadian life at the beginning of the twentieth century. Nevertheless, the recessional of the sacred was already much advanced as the new century moved towards the secularism which is one of its most distinguishing marks. In 1900 religious observance and discussion continued to occupy an extraordinary amount of Canadians' time, and religious belief much affected what Canadians could read, see, eat, and drink. Church steeples dominated urban architecture and even the rural countryside. Yet most serious religious scholars of the time spoke of a crisis in belief. What were its sources?[10]

First of all, there was science. Science, the Reverend G.J. Low wrote, 'ever adds to her domain.' 'As her empire extends she divides and subdivides her possessions into special sciences which increase and multiply until, today, the number of the various 'ologies seems beyond count.' Science had taken away so many of the mysteries which had traditionally inspired faith. The most dramatic impact came from Darwin's theory of evolution which by 1900 had undermined the nineteenth-century link between natural science and religion. So complete was the victory that evolutionary principles were being extended to the study of society. Second, sociological concerns replaced the theological focus even within the church. For many clergymen and university teachers of theology, the scientific achievements of the 'new age' promised the possibility of building a new heaven upon earth. Their attention fell upon this world, not the next. To many believers, this reductionism seemed to strip the church of its proper function and to define it as part of the world it had once stood beyond. In short, it fell off the pedestal. Third, some individual clergymen and some churches erected barriers against this 'modernism.' Throughout English and French Canada, denunciations of 'liberal' thought and contemporary materialism rung out from pulpits. Books were censored, dancing forbidden, and ostentation ridiculed. But the times made such actions more difficult: streetcars ran to distant dancehalls; printing presses were too common; and wealth came too easily. Finally, urban life seemed to threaten the rural intimacy which had strengthened the church in Canada. The French Catholic church especially feared the impact of urban life upon its flock, but it was not alone among Christian

10 This section relies on Ramsay Cook's valuable *The Regenerators: Social Criticism in Late Victorian English Canada* (Toronto 1985).

TABLE 2
Per Cent of Population in 1901 for each Faith

Roman Catholic	41.51
Methodist	17.07
Presbyterian	15.68
Anglican	12.69
Baptist	5.92
Lutheran	1.72
Others	5.32

churches in seeing the city as the enemy of religious observation. The social differentiation, complexity, sensationalism of the Montreal or Toronto *Star*, extremes of wealth and poverty, commercial greed, squalor of the slums, and social disorganization all presented an enormous challenge to the church – the greatest, it was said, since the schisms of the sixteenth century, and one whose outcome could not be forecast as the twentieth century began.

The church's presence in Canadian life remained overwhelming if we judge by late twentieth-century standards. Nearly all the small universities were church-affiliated, as were a few of the larger ones; religious studies and prayers were included in school curricula; clergymen influenced the public questions of the day, and virtually every Canadian declared his or her attachment to one faith or another. The Roman Catholic church and five Protestant denominations together accounted for over 94 per cent of the population, and only .09 per cent stated no religion (see Table 2).

Leading businessmen, prominent politicians, and even publishers of dubious newspapers attended services every Sunday and frequently went to conferences or meetings where theological questions were debated. The Queen's University's Alumni Conference of 1900, for example, featured lawyers, professors, publicists, and clergymen debating such topics as 'The Gnostics and the Fathers,' 'The Theology of St Paul,' 'The Creation Narratives,' and 'The Relations of Legislation and Morality.' Appeals for political change, such as the women's franchise, prohibition, and even streetcar timetables, were swaddled within religious arguments. All politicians professed faith. Many, however, had great private doubts, not least the nation's best-known Catholic, Prime Minister Wilfrid Laurier, who seemed to accept the church's tradition but not its God. In his person he symbolized the paradox of the times.

THE CITY

Most Canadians in 1900 would also have thought it paradoxical (had they known) that the strongest non-believer in Laurier's cabinet was minister of agriculture Sydney Fisher, for it was the city, not the country, where scepticism and agnosticism were supposed to flourish. The Methodist clergyman J.S. Woodsworth saw the modern city as Sodom, with Mammon as its God. In the modern city, Woodsworth declared, there were no neighbours, only individuals craving sensation and fortune. The city's charms, 'its shopping and concerts and sight-seeing,' were easily found by the occasional visitor from the countryside. But the rural visitor must look further, Woodsworth dourly warned, and if he did, 'The higher the buildings, the less sunshine, the bigger the crowds, the less fresh air ... We become weary in the unceasing rush, and feel utterly lonely in the crowded streets. There comes a wistful longing, for the happy life of "God's-out-of-doors" with the perfume of the flowers and the singing of birds ... As we penetrate more deeply into its life, we discover evils of which we had hardly dreamed. Pitfalls abound on every side; dark crimes are being committed; dreadful tragedies are being enacted in real life. We get behind the scenes; we see the seamy side. We look beneath the glittering surface and shrink back from the hidden depths which the yawning darkness suggests.'[11] This is an extreme reaction, but one which indicates how threatening the city was to one who cherished social order and who idealized rural life.

The cities, to be sure, were confusing. They were growing much too quickly, and sanitation, public services, and housing facilities could not keep up the pace. Montreal had swollen from 155,238 in 1881 to 219,616 in 1891 to 267,730 in 1901. Toronto proportionately grew even faster: 96,196 to 181,215 to 208,040. Vancouver appeared out of nowhere, expanding from 13,709 in 1891 to 42,340 in 1901. Not all cities shared in this rapid expansion. Quebec, Canada's second largest city in 1871 with 59,699 residents, had only 68,840 in 1901. The population of Saint John had in fact fallen from 41,325 in 1871 to 40,711 in 1901. Such cities, however, were the exception and were largely found in the Maritimes where economic opportunities were much fewer than in central Canada and the west.

The cities and towns of Canada were rarely places of physical beauty. The downtowns were a web of overhead wires, strung along a forest of poles. Sometimes the underlying physical structures were improved by the concealment which the wires provided, but rare was the artist who commemorated Canadian city centres. There was almost no control over the uses to

11 J.S. Woodsworth, *My Neighbor* (Toronto 1911), 22

which urban property could be put. Most buildings were still built of wood, although the fires which had been the bane of nineteenth-century Canadian cities were leading to the rapid introduction of new materials, especially steel and concrete, for office buildings. Although some cities, notably Montreal, had parks, avenues, and some distinguished stone buildings, the overall impression left by urban Canada was one of disorder. In Toronto, as in other Ontario cities and towns, there was a solid and ostentatious town hall, a classical revival courthouse, and a couple of firehalls fitfully seeking to emulate Italian villas, but these did little to raise the standards of the cities, or to replace squalor and disorder with dignity and seemliness.

Residential building was mixed. Many Ontarians seemed to like to live in narrow-fronted brick warrens, crammed together on tiny lots. In the 1980s the resultant 'Victorian streetscapes' command a certain sentimental admiration, but in terms of the amenities they offered such streets bore little comparison with contemporary arrangements in New England or the American middle west. Conditions were similar in the smaller cities of Quebec, except that brick was much less common. Only Montreal possessed any quantity of apartment dwellings; everywhere else Canadians lived in single-family houses or in 'doubles' and 'duplexes.' In Halifax and other Maritime centres there were impressive echoes of a more spacious tradition that seemed to come from New England. Halifax had its commons, parks, and open spaces, and Sydney a beautiful harbour setting, soon to be defaced by an ill-located steel mill. Prairie towns were laid out more spaciously than the cities of Ontario, and made some attempt to seize whatever natural advantages they might have. In British Columbia the natural settings overpowered any amount of municipal mismanagement, yet it is depressing to see how little was done to capitalize on the scenery.

It was not, however, the physical appearance of the cities which attracted the critics. Indeed, even Woodsworth could accept that rural folk should admire the block-long department stores of Eaton's or Simpson's in Toronto, the imposing columns of McGill University in Montreal, or the Winnipeg office buildings which commanded a view of the entire city. Rather, it was the moral and physical health of many of the city's inhabitants which was the focus of criticism.

The two largest cities, Montreal and Toronto, attracted the closest scrutiny and the strongest attack. Montreal's flaws were especially well-known because of a pioneering sociological survey carried out in 1896 by a wealthy young Montrealer, H.B. Ames. Ames's report on the St-Antoine and St-Anne wards was published in 1897 as *The City Below the Hill*. In this area of 38,000 people, almost evenly divided among English, Irish, and French, Ames starkly portrayed the extent and conditions of urban poverty. Most of the streets in the area were unpaved, clouds of dirt in summer, seas of mud in spring, and filled with the refuse of human and animal life. Over half the houses were served by the notorious outdoor 'pit privy,'even though these relics were recognized as a serious health hazard. So too were the communal watertaps which many residents still used. Life was precarious in Montreal, especially for the young. Over one-quarter of the newborn died before they lived a year. The percentage was double that of New York and, among large cities in the world, was exceeded only by Calcutta.[12]

Densely crowded together, terrified of disease and its many forms, these Montrealers must have yearned for release which seldom came even for the children. Many found relief in alcohol, for bars abounded in these working-class areas. The tavern became a community centre, offering entertainment, solace, and distraction from a drab existence.[13] It also became a target for reformers, who saw it as a symbol of disorder and of the frivolity which was the enemy of social progress.

By 1900 residents 'above the hill' were well aware that the conditions 'below' might affect the health of the entire city. One result was a move towards regulation and improvement of public health: the banning of pigs and other animals, the development of city sewage systems, and the provision of city water. By 1900 city water, which had first been developed to fight fires, was available in approximately eighty Canadian cities and towns, although not of course in all areas. Churches established missions to provide for the physical and moral health of the 'down and out.' Fresh-air funds were started in the 1880s to take slum children to the countryside in the summer. Temperance crusaders used local option – district plebiscites – to close down tavern after tavern when their attempt to bring in national prohibition failed. The existence of such misery and poverty enabled humanitarians like Woodsworth to tug at the sentimental hearts of the late Victorian age and play upon Christian guilt. The youthful student reporter Mackenzie King came to public attention in Toronto in the mid-1890s with a series of newspaper articles on city 'sweatshops.'

C.S. Clark, a Toronto moral reformer (albeit an eccentric one who wanted to legalize prostitutes so as to drain off the excess sexual energies of Toronto's young men), pointed to another response to urban ills on the part of the more prosperous: segregation. In his ironically titled 1898 study *Of Toronto the Good,* Clark noted the geographical separation of rich and poor:

12 Besides Ames's work, the more recent study by Terry Copp, *The Anatomy of Poverty* (Toronto 1974), is important.
13 For a fascinating description of nineteenth-century tavern life in Montreal see Peter DeLottinville, 'Joe Beef of Montreal: Working-Class Culture and the Tavern, 1869-1889,' *Labour/ Le Travailleur* 819 (autumn/spring 1981-2): 9-40.

'Living in the city is very expensive, the poor are obliged to live in the shaky, tumble-down houses of Centre Elizabeth, South Jarvis and Lombard and Bathurst and some other streets, while the middle classes and those of only moderate means reside in the suburbs, or a considerable distance from the business part of the city. They come down every morning to business in crowds between the hours of seven and nine, and literally pour out of it between the hours of four and seven in the evening.'[14] In smaller cities the separation was not so marked, nor was the streetcar network everywhere so extensive. Yet by the turn of the century even the new cities of the west and the smaller cities of Ontario were becoming more differentiated.

Despite the difficulties, the young flocked to the cities. Clark thought it the goal of 'almost every youth's ambition in the province to become eventually a resident of the Queen city.' Why, in view of the health hazards, noise, apparent immorality, and intense competition, should so many of the young crave urban life? The question was often asked in 1900, but the answer, now as then, cannot be definite. Some factors are well known but nonetheless important: the exhaustion of new good land in central Canada, the large size of rural families, and the opening up of jobs in cities for young women. Contemporary literature indicates that the excitement of the city must have lured many. The city was a continuing spectacle, and its streets bore many parades – of colourful militiamen, Orangemen and their papal foes, circuses, and union members. Grand occasions enlivened urban life, as in Hamilton where for Queen Victoria's Golden Jubilee the Hamilton Philharmonic Society assembled a sixty-piece orchestra and a choir of 1425 to mark the regal event.[15] Conversely, if the city offered more public spectacles, it also offered a privacy which village life made difficult. Woodsworth and others may have idealized rural community, but there is much other testimony to the stifling character of the small village, where outsiders were shunned and moral opprobrium generously dispensed. A medieval saying, *Stadtluft macht frei* (city air brings freedom), still bore a certain truth.

The city at the turn of the century captured far more attention than its numbers merited. After all, in 1900 only 8.86 per cent of Canadians lived in Montreal and Toronto and only 12.24 per cent lived in cities over 50,000. This is hardly what late twentieth-century Canadians would think of as an urban society. Yet the influence of Montreal, Toronto, and other urban centres in 1900 cannot be denied. These cities dominated the flow of information with their publishers and presses; they directed spiritual life; they linked Canadians with intellectual currents flowing through Western socie-

14 C.S. Clark, *Of Toronto the Good* (Montreal 1898), 3
15 See John Weaver, *Hamilton: An Illustrated History* (Toronto 1982), 118ff, for a good description of the riches of cultural and sports life in a moderately sized city.

ty; and they were the testing ground for the exciting ideas and innovations of a new age. The cities, as Clark recognized, were the centres of opportunity. Horatio Alger died in 1899, but his success parables continued to animate young Canadians as well as Americans and to bring them to the great commercial centres. Prime Minister Laurier explained the loss of good men in politics by pointing to the attractions of business. Business was preeminently of the city, and its barons built their castles upon the elegant avenues. In 1900 the farmer may have lived a worthy and relatively prosperous life, but the rewards of status and wealth came to the young men who left the small towns to make their fortunes in the city. They reaped the knighthoods; they compelled attention. Capitalism had come to Canada, and its values were firmly in place.

CAPITALISM

Whatever 'capitalism' might be, it was not new. Nineteenth-century Canada had plenty of rich men, indigenous entrepreneurs, and propertyless wage-earners. In 1900 wealth must have been very unequally distributed, although no one can possibly know the extent of this disparity. Sometimes romantics hark back to a time when Canada, or some region of Canada, was a 'propertyowning democracy.' Although in 1900 some agricultural regions might have given that impression, for the nation as a whole the reality was very different. Nonetheless, wage-earners were still a minority, chiefly because 40 per cent of Canadian workers still laboured in agriculture, where most were self-employed; furthermore, in non-agricultural work, especially in commerce and in small-scale production, self-employment was widespread. But in the larger cities, the typical resident had become a wage-earner by 1900.

Such folk were more dependent on their wage-earnings than earlier generations had been. The crowding in working-class sections of cities meant that gardens disappeared. Health regulations drastically reduced the number of animals that could be kept. Households produced fewer of their own needs, depending on the new factories for more of their clothing and bread products. Bettina Bradbury has concluded that, for the Montreal working class, the means to supplement wage income had almost disappeared by 1900, so that wage dependence was virtually complete.[16] Yet in other cities many wage-earners owned their own homes, and filled the spare rooms with boarders. Savings deposits, especially in the government's postal savings system, were far from uncommon. Private charity, largely operated through the

16 Bettina Bradbury, 'Pigs, Cows, and Boarders: Non-Wage Forms of Survival among Montreal Families, 1861-1891,' *Labour/Le Travailleur* 14 (fall 1984): 13

churches, provided some protection against the uncertainties that came from wage dependence and from the swings of the business cycle. Various factory acts prevented the worst abuses of child and female labour, while public health acts had begun to be passed. Yet the state's defensive structure was exceedingly primitive by modern standards, and, as labour historians have emphasized, certain traditional craft protections were dissolving in the factories that the industrial capitalists operated.

Some economic historians have wondered whether Canada's capitalism was genuinely Canadian, or whether it was simply an importation of foreign capital: Canadian capitalism as opposed to capitalism in Canada. The question arises because, already by 1900, there were American branch plants in Canadian industry. Their number would increase in the coming decades. But there were plenty of Canadian-owned businesses too, and these showed a healthy vitality both then and later. Furthermore, after the hectic growth of the Great Boom, 1900-13, the Canadian economy seems to have saved more than enough to provide for all the new plant, equipment, inventories, and housing that the economy was accumulating – not in every year, but taking one year with another. Why then would anyone think that Canadian capitalism was not a locally grown plant?

The main reason is that from 1900 to 1945 Canada contained a great and growing number of American-owned and British-owned businesses, especially in manufacturing and in the extractive industries. Some Marxist observers believe that the mere presence of such firms indicates some defect in the development of Canadian capitalism. They argue or imply that if the capitalist system had grown 'naturally' there would have been a fully autonomous Canadian capitalist class to exploit all available investment opportunities within the dominion. The presence of non-Canadian capitalists is therefore thought to be symptomatic of a distortion in the Canadian economic system, such that the capitalists were unable to come to their full natural flowering – the indigenous control of the national economy. One such distortion, according to some observers, is an excessive interest in finance and the import-export trade, so that Canada's capitalists were unwilling to switch into the 'industrial capitalism' of city, mine, and factory. Further, it is suggested, Canadian banks and other financial institutions were unduly conservative and risk-averse, diverting the flow of funds into 'safe' channels and denying finance to nascent miners and industrialists. The field would thereby be left open for the British or American capitalist who could come to Canada, bring capital and expertise with him, and occupy industrial fields which could and should have been occupied by Canada's own industrial capitalists – if only our capitalists had spotted the opportunities, or if only our banks had been sufficiently willing to lend.

If the Canadian capitalists had really been like this, the characteristics would have been obvious in 1900. But the more we learn about Canadian economic history, the more distorted this view comes to appear. First, Canadian financial institutions were by no means averse to risk, whatever their leaders might find it prudent to say. Many very risky loans were made and many industrialists were floated off, directly or indirectly, by bank finance, while others did well out of the money of the insurance companies. Second, there was plenty of indigenous 'industrial capitalism,' and plenty of profit which could finance its expansion. It is simply not true that all, or most, of the new firms in industry and mining were foreign promotions, however 'foreign' may be defined. And defining the 'foreign capitalist' is no small problem, because so many energetic folk came to Canada from Britain and the United States, founding Canadian busineses and making their careers in the dominion. Consider John Northway, who came from Britain, settled in a small town as a dry-goods merchant, and later built up a large business both as department store owner and as clothing manufacturer.[17] Or consider Messrs Goldie and McCulloch, who came from Scotland to Galt in 1844. Starting in a small way, they gradually built up a large foundry and engineering business which was, by 1900, an important producer of steam engines and other complex machinery. These individuals are Canadian industrial capitalists – regardless of birthplace.

No doubt banks sometimes overestimated the riskiness of particular projects; probably some businessmen did not get the finance they wanted on the terms they were willing to accept; it would be surprising if there had been no deficiencies of vision, such that foreigners seized oportunities which Canadian businessmen could just as well have taken up. But the same could be said of any modern industrial state.

Canada was different from other countries because, first of all, she had common citizenship through the British connection in a much larger international entity, the British empire. Second, because her majority language was English, her economy was open to external penetration both by Americans and Britons. Third, because her legal system was familiar and her laws were properly enforced, British and American businessmen felt comfortable in Canada – far more than in, for instance, Mexico or Russia. Finally, she was a small economy with an immense territory offering great profit potential to the skilful entrepreneur, whether that person sought profit from current production or capital gain from speculation and promotion. It was the combination of these circumstances, and especially the potential for profit, which produced Canada's characteristic mixture of resident and external owner-

17 See Alan Wilson, *John Northway: A Blue Serge Canadian* (Toronto 1965).

ship and control of capitalist business, in manufacturing, the extractive industries, and public utilities and transport.

It used to be thought that in the history of Canadian capitalism, Quebec was somehow 'different.' Observers noted the special respect which the clergy received, the particular role which the church played in the shaping and leading of society, the anti-capitalist and pro-agrarian ideology which the church was believed to espouse. Observers also noticed that in Quebec the large firms tended to be owned by anglophones or foreigners, while francophone businesses were generally small, partly because the church and the learned professions attracted many young men of talent. Nevertheless, the actual course of capitalist development in Quebec was not much different from in Ontario. Because industry meant good and regular jobs, the church was anxious to encourage its development, especially in rural areas and smaller towns. The path of urbanization and the rate of industrial growth was much the same in Quebec as in Ontario. It is true that the proletariat was disproportionately francophone and the capitalist group disproportionately anglophone. But there were plenty of poor anglophone wage earners, especially among the Irish, and plenty of small francophone capitalists. Quebec capitalism is odd chiefly because the great firms in industry, finance, and the utilities were overwhelmingly 'anglo.'[18]

In Ontario, as in Quebec, the churches were full of anti-capitalist and anti-urban ideology. Methodists such as Woodsworth and Presbyterians such as Charles Gordon worried lest their flocks be dispersed and corrupted in the wicked cities: to ministers the rural life of the farmer and small artisan appeared to be more 'natural.' With the settlement of the West and the export of Protestant missionary ministers to prairie manses, this anti-urban ideology was exported too; by the early 1920s it was helping to shape prairie populism, and it provided much of the driving force behind the urban reform movements from Winnipeg to Vancouver. Yet no one would call Ontario and western Canada un-capitalist or anti-capitalist.

The inhabitants of the Maritimes worshipped in the same churches as the 'upper Canadians' and in all likelihood heard similar sermons. Given Maritime circumstances, the most important virtue to preach about would have been the virtue of thrift. Although Maritime economic evolution diverged from that of Canada as a whole, this divergence can be exaggerated. Between 1900 and 1914 there was considerable industrial development in northern Nova Scotia especially on Cape Breton Island, while in Halifax

18 See W.F. Ryan, *The Clergy and Economic Growth, 1896-1914* (Quebec 1966), André Raynauld et al., *Croissance et structures économiques de la Province de Québec* (Quebec 1961), and René Durocher and Paul-André Linteau, *Le 'Retard' économique et l'infériorité économique des Canadiens français* (Montreal 1971).

there was a small but active and well-connected financial centre. Capitalism, whether industrial or financial, was alive in the Maritimes, though development was slower and much more uneven. What had gone wrong?

This question has perplexed economic historians of the Maritime provinces for at least two generations, yet there is no agreement on the answer. It has long been clear that Maritime capitalists did not manage to make the transition from a maritime economy of wood and sail to a seagoing economy of iron, steel, and steam. At Confederation, Maritime merchants were still prospering in the Atlantic carrying trades; by 1900 these trades had dwindled almost to nothing in spite of the immense contemporary increase in the volume of transatlantic cargo. It has been suggested that Maritime capitalists were too readily attracted by the National Policy tariff of 1879, placing their funds in factories, especially textile mills, which they did not know how to run. Failing in textiles, they were then too impoverished to try anything else. Another suggestion related to the accidental and unintentional 'pumping out of surplus' from the Maritimes by central Canada. After Confederation this process might be imagined to occur in at least two ways. First, thanks to the dominion's protective tariff, central Canadian manufacturers could make profits by selling in the Maritimes, while Maritime manufacturers were not so successful in central Canada; profits, therefore, would in a sense flow west. Second, as branch banking spread through the Maritimes and as local banks established better connections with larger financial centres, local savings might have been mobilized and made available for lending outside the region while national branch bank systems might be unresponsive to Maritime needs. Both developments probably happened; neither, taken by itself, really explains very much. Two questions remain: Why were Maritime factories less able to win external markets? And why did the banks not find enough willing borrowers within the Maritimes?

The answer to both questions probably lies in the interregional and international movement of labour. Talented businessmen could and did leave the Maritimes in considerable number. They might have done well in Pictou, Summerside, or Moncton, but in Montreal, Hamilton, or Boston they expected to do better. If so, the Maritimes must have suffered from a steady draining-away of entrepreneurial talent, leaving, on the average, badly managed factories and little demand for loanable funds. Hence, perhaps, the lack of competitiveness and the draining away of savings.

CANADIANS IN THE NEW CENTURY

By 1900 industrial capitalism had made its deep imprint upon much but by no means all of Canada. As we have seen, relatively few Canadians lived in the industrial cities; far more still gained their livelihood from the land. Canada thus began the twentieth century as an agricultural country, and most Canadians, reflecting on the bounty Canadian harvests had brought and the vast western lands to be opened, expected that agriculture would retain its pre-eminent place. The nation had become a more complex country, a more differentiated country, but still recognizable for those who were alive at Confederation.

There was, nonetheless, a sense in 1900 that the patterns of the past would not be those of the future. Canadians, like others, were in awe of science and its most fruitful marriage with technology in the nineteenth century. The scientific temper was critical, and established institutions and beliefs were receiving a sharper scrutiny. In Canada there were only faint echoes of the modernism in literature and thought exemplified in 1900 by the publication of *The Meaning of Dreams* by Sigmund Freud. Still, the secularism and the quest for the new which are at the core of the modernist temper were powerful forces within Canadian society in 1900. Canadians, unlike most of the world, were part of a western tradition that was to undergo a fundamental transformation in the twentieth century. Inevitably, Canada too would be transformed.

In 1900 Canadians sensed that the revolution in communications and transportation, which had such a large impact on the country in the last part of the nineteenth century, was far from over. The next year, 1901, Marconi sent the first wireless signal across the Atlantic. Two years later the Wright brothers made their first flight, and Henry Ford founded his motor company. By the end of the decade Canadians had made flights too. The motorcar, so rare at the century's beginning, was a common sight on Canadian streets by 1910. The newspapers of the day welcomed the twentieth century with tributes to a new age. In this case the ritual had genuine meaning, for the new century would bring much that was new and much that was unexpected.

The twentieth century was to bring a new meaning to politics. Thus, before we can discuss Canada's path through the twentieth century, we must first describe the Canadian political setting when the new century began.

2

A Nation and its Parts

CONSTITUTIONAL CONVENTIONS

Canada's constitution was already thirty-six years old in 1900. The basic arrangements had been worked out by colonial politicians at the Charlottetown Conference and the Quebec Conference in 1864, and in 1867 the Imperial Parliament at Westminster placed its imprimatur on them. Behind the formal constitutional planks which were spelled out in the British North America Act were various pre-existing and continuing understandings about the relations among the various components of the governmental apparatus, both in Canada and in the United Kingdom. There was also a subsequent accumulation of precedent and understanding, partly the work of the British and Canadian courts and partly that of the politicians, which changed the character of the original plan. Thus, by 1900, Canada's constitution, like that of the Mother Country, was not written; although some components were embedded in the British North America Act, as amended, others came from quite different documents as well as from custom or tradition.

Strictly speaking, in 1900 the Dominion of Canada was still a British colony whose head of state was Queen Victoria and whose legislature was not fully master in its own house. It had always been possible for the Imperial Parliament to legislate for the colonies; that power continued, although it was no longer exercised except in relation to the British North America Act itself. The Imperial government could disallow any colonial statute and that power also continued, although it lay in abeyance. Indeed, it was by analogy with the imperial power of disallowance that Ottawa exercised the power to disallow provincial measures. Imperial treaties bound all Her Majesty's possessions, except when particular territories were specifically excluded. Imperial statutes might well apply in the colonies, or in some of them. Imperial common law and the accumulation of legal precedent formed part of the basis on which colonial lawyers and courts, such as the Canadian, had to do their work, except in areas such as Cape Colony and Quebec where a different civil law was established. British legal precedents were relevant and were cited regularly; American precedents were not. And although Canada possessed its own Supreme Court, the ultimate court of appeal for the dominion was the Judicial Committee of the Privy Council in London. Indeed, it was not at all uncommon for appeals to proceed directly from the local Canadian courts to the Judicial Committee, entirely bypassing Canada's Supreme Court.

Among the unwritten constitutional conventions were those which provided the framework for responsible parliamentary government. In theory, the cabinet consisted of the ministers whom the sovereign had summoned to advise her and to carry on her administration. In the dominion, the governor general was presumed to act as the sovereign's viceroy. The BNA Act did not say that the ministers had to be drawn from the members of the dominion Parliament, whether Senate or House of Commons. It did not say that the sovereign or her viceroy had to choose the leader of the largest parliamentary party as her chief minister. It did not describe the conditions under which the governor general could, or must, dismiss a ministry, summon another, call an election, or whatever. The BNA Act provided that no Parliament should last more than five years; it did no more. It was parliamentary convention, almost entirely borrowed from the parliamentary life of the United Kingdom, which ensured that the prime minister would be the person who led the largest party in the Commons and would therefore generally command a majority. Convention also ensured that a ministry could not cling to office if it lost the confidence of the House, at least on a matter of importance. Hence the significance of 'votes of confidence.' Furthermore, it was the conventions, not the written constitution, which prescribed the forms by which Parliament would regularly vote funds for the sovereign's government, impose taxes to provide these funds, and plan the government's expenditures in the course of making the votes.

Canadian politicians were accustomed to these conventions because the legislatures of the three federating colonies – the Province of Canada, Nova Scotia, and New Brunswick – had conducted their affairs along the same lines. Indeed, the literate political community would have seen the conventions as part of Canada's British heritage – one of many things which made the dominion different from the perfidious American nation to the south. In Canada, as in Britain, furthermore, it was convention and certain ancient British enactments, rather than a written constitutional provision, which protected the basic freedoms of the citizenry. Not for the dominion 'a bill of rights.' It is reasonably clear that the politicians of the 1860s deplored such a charter. Their successors in 1900 would have found the idea equally uninteresting and thoroughly dangerous.

Thanks to the weight of convention and tradition, the federating colonies had been able to operate their parliamentary 'responsible governments' without any constitutional documents at all. The same was true of the other colonies – British Columbia, Prince Edward Island, and Newfoundland – which entered the confederation later. To this day the Canadian provinces, unlike the American states, have no constitutions of their own. The federating colonies were not sovereign states. Indeed, two of the new provinces – Ontario and Quebec – had not existed since 1841, when Upper and Lower Canada had been united. If the federating colonies had wanted to form a simple legislative union with a single legislature and government, they could have managed after 1867, as before, with no written constitution at all. There need have been no imperial statute, although a measure might well have been thought convenient or prudent. Her Majesty could have appointed a single governor, convened a single Parliament, called forth a single body of advisers, and that would have been that. But although the Fathers of Confederation had wanted a strong central government, they were not prepared to suppress the pre-existing legislatures completely. They wished to provide new legislative bodies for Ontario and Quebec so that certain disputatious matters which had disturbed the peace of the old Canadian legislature could be delegated to the two provincial houses, which would then treat these contentious issues separately. But if there were to be two levels of government, there would have to be understandings about the division of powers, functions, and funds. In addition, there had to be provisions for constituting the central Parliament and for duly subordinating the regional legislatures. All these provisions are found in the BNA Act.

The Fathers of Confederation wanted their new state to take charge of economic development. Hence they gave it unlimited power to spend, borrow, and tax, and they assigned it control over such crucial matters as railways, canals, navigable waterways, banking, and currency. Property and civil rights, however, they confided to the provinces, largely because the civil code of Quebec was different from the common-law traditions of the other regions. Education, roads, social welfare – poor relief, hospitals, some prisons, and the like – went to the provinces. The question of education had been a divisive one in the pre-1867 Province of Canada, and roads and social services were neither interesting nor expensive. By 1900 these areas of provincial jurisdiction had caused no particular trouble; the dominion had shown no eagerness to enter them, and so the provinces had not had to fight to defend their jurisdiction. Municipalities, which everyone agreed were 'creatures of the provinces,' administered and in large part financed these 'provincial activities.' This was just as well: the BNA Act allowed the provinces to levy only 'direct taxes,' which were very unpopular. They could also collect licence fees and garner revenues from crown lands, which they administered. It was indeed no accident that the provinces were allocated the visible and unpopular taxes. The dominion distributed a permanent fixed subsidy to each province and looked after the former provincial debts, while collecting all the tariff and excise revenues which before had flowed to the provinces. The results were painfully constricting for some provinces, such as Quebec, which regularly demanded a better deal from Ottawa. By contrast, until 1900 Ontario had been willing and able to live within its means.

Crown domains were valuable: lands could be sold, timber rights leased, mining resources rented or otherwise disposed of. In the 1870s and 1880s Ontario fought hard to expand its frontiers at the expense of Manitoba and the North-West Territories, chiefly to increase the lands which it could administer, sell, and rent out. Except in that way, however, by 1900 the dominion and the several provinces had not begun to argue about natural resources. On entering Confederation in the early 1870s, Prince Edward Island had kept all its natural resources, and British Columbia most of its potential wealth. When the dominion purchased Rupert's Land from the Hudson's Bay Company, the federal government acquired most of the company's territories as crown lands and, as new provinces were erected in the territories, beginning with Manitoba in 1870, the dominion kept the crown lands, alienating them partly for railway subsidy and partly for settlement. Subsoil rights, in general, were not alienated even when the surface was disposed of.

By the 1870s it was clear that the BNA Act was sometimes ambiguous. The act assigned certain powers to the provinces and to the central government, reserving all unspecified or residual responsibilities for the federal authority. This arrangement not only restricted any increase in provincial power but it underlined the differences between the Canadian system and the American, where the federal government received only specified powers and the state governments fell heir to all the unspecified powers. One of the sixteen specified areas of provincial responsibility was property and civil rights, while another was 'generally all matters of a merely local or private nature.' These items were interpreted, partly by provincial legislatures and partly by the courts in Canada and Britain, in such a way as to broaden the provinces' areas of activity, creating some dominion-provincial conflict and identifying many areas of 'concurrent jurisdiction.' Thus, by 1900, no one knew who was to arrange for conciliation in labour disputes, and both levels of government were chartering corporations, regulating trust, mortgage, and insurance companies, and subsidizing railways, both by grant and by guarantee.

The constitutional arrangements of the BNA Act certainly expressed the idea of subordination. The dominion government would have the power to disallow any provincial statute, for any reason or for no reason at all. It would appoint the lieutenant-governors, who could withhold assent to any provincial measure or, on Ottawa's instruction, reserve provincial bills for the dominion's consideration. Acting in this way, the lieutenant-governors would be functioning as Ottawa's representatives, not as the queen's, and they would have more authority vis-à-vis the provincial legislatures than the queen enjoyed vis-à-vis the Imperial Parliament.

Although in theory these arrangements of subordination still exist, in practice they broke down very soon. Lieutenant-governors came to be seen as the queen's representatives, not Ottawa's. They acquired ceremonial powers, such as the right to create queen's counsels, which certainly were not foreseen or intended in the 1860s. It became almost inconceivable that a lieutenant-governor could deny his assent to a provincial legislative measure, and both lieutenant-governors and the central government were increasingly circumspect in employing reservation and disallowance. Even Sir John A. Macdonald came to believe that the dominion should not disallow any provincial enactment, except where a measure was clearly contrary to the general policy of the dominion itself. Similarly, although the central government could override the provinces' control over natural resources, property, and civil rights by declaring some work to be 'for the general interest of Canada,' by 1900 it was well understood that the dominion would always be most reluctant to do so.

The BNA Act made no provision for constitutional review, but it was always possible for the disgruntled to argue that some action of the dominion or of a province was inconsistent with the act, thus taking the question to the courts. Similarly, ordinary common-law proceedings could, on appeal, generate pronouncements which could and did affect the constitutional conventions and understandings. Increasingly, too, intergovernmental disputes of a constitutional character came to be submitted, by agreement, to the courts as 'reference cases.' The net effect of all this juridical wrangling, in which the Judicial Committee of the Privy Council played a prominent part, was to establish that the provinces were 'gradually recognized as co-ordinate jurisdictions with the central government, fully sovereign within their sphere of authority and not at all like the glorified municipalities originally envisaged.' In 1892 the Judicial Committee decided that the BNA Act had not meant to subjugate the provinces to federal authority, but to allow each province to retain its own autonomy in its sphere. How provinces such as Ontario and

Quebec, which had not existed before 1867, could be said to have 'retained' anything must be left to the learned judges. But for the Maritime provinces and British Columbia, which *had* enjoyed prior and separate existence, a better case could be made. In any event, well before 1900 the pattern had been set.

Besides distributing sanctions and funds, the BNA Act had to contain rules for creating and constituting the new central legislature. There would be two houses of identical powers. The Senate would be appointed, with equal representation from Quebec, Ontario, and the Maritimes. The House of Commons would be elected, with seats distributed in proportion to population. Constitutional conventions would ensure that the Commons would be the dominant House, and that the Senate, like the British House of Lords whose non-elective character it aped, would in general not obstruct the will of the Lower House. In later years, as the dominion added provinces, the Commons and the Senate added members. There were no pensions for MPs, but senators served for life. In both cases, the people's representatives were exclusively male.

The act did not say who could vote. There being no idea of a separate Canadian citizenship, any male British subject could vote so long as he resided in Canada and satisfied the local requirements. At first, the dominion continued with the various kinds of franchise which had defined the electorates in the three federating colonies. Based on property to some extent, these arrangements had their oddities, and many adult males had no vote. By 1900, in most provinces, there was 'universal manhood suffrage for British subjects of 21 years and older,' except for Indians residing on reservations and Eskimos, who could not vote because they were regarded as 'wards of the government' – children in all important respects. Women's suffrage was an idea very much in the air, but its likelihood seemed remote. There were no female MPs, senators, judges, senior civil servants, or, except in certain cases in municipal elections, voters.

These constitutional arrangements were not final. Having established their autonomous status, the provinces were already pressing the dominion for larger subsidies – unconditional grants which the provincial governments could spend as they liked. The dominion would shortly increase its subsidies but its help was not enough to keep the provinces from exploring new kinds of direct taxation. By 1900 most provinces were already taxing corporations and estates, a few were taxing personal incomes, and in the next thirty years they would tax motor vehicles, gasoline, and the drink trade as well. As yet the dominion gave no 'conditional grants,' the sort which required coordinate provincial legislation and joint spending on some agreed program. After the First World War, following some earlier legislative wranglings, such grants would come – first for labour exchanges, housing, and roads, then for old-age pensions, and, in the 1930s, for relief. Court 'references' and court battles would continue, narrowing the area of co-ordinate jurisdiction and allocating new fields, by analogy, to one jurisdiction or the other. From time to time the BNA Act itself would have to be amended, if only to rearrange the representation in the national Parliament as new provinces were erected.

On what basis could the act be altered? A statute of the Imperial Parliament, it could be amended only by that body, which acted on petition from the dominion government. Nothing was said about dominion-provincial consultation, and there was certainly no provision, written or conventional, by which any one province could veto proposals for change. Indeed, sometimes the dominion government sent proposals to London without consulting the provinces at all, and sometimes it forwarded proposals which were opposed by one or more provinces. However, it is doubtful that the dominion would have acted without provincial acquiescence if an amendment would abridge provincial powers, especially respecting education and natural resources, in any substantial way. As a matter of fact, between 1867 and 1940 no such amendments were ever transmitted to London, and the provinces did not dispute the amendment of 1940 which gave the dominion the power to create an unemployment-insurance system.

As for the Indians and Eskimos, to the observer in the 1980s their constitutional position was somewhat surprising, but in 1900 it appeared natural and entirely appropriate. The BNA Act assigned them to the dominion, in effect as successor to the Imperial government. With respect to constitutional change, no one thought of consulting Canada's 'first peoples,' and there was no provision for doing so. The relations between the dominion and its Indian and Eskimo dependants were regulated by a network of purchase agreements and treaties which stretched well back into the eighteenth century. The treaties gave the first peoples certain entrenched rights and, although the dominion might not honour all these points, it could not unilaterally remove the treaties' protection. Within their bands and on their reserves, the Indians possessed limited powers of self-government which certainly formed part of the nation's constitutional framework, even though few such rights had been spelled out in writing, and the BNA Act ignored the powers completely.

Politicians and opinion-makers in 1900 believed there was an 'Indian problem,' but one of assimilation and 'civilization,' not of constitution-making. The 'non-treaty Indians' and Métis, however, had no special status, either by law or constitution. No one would have denied that Canada's 'first peoples' were in a sense 'founding peoples,' but the Canadians of European extraction did not much like the foundations the Indians had laid and were anxious to erect a very different way of life.

It is clear that the Indians and Eskimos formed no part of a 'compact.' But what of the provinces and the linguistic groups? Was Confederation an agreement among Ontario, Quebec, Nova Scotia, and New Brunswick? A compact between Anglophones and Francophones? Or what?

For years, Canada's politicians, lawyers, historians, and political scientists have been debating these issues, and there is as yet no agreement. Some scholars observe that because neither Ontario nor Quebec existed in 1867, they cannot be said to have formed part of an agreement, either as political entities or as representatives of linguistic ones. Others observe that before 1841 the antecedent colonies of Upper and Lower Canada, though not possessing responsible government, had been separate political and constitutional entities. It is also noted that in the united Province of Canada there were elements of dualism: laws and legal codes were not the same in 'Canada East' as in 'Canada West,' while for some topics there were parallel departments of government – and even parallel ministers of the crown. Indeed, in the pre-1867 Canadian Parliament the eye of faith can detect the germs of two separate and parallel legislatures, merged and working together for most purposes but not for all.

Nevertheless, the question of an Anglophone-Francophone compact is a more relevant idea, and a persuasive one, which gives plausibility and perhaps legitimacy to many of the claims that, in the course of the twentieth century, would emanate from the Province of Quebec. However, there is a difficulty: Quebec has never contained all Canada's Francophones, nor do all Quebeckers speak French. The result has been a tangle between linguistic rights and provincial ones. It had begun to surface by 1900, and in later decades it would become more noticeable. Only after 1945, however, with the expansion of the dominion's activities in education, culture, and welfare, would it become pressing.

No well-informed historian or political scientist would now maintain that the BNA Act or the constitutional conventions of 1867-1900 actually expressed any interlinguistic compact. But surely it was there, a convention which lurked in the unspoken assumptions on which the Fathers of Confederation had erected their new state. The dominion's parliament and courts would be bilingual. Quebec would retain its own civil code and could arrange its educational system as it wished. In the subsequent operation of the new dominion, parties would not organize themselves on ethnic grounds, but neither would the Anglophone majority feel free to coerce the Francophone minority, even though the Francophones could not be given a formal blocking veto with respect to any and every action which the dominion might want to take.

The result might be called an indelicate balance. As yet, by 1900, the division of powers was not a serious problem because, as we have noted, the dominion showed no inclination to intrude itself into the provincial sphere by using its spending and taxing powers. Nor did the dominion interest itself in matters of education and culture. But the operation of the dominion government itself was already a problem, involving what the sociologist might call intergroup interaction. Francophones frequently believed that their views were ignored and their interests overruled by their English-speaking colleagues. Anglophones, in turn, were sometimes heard to observe that the presence of the French was a damned nuisance. In other words, from time to time each group felt constrained or wounded by the presence of the other within the bosom of a single state. In the 1860s the politicians of Canada West had hoped that by creating a broader union they would be able to outvote the French, thus avoiding some of the irritating paralysis which had afflicted responsible government in the St Lawrence Valley. From Quebec's point of view, after 1867 those Anglais from Toronto had got their way; from Toronto's viewpoint, the Anglo victories were far too few.

THE REALITY OF THE POLITY AND THE POLITICS OF REALITY

Although some provinces were increasingly anxious to assert themselves, Canada in 1900 was still a state in which the central authority – the dominion government – counted for much more than the provincial governments. This was partly because some provincial governments had little or nothing by way of administrative skill. It was also because so many functions of modern government which the BNA Act assigned to the provinces – education, roads, and most aspects of social security and human welfare – were as yet of little concern at any level of government above the local. Universities, for instance, depended almost wholly on fee and endowment income, and most of Canada's universities had begun as private foundations, which in 1900 still received no money from any government. Equally important was the fact that the dominion controlled those parts of the nation's economic life which were central to the shaping of the new nation – the protective tariff, the railway system, and the virgin lands of the prairie. In addition, the banks and insurance companies, the only really important financial institutions in the country, operated under dominion regulation, as did some of the loan and trust companies which pumped funds into mortgage lending. Provincial legislatures could regulate factory conditions, give grants to schools and businesses, even incorporate business corporations. But the big questions would be settled in Ottawa. And at all levels of government, politicians and businessmen knew it.

The biggest of the questions related to the physical expansion of the country and the populating of the virgin lands in the west. The important decisions had already been taken by 1880, and in many respects the life of the dominion, at least until 1929 and probably long thereafter, was the working-out of these decisions. First of all, the little dominion along the St Lawrence and the Atlantic shore would expand until it included all of British North America. This part of the operation was almost completed in 1873, with the accession of Prince Edward Island. Second, railways and canals would be built. Third, manufactures would be encouraged, partly by protective tariff and partly by bounty.

The dominion government was not rich and there were limits to what it could do. By the standards of the late nineteenth century, Canadians were a prosperous folk, but they did not like to pay taxes. Hence the utility of the tariff: collected at the frontier, it was not directly visible to the citizenry, unless they paused and thought about things. In most of the years since Confederation the dominion had been a borrower: funds were needed for national development, and the tax base did not meet that need. The dominion also was responsible for the old debts of the several provinces, a burden it had shouldered at Confederation. In 1900, 20 per cent of its outlays consisted of debt service and another 7.7 per cent were subsidies to the provinces; defence swallowed 5.8 per cent, while transportation, communications, resources, and development engulfed 52 per cent of budgetary outlays. Since Confederation, the dominion's debt had risen from $94 million to $292 million.

The provinces, in turn, depended heavily on dominion funds. As the provincial public accounts are a morass through which researchers are only now clearing trails, it is not possible to be sure just how dependent. Ontario's data have been unravelled, and the result is quite striking. In 1900, 31.5 per cent of the province's revenues came from the dominion. Furthermore, the absolute subsidy figure of $1,439,000 in 1900 was almost exactly the same as the figure for 1868, and in the intervening years the changes had been small. The basic subsidy under the BNA Act was $1.2 million in 1874; in 1900, and indeed in 1902, it was still the same.

The dominion-provincial subsidies were intended to be permanent, unchangeable, and non-negotiable. The dominion paid them; the provinces could do what they liked with them. Naturally, the constitutional facts had not prevented the provinces from pressing for more dominion generosity. The dominion, however, had resisted, although some minor readjustments had been made for certain provinces. The reader can understand why. The dominion had to shoulder most of the burden of nation-building, and the debt that went with it. Its tax system was simple; its revenues depended not so much on policy as on the level of economic activity. If the provinces wanted to spend more, let them invent their own taxes and collect them. The dominion had left them plenty of room to do so.

CONCLUSION

The form of Canada's constitution was much the same in 1900 as in the late 1930s, and not markedly different from that of the late 1970s. The substance, however, was very different. In 1900 the dominion counted for much more, and the provinces for much less. This is to be explained on the basis of the distribution of tasks and powers, as well as on the significance which contemporaries attached to these matters. In 1900 Canada was normally called a 'dominion,' and its national authority, the 'dominion government.' The usage was common to English and to French, and it was embedded in the BNA Act. It did not connote subordination to an external power, such as Great Britain; rather, it implied the subordination of the parts to the whole. The Dominion of Canada was not just the sum of its parts; it was more than that.

The country, however, was not an international actor. It could not amend its own written constitution; its legislation could be disallowed in London; it had no diplomatic relations with foreign powers; and, without Britain's participation and consent, it could not negotiate treaties or sign them, yet it could be bound by Britain's own treaty-making.

In 1900 few Canadians worried about these things, and almost no one agitated to change them. The British connection brought important advantages, and London did not interfere. Full independence would be expensive and perhaps it would be impossible to sustain: the Americans were talking of manifest destiny, and Washington might be quick to swallow an undefendable and underpopulated nation on its northern border. As things were, little Johnny Canuck could shelter behind Britannia's skirts. Many Canadians, especially in Quebec, disliked Britain and the British. Nevertheless, autonomy behind the skirts was better than absorption into the United States. For Canadians, the British link meant much more than simply the heritage of parliamentary government and legal and constitutional traditions. In the first decade of the century, Prime Minister Wilfrid Laurier learned how tenacious these links were.

3

Politics and Political Culture

Sir Wilfrid Laurier dominated the political landscape in the first decade of the new century. When he first became Canada's prime minister in 1896 he was still a stranger to most of the country. At first glance the fifty-five-year-old French Canadian seemed too frail to endure the harsh climate of Canadian politics. In 1891 he had flirted too intensely with the Americans; in the following years he seemed helpless before the religious and cultural passions which beset Canadian politics. By 1896 he had gained some mastery over his party; nevertheless, his victory appeared more a Tory defeat than the victory of a strong alternative government. Many doubted that he had the stamina and the will to govern a country divided in many ways. His gentle lines and his evocative gaze did not yet reveal the harder and more complicated man that Laurier was. To most Canadians he was merely a man who promised 'sunny ways.'

But the 'sunny ways' did come, and by 1900 Laurier was recognized as a skilful and ruthless politician. His eloquent speeches and the lofty visions they often portrayed captured the imagination of most Canadians. He radiated optimism, and he left a rich legacy for speakers on occasions when optimism is required. There were, however, reservations which were rarely noticed. When Laurier elaborated on his visions, his essential practicality came through. And to his closest friends his pessimism about human nature, his times, and his nation were most apparent. He loathed photographs, telephones, and automobiles. He thought the eighteenth century was far superior to what had come since.

Laurier was a Catholic, as the philosopher George Santayana was a Catholic: devoted to the mystery, the elegance, and the history of the church. Like many in his time, he regretted the ebbing of traditional faith and feared the new creeds that would struggle in the future. He knew that old prejudices derived from faith would be replaced by new and perhaps more frightening ones. In the swirl of bias and change he considered that political positions were often mere posturing. He told his biographer John Willison that politics in Canada meant only beating the other man. Willison regarded the remark as horrifying, but he misunderstood Laurier's meaning.

For Laurier, politics was a theatre where symbols and gestures represented and, indeed, moderated fundamental human passions. He was, therefore, deeply committed to politics in itself. Because politics were such a human activity, perfection was impossible. This made Laurier appear cynical and old-fashioned to those Canadians who demanded that politics be 'purified.' For Laurier, it was most important that politics simply exist, and that Canadian politics modify the tensions and divisions within Canadian society. He did not share the belief in perfectibility which was at the core of nineteenth-century liberalism, but he did believe most profoundly in the principles of toleration and pacific settlement of international and national strife which British liberalism upheld.

Laurier's genius was that of a great actor. He could convey most directly, through the simplest of his gestures, the complexities of the human heart and mind. And thus this period in Canadian history became very much his own. Laurier's pre-eminence in the first decade of the twentieth century made it difficult for others to play meaningful roles on the stage. Yet his cabinet in 1896 was impressively talented. Three provincial premiers, Sir Oliver Mowat of Ontario, A.G. Blair from New Brunswick, and W.S. Fielding of Nova Scotia, came to Ottawa, as did the brilliant Manitoba attorney-general, Clifford Sifton. Such political veterans as Sir Richard Cartwright, Sir Henri Joly de Lotbinière, and the former Conservative, Israel Tarte, added strength, although their views diverged widely. Laurier's first cabinet indicated his moderate approach to political affairs and his apparent willingness to try to work with those who differed from him. In fact, Laurier's desire for compromise and balance was accompanied by a frequent impulsiveness in decision-making and a refusal to let others have a similar freedom of action in their own political preserves. Partly as a result, Laurier's cabinet by 1905 was significantly weaker than in 1896. Mowat, who had brought prestige to the cabinet, was too old and had left early. Blair departed after Laurier failed to consult with him fully on the building of the new railways. Sifton resigned in 1905 when Laurier, in the Autonomy Bills which established the new provinces of Alberta and Saskatchewan, seemed to renege on earlier commitments in regard to separate schools. Tarte returned to his old Tory loyalties and began to scheme for Robert Borden as he had done for Laurier earlier – this time with less success.

In Ontario and Quebec, particularly, the lack of eminent ministers hurt the Liberals after 1905. In Quebec, Henri Bourassa, a Liberal member who had resigned over the issue of Canadian participation in the Boer War, led many of the young and politically enthusiastic away from party affiliation and towards political independence. In Ontario it was thought that the best young men shunned politics in favour of business careers; Laurier shared this belief. Even worse, men entered politics to advance their special business interests. Thus, when young and clever Mackenzie King left the bureaucracy to join the political rough and tumble in 1908, he astounded commentators in his choice of a political career. Even more surprising was King's willingness to talk about politics as a vocation at a time when very few Canadians did. Despite the entry of King, Laurier's overall record in replenishing the talents of his cabinet was not good. By 1910 this failure was affecting the ability of his government to respond to challenges which it faced.

The opposition, however, had its own problems at that time. Essentially, the Tories seemed bereft of ideas as well as leadership. Robert Laird Borden had become leader of the Conservative Party in February 1901, imposed upon a Conservative caucus which lacked the will and resources to resist by former party leader Sir Charles Tupper. Borden, MP for Halifax and law partner of Tupper's son, was forty-seven years old, married but childless, and the epitome of the upper middle-class Nova Scotian. He was unilingual and his speeches were workmanlike rather than inspiring, as befitted a self-made man. With his thick thatch of hair parted neatly in the middle and a bushy moustache hiding all but half of his fleshy lower lip, Borden exuded Victorian respectability and reserve. His apparent dullness, however, concealed intelligence and determination. Like so many Victorians, he was entertaining in private while boring in public. Canadians would eventually learn that there was more to the man than there seemed. There was also more to the Conservative party than its political failures and bitter internal quarrels led critics to believe.

In fact, there was a great deal more to both parties than met the eye. By the early 1900s the national two-party system had extended its web across the continent. Political non-partisanship, which had flourished at the time of Confederation, had all but vanished at the federal and provincial levels. Party governments existed in all provinces, including the newly created Alberta and Saskatchewan after 1905. In Quebec, nationalists found they had little success when they tried to work outside the party system. If the Liberals were not to their taste, their political survival depended on some kind of alliance with the Conservatives. Similarly, all kinds of political independents, cranks, and ideologues found that they could best be heard within the confines of the existing parties. Thus, Borden had to wrestle with Conservative candidates who espoused socialist views, and Laurier had to deal with single taxers and religious mystics who cropped up within Liberal ranks. This diversity of opinion within party ranks reflects not only the lack of ideological distinction in Canadian politics but also the political inexperience of many Canadians.

The Canadian party system received much criticism from a variety of directions in the early years of this century, yet it accomplished tasks of enormous importance which other national party systems failed to carry out. In the late nineteenth century, as the franchise was extended to the working class, working men generally found their political place among the ranks of Conservatives or Liberals rather than in any new political movement. The party system also did not fracture on regional lines as it later did. In 1900, for example, the Conservatives received 47.4 per cent of the vote overall but in no province was their percentage higher than 49.7 per cent (Ontario) or lower than 40.9 per cent (British Columbia). Even in areas where the Conservatives were considered weak, notably the prairies, their percentage of the vote between 1900 and 1911 never fell below 36.8 per cent (Saskatchewan in 1908). Although seat totals would suggest that the Conservatives were weak in Quebec in this period, in fact their percentage of the Quebec vote never fell below 40.8 per cent (1908), and in 1911 the party won almost 50 per cent of the votes. In short, this was a truly national party system.

This stability in the party system is all the more remarkable considering the 1,750,000 immigrants who entered Canada during the period 1901-11, a number equal to almost 40 per cent of the 1901 population. These immigrants came from a wide variety of backgrounds and political experiences. Some, such as the Ukrainians, had no experience of democratic elections. Others, such as the Germans, came from areas where political debate was highly ideological and touched by Marxism and socialism as well as by traditional religious concerns. Great Britain, the home of most of the immigrants, also had a two-party system, Liberal and Conservative, which had developed a high degree of sophistication. The Canadian party system integrated British and even non-British immigrants with remarkable ease. Political scientists declare that a party system's success can be judged by the degree to which it integrates newcomers and new political debates within its framework. If this is so, the Canadian party system deserves high marks.

Successful integration occurs at several levels, economic, social, and intellectual. The best-known is the level of political events, followed by the continuing organizational structure of the parties and the electorate. The relationship among these levels is organic; each affects the other. Indeed, the degree to which each level influences the other is the best measure of the strength of a political system. If, for example, the party organization is remote from the control of the party voters, the overall strength of the party is diminished. Similarly, if the party's parliamentary actions do not reflect the interests of its constituency workers, atrophy of the party is inevitable.

Critics of the Canadian party system before the First World War mostly focused upon the absence of ideas in Canadian politics. André Siegfried's brilliant study of prewar politics, *The Race Question in Canada,* echoes this view when it declared that Canadian parties were simply machines for winning elections. There was no place for ideas or doctrines; there were, rather, 'only questions of material interest, collective or individual.' Elections were simply battles between the ins and outs: 'Whoever may be the winner, everyone knows that the country will be administered in the same way, or almost the same.'[1] Yet Siegfried was puzzled by the 'fury and enthusiasm' which he found at the constituency level in the 1904 general election. Such fury found no parallel in his native France, and he could find no convincing explanation for it.

Siegfried's analysis derived from his European background, which predisposed him to evaluate parties on the extent to which they reflected socioeconomic factors. In Canada, these factors appeared to be absent. Thus, Canadian elections were to him simply contests 'between two parties equally Conservative.' Both parties accepted the strategy of national development set out in the nineteenth century, and, in contemporary terms, both were wedded to capitalist ideology. For both parties, government intervention in the economy was pragmatic, not a reflection of intellectual commitment. But differences there were, and they emerged at every election.

ISSUES AND ELECTIONS

Two particular issues were significant in the elections which took place in 1900, 1904, 1908, and 1911: Canada's relationship with the British empire and with the United States. This is not to say that foreign policy dominated those elections; indeed, it would be more accurate to state the opposite. What is important is the extent to which those two issues defined the Canadian political identity. Along with religious ties, they were the factors which brought the fury to Canadian politics. In the eyes of those Canadians who beheld prewar politics, they had deep meaning.

The two elections of the 1890s had established the framework for the political debate of the new century. After the defeat of 1891, the Liberals moved away from their commitment to closer economic ties with the United States. After their 1896 defeat, the Conservatives became less disposed to proclaim their attachment to the 'old flag.' Nevertheless, the perceptions of

1 André Siegfried, *The Race Question in Canada,* trans. E. Nash (1907, Toronto 1966), 113, 117

each party led Canadians to identify Liberalism with a more 'North American' outlook and Conservatism with a more 'imperial' point of view. On the whole, the perceptions were accurate.

The 1900 general election occurred in the midst of the Boer War. The war had aroused considerable imperial enthusiasm among urban English Canadians, especially in Ontario. Although Conservative leader Sir Charles Tupper was not militantly imperialist on the issue, some of his colleagues such as Sam Hughes most certainly were. The Conservative press in English Canada rallied British Canadians to the cause of British Africans, who, thousands of miles away, were denied their British rights. The Boers, the press pointed out, had attacked the British first. Laurier did allow Canadian volunteers to participate in the war, but his agreement came after a serious cabinet division on the subject. As Charles Stacey has observed, never was a Canadian cabinet so divided on the issue of war.[2] Laurier's decision was too timid for some of his English-Canadian colleagues, but it was almost too much for Israel Tarte and more than Henri Bourassa could stomach. Bourassa resigned and tested the feelings of his constituents on the subject of the war. The electors of Labelle – where he was *seigneur* – endorsed his decision.

This defiance so infuriated many English Canadians who had heard rumours of the extent of French-Canadian opposition to Canadian involvement in the war. In the election campaign of 1900 the *Toronto News,* which billed itself as an independent newspaper, demanded that Toronto voters defeat the Liberals 'who have been stirring up race feeling in Quebec as a preliminary to restoring Canada to French dominion or building up an independent French state. Canadians must decide now between Mr. Tarte's ideals and the movement to knit the Empire into one vast union.' This was the heyday of the Imperial Federation spirit, and that spirit infused political debate in Ontario. The editor of the Toronto *Globe,* John Willison, knew how hard Laurier had tried to maintain a balance, but he saw that many of his friends considered the attempt to be pointless. In Ontario, therefore, the balance tipped. The Conservatives held Ontario; Laurier, however, took Quebec. (See Appendix 1.)

Laurier had a solid majority, but that majority was based on Quebec. Conversely, the Conservatives relied on Ontario in a way that John A. Macdonald never had. This meant that Quebec had considerably less influence in the Conservative caucus than it had in Macdonald's day and that Ontario was somewhat weaker in the Liberal caucus. The effects of this balance are apparent in the behaviour of the party leaders between 1900 and 1904, when

2   C.P. Stacey, *Canada and the Age of Conflict,* volume 1 (Toronto 1977)

the next general election occurred.

The new Conservative leader, Robert Borden, flirted with the notion of a closer imperial union. He knew that his party could never recover office unless it improved its standing in Quebec. He tried to find a Quebec lieutenant, a task which drew him into questionable dealings with some Quebec businessmen. Despite his efforts, Borden found the political footing in Quebec too slippery; the old Tory position could not be recovered. In framing policy, the voice of Ontario was the loudest in Conservative councils.

Laurier was more fortunate in that his party had strength throughout the country, and compromises were more easily struck. After the 1900 election, Laurier's genius for striking compromises was more apparent. So was his political shrewdness. When, for example, the Alaska boundary decision went against Canada, Laurier used Canadian anger to gain support for his policy of national development and to gain freedom to manoeuvre in Canada's relationship with Great Britain and the United States. By 1904 the imperial issue which had stirred Canadian politics during his first term was much less troubling to Laurier and, for that matter, to Borden. The major concern of Canadians was the nation's remarkable expansion. The boom had begun under Laurier and, in 1904, he harvested its fruits with another solid majority.

These results depressed Borden, who had actually expected a small majority. He tried to resign, but his party had few alternatives and he remained leader in response to his colleagues' pleas. His determination to remake the party became stronger. He believed that such party renovation required a clearer definition of policy, and, in defining this policy, Borden was aware that his party had to appeal to the west as well as Quebec; it had to escape from too much dependence on Ontario. Still, Ontario's support could not be risked. The 1904 election was the third consecutive election in which Ontario results ran counter to the national result. Conservative strength had grown in all parts of the province, especially in the old Liberal heartland of southwestern Ontario. Murray Beck has conjectured that the 'old Grit strongholds in western Ontario tended to become Conservative as Quebec became more and more the preserve of the Liberal party after 1896.'[3] Events after 1904 confirmed the trend.

In 1905 the new provinces of Alberta and Saskatchewan were carved out of the Northwest Territories. The celebration which should have accompanied this event was marred by a bitter fight over the educational rights of the Catholic minority in the new provinces. French Canadians demanded guarantees that French and Catholic rights be respected in the new

3   J. Murray Beck, 'The Democratic Process at Work in Canadian General Elections,' in John Courtney, ed., *Voting in Canada* (Scarborough 1967), 6

provinces. The cabinet divided on the question, with Sir Clifford Sifton eventually resigning on the issue. The Conservatives were allowed a free vote by Borden. The Quebec members voted with the government, and the leading French-Canadian Conservative, Frederick Monk, accused Borden of ruining the future chances of his party in Quebec because of his behaviour during the Autonomy Bills debate. Borden, Monk thought, had little sensitivity to the concerns of French Canadians. Borden, in contrast, found the French Canadians' concern for special rights peculiar. They should be 'content to be Canadians.' Worry about whether 'ancestors were English or French ... only tends to keep alive ideas which really have no useful place in the life of this country.' Lacking French-Canadian colleagues who could tell him why such ideas had a place, Borden and his party drifted farther away from an understanding of French Canada.[4]

Since traditional religious and cultural ideas had no place in his mind, Borden sought to inject a broader discussion of socio-economic issues into Canadian politics. His 1907 Halifax Platform represented an attempt by the Conservative leader to redefine the ideas which formed the core of Canadian political debate. The platform reflects the influence of American progressivism and other advanced social thinking at the time. Government intervention was readily accepted, and the notion of a patronage-free system of administration was strongly emphasized. The platform said little about imperial matters beyond a hint that imperial preferential tariffs should be promoted if it were found that they made economic sense. The platform also studiously avoided problems of race and religion; indeed, it seemed to relegate them to the realm of the non-political. But that was at best a fantasy.

In the 1908 election campaign a leading Ontario Conservative, H.C. Hocken, wrote a scurrilous pamphlet entitled 'The Duty of the Hour' which called upon Protestants to expunge the influence of the Papists and the French upon their national government. Both sides used the pamphlet, the Conservatives in Ontario, the Liberals in Quebec. In another sense, both sides used the Halifax Platform, as Laurier reacted to the good ideas contained in the Tory proposals by including some of them in legislation. The debate on developmental policies which the platform was intended to provoke did not occur. The election results reflected once more the patterns established in the early Laurier years, as Quebec remained strongly Liberal and Ontario reaffirmed its Conservative tendencies.

The Conservatives did improve their position in western Canada where both British Columbia and Manitoba had strong provincial Conservative

4   The outstanding biography by R.C. Brown, *Robert Laird Borden: A Biography,* 2 volumes (Toronto 1975, 1980), is essential reading for students of this period.

administrations. These Conservative governments, along with that of Ontario, were vocal in their support for closer imperial ties and in their rejection of concessions to French Canada. After 1909 the imperial issue which had been quiescent since the Boer War returned to the centre stage of Canadian federal and even provincial politics. The Conservative war horse Sir George Foster moved a resolution in 1909 which called for Canada to take more responsibility for its coastal defence, and the question of what Canada should do to aid the motherland, whose supremacy on the seas was being challenged, remained in the forefront of Canadian political debate. Both Laurier and Borden feared the entry of the imperial issue into the political arena, and the initial result of the Foster resolution was a compromise which the party leaders believed would satisfy all but the extremists on both sides. It did not. By 1910 Quebec nationalists were grumbling that Canada was beginning to arm for a British war. The precedent of the Boer War seemed ominous. Imperialists, however, saw Britain threatened. For Canada, this brought both opportunity and duty.

Urged on by Conservative provincial premiers, especially Richard McBride of British Columbia and James Whitney of Ontario, Borden retreated from the compromise he had struck with Laurier. Laurier's navy became the 'tin-pot navy,' an inadequate and ungrateful response to the motherland's entreaties. The Quebec branch of the Conservative party also denounced Laurier's navy, but from an anti-imperialist perspective. Acting independently, Monk called for no naval contribution and no Canadian navy unless a referendum were held. His remarks infuriated Conservative supporters such as the Toronto businessman Joseph Flavelle, who warned Borden that English-Canadian Conservatives would not tolerate a 'policy which cribs, cabins and confines the actions of the Conservative Party upon public issues of high importance within the limits set by Quebec.' Actually, Monk's notion of a referendum did offer a way out for Borden. Far from confining the Conservative party, its Quebec wing's stand permitted the party to ally with the increasingly strong Nationalist movement in Quebec.

A by-election in Laurier's old constituency of Drummond-Arthabaska revealed how strong Nationalist sentiment was in Quebec. The constituency seemed so Liberal that the Conservatives did not bother to run a candidate. Monk, however, joined with Henri Bourassa and other Nationalists to back an independent who made the naval issue the central concern of his campaign. The victory of Arthur Gilbert in November 1910 stunned the Nationalists, the Conservatives, and most of all the Liberals. No longer could Laurier count on a solid phalanx from his home province. For the Conservatives, alliance with the Nationalists offered enormous opportunity. Thus the 'unholy alliance' was formed. Conservatives and Nationalists in Quebec joined forces to tear down the fabric of Laurier Liberalism.

The alliance presented dangers for the national Conservative party where, after all, most Canadian imperialists found their political haven. Bourassa was anathema to many Conservative parliamentarians, and the English Conservative press often treated him as the anti-Christ. If the naval issue had remained the focus of attention in English Canada, the contradictions in the Conservative stand would have become apparent. In late January 1911, however, Finance Minister W.S. Fielding's announcement of a Reciprocity Agreement with the United States stunned the House of Commons. Initial reaction suggested that reciprocity was an enormous accomplishment which would perpetuate the Liberal ascendancy, and most Conservative parliamentarians reacted with despair.

Within the next few weeks, however, the Conservative members discovered that many of their constituents did not agree, especially in the industrial area of Ontario. Many Liberal members in Ontario also found that their followers did not like the path Fielding proposed to take. In February, eighteen Toronto businessmen and financiers, some of whom had been identified with the Liberal party, signed a statement opposing reciprocity. The anti-reciprocity campaign soon gained a highly skilled and surprising leader, Sir Clifford Sifton, the erstwhile minister of the interior. Sifton cleverly linked Laurier's ambiguous commitment to imperial defence with his hasty embrace of reciprocity: 'Up to this present time we have been somewhat of a nuisance to the Empire, but now we come to a point where we may be of use to the Empire, when we can send men and ships if necessary, to her aid[;] then, when we can be of some use to the Empire that gave us our liberty and our traditions of citizenship – at the first beckoning hand from Washington we turn to listen; the first time anyone beckons we turn from the path that leads to the centre of the Empire and take the path that leads to Washington. So far as I am concerned, I say, "Not for me."'[5] And it was no for many others too.

Borden found it much easier to ally with these English-Canadian nationalists than with their French-Canadian counterparts. He quickly accepted the terms of the alliance which Sifton and the Toronto businessmen demanded. They insisted that Quebec and the Roman Catholic church should not have influence over the policy of a Borden government. At the same time, they argued that their group should have considerable influence. A Borden government should contain some men who had acquired 'outstanding nation-

5 *House of Commons Debates,* 28 Feb. 1911

al reputation and influence' in order that the authority of the 'progressive elements of the country' could be assured. The progressive elements, it was clear, were to be found among the ranks of those English Canadians who saw the imperial commitment as central to nationhood and to national prosperity. These men identified that nationhood with the interests of the industries they created, the railways they invested in, and the churches in which they worshipped. Their vision was narrow; it gained its strength from its cohesiveness, its historical sense, and the assurance that it was threatened by Americans, French-Canadian Nationalists, and Wilfrid Laurier, whose true self had been finally revealed.

In 1904 André Siegfried could find no cause for the fury which he discovered in the constituencies. In 1911 he would have witnessed an election where the fury of the constituency reflected the issues of the national debate. The parties defined their differences in the starkest terms. In Ontario, the Conservatives issued an appeal to 'those of British blood.' In Quebec, Laurier Liberals reminded French Canadians that Laurier was one of their own. Bourassa, however, accused Laurier of betraying his own race. Borden kept quiet, leaving Quebec to Bourassa and Monk. In Quebec, the Conservative-Nationalist alliance directed its anti-imperialist fire against Laurier's navy. In the other provinces the Conservatives championed the imperial connection and denounced reciprocity as a device which would surely sever the connection. Laurier knew he was trapped: 'I am branded in Quebec as a traitor to the French and in Ontario as a traitor to the English ... In Quebec I am attacked as an Imperialist, and in Ontario as an anti-Imperialist.' Dark clouds came over the man of 'sunny ways.'

Borden knew that his alliance with Bourassa would cause him future problems. He realized that stoking the imperialist fires in English Canada presented dangers too. In his mind, the gravity of the issue justified what he did. Canada, Borden believed, stood at the parting of the ways: 'We must decide whether the spirit of Canadianism or of Continentalism shall prevail on the northern half of this continent.' The choice was today; the future was tomorrow's problem. In September 1911 Canadians chose their future – a Conservative government.

The Conservatives gained sixteen more seats in Quebec and twenty-five more seats in Ontario than they had in 1908. Their percentage of the popular vote had risen over seven points in Quebec and just over five points in Ontario. But Borden knew that the Quebec success belonged to Bourassa and Monk. Moreover, his promises to Sifton and the others who had helped him included the pledge that he would restrict the influence of 'the French and the Church.' Although he did consult with the Nationalist leaders on the composition of the new cabinet, Borden relegated his French-Canadian ministers to less significant portfolios than they had a right to expect. More seriously, the private counsels which Borden heeded included no French Canadians, but numerous individuals who were most resentful of Quebec's influence in national life. As a result, it did not take long for the fragile co-alition which captured power in 1911 to break apart.

In its first summer, the new government had to confront the naval prob-lem. Borden believed that he had Monk's promise that he would support a contribution to Britain if there was a genuine emergency. He tried to per-suade his colleague to accompany him on a fact-finding visit to Britain where he hoped Monk would succumb to British charm and eloquence. But Monk refused the invitation.

Borden's journey to Britain in 1912 convinced him that there was indeed an emergency which required Canada's assistance. Moreover, British First Lord of the Admiralty Winston Churchill told Borden that he was 'quite willing to play the game' and 'give assurance in writing' of the necessity of an emergency contribution. He also got a vague promise from Prime Minis-ter Asquith that Canada would be invited to meetings of the Committee on Imperial Defence whenever its discussions might affect Canada. These promises seemed sufficient to stave off criticism from two important direc-tions; first, that there was no emergency and, second, that Canada had no voice in British decision-making as Britain made decisions which might lead to war.

Borden's hopes were dashed when Monk refused to agree to a contribu-tion unless a referendum were held on the naval question. He had no choice. In the pages of his increasingly influential newspaper, *Le Devoir,* Henri Bou-rassa warned Monk that the Nationalists would not accept betrayal on the naval question. In October 1912 Monk resigned, stating that Borden's naval policy was 'at variance' with his election promises. In November the Quebec Conservatives split on the vote on the contribution. Bourassa denounced those who voted with Borden as traitors; the Nationalist-Conservative alli-ance was in shambles. The bitterness in Quebec matched the mood at Otta-wa, where resentment between the parties reached a pitch unknown since Confederation.

In 1905 Siegfried warned of the fragility of the Canadian party system. In the future 'some great wave of opinion' might sweep over the country and wash away 'the sordid preoccupations of patronage or connection' which, in his view, marked Canadian politics. The problem after 1910 was that not one but several waves arose. They met violently, and the resulting clash threatened the structure of Canadian political parties. But they did not over-whelm it. The tidal wave came later with the war.

PARTIES AND VOTERS

So much for the level of political events which, in turn, affect party organization and individual voting behaviour. In a two-party system where the two parties are relatively closely balanced, independents play an important role. Research into voting behaviour has shown independents to be better informed than those who are unflinching adherents of a single party. In prewar Canada there were certainly more stalwarts than independents, but this served to exaggerate the importance of voters willing to switch. As we have seen, the differences in terms of popular vote between the two parties in all provinces was relatively small. Moreover, the constituency system of representation meant that a relatively small shift in the popular vote could have a dramatic impact on the number of seats a party held. Thus, in 1911 the Liberal percentage of the popular vote fell only 2.7 per cent from that of 1908, but the party lost office and forty-eight seats.

The task of Borden and Laurier as party leader was two-fold; to maintain solid ranks and to woo the independents. There is much evidence that the former was easier than the latter. The strength of party attachment was the most significant factor affecting the individual decision to vote. The party meant much more than the individual candidate, as is clear in the behaviour of voters in the three double-member constituencies which existed between 1904 and 1911. Only once during that period did the margin between the candidates of the same party vary more than 6 per cent. Electors, therefore, thought mostly of the party, not the man.

How did voters come to identify either the Liberal or Conservative party as their favourite? In the absence of modern polling devices, this question must necessarily remain speculative. Students of voting behaviour in prewar Canada have identified ethnicity as the major factor affecting party identification. In the 1908 election, for example, the strongest correlations are found between English-Canadian concentration and Conservative votes. Conversely, the Liberals did well wherever there were more French Canadians. In the case of the third largest ethnic group, the Germans, there was a disposition to support the Conservatives in the east and the Liberals in the west where, it should be noted, the Germans, unlike those in Ontario and Nova Scotia, were recent immigrants.

In 1908 it did not matter whether a voter lived in a rural or urban area. This changed in 1911 when reciprocity was the major issue in English Canada. In that election, rural voters, whom reciprocity appeared to benefit most, swung sharply towards the Liberal party and away from the Conservatives. This was especially true in western Canada. The Conservatives won the election on the basis of their better showing in urban ridings, where industrial leaders and workers thought that reciprocity might imperil their livelihood. As the Tory Ontario leaders believed, the British-born in that province were good targets for their appeal. In the four elections in the first eleven years of the new century, the Liberals with their French-Canadian leader consistently lost ground in Ontario. This was especially true in southwestern Ontario, where George Brown's Grits had earlier found such fertile ground for their party among the rural voters. At the same time, French Canadians outside of Quebec became more attached to the Liberal party. The trend was the same in Quebec until 1911, when the Conservative-Nationalist alliance made inroads among the French Canadians in Quebec. For them, the naval issue was the only issue. For French Canadians elsewhere, the naval issue did not play a large part and their allegiance did not change.

These tendencies in voting behaviour were the foundations on which party organization was built. The Nationalists' disillusionment with Borden after the election of 1911 was quickly followed by a weakening of Conservative organization in the province. A veteran Quebec Conservative politician complained to Borden in August 1913: 'There is nothing doing here; no organization; no stirring up of the masses; no educational campaign; no telling our people what we have done, or what we intend doing; nothing to inspire the young men with confidence in the future of the Conservative Party. I am told, and I really believe that it is true, that the young men are discouraged and are gradually dropping away from us.'[6] Laurier had heard the same complaints several years earlier when Bourassa and the Nationalists had attacked his policies. What this quotation indicates is the importance of political enthusiasts in the organization. In the 1911 campaign in Quebec the Nationalists breathed fire in the direction of Laurierism and life into the largely moribund Conservative organization. However, the reinvigoration was temporary.

Bourassa linked up with the Conservatives because of his commitment to scuttling Laurier's navy. It was this issue above all which attracted him and his friends to the Conservative alliance. But Bourassa would have seen no gain in linking his fate with the Tories were it not for the solid base the party enjoyed in the province already. Its organization was weak but its tentacles extended widely. The extent of these tentacles for both parties in all

6   Public Archives of Canada, Borden Papers, vol. 28, Thomas Casgrain to Borden, 17 Sept. 1913. Information on prewar voting behaviour on which the above discussion is based is found in several sources: Douglas Baldwin, 'Political and Social Behaviour in Ontario, 1879-1891: A Quantitative Approach' (PhD thesis, York University, 1973); Donald Blake, 'Regionalism in Canadian Voting Behaviour 1908-1968' (PhD thesis, Yale University, 1973); M. Janine Brodie and Jane Jenson, *Crisis, Challenge and Change: Party and Class in Canada* (Toronto 1980); and K.M. McLaughlin, 'Race, Religion and Politics: The Election of 1896 in Canada' (PhD thesis, University of Toronto, 1975).

areas of Canada explains the dominance of the two-party system in prewar Canada.

First, there were affiliated groups whose relationship with the parties was almost symbiotic. The papers of Conservative party organizers in Toronto, for example, reveal that in the first years of the century the Conservatives and the Orange lodges often shared meeting halls and that lodge membership constituted a strong recommendation for a patronage position. It was no coincidence that Robert Birmingham, the chief Conservative organizer and dispenser of patronage in Toronto for the Conservatives, also held high office in the Orange Lodge. J.S. Carstairs, a colleague of Birmingham in the sorting out of patronage questions, reflected other interest groups which coincided with the Tory party: he was involved in the militia, the Freemasonry movement, and the United Empire Loyalist Association. Both were Anglicans, and most Anglicans were Conservative. In a very real sense, private and political life were intertwined.

Similarly, working life and party life were often integrated. In the 1880s the socialist Phillips Thompson lamented the hold which the political parties had established over working-class political behaviour. The politicians, he complained, 'have been able to use labour because working-men have put party first.' 'Energy and intelligence which ought rightly to be devoted to the solution of the labour problem are worse than wasted over the petty, misleading, idle issues which partyism keeps in view ...' In the last decades of the nineteenth century the Canadian parties wrestled with the spirit of political independence which often cropped up in labour movements. By the mid-1890s the parties had largely won the tussle.

Patronage was a key means by which the traditional parties restrained independent labour politics. By the 1880s, Gregory Kealey points out, several labour leaders had received rewards from political commitment. J.S. Williams, a printer, had become a full-time Conservative organizer. John Hewitt, a cooper, became the assistant editor of the *Orange Sentinel* where his boss, E.F. Clarke, had been a leading agitator during the printers' strike of 1872. Clarke eventually became a prominent politician, serving as Toronto's mayor, an MPP, and an MP. On the other side, the Liberals rewarded labour leaders D.J. O'Donoghue and Alfred Jury with provincial appointments.[7]

Such patronage appointments, Laurier believed, were 'the most important single function of government.' Provincial leaders would have agreed. In his study of Saskatchewan Liberalism before 1917, David Smith points to the great attention that party gave to patronage questions. Patronage was 'clearly federal or provincial in origin, but either might be rewarded to

---

7 Gregory S. Kealey, *Toronto Workers Respond to Industrial Capitalism 1867-1892* (Toronto 1980), 217

individuals whose claim rested on service in the other realm.'[8] In this sense, patronage was a powerful glue between federal and provincial components of the same party, and it was probably a nationalizing force, restricting tendencies towards third parties in new areas. In older areas such as the Maritimes and the central provinces, patronage lubricated the party's organizational gears.

The hope of appointment – as a mailman, customs clerk, census taker, or senator – brought forth party workers in election campaigns. There was virtually no restriction upon the activities of government employees in political campaigns. Only the fear of firing by a new government curtailed the worst partisan excesses by government employees. But this fear was not always effective. In Manitoba, government employees, on the instructions of the 'Hon. Bob' Robert Rogers, drilled wells with government equipment on government time for potential and actual Conservative voters who settled in the province. Sometimes, however, Clifford Sifton's 'army' of immigration agents and land agents had got to the new Manitobans first, and captured them for the Liberals before the well was drilled.

The government thus indirectly supported the existing party system by permitting political action by government employees on a large scale. These efforts, however, did not encompass the full range of patronage in the Canadian political system. Campaigns were very expensive, and sustaining the party between campaigns also required funds. Again in Manitoba in 1915-16 the investigation of how the contracts were awarded for the building of the legislature revealed the dependence of parties (in this case the Manitoba Conservatives) on donations from business interests. It also revealed fraud: in return for an 'extra' payment of $892,098.10, the contractor Thomas Kelly paid 'large sums' of money to Dr R.M. Simpson, the president of the Provincial Conservative Association. Other investigations and trials revealed similar occurrences in the granting of road-building contracts and the construction of other government buildings. Nor was the practice restricted to Manitoba and the Conservatives.

The world of political fund-raising in prewar Canada abounded with stuffed envelopes quietly passed on street corners, nervous winks, and even telegraph taps. The papers of contemporary politicians reveal the pressure they faced because of the need for party funds. It was a nasty business that brought politicians into contact with some remarkably nasty people. Generally, the party tried to protect its leader from the nastiest, but this was not always possible. In 1903-4, for example, Robert Borden faced his first

8 O.D. Skelton, *Life and Letters of Sir Wilfrid Laurier* (Toronto 1921), volume 2, 270; Da Smith, *Prairie Liberalism: The Liberal Party in Saskatchewan, 1905-71* (Toronto 1975), 42

election as Conservative leader and found party funds exceedingly scarce. He turned for help to Hugh Graham, publisher of the *Montreal Star,* who loved political intrigue and titles. The future Lord Atholstan drew Borden into a silly plot which involved secretly buying *La Presse,* getting Liberal candidates in Quebec to resign their candidacy just before election day, and having some railway interests supply ample quantities of campaign funds. The scheme collapsed under its own light weight. Borden would be more careful in the future, but the need for funds persisted.

As unpleasant as Graham was, he could provide funds. And money was needed to help the Tories in areas such as Quebec where the Liberals governed provincially and, with their federal brethren, controlled all government patronage. He also owned one of the most powerful newspapers in Canada. Its influence had been proven in the agitation Graham led to commit Canada to participate in the Boer War. In some ways, however, Graham's newspaper was exceptional in that it had financial independence. In smaller cities and with newspapers of smaller circulation, closer attachment to a political party was characteristic of the press. And this was true of many larger city dailies as well. The rapid growth of newspapers throughout post-Confederation Canada may be attributed to 'politicians and their minions who strove to construct countrywide networks of outright organs.'[9] These newspapers were sometimes owned directly by the party, but in most cases the control was indirect. The party might have provided some venture capital to a sympathetic Conservative or Liberal who wanted to start a newspaper. After that, there would be government advertising in addition to the knowledge that good party people would read only good party newspapers.

The importance of the party press at this time rested on the absence of alternative media as well as the near universal literacy which obtained in Canada by 1900 (see chapter 1). The price of newspapers had declined greatly since Confederation and, as a result, they were much more widely read. Some newspapers, such as Graham's *Star* and John Ross Robertson's *Toronto Telegram,* could well afford to be independent; they were highly popular and profitable mass newspapers. Nevertheless, pure habit and the partisan spirit of their owners made their editorials and their news reports one-sided. The *Telegram* made every Borden speech a Periclean performance in which vast throngs cheered the brilliance and the eloquence of the leader. In the *Globe,* in contrast, Borden invariably spoke to an empty hall and droned out a lacklustre squib. The opposite applied to Laurier. No matter, the readers had had their bias stroked.

9 Paul Rutherford, *The Making of the Canadian Media* (Toronto 1978), 49. See also Brian Beaven, 'Partisanship, Patronage and the Press in Ontario, 1880-1914: Myth and Realities,' *Canadian Historical Review* 64 (Sept. 1983): 317-51.

In the view of John Willison, editor of the *Globe* in the 1890s, the Canadian press was more partisan than in any other 'civilized country in the world.' Willison and Joseph Flavelle tried to make Toronto more 'civilized' by founding a truly 'independent' newspaper in 1902. The Toronto *News* lasted six years before its poor balance sheet forced its sale to a Conservative syndicate. The attempt to found an 'independent' newspaper and the arguments used to justify it, are significant. For a great number of Canadians, partisanship was becoming less 'civilized.' Moreover, the flurry of new newspapers and periodicals which sprang up after the turn of the century reflected an economic or social interest not directly related to the activities of either political party. The best examples were the numerous papers in western Canada which spoke for regional interests or for a disgruntled economic grouping.

The Canadian party system had remarkable success in embracing a diversity of interests in the period of rapid growth and change which occurred after 1896. Until 1911, the parties had worked to obscure issues upon which Canadians felt deeply, thereby making both Liberalism and Conservatism palatable to the taste of nearly all Canadians. Some, however, believed that they were tasting warm gruel and that the texture and the taste could be markedly improved. These Canadians included individuals with such diverse views as Henri Bourassa, Clifford Sifton, and Stephen Leacock. The number of articulate and influential Canadians who had broken free of party restraints grew rapidly after 1900. Their number permitted Borden to build his coalition which tumbled Laurier from office in 1911, but he soon found that their independence was real. They asked what a party could do to serve their diverse aims, and they founded associations and institutions where the touch of party was light. The hostility of these independents grew as the parties refused to embrace their aims. Their visions were exclusive; the Canadian party system was not. A clash was inevitable.

4

The Great Boom of 1900-13

From the turn of the century until the outbreak of the First World War, Canada experienced the greatest economic boom in its history. The development was not unprecedented; there had been booms before, and we know that the years from Confederation to the early 1890s had seen a quite impressive development of industry in central Canada. But the Great Boom of 1900-13 captured the imagination of contemporaries in not only Canada but also Britain and the United States. It has continued to fascinate historians.

During these years the fields and mountains of the Canadian west became as populated as they are ever likely to be. Farmers settled in the thousands on the wheat fields of the prairie provinces; prairie cities grew many-fold. In northern Ontario and Quebec, new mines, fields, and paper mills appeared. In British Columbia, mining and forestry developed apace; the city of Vancouver became the metropolis of its province and a major seaport not only for British Columbia but for the prairies as well. At the same time, rapid urbanization and industrial development occurred in central Canada and Cape Breton Island. The railway network was transformed, as was the financial system which came to resemble the arrangement we know.

PEOPLING AN EMPTY LAND

In 1900 Canadians could look back on thirty years of demographic disappointment. Immigrants had come to Canada in some numbers – in particular from the British Isles, and chiefly to the Province of Ontario and the Montreal area – but emigrants had left in somewhat larger numbers, so that the country had not retained the natural increase of its population. The Canadian Pacific Railway and the dominion government both wanted to attract agricultural settlers, but neither Ontario nor Quebec had much of an agricultural frontier, and as yet it was not profitable to produce prairie wheat west of Manitoba. In Quebec the Catholic church and the provincial authorities had been anxious to encourage 'colonization' on the fringes of the Canadian Shield, but the land was not enticing and there did not seem to be enough to keep the Québecois from emigrating – partly to Ontario, but mainly to the New England states. In the Maritime provinces, similarly, there was not much of an agricultural frontier, and the area received virtually no immigrants; most of its natural increase flowed outward, to Ontario and New England. From Ontario, farm boys drifted to Manitoba and the fields and factories of the United States. In the North-West Territories and in British Columbia in-migration had fuelled a considerable growth of population, but still only 343,000 dwelt in the coastal province.

When Clifford Sifton became minister of the interior in the autumn of 1896 there were no controls over people who came to Canada by rail and, at the ocean ports, only three classes of migrants were proscribed: the diseased, the criminal or vicious, and those who appeared likely to become public charges. Prime Minister Sir Wilfrid Laurier believed in wide-open immigration, but Sifton, though willing to encourage migrants, was not anxious to see Canada's cities grow.

In their attitude to migrants, Sifton and his department may well have been more liberal than most Canadians, but they were not free of prejudice. There was already a $50 head tax on Chinese immigrants; Sifton raised it to $100 in 1900 and to $500 in 1903. The result, of course, was an end to immigration from China. Sifton was worried about the Japanese migrant as well, but could not take measures against them, largely because of the alliance between the British empire and Japan. When he left the ministry in 1905, however, the dominion's southern and eastern borders were as open as they had been in 1896. In continental Europe the borders were anything but open. It was in general not possible to 'incite emigration.' Sifton therefore devised, in 1899, a secret agreement with a group of German travel agents, by which the Canadian government would pay bonuses whenever agricultural migrants were diverted to Canada. The arrangements were later extended, so that by 1902 they covered the area from northern Italy to Finland, and from Belgium to Bulgaria and Romania. These arrangements lapsed soon after Sifton left office, in 1905. They had never extended to France, which was actively anxious to discourage emigration, or to Britain, where there were no rules respecting the outward movement of people.

The new Immigration Act of 1906 appeared to set the free-entry policy officially to rest. Now there was control along the American border; new provision for the deportation of immigrants who might become criminals, public charges, or infirm; new rules for the exclusion of the same groups, as well as prostitutes and procurers; and means by which the government could fix a necessary minimum 'landing money' and make other regulations as well. In 1907, consequently, there were regulations to exclude certain subsidized migrants and to require from $25 to $50 in landing money, except from agricultural workers, domestic servants, and immigrants who were coming to join close relatives. Immigrants were obliged to come by direct continuous journey from their homeland, the Japanese government was persuaded to restrict emigration to Canada, and Asian immigrants who were neither Chinese nor Japanese were obliged to possess $200 in landing money. The 'continuous journey' provision, of course, did not apply to American citizens, even if they had begun their lives in some other country. Nor could it be applied to people from the British Isles, with whom Canada shared a common citizenship. However, people from Britain could be excluded, if they did not have the landing money or if their passage had been subsidized in certain ways. Paupers, in particular, were unwelcome. British immigrants could be, and were, deported. In 1910 it was established that 'no person may enter Canada as a landed immigrant if his way has been paid by a charitable society unless that charitable society has been approved by the Canadian Government.'[1]

In British Columbia, meanwhile, there was increasing fear about oriental immigrants, who were arriving not only via CPR steamships but across the American border – the latter movement not being reflected in the statistics reported above. In 1907 'there were ... only about 100,000 adult males in British Columbia of whom perhaps 75,000 were whites and 25,000 already Asiatics.'[2] In no time, unless something were done, it was thought that British Columbia would have an Asian majority. The legislature of British Columbia regularly passed oriental-exclusion legislation, which the dominion always disallowed. The Anglo-Japanese Treaty, which included Canada, provided for the free movement of the nationals of the two countries. In accepting the treaty, the Laurier government believed that the Japanese government would maintain the existing informal and secret arrangements for the control of Japanese emigration. The populace, naturally, knew nothing about these arrangements, so it was necessary to negotiate with Japan. Rodolphe Lemieux and Joseph Pope went to Tokyo in November 1907, and agreement was quickly reached: 'for diplomatic reasons,' in an early form of 'voluntary quotas,' the Japanese government would allow no more than 400 migrants to go from Japan to Canada each year. In January 1908 Ottawa decreed its 'direct voyage' regulation, thus ensuring that Japanese and Indi-

---

1   Mabel F. Timlin, 'Canadian Immigration Policy 1896-1910,' *Canadian Journal of Economics and Political Science* 26 (Nov. 1960): 523
2   Ibid., 524

ans could not evade the controls by using Honolulu as a transfer point. In the same year, lest Asian migrants evade the 'passage money' requirement by travelling via the United States, the immigration controls on the American border were at last set up.

In 1910 another new Immigration Act strengthened and codified the government's power to issue orders respecting immigration. It also proscribed subversive immigrants and allowed the government to make new sorts of regulation respecting the presentation of passports and certain other documents. By this point the government's purpose was to discourage immigration not only from Asia but also from southern and eastern Europe.[3] The plan, however, was not carried into effect: in the years 1911-19 immigration rose year by year, reaching, incredibly, the 400,000-person mark in 1913. Meanwhile, immigration from southern and eastern Europe was rising too, so that in 1913, 27 per cent of the immigrants came from those areas.

At the time, and in the 1920s, many Anglo-Canadians worried about the size of this inflow. Could so many aliens be Canadianized, and, if so, how? Much of the work would fall upon the schools, especially in the three Prairie provinces. There was no question of 'multi-culturalism.' The public schools would work in English. The values and attitudes would be Anglo-Saxon. Immigrant communities could preserve their own traditions and languages only with their own money and on their own time.

From 1900 to 1921, besides the wave of immigration, Canada's own demographic engine was pushing up the population and the labour force at a considerable speed. The available estimates exclude children less than ten years old. They suggest that between 1900 and 1921 natural increase raised Canada's population by at least 1.5 million – 36 per cent of the comparable population in 1901, and 27 per cent of total population. Whereas before 1900 much of this natural increase would have flowed abroad, the reverse occurred between 1900 and 1931 and even in the 1930s emigrants were few compared with the natural increase of the population. The twentieth century might or might not belong to Canada, as Wilfrid Laurier had said, but at least, after 1900, most of the Canadian-born would spend their lives in Canada.

This is not to say that no Canadians went abroad. A few settled in Britain and the West Indies; rather larger numbers went to the United States. Thanks to the common empire citizenship, Canadians could move freely to Britain; because the United States did not regard Canadians as an ethnic threat, Congress imposed no limits on Canadian immigration even after Washington began to fix quotas for most migration. A few Canadians would

3   See Canada, Department of Manpower and Immigration, *The Immigration Program* (Ottawa 1974), 8.

always find special attractions in the tropics or in the 'Old Country'; more would be drawn to the United States by higher living standards and, often, wider opportunities. Thus Max Aitken, later Lord Beaverbrook, left Montreal for London, and John Kenneth Galbraith moved from southwestern Ontario to Massachusetts and Washington, before settling eventually in the Swiss Alps. Nevertheless, from the turn of the century until the end of the 1920s the opportunities in Canada were better than ever before; most Canadians stayed at home.

If twentieth-century Canada was attractive to its own native sons and daughters, it proved enormously attractive to those who came from elsewhere – especially from Britain and the United States. US immigrants, especially important in the settlement of the Prairie provinces, were often Canadian-born, or children of Canadian-born, who had earlier migrated to the south. In 1900 most Americans and other people could and did cross the border without anybody paying the slightest attention: in those days before quotas, visas, 'landed immigrant status,' and SIN numbers no one knew just how many immigrants there were. The arrivals from overseas were more carefully recorded. Passports were the exception rather than the rule; there was no such thing as 'Canadian citizenship,' and British subjects from the United Kingdom could and did work, vote, and take part in public life with little formality and no red tape.

We might wonder where the immigrants had previously lived, what their ethnic origins were, and where their trip to Canada began. The available data record the pattern only incompletely. As for the point of departure, 60 to 80 per cent of all Canada's immigrants arrived from the United Kingdom and the United States. As for ethnic origin, almost 60 per cent of the recorded immigrants were of 'British and Irish stock,' while almost none of them were of French – just over 1 per cent of the total. Jewish immigrants made up 3.9 per cent of the total; most of them seem to have come from northern, central, and eastern Europe, regions which provided 29 per cent of the immigrants. Italy and the Mediterranean provided 6.5 per cent, and all of Asia and Africa only 3.8 per cent – a very different pattern from that of the 1960s and 1970s. Indeed, as a result of the dominion's punitive measures, in 1903-4 there were no recorded immigrants from Japan and China, while in 1900-1 there were a total of fifteen. Canadian immigration policy was anything but colour blind: in spite of the common imperial citizenship, Canada did everything it could to ensure that imperial subjects from the West Indies, Africa, and India would not settle in the dominion. The topic was especially sensitive in British Columbia, where a small colony of Indian Sikhs had established itself well before 1900. 'British,' therefore, almost always meant 'white.'

Before 1914 this torrent of immigrants had an immense demographic impact. It was changes in migration flows, not changes in vital statistics, which altered Canada's demography between 1900 and the First World War. If we consider the population that was ten years of age or over, we find that net immigration was considerably larger than natural increase. Between 1901 and 1911 Canada's population grew from 5.4 million to 7.2 million, an increase of 34 per cent, and 39 per cent of the growth came from net immigration. Both of these percentages are extraordinarily high; nothing like them had been seen before or since. As for natural increase, some contribution came from a decline in the overall death rate, which had been 16.2 per thousand in 1891-1900 as against 12.9 per thousand in 1901-10. The crude birth rate was slightly higher than it had been in the 1890s, although it was much lower than in the middle of the nineteenth century. The flow of immigrants rose from a low of 16,835 in 1896 to 272,409 in 1907, receded in 1908 to 143,326, and then rose to an all-time peak of 400,870 in 1913.[4]

Thanks to the development of the west, the distribution of Canada's population had changed by 1911, and even more so by 1921. The Maritime provinces, which attracted almost no immigrants and which continued to export much of their natural increase, contained 8.4 per cent of Canada's population in 1921; twenty years earlier their share had been 16.8 per cent. Ontario and Quebec, which had been demographically dominant in 1901 with 71.3 per cent of Canada's people, accounted for only 60.3 per cent in 1921. The share of the Prairie provinces went up from 7.9 per cent to 21.9 per cent. British Columbia and the Territories accounted for the rest, British Columbia's share nearly doubling. In these two decades, 150,000 native-born Ontarians settled elsewhere in the dominion, as did 39,000 Quebeckers and 37,000 Maritimers. Many of the Quebeckers and some of the Maritimers were moving to Ontario, but almost everybody else was going to the Prairie provinces and British Columbia. The result was to make the prairie population much more 'Ontarian' than it was to become in later decades and to establish a substantial 'Franco-Ontarian' population not only in the far eastern part of the province but in the mining and forestry areas of its northeastern region.

Some Canadians returned from the United States to settle the prairies, and many Americans came too, as did substantial numbers from the British Isles. There were problems about the British: since most were from cities, few wanted to settle on farms; nevertheless, especially in Saskatchewan, there were considerable numbers of new British farmers, and in Alberta there were British ranchers, including members of the Royal Family.

4   Warren Kalbach and Wayne McVey, *The Demographic Basis of Canadian Society* (2nd edition, Toronto 1979), table 2:1. Statistics which follow are from this source.

Thanks to the recruiting efforts of the dominion government and the railways, there were also large numbers of immigrants from Austria-Hungary and the Russian empire. There was no Polish state, and the folk we call Ukrainians might come from the Ukrainian districts of the Russian empire or from Galicia, a part of Austria-Hungary, which also contained many Poles and Jews. Hence, when minister of the interior Sir Clifford Sifton spoke of 'Galicians in sheepskin coats,' he was talking of agricultural immigrants from Russia or Austria-Hungary who might speak Ukrainian, Polish, or even Russian. The central Europeans were especially welcome because they could be trusted to settle on the land and to stay there. Conditions were hard, and disappointments common, but in general things were better on Canada's prairies than on the Ukrainian steppes.

Agricultural immigrants, however, were fewer than expected at least in relation to total immigration from overseas. From 1904 through 1914, 395,000 overseas immigrants said they were going to farm – but this number represented only 28 per cent of overseas migrants. Furthermore, an immigrant might say his intention was to farm, yet move to other work at once, or after a period of trial.

Thus, most of the immigration was non-agricultural. Where did these people settle, and what did they do? British Columbia attracted almost all the Asian immigrants, who took up fishing, truck-gardening, and retail trade. But most of the immigrants to British Columbia were British, and these people worked in mining, forestry, and the whole range of urban occupations. Jewish immigrants settled overwhelmingly in towns and cities, especially in Toronto, Montreal, and Winnipeg, where they soon became prominent in commerce and manufacturing. Italians, also, congregated in Toronto and Montreal; immigrants from Britain and northwestern Europe were also drawn to the cities and towns. For central Canada, economic growth meant industrialization and the exploitation of new mineral resources; both developments meant urbanization, not only in such large centres as Montreal, Toronto, Hamilton, and London but in mining centres such as Sudbury and Cobalt and transport foci such as Fort William. Even in Ottawa and Hull, where government was not yet a 'growth industry,' forest-products industries were far from dead and new goods, such as paper, carbide and streetcars, were manufactured.

Such new developments pulled immigrants from central Europe. Thus, for instance, by 1914 there were substantial numbers of Poles in the Hamilton steel mills and in the mining camps of northern Ontario. Even so, in 1921, 92 per cent of the Quebec population and 87 per cent of the Ontario population was Canadian-born, and a large fraction of the residual came from the British Isles. The west had been populated by non-francophones, yet in 1921 Canada still contained only 107,000 Ukrainians, 53,000 Poles, 67,000 Italians, and 126,000 Jews.

In demographic terms, the 'two founding peoples' were still dominant. In 1901 people of British and Irish origin made up 57 per cent of Canada's population; in 1921, after twenty years of hectic immigration and diversification, the fraction was 55.4 per cent. As for people of French origin, they made up 31 per cent of the nation's population in 1901, and 28 per cent in 1921. In linguistic terms, of course, things might be different: many of the non-French immigrants spoke English on arrival, or learned it soon afterwards; few learned French. There was, nevertheless, little sign that the French-speakers were really in danger of being swamped, even in Montreal where the anglophone percentage of the population had dropped considerably since Confederation.

THE COURSE AND CAUSES OF THE BOOM

The Great Boom has attracted considerable scholarly attention. Two descriptions have enjoyed special popularity: one characterizes the period as Canada's 'take-off into self-sustained economic growth,' a view popularized by the American economist W.W. Rostow; the other describes it as a 'wheat boom' fuelled by the burgeoning wheat economy of the prairies. Both these views have some merit and truth behind them, but they do not tell the whole story.

That story is much more complex. First, the 1896 boom had its predecessors. There was considerable industrial growth in Canada in the years before 1896; if there was a 'take-off' it occurred then and not in the twentieth century. Second, the Canadian economy is too regionalized, too specialized, to be entirely dominated even by the great railway-and-settlement boom on the prairies under the Laurier government. What is true is that forces making for growth in British Columbia, central Canada, and Cape Breton interacted with the boom on the prairies, producing a kind of economic explosion.

Clearly, the expansion was 'demand-led,' not 'supply-determined' – that is, an expansion in the demand for output induced an expansion of the economy, pulling into Canada large quantities of labour and capital from abroad. Present-day economic theory would suggest that such a demand-led expansion is almost certain to originate with exports, domestic spending on new plant, equipment, and housing, and new government spending. These factors might be present singly or in combination; they might or might not interact with one another. How important was each of them?

Between 1896 and 1913 there was an impressive expansion of exports, especially from agriculture. Exports of animal products went down, as Ontario milk producers diverted their output from the British market to the rapidly growing local market for milk, butter, and cheese. Reflecting the settlement of the west, grain exports surged ahead.

However, a comparison of investment data with export data shows that more stimulus came from the growth of investment than from the growth of exports. The value of new and repair construction increased by almost 400 per cent, while the value of exports went up just over 100 per cent. The size of the railway system and the quantity of residential housing increased much more rapidly than the volume of exports. Government construction also increased rapidly, but the absolute increases were small relative to exports and the rest of investment. Government's contribution, in other words, came through its stimulation of other investment spending, not through the growth of its own outlay.

Moreover, to some degree domestic production replaced imports in this period. Canada first produced steel in 1894 and steel rails soon after; after 1900 the domestic iron and steel industry satisfied a growing proportion of Canada's internal demand. This diversion of demand was a further stimulus to domestic expansion. Some of the results may appear startling. These were great years of railway building, for example, yet during this period Canadians consistently spent more on new housing than on the expansion of the railway system. Residential construction was needed because the cities, particularly in central Canada, were growing, and that growth derived in part from the expansion of the whole economy, including prairie development and the transport system.

No historian doubts that the prairie wheat boom was important as a spur to growth, but why did it happen when it did? At one time people thought that the 'closing of the American frontier' deserved the credit; that immigrants were diverted to Canada because in the United States there was no more free land. That, however, is not the whole story. Prairie farmers came to the Canadian west not merely to feed themselves; they wanted to sell and to export. Unless the expected returns were adequate, no rational man would bring his family to the Canadian prairies. It is reasonably clear that in the 1880s most of the prairies west of Manitoba were beyond the margin at which wheat growing was profitable. In the 1890s, however, conditions changed. From 1897 until 1914 the price of grain and fodder rose steadily and considerably, while prices of consumer goods in general rose far less rapidly and those of many agricultural inputs, such as machinery and building material, rose less rapidly still; some inputs, indeed, such as cement, actually became cheaper. The terms of trade were moving in favour of the farmer, who was also learning to grow new quick-maturing kinds of wheat and to cultivate arid lands with new dry-farming techniques. Also, at home and on the oceans, the transport system was becoming more efficient and competitive. Thus, the prairie farmer received a higher proportion of the European grain price and the railroads could profitably extend their networks of branch lines. The figures tell the story. In 1886 it cost 35.2 cents to move a bushel of wheat from Regina to Liverpool, of which 19.8 cents was the cost of shipment as far as the Lakehead. In 1913-14 the cost of moving a bushel of wheat from the prairies to the British market was less than it had been at any time before the turn of the century. Meanwhile, as Canada's railways learned their own business better, and as the total flow of traffic increased, the unit costs of operating prairie lines declined as well. New branches, therefore, were profitable, and the 'feasible region' for wheat farming grew larger.

Settlement, therefore, spread over the prairies, and a network of railway branch lines accompanied that spread. Just as the railways needed the farmer, so the farmers needed the railways and the small mercantile towns which quickly appeared along the tracks. In the process, millions of acres passed from large owner to small occupant. When the dominion purchased Rupert's Land from the Hudson's Bay Company in 1870, the company retained 20 per cent of the acreage in the 'fertile belt,' an amount which, after downward adjustments because of Indian reserves, national parks, and forest reserves, came to rest at 6,639,059 acres. The rest of Rupert's Land consisted of 'Dominion lands' and reserves. On entering Confederation in 1871, British Columbia transferred 14,181,000 acres to the dominion as a railway land grant. Much of the 'Dominion land' was passed on to the railway companies as a form of construction subsidy. Altogether, the dominion granted 31,783,654 acres of its lands to railway companies, of which 26,055,463 passed to the Canadian Pacific and its subsidiaries and the rest to the Canadian Northern, whose Toronto promoters, William MacKenzie and Donald Mann, had excellent connections in Ottawa.

The HBC and the railway companies did not always sell the land directly to settlers. Often they sold off large blocks to speculative land companies, which in turn would sell the land at a profit to farmer-occupants. It was precisely because prospects for wheat were buoyant that the land grantees could dispose of huge areas on increasingly favourable terms. Without willing occupants who could foresee a profit from wheat growing, the land grants would have been worthless. The dominion, furthermore, was willing and indeed anxious to sell its remaining land, both *en bloc* and in small parcels. The demand for purchased land, however, was limited by the availability of free or cheap 'homestead land.' Ever since 1871 it had been possible for a settler to occupy and eventually to own a free homestead that was normally 160 acres in size. Title would pass to the homesteader after three years of occupancy, so long as certain improvements were made, on payment of a small fee. In 1908 it became possible for homesteaders to buy an additional 160 acres, or even more, at low prices.

During the wheat boom period large areas were alienated by the dominion through the homestead system. Homestead land was cheap at 17 cents per acre, not including the necessary improvements. New free homesteads amounted to 24.1 million acres; in Alberta and Saskatchewan there were 30,498 new entries in 1913 alone, and in the three Prairie provinces, from 1900 through 1913, 407,603 entries. In addition, from 1909 through 1913, 66,159 homesteaders obtained extra dominion land on favourable terms, through purchase and pre-emption of adjacent quarter-sections.

As rural settlement grew, so did urbanization. It didn't take much to be urban in Canada, where 'urban' meant any incorporated place, or a densely settled, built-up place containing more than 1000 persons. Thus, 35 per cent of Canada's people were urbanized in 1901, 42 per cent in 1911, and 47 per cent in 1921. The Prairie provinces were the least urbanized, and the rapid growth of their populations ensured that for the dominion as a whole the figures would not be dramatic. But even on the prairies the urbanized proportion went up from 19 per cent in 1901 to 29 per cent in 1921, and in British Columbia, which also was growing quickly, the proportion went from 46 per cent to 51 per cent. In In all other parts of the country, urbanization made rapid progress. In Ontario the proportion rose from 40 per cent in 1901 to 59 per cent in 1921; in Quebec, from 36 per cent to 52 per cent; in the Maritimes, from 25 per cent to 39 per cent.

The cities were growing partly because the prairie farm economy was growing, creating a large and rapidly expanding outlet for the manufactures of eastern Canada and the Maritimes. To move goods to and from the prairies the country needed a larger 'infrastructure' – railways, ports, canals, financial and commercial institutions – all of which were based in and run from the towns. Furthermore, railway building and farm development created a growing demand for various 'capital goods' – everything from steel rails through locomotives and harvesters to electrical generating equipment and telephone exchanges – which came from the city factories of central and eastern Canada.

However, the city-based manufacturing industries of central Canada had been developing quite speedily for a long time before 1901, on the basis of local markets. Such development would have continued, although at a more leisurely rate, even if the western prairies had consisted of nothing more useful than granite. Also, central Canada and British Columbia were the beneficiaries of developments which had nothing at all to do with the prairies, and which might have been expected to produce unusual prosperity between

1900 and 1913 even if the prairies had not existed at all.

These were the years, for example, in which a real forest-products industry became established in British Columbia. The market for BC lumber was partly on the prairies but also in the United States and overseas. The same might be said of the British Columbia fisheries, and of pulp and paper and non-ferrous metals (eg, copper, zinc, or silver) mining and refining both in British Columbia and central Canada. In all parts of the dominion, but especially in British Columbia, Ontario, and Quebec, the development of hydroelectricity meant plenty of construction, and the industry of central Canada was able to produce much though not all of the heavy electrical equipment that was needed. Similarly, it was after 1900 that the automobile industry came to Canada, with important effects for the producers of steel, rubber tires, glass, petroleum products, and so on.

How did these developments affect Canada's market place? Even as late as 1921 the dominion's domestic markets were *not* predominantly in the west, which still contained less than 30 per cent of Canada's people. Western development presumably stimulated such industries insofar as it made Canadians more numerous and more prosperous. But that development was not the only spur to growth. The farm implements industry, whose protected status so annoyed prairie farmers, had a large and thriving market in central Canada. By 1910, after more than a decade of rapid prairie development, farm implements accounted for less than 10 per cent of the gross value of Ontario manufacturing.

In effect, what Canada had was a very complicated kind of boom, fuelled by new technology, new products, and new needs, as well as capital formation and the growth of exports, with many interactions among the elements of expansion. In the process, all the settled areas of the country, without exception, were dotted with new construction and new investment projects.

The most dramatic and best-known investment projects were connected with railway building. The Canadian Pacific expanded its prairie branch-line network, double-tracked its line from Winnipeg to the Lakehead, and built a new southern main line from Alberta through the Crowsnest Pass to join its original main line at Hope near Vancouver. The Canadian Northern first expanded its own branch lines in Manitoba and then began to extend itself eastward and westward, eventually producing a main line from Vancouver through the Yellowhead Pass to the Lakehead, Toronto, and Montreal. The long-established and British-owned Grand Trunk built the Grand Trunk Pacific from Prince Rupert to Winnipeg, where it connected with the dominion-owned National Transcontinental that continued to Quebec and Moncton. In Ontario the provincial government pushed its Temiskaming and Northern Ontario line from North Bay into the mining and agricultural zone of the Great Clay Belt. Around the Soo, private promoters built devel-

The Growing Time for Trans-Continental Railways.

The Premier: 'The people pay for and give you the Railways, and make you a present of the country; but what do they get as a quid pro quo?'
Chorus: 'The people – as represented by the Government – will get our vote and influence, you know.'
Laurier explains his railway policy to a hopeful audience
Bengough, 1901

opment lines, and other promoters tried to build a line northward from Vancouver to the main Grand Trunk Pacific Line at Prince George. In southern Ontario, electric 'radial lines' sprang up like fungoid growths. On the West Coast the British-owned B.C. Electric Company built its own radial seventy miles eastward from Vancouver. Huge sums of money were spent on lines and rolling stock. It is indisputable that many unjustified and imprudent lines were constructed, but equally obvious that the construction mightily stimulated the Canadian economy. And if each and every lunatic railway project of those years had actually been built, the boom would have been still greater.

Urbanization, in turn, implied enormous outlays on residential building and the provision of services, both public and private. In the mid-1890s Canada was completing fewer than 20,000 residential dwellings each year. For 1906 the figure was already nearly 50,000, and for 1912, over 80,000. The construction materials industries responded proportionately. For instance,

Ontario brick production rose from 117 million in 1896 to 490 million in 1913, and over the same period the province's production of Portland cement rose from 78,000 barrels to 3.8 million barrels. The country, it seemed by 1912, would soon be hip deep in bricks and cement – insofar as it was not covered with railway tracks.

THE CENTRE AND THE MARGINS

The Maritime provinces did not fully share in the great economic developments of the boom. They exported population and attracted few immigrants; their shipping and shipbuilding received no useful stimulus, and their fisheries were aided indirectly or not at all. However, even in the Maritime provinces there were signs of growth and change. Most obvious, perhaps, was railway development. The dominion-financed National Transcontinental, straggling through wilderness across New Brunswick to Moncton, created a great deal of work during the long period of construction. The Intercolonial, still subsidized from the dominion's exchequer, made a good many modest improvements. Although the dominion could not compel western wheat to move through the ports of Saint John and Halifax when Montreal, New York, and Portland were more convenient and cheaper, it did what it could to generate and channel trade to and from the Maritime ports, which inevitably found their trade expanding with the growth of the national economy. Regrettably, in serving the markets of central and western Canada, the manufacturers of Ontario and Quebec enjoyed enormous locational advantages, and the disadvantageous location of Maritime manufacturing firms translated into slower growth and lower wages. Nevertheless, thanks to the National Policy tariffs, the subsidized freight rates on the Intercolonial, and the dominion's bounty policy during the period, Nova Scotia did see some important industrial developments.

The demand for new railway rolling stock was such that many orders came to Nova Scotia firms, and the iron and steel complexes of Cape Breton were brought into existence. The task was far from easy, and success came slowly. Nova Scotia had plenty of coal, a little iron ore which was hard to smelt, and a poor location vis-à-vis the Canadian market. Fortunately, there was iron ore at Bell Island off Newfoundland, and insofar as it too was difficult to process, ore could be brought cheaply from Europe. Unfortunately, the chemical properties of both ore and coal made successful smelting difficult. But for some years the dominion paid bounties on coke pig iron and on steel rails and the railway boom created a massive though temporary demand not only for rails but for foundry iron; thus, the iron and steel companies persevered and, by 1913, just in time for the collapse of demand, their works appeared to be well established. Later generations would wonder whether the dominion had been wise to use subsidy and forced-draft demand to create the Sydney industry, given its dismal later record. But for the time being, Ottawa, and the Liberal politicians who were deeply involved with the Cape Breton enterprise, could claim it as the one great Maritime success from the period of the wheat boom.

In financial matters, also, the period saw some interesting Nova Scotian developments. In 1900 the Halifax business community was deeply involved with banking in the West Indies and by 1905 this interest had broadened to include company promotions – utilities projects for Jamaica, Puerto Rico, and other areas as well. New securities houses, such as Royal Securities, were formed to arrange for the distribution of bonds; new entrepreneurs, especially Max Aitken, found a lucrative business in company promotion and bond selling. Nor was Halifax finance cut off from the developments on the north shore of the Nova Scotia mainland or in Cape Breton. Although American and British capitalists were active in the Nova Scotia iron and steel industry from time to time, the businessmen of the province were by no means shut out from it.

Later generations wonder whether a more self-conscious policy of regional development might have produced a better balanced growth between 1900 and 1913. More specifically, was it really necessary or desirable for industry to concentrate so strikingly between Windsor and Quebec City? In hindsight, of course, it is impossible to tell whether manufactures might not have been shifted to the west, or the east – perhaps even to Prince Edward Island.

It must be admitted that if governments are prepared to regulate and subsidize sufficiently, almost anything is possible. Thus, in the abstract, the dominion could have caused oil refineries to sprout in Calgary, where oil had not yet been found, or shifted blast furnaces and rolling mills to Vancouver, 2000 miles by rail from Mesabi ore, or arranged for the conversion of trees into wood pulp at Charlottetown, where the potato was king. These things did not happen, but others were dreamt of and some were actually implemented.

The contemporary ideologists of Quebec could and did regret the drift of the *habitants* to the evil ways of the city. Winnipeggers hoped to become an industrial focus, and to some extent they did. Both in Ontario and Quebec there were serious and entirely misconceived efforts to plant new agricultural offshoots on the inhospitable clay and rock of the Canadian Shield. Fortunately for Canadian taxpayers, although local industrial development was a plentiful source for patronage both direct and indirect, the dominion government of the day had no idea about 'regional balance,' 'the equalization of regional disparities through industrialization,' or whatever. Almost certainly, it was well that they did not. For the locational pull of central Canada was very strong. It could get the coal and the quality iron ore; it had the population, the oil, plenty of water power and lots of timber, a decent educational system, and a well-developed commercial-financial infrastructure. The local market of central Canada was as concentrated, prosperous, and acquisitive as any which the dominion was ever likely to possess. To overcome this locational pull, the manipulations and subsidizations would have had to be enormous. And to what end?

The ideologues of later times would regret the fact that so many Maritime 'lads o'pairts' had to pack their suitcases and head for the high timber of British Columbia or the fleshpots of 'upper Canada.' But did the actual wanderers care? Perhaps they did not. So far as anyone can tell, Max Aitken moved from New Brunswick to Halifax, then to Montreal, and finally to Britain without detectable pangs of regret. He moved to better himself, and he certainly succeeded. Others did the same.

THE TARIFF, THE DOMINION GOVERNMENT, AND THE GREAT BOOM

In the literature of Canadian economic history we are often told that in the Great Boom there was a Grand Design. The dominion, it is suggested, wanted to build a nation by a mixture of prairie settlement, which would create exports; railway building, which would unify the country and serve the prairies; and tariff protection, which would stimulate manufactures – these depending, in turn, on the prairie markets. Hence it was eminently logical for the Laurier government to embark in 1903 on a massive program of railway subsidy, simultaneously distributing western lands and maintaining Macdonald's National Policy tariffs. However conscious the design may have been – and political historians are less inclined than economic historians to believe in it – no one would deny that dominion economic policy did centre on the three elements: land, railways, and the tariff. We have already discussed the first two; now we must glance at the third.

The tariff was not only a protective device; it also produced most of Ottawa's revenue. In 1901, 54 per cent of Ottawa's revenue came from customs and another 20 per cent from excise taxes, while the gross revenues of the post office produced 6 per cent and dominion lands only 3 per cent. In 1913 the tariff produced 66 per cent of the total, excise taxes 13 per cent, dominion lands 2 per cent, and the post office 7 per cent.[5] In principle, therefore, the dominion authorities faced a difficult problem. If duties were pushed too

5   J.H. Perry, *Taxes, Tariffs and Subsidies* (Toronto 1955), volume 1, 107

high, the protective effect would cut off the flow of imports, bankrupting the dominion unless new taxes could be devised. If duties were too low, revenue might suffer, and so would the political reputation of the government in the urban manufacturing ridings, though not in rural areas. Already by 1910 the western farmers had noticed that the protective tariffs forced them to pay more for their purchases, while they had to sell their produce in world markets. Before 1900, when Canada contained no large single-crop agricultural exporting areas, it was always possible for the government to argue that insofar as the tariff caused cities to grow, it created new local demands for the produce of Ontario and Quebec farms. The argument was a mixture of truth and falsehood, but it could be politically effective. After 1900 the argument could still be used in central Canada, but in the burgeoning agricultural economy of the prairies, or in British Columbia, it did not commend itself even to the most unsophisticated. Indeed, in those parts of the country, critics were much more likely to ignore the fact that the dominion's port and railway works depended on the security of its credit, which in turn depended on its revenue, which further depended to a depressing extent on the tariff.

Canada began the twentieth century with a 'two-column tariff.' There was a general schedule and a preferential concession. When first introduced in 1897, this preferred rate could be given to any country which granted Canadian goods favourable treatment; in 1898 it became an exclusively British preference, extended at first to goods from the United Kingdom, the West Indies, New South Wales, and India. In 1900 the preferential concession was increased to a flat reduction of 33-1/3 per cent. In 1907 the flat-rate concession was replaced by a more variegated system of imperial preferential rates, and a third column of intermediate rates was introduced so that Canada could make concessions to non-empire countries without conceding the full margin of Imperial Preference.

The external economic policy of the dominion, like domestic policy, centred largely on the tariff. Ottawa pressed Britain at various imperial conferences to introduce a measure of tariff preference that was symmetrical with Canada's concessions. As all Canadian goods then entered Britain duty free, this 'concession' meant that Britain would have to impose a duty on competing goods from non-empire countries. So far as Canada was concerned, the goods which mattered were wheat, cheese, and bacon. Although some British politicians sympathized with this idea of 'Imperial Tariff Reform,' especially if the result would be wider empire markets for British manufactures, the British electorate was not attracted by the idea of a tax on its diet: since the empire could not produce enough wheat and animal products to satisfy the British market, a duty on foreign supplies would naturally raise the price in Britain, probably by the full amount of the duty. In 1906, not surprisingly, the British electorate defeated the party which favoured the idea.

The empire was already of importance for some Canadian manufacturers, although the impact was less marked than might have been expected. In the 1903 agreement which established Ford of Canada, the Windsor factories were given the entire British empire – minus Britain itself – as a happy hunting and selling ground. Thus, by 1914, Canadian-made Fords were being shipped to India, Africa, and Oceania, as well as to the West Indies. Other manufacturers benefited from preferential entry to some empire markets, but Britain herself still placed no duties on manufactures. Thus, Canadian producers had to compete on equal terms in the largest industrial market outside the United States. No wonder Canada's transatlantic exports consisted overwhelmingly of the primary products in which the dominion had a natural comparative advantage.

Thwarted in their efforts to manipulate the British tariff structure, the Laurier government welcomed the American approaches of 1911. It is far from clear just what these would have meant for Canadian industry and trade. The proposal covered natural products and a short list of manufactures. Canadian manufacturers were worried lest the list grow longer in future; they did not expect that the American's duty reductions would give them more of an outlet in the American home market, where the high American tariffs had long excluded Canadian manufactured goods. As for Canada's fishermen, foresters, and farmers, in general they produced the same natural products as their American opposite numbers and sold them in the same foreign markets on the same terms. By 1911, in other words, free trade in natural products would have been of little consequence for either the United States or Canada, although a few small groups, such as fruit and grape growers, might have suffered.

Given the fact that American products so often competed with Canadian, it is hardly surprising that before 1914 the United States market, although Canada's second largest, was far less important than the British market. In the period 1900-14 Britain normally took about half of Canada's exports, the United States well under 40 per cent, and most of the rest went to continental Europe, with small sales to the other parts of the British empire. As a supplier, however, the United States was far more important than Britain, providing about 60 per cent of the dominion's imports as against some 25 per cent that came from Britain. Canada sent some manufactures to the empire, food products to Britain and Continental Europe, and non-ferrous metals, lumber, pulp, and paper to the United States; from the United States she bought manufactures, raw cotton, petroleum, and tobacco, while from Britain she bought almost nothing but manufactures.

Canada thus took part in a system of international specialization and division of labour which was shaped by her own tariffs, the tariffs of other countries, and her own advantages and disadvantages in production. A high-income country with a small population, Canada would naturally tend, on balance, to import manufactured goods, as well as tropical and semitropical products which she could produce only at high cost, if at all. Her own tariffs restricted these imports somewhat, just as American tariffs restricted the dominion's exports of manufactures – even simple ones, such as newsprint paper, from which the Americans removed their duty in 1913 after some Canadian provinces imposed a 'manufacturing condition' on the export of pulpwood cut from crown lands. Given her advantages with respect to natural resources, Canada could and did export a wide range of products – wheat, flour, timber, nickel, other non-ferrous metals – to duty-free markets such as Britain and to protected markets such as France, whose duties were low enough for Canadian goods to 'jump.'

In the years between 1896 and 1914 the international division of labour was good for the dominion. Canada found new and buoyant markets for the things she could do well; the world economy supplied her with plenty of labour, capital funds, and the manufactures and raw materials which her growing and prosperous economy was eager to absorb. In future years, things would not always go so well.

GOVERNMENT AND THE ECONOMY

In earlier sections we saw that the dominion was concerned with the tariff, railways, and the distribution of dominion lands. Those three items did not exhaust its agenda for economic policy, but they came close to doing so. Similarly, the provincial governments, administratively weak and sometimes corrupt, were primarily interested in simple sorts of 'development,' concentrating their attention on transport and, in British Columbia and the central provinces, the management of crown lands. What is striking is how little governments did: interventionism and collectivism were remote, and any sort of socialism or overall planning was more remote still.

To an extent which later generations would find almost unbelievable, governments left the financial institutions alone. True, there were bank acts, which provided for the incorporation of chartered banks, regulated their investment policies, and controlled their power to issue their own banknotes, while enforcing the convertibility of these notes into gold or dominion notes. There was a Dominion Notes Act, which regulated the quantity of the dominion's own paper currency while ensuring the convertibility of that currency into gold, on demand, at a fixed price. But there was nothing we would call 'monetary policy,' no reserve requirements, no Bank of Canada, no one in Canada from whom the banks could borrow in moments of need. Insurance, trust, and mortgage companies operated in a complex legal morass. Admittedly, every such institution was regulated by some statute or other. But such companies, unlike the chartered banks, could opt for provincial or dominion incorporation, and in general they would be regulated by one, the other, or sometimes both. Furthermore, a disconcerting number of companies operated either under special legislation, or under the provisions of the general law as it had existed at the time of their several incorporations. 'Grandfathering' could have gone no further.

Since 1889 Canada had possessed anti-combines legislation, but it was toothless and ill-enforced. In 1910 the Liberal government brought in a new 'combines investigation' measure, but the law did not change the basic situation. Nor was it clear just how an effective measure could be devised, even if some government had wished to do so. Companies could incorporate under dominion or provincial law, and, as we saw in Chapter 2, the British North America Act gave the provinces jurisdiction over 'property and civil rights,' except where specific alternative provision had been made, as for banking and railways. The dominion could produce general anti-combines legislation only by using its power to create and modify the criminal law, which it did in measures in 1889 and 1910. But criminal law implied stricter standards for proof of wrong-doing, a tendency to provide penalties that many observers thought unconscionable, and severe difficulties in devising combines legislation which, like the American law, could enact some general vision of economic and social organization.

Although there had been important mergers before 1900 in such industries as bicycle making, farm implements, oil refining, and cotton textiles, it was really only after 1900, and especially in and after 1909, that concentration of economic power became a highly visible aspect of Canadian economic life. In the manufacturing industry, many of the newer lines, such as electrical apparatus, motor cars, and rubber goods, tended to be organized in huge enterprises. Thus, new firms such as Algoma Steel, Ford of Canada, Canadian General Electric, Canadian Westinghouse, and Canada Foundries were doing business on a massive scale, and they were growing fast. In addition, in 1909 low interest rates stimulated a remarkable wave of mergers which created some very large enterprises, such as the Steel Company of Canada and the Canada Cement Company, financed through industrial bond sales in Britain and Canada. The chance was seized by the new and imaginative bond houses, such as Toronto's Dominion Securities and Max Aitken's Royal Securities in Montreal. Meanwhile, in retail trade, the boom gave a new stimulus to the growth of the great retail stores – Eaton's, Simpson's, the Hudson's Bay Company, and such lesser regional enterprises as Vancouver-based Spencer's and Woodward's and Montreal-based Morgan's. By 1914 the department stores, great palaces of trade and temples of consumer prosperity, had come to dominate Canada's central cities. Except for such variety stores as Woolworth, chain merchandizing had yet to establish itself in any serious way, but by 1900 retail merchants were already complaining about the 'unfair competition' of the department stores and their mail-order operations. However, there was no dominion or provincial response to protect small business.

No one was interested in the devices which a later generation would call the 'welfare state.' Conditions in the workplace were improved sporadically from the 1880s by means of provincial legislation. Furthermore, several provinces made new arrangements for workmen's compensation, often extending or remodelling plans which had been introduced in the 1880s. But neither Canadian governments nor the fashionable 'reformers' were much interested in sickness insurance, old-age pensions, disability insurance, or unemployment insurance (not to speak of day-care centres!). Imperial and undemocratic Germany had provided sickness insurance and old-age pensions since the 1880s. Britain introduced such pensions, and a form of health insurance, in 1911, and New Zealand had already done likewise. These examples were not followed. Indeed, Canada's governments were even slow to look after their own employees. Ontario, for instance, provided teachers' and civil servants' pensions only in 1921.

Labour unions were of interest to governments only insofar as they might annoy capitalists or disrupt public order. We discuss their fate more fully in Chapter 5. Nor did anyone try to redistribute income through government taxing and spending. The dominion did not tax personal incomes, corporation profits, or inheritance. Only Prince Edward Island, British Columbia, and a few municipalities taxed personal income. In accord with ancient English and Scottish tradition, local governments had to aid the needy, although some provinces provided help for special groups of people – the insane, blind, deaf, orphans, and destitute who needed hospital care. Arrangements naturally differed from one province to another, but by the standards of the 1980s, or by contemporary standards in the Antipodes and some European countries, assistance was pennypinching, inadequate, and mean.

As for 'social ownership of the means of production,' or nationalization for short, most politicians did not want it; nor did the public, which regarded 'national' services like the Public Works Department, Post Office, and Intercolonial Railway, all of them believed to be sinkholes of patronage, as painful necessities that ought not to be duplicated. Admittedly there were exceptions, most importantly in Ontario, where the provincial government went into the railway and power-distribution businesses, and in the Prairie provinces, where governments bought the telephone systems from Mother Bell. Here and there municipal reformers hoped that a city-owned power plant, telephone exchange, or streetcar line would lower local charges and sweep corruption out of city hall. Now and then such reformers got their way, although in 1914 the great private utility companies still operated in Canada's cities. Sometimes, as in Ontario, private capitalists coexisted more or less uneasily with the new public enterprises.

Except where utility rates were in question, politicians also gave little thought to the terms on which most capitalists sold goods or services. Here the only important innovation was the introduction of rate regulation for the railways (1904) and for telephone service. The famous 'Crowsnest Pass Rates,' which governed the price of moving grain from the Canadian west, might be regarded as price control. But they should better be seen simply as a bargain. The rates arose out of CPR's desire to extend a branch line into the mining country of southeastern British Columbia and its hope that the government would help to pay for it. The Laurier government agreed to give the expected subsidy, $3.4 million, but in return the CPR agreed to reduce its rate for shipping grain by 19 per cent – in perpetuity. This was nothing new, and there were subsequent parallels in the experiences of other railways. Those other railways were obliged to match the CPR rates, even though they received no subsidy. That they could do so is testimony to the fact that railway operation costs were falling during this period. Hardly a punitive measure, from the capitalists' viewpoint! Indeed, American historians have suggested that rate regulation is basically in the capitalists' interest: among railway companies, it prevents destructive competition which bids rates down, while in the telephone business it guarantees at least a minimum rate of return on the large capital outlay the company has to make. Mother Bell, in other words, might have cried – all the way to the bank.

The dominion was subsidizing and building new railway lines, but it did not propose to operate them: the foolish and unnecessary National Transcontinental from Winnipeg to Moncton via the Canadian Shield was to be leased to the Grand Trunk Pacific. Sir Wilfrid Laurier may actually have believed that the line would be needed to move grain from the west; he had failed in his efforts to induce the Canadian Northern promoters and the Grand Trunk owners to co-operate, and he owed political debts to the Toronto interests who stood behind the Canadian Northern; he thought that a line through northern Quebec and New Brunswick would earn new political returns. It was convenient that in 1903 the dominion appeared to be in splendid financial shape, and that borrowing costs in London had never been lower.

MONEY AND FINANCE IN THE BOOM

Canada's financial institutions – the banks, trust companies, mortgage companies, insurance companies, bond dealers, stock markets, and credit unions – benefited from the boom and facilitated it in various ways. It is true that Canada contained no 'development banks' which would direct attention towards long-term industrial finance, that the nation's chartered banks could not make mortgage loans, and that the banks talked as if they restricted themselves to the financing of production, trade, and commerce, not long-term investment. It is also true that some banks and trust companies made errors and came croppers. Nevertheless, it is hard to fault the system as a whole. The mortgage and insurance companies were eager and willing to finance urbanization and western development through mortgage lending. The bond houses succeeded in developing an active domestic market for Canadian bonds, and with the help of the banks and the trust companies they became skilful at the tilling of financial fields in London and New York, thus facilitating the inflow of portfolio capital. It does not appear that in their lending policy the banks discriminated against manufacturers, the west, the Maritimes, or whatever. Some banks and some insurance companies were quite willing to make risky loans for the development of industry and transport, and for public utilities. One set of populists tends to criticize such loans for their riskiness; another set – or sometimes the same set – criticizes the financial system for not taking enough risks. It seems that banks and insurance companies cannot win.

It was during the period 1900-14 that Canada's banking system took on more or less its present shape. Branch banking, of course, had existed for a long time, but in the 1890s only a few banks had anything approximating to nation-wide branch networks, and there were a good many small banks which had only one or two offices. Also, there were scores of 'private banks,' especially but not exclusively in Ontario and western Canada. Finally, there were no credit unions or *caisses populaires*. After 1900 there were several new bank-charterings, but the number of chartered banks tended to fall as the larger institutions joined with smaller, regional banks. Regional banks either merged or migrated. Thus, the Merchants Bank of Halifax moved to Montreal and became the Royal Bank of Canada, while the Bank of Nova Scotia moved its executive offices to Toronto, where the Bank of Commerce was energetically and somewhat dangerously financing the railway adventures of William MacKenzie and Donald Mann. Branch offices, meanwhile, extended from coast to coast, as the Toronto, Montreal, and Hamilton banks spread their wings. Credit unions had not appeared by 1914, but in 1903, at Levis, the Desjardins *caisse populaire* movement, which has since scattered this special sort of credit co-operative through Quebec and into Ontario, was born. Although the model was European, the import was quickly domesticated. During the same period, trust companies and mortgage-loan companies were proliferating. Both kinds of firms drew funds not only from Canada but from Britain and France; both kinds were rapidly developing the 'semi-banking' business with which Canadians are now so familiar.

Contemporaries knew that prices were rising. We now know that the money supply was rising too, and most economists would blame the inflation partly on the boom and partly on the general upward drift in the world price level – a marked feature of the period. But the price advance was very gentle and by no means universal. Our best available measure of general prices stands at 55.9 in 1896 and 83.4 in 1913, where the price index is expressed as percentages of the 1935-9 figures. But the price of many manufactures rose little or not at all, while some manufactured goods actually became cheaper. It was primarily the price of agricultural produce, pulled up by developments in Europe and spurred further by reductions in domestic rail changes, that was rising. In many urban areas, rents and land prices, stimulated by the rapid growth of cities and by speculation, also increased very fast. But just as a fall in transport costs ensured that farmers would gain more benefit from improvements in world markets, that fall also reduced the delivered price of manufactures, whether imported or locally produced.

The businessmen and governments of the dominion were accumulating far more than the citizens of the country were willing to save. In 1900, it is believed, gross domestic capital formation was about 13 per cent of Canada's gross national product, and about 30 per cent of this capital formation came from abroad, so that Canadians were actually saving about 9 per cent of national output. By 1910 domestic savings had risen from 9 per cent to 13 per cent of national output, but capital formation had risen more rapidly still – to over 26 per cent of GNP – so that roughly half of all the new capital formation was financed from abroad.

The import of capital funds was continuous and, from 1900 to 1913, they cumulated to a total of $2.4 billion. Given the rate of growth and the pace of capital formation in the small Canadian economy, such imports of capital were inevitable, in the sense that they could have been avoided only if Canadians had consumed a great deal less. Even so, it was by no means clear that the country could have exported enough to push up its earnings sufficiently to pay for necessary imports.

Almost all the external money came from Britain and the United States, with Britain providing the larger share. In 1900, it has been estimated, 85 per cent of Canadians' external obligations were owed to Britons, and only 14 per cent to Americans; by 1916 the figures were 66 per cent and 30 per cent, respectively. The United States, in other words, was already an important financier of Canada's growth, but Britain provided more money, and the Canadian domestic economy still more.

American funds came largely as direct investments – that is, in connection with American ownership and management of an enterprise in Canada. In 1909 American direct investments seem to have been worth about $254 million, as against $121 million worth of British direct investments. The American firms tended to concentrate on branch plants in manufacturing, and on lumber, timber, pulp and paper, though American firms were found in other industries too. By 1900, for instance, Imperial Oil had come under American ownership through purchase. Canadian Westinghouse was established in Hamilton as a branch plant, and soon after the turn of the century Ford of Canada began operations as a joint venture of Canadian capitalists and the American Ford company. Canadian General Electric, however, was until the 1920s Canadian-owned.

British direct investments, in contrast, were much more dispersed. Only 13.5 per cent of the total investment was in manufacturing, while land, mining, oil, finance, and utilities attracted considerable British interest. In Ontario and on the prairies, various British financial firms were active; the Bank of British North America was owned in Britain; and the British Columbia Electric Railway Company, which ran all the utilities in Vancouver and Victoria, was owned in England and, to some extent, managed from there.

Although British businesses were not anxious to set up branch plants, especially in manufacturing, the British investor was willing and eager to lend to Canadian government and business. From 1900 through 1914 Canadian governments and businesses raised $1,390.6 million by floating securities on the British new-issue markets. In addition to these public issues of bonds and stocks, a good many issues were privately distributed in Britain. As economic historians William Marr and Donald Paterson report, 'Canada depended on Great Britain for over 85 per cent of imported portfolio capital prior to 1914.'[6] Not much could be raised by selling common stock; bonds were preferred, especially if they came from a government – the dominion, a province, a large municipality – or if they bore the guarantee of some government or other. Vancouver borrowed to build sewers; the dominion borrowed to build canals and railways; the Grand Trunk Pacific and the Canadian Northern did likewise, assisted by dominion or provincial guarantee; manufacturing firms borrowed to expand plants, buy out competitors, or reduce their obligations to Canadian banks; mortgage companies borrowed

6 *Canada: An Economic History* (Toronto 1980), 278 and table 9:4

so they could lend more in Canada, especially on the prairies and in British Columbia.

It is sometimes suggested that this massive inflow of funds, especially insofar as it involved direct investment and the operation of branch plants, represented some sort of cosmic failure of indigenous capitalism. But this is not so. Most of the inflow was portfolio investment, which by its very nature involved no element of foreign control. The borrowings reflected the decisions of Canadian entities – governments and businesses. It is true that if they wanted to go on borrowing, both governments and businesses would have to avoid annoying the British private lenders from whom most of the loans came. But it does not appear that in this period they were tempted into decisions which might have annoyed many capitalists, domestic or foreign. As for foreign and British direct investment, this was generally welcomed by the governments of the day because it created jobs, taxes, and a larger flow of goods and services. British and American entrepreneurs had to share the Canadian field with a large, imaginative, and enterprising crop of home-grown talent. Canadian businessmen were active in railway building, wholesale and retail trade, finance, and manufacturing; they were especially noticeable in iron and steel, machinery building, shipbuilding, the automobile industry, and everything connected with the rapidly expanding electrical industries. Foreign businesses were not coming to Canada to take advantage of an entrepreneurial vacuum; they were coming to jump the Canadian tariff, exploit valuable patents, make capital gains through speculation in land and minerals, and simply to make profits by serving the rapidly growing Canadian market with manufactures and the expanding world market with products such as pulp, paper, and nickel.

WHAT IT ALL MEANT

Most obviously, the boom transformed Canada both economically and politically. There was a significant population in the west and, sooner rather than later, the political system would have to take account of its wishes. At the same time, the weight of the Maritimes had been much reduced, simply because much of the new industry, and almost all the new people, were elsewhere. The country now produced many more sorts of manufacture, such as primary aluminum, steel, motor cars, and tires; production of most other manufactures, such as brick, cement, agricultural implements, and heavy electrical equipment, had expanded several-fold. So had the cities and their wage-earning industrial and commercial populations. Far more women now worked for wages. External trade, too, had been transformed, because Canada had the potential to export really large amounts of wheat, non-ferrous metals, forest products – and motor cars. In 1913 the Canadian economy produced manufactures which later statisticians have valued at $1,410 million; in 1900 output was only $550 million, and in 1895, only $375 million. Nor did inflation offset much of this advance.

As for the wage-earning masses whose numbers increased so greatly, their fate in terms of living standards remains obscure. All the big cities came to contain congested, slum districts, and in 1913, as in 1900, there were many families which made ends meet only with difficulty, depending on wives' and children's earnings and on the renting of rooms. Real earnings and real wage rates – money earnings corrected for changes in purchasing power – have yet to be accurately measured. The old saw has it that there are three sorts of untruth: lies, damn lies, and statistics. During the period of the Great Boom the dominion dealt with the last sort of untruth by gathering almost no economic data beyond the census tabulations, information about unions and strikes, and, after 1907-8, a good deal of annual information on agriculture. Administrative routines yielded some extra information on such things as imports, exports, telephones, and electric stations. But the result was only a sketchy and incomplete account of economic life. Some provinces tried to fill the gap, but their efforts were not impressive; most of the results are uncertain at best.

Serious study of prices and earnings began only in 1915, when the dominion published an *Enquiry into the Cost of Living*. The enquirers had to generate their own data, and many of their methods were anything but sophisticated. They concluded that in terms of food, wages had kept ahead of prices, but that in terms of rent, that was not so; therefore, real wages might be supposed to have stayed more or less unchanged. Their study included almost no manufactured goods such as clothing – the goods whose prices were rising the least. It was also unsystematic in the way various goods were combined into an overall measure of living costs. But there things remained until the 1970s, when scholars returned to the topic. Close analysis of working-class standards in Montreal and Toronto suggested that, at best, living standards may have remained unchanged during the boom. The Montreal study is persuasive; the Toronto study, when examined closely, less so. Meanwhile, economists had tried to recalculate better indices of money wage rates and prices: sad to say, their estimates often point in different directions.

In thinking about these matters, we should remember that the boom conditions were such that workers could not expect much immediate gain. First of all, governments were doing little to protect them. Second, the boom attracted many immigrants to the cities, increasing the competition for jobs. Furthermore, a high proportion of the nation's output was being accumulated; that effort would increase the flow of consumer goods and services only after a lag – or, if the investment plans were ill-conceived, not at all. Thus, working conditions remained hard, hours long, and earnings often insufficient to support a family.

Money wage rates and annual earnings rose, but at different rates, reflecting the uneven balance between supplies and demands for various groups of workers. Immigration affected this balance in that new arrivals found it easier to enter certain kinds of jobs. Prices were rising also, although in comparison with the experiences of the 1970s and early 1980s the increases were modest indeed. Thus, for some workers, such as railway employees, construction workers, and supervisory and office staff in manufacturing, general wage rates and earnings seem to have outrun prices. It also appears that in Ontario manufacturing, average annual earnings rose by more than the price level. For some groups, however – coal miners, metal miners, loggers – it is clear that real wage rates declined.

However, in evaluating the situation we have to be aware of the many uncertainties. Average wage rates may give a misleading impression if the number of work-hours changes – for instance, if a boom gives more regular employment, or if a slump, such as that of 1913-15, produces layoffs. The starting point and stopping point of any comparison is therefore very important. The year 1912, the height of the boom, must have been more favourable for many workers than 1913 or 1914, when in many industries there was a deep slump, or 1917, when wartime inflation had taken off. Also, we must remember that the underlying general indices are often quite primitive, as American studies have shown during the past quarter century. For many years it was believed that American real wage rates had stagnated between 1900 and 1913; when better price indices were constructed, it was found that real wages had risen. This finding is doubly relevant to Canada: since both Canadian and European workers could freely enter the United States, it is hard to see how Canadian industry could have attracted workers if its rewards consistently lagged behind rewards in the United States. In other words, if Canadian real earnings stagnated or fell while American real real wages or earnings rose, why did anyone come to work in Canada? And why did anybody stay in Canada to work?

In fact, the data seem to show that it was precisely those occupations which were most closely associated with the boom – construction, railways, Ontario manufacturing – where wages and earnings outgrew the price level. In some of these activities, such as railway work, unionization may also have played a part. Conversely, the decline in real wages in logging and mining may help to explain the relatively rapid penetration of labour unions in those industries – and the radical stance which such unions often adopted.

On the new prairie farms, furthermore, the course of real earnings is hard to trace. Certainly there were many disappointments, and many farmers found conditions much harder than they had expected. At the same time, throughout the period of the boom, things were going the farmers' way. Wheat prices were rising in relation to the price of inputs and consumer goods, while some rail rates and tariff rates were stable and others were declining. Yet many farmers felt they had somehow been cheated. Immigration agents and the farmers' own over-optimism had done the dirty deed, not the dominion government or the big interests back east.

The boom occasioned speculation – in timber lands, urban real estate, and also in manufacturing. Especially in western Canada, there was a natural tendency to believe that the boom was here to stay, and to make commitments accordingly. The small recession of 1904, and the more important one of 1907-8, were readily forgotten in the euphoria of 1909-12. But such a boom could not go on forever, even if world financial markets did not turn sour, as indeed they had begun to do by the middle of 1913. In western Canada speculative building had often outstripped the immediate demand for houses, shops, and factories. The same may have happened to some extent in eastern Canada. Although the new transcontinental railways were not yet finished, much of the most expensive work had been completed, so that the pace of construction slackened somewhat. In industry, too, there must have been many firms which found that, for the time being, the frantic construction and expansion of the past decade had given them more plant and equipment than they could profitably use. There may also have been a reduction in inventories, especially given the fact that money had become tighter than it had been for some years past. All these things would imply a decline in investment – a temporary cutback, doubtless, but painful nonetheless.

Thus, in 1913 the Great Boom ended, and when war broke out Canada's industrial economy was sunk in deep depression, even though the great railway projects were neither finished nor fully equipped, and even though prairie settlement still continued apace. The slump, and the subsequent recovery, are treated in Chapter 13. For some observers, especially those who deplored congestion, factories, and the uncertainties and insecurities of urban wage-earning life, a pause for regroupment might have its attractions. As we shall see in Chapter 5, during the period of the boom Canada had spawned a plethora of reformers, even if by 1913 they had yet to achieve their aim of 'national renewal.' The course of the Great Boom would have been much the same even if Canada had been purged of the Demon Drink at an earlier date. At the end of the boom, however, there was still a long agenda for social-economic reform, and many decades would pass before that agenda was completed. Meanwhile, capitalists had to adjust to a sharp drop in profits and expectations, and workers to a sharp rise in joblessness. Neither adjustment was pleasant.

5

Drink, Labour, Public Ownership, and Corruption, 1900-14

In the city, the Mausoleum Club stood on the quietest corner of the best residential street. Its imposing stone structure on Plutoria Avenue was surrounded by great elm trees on whose branches perched and sang 'the most expensive kind of birds.' But 'just below Plutoria Avenue and parallel with it, the trees [died] out and the brick and stone of the City [began] in earnest. Even from the Avenue you [could] see the tops of the sky-scraping buildings ... and [could] hear or almost hear the roar of the elevated railway, earning dividends. And beyond that again the city [sank] lower, and [was] choked and crowded with the tangled streets and little houses of the slums.'

The city was Stephen Leacock's Montreal where, on the mansion-studded boulevards, you could see 'a little toddling princess in a rabbit suit' who owned fifty distilleries, and 'incalculable' other infants who waved 'their fifty-dollar ivory rattles in an inarticulate greeting to one another.' But below the hill where the toddlers frolicked swarmed a dense humanity which lived in conditions of now unimaginable crowding and filth. Infants died as often in downtown Montreal as in Calcutta, and the streets reeked of open sewage and decaying garbage. Leacock saw this disparity – and he wanted reform.

Yet he distrusted the reformers whose panaceas he thought often reflected their own self-interest. When members of the Mausoleum Club found the city's politicians reluctant in their support for some of their projects, such as renewal of the franchise of the Citizen's Light Company, they too called for reform: 'The thing came like a wave. People wondered how any sane, intelligent community could tolerate the presence of a set of corrupt scoundrels like the twenty aldermen of the city.' Thus the Clean Government League, with its president Lucullus Fyshe, determined to throw out the rascals.

Election day was a total triumph for the cleans, thanks to the enormous commitment of their supporters. Never had an election been so pure; the league ensured that it was: 'Bands of ... students, armed with baseball bats, surrounded the polls to guarantee fair play. Any man wishing to cast an unclean vote was driven from the booth: all those attempting to introduce any element of brute force or rowdyism into the election were cracked over the head.' The Mausoleum Club celebrated the city's salvation long into the night. A rousing cheer greeted the news that the Citizen's Light franchise would be made for 200 years so that the company would have a fair chance to serve the citizens. 'So the night waxed and waned till the slow day broke, dimming with its cheap prosaic glare the shaded beauty of the artificial light, and the people of the city – the best of them – drove home to their well earned sleep, and the others – in the lower parts of the city – rose to their daily toil.' And still Leacock remained a reformer.

Leacock's wonderful book *Arcadian Adventures with the Idle Rich* (1914) expresses well the ambiguity of reform in prewar North America.[1] So much fell under the reform umbrella, and many scoundrels took shelter under it. As Leacock said, reform 'came like a wave' which was felt in all parts of the country. Some reformers demanded clean government, others wanted prohibition, others thought a simple tax on land would eliminate the nation's problems, while still others believed public ownership was the best panacea. Reformers seemed to share only indignation, but in actual fact they had more in common.

Stephen Leacock's teacher, the American economist Thorstein Veblen, understood what was happening to his times. It was not easy, he argued, 'indeed it is at times impossible until the courts have spoken – to say whether it is an instance of praiseworthy salesmanship or a penitentiary offense.' The rapid changes in society which occurred in the late nineteenth and the early twentieth century changed the way North Americans saw their world, and this in turn altered what they thought. When a society's self-proclaimed values conflict with the behaviour that society rewards, the perception is distorted – as in Veblen's example, or in Leacock's satires. Thus, Bob Edwards called his newspaper which roasted corrupt politicians and businessmen *The Calgary Eyeopener*. He believed he opened westerners' eyes to the contradictions he felt surrounded them. In one celebrated episode he printed a character reference for a notorious horse thief from Lord Strathcona of the Canadian Pacific Railway. The thief, Strathcona supposedly wrote, was a fine fellow who simply employed on a smaller scale the methods which had brought himself fortune and a peerage. Is this not Veblen's point? It all depends how one sees it.

1   Quotations from New Canadian Library edition (Toronto 1959), chapters 1 and 8. On reformers generally see Ramsay Cook, *The Regenerators* (Toronto 1985).

As Leacock recognized, the dominant forces in early twentieth-century Canada were capitalism and religion. Both established the ethos which marked the age; and in the four decades since Confederation, both had changed. As the organization of economic life shifted away from a rural and individual base, both religion and capitalism faced a crisis. As capitalists combined and fixed prices, their attacks on labour unions for 'combination' and for interference with a free market system rang hollow. These contradictions were not missed either by workers or, increasingly, the churches. Indeed, Leacock's competition as Canada's best-selling author, the Reverend Charles Gordon, or Ralph Connor to the many fans of his romantic parables, was also eager to point out these contradictions and enlist the churches against the ills which, in his view, contemporary capitalism had brought.

In early March 1914 Gordon gave a stirring address to the meeting of the Social Service Congress in Ottawa. This meeting brought together representatives of the Protestant churches with labour representatives, government officials, and others concerned about 'social' questions. The congress had grown out of the Moral and Social Reform Council of Canada (1907), which in turn had institutionalized the alliance of church and labour bodies that had successfully fought the battle for the 'Lord's Day Act.' Gordon rallied the congress to new causes, and, in his own words, to a 'New Church' which worshipped a God who was 'a good man with goodness raised to the highest power.' This 'New Church' would have a 'passion for men' and would seek the Kingdom of Heaven on this earth, not in the next. God's immanence meant that Christians must reconstruct their society. The emphasis, therefore, was upon the community, not upon the individual. The 'New State' and the 'New Christianity' would free themselves from the 'Big Individual' and 'Big Business' which controlled Canadian politics. In the preface to the congress report, Gordon expressed his passionate conviction that Canadians would come to see, as he did, that the capitalist system challenged Christian principles. All might be well, however, for there was 'in our nation so deep seated a sense of righteousness and brotherhood that it needs only that the light fall clear and white upon the evil to have it finally removed.' Once again, it was a matter of seeing clearly.

The reform movement after 1900 derived much of its strength from the pervasiveness of religion in Canada. A Social Service Congress held in 1914 enlisted support from groups not formally associated with the church, such as labour unions, but, even in case of labour, many of its most vigorous spokesmen were also active within churches. For example, James Simpson, the vice-president of the Social Service Council of Canada, was also extremely prominent in Methodist circles and was the vice-president of the

Lord's Day Alliance. Simpson's career pattern reflected that of many other early labour leaders.

The reform movement emanating from the Protestant churches was known as the Social Gospel. The term is an elastic one, but its history is comparatively straightforward. This Social Gospel was not an indigenous Canadian outgrowth.[2] In the latter part of the nineteenth century, several Protestant churches shifted their social philosophies from a strongly individualist bias to a collective outlook. The emphasis changed from saving souls to improving social conditions on earth. This idea received a theological foundation in the writings of the German Albrecht Ritschl and the American Walter Rauschenbusch which closed the gap between God and man, thereby making the moral perfection of mankind possible. The church thus becomes an agent in the achievement of that moral perfection. The burden of original sin and the fear of the harsh judgment of the Old Testament God disappear from this theology. Moreover, this interpretation fitted neatly into the strong evangelical tendencies of Protestant Christianity in North America.

It was no coincidence that the Methodists were the dominant force within the Social Gospel, for within that church the emphasis upon evangelicalism was strong. Through repentance, the sinner could achieve perfection. In the Social Gospel, the sinful society was called upon to repent. There was also the influence of the new secular thought upon religion. Debate over theology – about the nature and existence of God or the historical accuracy of the scriptures – was deeply affected by the scientific revolution of the nineteenth century. The rising middle classes had reinvigorated Protestant religion, especially Methodism, in the nineteenth century, but this class expanded its ranks and wealth greatly as a result of the scientific and technological revolution of that century. The middle class thus stood in awe of scientific achievement in the secular world, and for that reason it could not reject the impact of scientific discovery, notably the theory of evolution, upon religious doctrine. By the twentieth century, many of the Protestant divinity schools had accepted the so-called higher criticism of the Bible and had introduced numerous courses on the social aspects of Christianity.

Mention of the middle class and its influence on the church points to another reason for the turn towards the Social Gospel: the fear that the working class was losing its tie with organized religion. In the new cities, traditional associations broke down. Rare is the religious tract of the time that does not lament the church's weakness in reaching out to the rapidly expanding working class. There was a sense that industrial and urban

2 See the informative study by Richard Allen, *The Social Passion* (Toronto 1973), upo which much of this account is based.

development had divided people in a way unknown in earlier times. Thus, the Methodist minister J.S. Woodsworth wrote that 'In country districts people are to a large extent on a level but in the cities we have the rich and poor, the classes and the masses, with all that these distinctions involve.' What these distinctions might mean for the church is a disintegration based upon the division which marked industrial society itself. Ultimately, the church would atrophy unless it could extend its urban embrace.

Woodsworth cared deeply about the masses, but in his prewar writing he also worried about the disorder which rapid immigration introduced. Through its diversity, immigration threatened what earlier generations had created. In this sense, the Social Gospel and Woodsworth were profoundly conservative. In many speeches and documents the disorder of contemporary times is contrasted with a supposed unity or integrity of an earlier period. Woodsworth should have known that society was not 'level' in the preindustrial past. Certainly, his father who travelled the plains in the 1880s knew – and did not criticize the inequality he saw. What provoked Woodsworth and many other Christian reformers was the disorder and uncertainty of the times. Their reform proposals had two major thrusts: first, to end economic hardship and reduce inequality; second, to impose regulation upon the apparent chaos of contemporary social organization. This latter direction allowed Social Gospellers like Woodsworth and James Simpson to work with leading capitalists (and fellow Methodists) like J.W. Flavelle as fellow reformers, purging politics of corruption and Canada of drink.

There was, finally, the simple excitement of reform for the Social Gospellers. For a religion whose intellectual supports were shaken, social reform offered a refuge. As Richard Allen pointed out, the years before the war 'were exciting ones for progressive churchmen.' Reform, in modern parlance, was where the action was. Reform enthusiasm, not religious commitment, kept many such as Woodsworth and A.E. Smith in clerical garb; later, when reform faltered, they cast off their old garb and took on the new raiments of socialism and communism.

If the sources of reform were various, so were its expressions. Prohibition, in the late nineteenth and early twentieth century, often seemed the reform which had to precede all others. According to social historian James Gray, 'From Winnipeg to the Rockies, whisky kept the prairies in a ferment for fifty years. Other causes flared brightly for a decade or two and expired. The crusade against whisky went on and on.'[3] For Social Gospellers, alcohol was the devil's own drink and the saloon Satan's earthly lair. Drink dissolved family ties, destroyed the work ethic, and led to the degeneration of the

3   James H. Gray, *Booze* (Scarborough 1972), 1

race. The song which female prohibitionists sang outside the taverns expressed their view that drink was a national and personal menace:

Who hath sorrow? Who hath woe?
They who dare not answer no;
They whose feet to sin incline,
While they tarry at the wine?

The prohibition movement drew upon fear of urban life and the search for a more efficient society. It also reflected nineteenth-century medical research, which seemed to prove that drinking was indeed highly deleterious to health. Given the reverence for science in the late nineteenth century, it is not surprising that these 'discoveries' had an impact. The old saw of soldiers, sailors, and frontiersmen generally, 'Have one, it's good for you,' could no longer be believed. What was increasingly believed was the existence of a conspiracy to inflict liquor upon society. In the view of Nellie McClung, originally a temperance crusader who became a leading suffragette, it was the liquor interests which corrupted the 'foreigners' – 'around the bar they get their ideals of citizenship.' And it was the liquor interests who kept women from voting, because they knew that when women voted they would use 'their ballots to protect the weak and innocent, and make the world a safer place for the young feet.'

The belief in conspiracy became easier in 1898 when a plebiscite was held on the question of prohibition. Sir Wilfrid Laurier held the plebiscite because of pressure from his English-Canadian colleagues who were most often strong temperance supporters. The result was a victory for prohibition (278,000 for, 265,000 against), but a narrow and unbalanced one which lacked, above all, much support in Quebec. The victory was close but clear; Laurier, however, refused to heed it. He saw that his fellow French Canadians had voted overwhelmingly against prohibition, and he feared that the imposition of prohibition would divide the country. French Canadians would regard prohibition as the imposition of the religious values of militant Protestants upon them. What might come next?

Faced with Laurier's refusal to act, and a Conservative party which had been traditionally hostile to prohibition, the prohibitionists turned to the provinces and to the device of local option. Under the Scott Act of 1878, individual constituencies could vote themselves dry. Provinces could act to control liquor trafficking within their boundaries. In the western provinces, as hundreds of thousands of newcomers arrived in the early years of the century, the campaign against liquor became almost a crusade. The lead was taken first by the Presbyterian and Methodist churches. The Anglican church and the Roman Catholic church held back, as they did generally in the reform wave which swept the west. In 1907 the Presbyterians created a Board of Social and Moral Reform, which led to the founding of a Moral and Social Reform Council of Canada. (This evolved into the Social Service Council described earlier.) Charles Gordon was asked to be president for Manitoba; his anger with the refusal of Manitoba's Conservative government to enact prohibition, despite the province's overwhelming support for it in a plebiscite in 1898, roused him to action. Writing in the third person about his decision to accept the presidency, Gordon seemed to see reform almost exclusively as the defeat of the liquor interests: 'It meant time and work, and what with his congregation and his writing and all that that involved he had little enough time and strength to spare for a fight with the liquor forces entrenched behind the impregnable defenses of the Conservative Party. He had no illusions about the nature of the fight. It would be bitter, dirty and ruthless.'[4] Needless to say, he accepted, and the Christian soldiers marched onwards.

Many other causes fell into line behind the temperance banner. The most vigorous campaigns were waged in the west, although Ontario Liberals fought a campaign in 1914 on the sole issue of 'Ban the Bar.' The leader of the Ontario Liberals, Newton Wesley Rowell, identified his party almost completely with the prohibition movement. The election issue was clear to Rowell: 'You have on the one hand organized Christianity, and on the other hand the organized liquor interests.' This attempt to reduce politics to a single issue failed dismally, as the Liberals actually lost votes as a result of the campaign.

In the west the prohibition forces also reached their peak in 1914, especially in Manitoba. Premier Roblin denounced the 'Prohibitionist cranks and clerical politicians' who attacked his Conservative government for its failure to regulate the liquor traffic. Not all clerics, however, approved of the involvement of people like Gordon and others in the Liberal party campaign in 1914. The Roman Catholic church was especially disturbed by attacks upon the church, Catholic immigrants, and separate schools. The Catholic concern was hardly surprising since the Methodist church had passed a convention resolution stating that 'there could never be a compromise between the Christian Church and the Liquor traffic, and that bilingual schools were a menace to the welfare of the nation and must be discontinued.' The same Protestants who were most vigorous in their denunciation of church control of the state in Quebec were trying to enforce their morality and religious interests upon others. So it seemed to most Manitobans, and the Roblin gov-

4   Charles Gordon, *Postscript to Adventure* (Toronto 1975), 162

ernment was returned with a small majority.

Prohibitionists had not won their battle by August 1914. Nevertheless, the most powerful ammunition in support of their pleas exploded in Europe in that month. They already had their opposition on the run; in wartime they could rout their foe.

The prohibition movement was a school for reform. This was especially true in the case of women. Prevented from voting or holding office, women got their first taste of politics in the movement to abolish the bar. The Woman's Christian Temperance Union was the major force behind the greater political involvement of women in prewar Canada. The union's aim was at first narrow, as the word 'temperance' in its name indicates. By 1914, however, it had established a much wider ambit for its activities. It developed a rudimentary social service system, including homes for unwed mothers and family counselling offices. It joined in the campaign for the observance of the Lord's Day, and was especially vigorous in its opposition to prostitution and the abuse of women workers. Closely associated with the Protestant churches, the WCTU was an effective organization for its many purposes.

In the twentieth century the WCTU embraced the cause of women's suffrage. When Canada's leading suffragist Nellie McClung began her illustrious career in 1897 she joined the WCTU, the 'most progressive organization' in Canada. The temperance platforms often heard Mrs McClung promote women's suffrage. The logic employed was disarmingly simple: if women could vote, politics could be cleansed of corruption and Canada would be rid of liquor. In the prewar west it was a potent argument, especially to middle-class women who had a freedom from domestic tasks which women in earlier centuries had not possessed. McClung herself was representative of this group in her attitudes – her vigorous Protestantism, nativism, her fear of the degeneracy of urban and industrial society – as well as in her articulateness.

It is fashionable to point to the conservatism of the suffragists in Canada. Certainly they continued to celebrate the values of the home and, in particular, the importance of motherhood. The middle-class women expressed great anxiety about the lot of the working woman; indeed, the National Council of Women termed itself Canada's 'national mother' and claimed it had a special role in protecting the poor working women. This protection, however, expressed itself in such crusades as the one for separate lavatories. Two scholars have argued with considerable force that the major focus of concern was the woman as a future mother, 'the sacrifice of whose health would degrade the community.'[5] Prewar feminism undoubtedly did have a middle-class bias; nevertheless, it is ahistorical to term it conservative.

5 Alice Klein and Wayne Roberts, 'Besieged Innocence: The "Problems" of Working Women – Toronto, 1896-1914,' in *Women at Work* (Toronto 1974), 215

At the time, men and women believed that women's suffrage would bring fundamental changes in society. The debates within the National Council of Women and other organizations about whether they should support the suffragists reveal the extraordinary conviction that fundamental change would occur if women voted. The council took many years before it finally agreed that it supported women's suffrage in 1912. Similarly, the opponents of women's suffrage believed that all kinds of catastrophe would follow the entry of women into politics. In the minds of McClung and her colleagues, the effect of women on government would be a moral revolution. In hindsight, we know that women's suffrage had no such result, but to suggest that the suffragists failed because they did not cry out for day care and other modern causes is the worst kind of present-mindedness.

There has been some present-mindedness as well in the study of prewar labour organization. Because of the prominence of labour unions in contemporary Canadian life, much attention has been lavished upon the stirrings among the workers in the late nineteenth and early twentieth century. Yet in 1914, only 166,000 of Canada's almost three million workers were members of labour unions. Not surprisingly, the influence of unions upon politics and upon economic affairs was considerably less than it was to become later. In marked contrast to their counterparts in Britain and the United States, Canadian political leaders like Borden and Laurier wasted little time in their correspondence worrying about what labour leaders wanted.

There are, nevertheless, several reasons why labour reformers deserve some attention here. First, other reformers heeded the views of labour spokesmen, as is illustrated by the example of James Simpson of Toronto. Simpson played a major role at the 1914 Social Service conference not because of the position he held in labour circles but because he was believed to represent the views of others beyond the ranks of organized labour who were themselves largely inarticulate. Second, there is evidence that organized labour would have been a considerably stronger force if many employers had not striven to prevent their workers organizing. In his remarkably frank testimony to a 1904 royal commission, British Columbia magnate James Dunsmuir admitted that he would do almost anything that was legal to keep unions out of his mines. Other evidence suggests that he was not above doing some things which were illegal, such as threatening workers who did little more than mention the word union. Dunsmuir kept the unions out. He also made his workers bitter and receptive to pleas from more radical voices in the labour movement. Third, younger politicians, scholars, and journalists paid special attention to the so-called 'labour question.' That shrewd judge of where ambition would reap the richest reward, William Lyon Mackenzie King, chose labour as his field as early as the 1890s because he believed that the 'labour question' would become the centre of political debate in Canada as it was already in Europe. The Canadian Manufacturers' Association agreed, often speaking in its journal *Industrial Canada* of the struggles between capital and labour which were to come. What King, the CMA, and the labour unions shared was a belief that the enormous changes which had occurred in the workplace would have, and were already having, a large impact on the way the society was organized.

Since the early 1870s, unions had enjoyed certain exemption from common and criminal law penalties relating to such things as liability for damages and conspiracy. The anti-combines laws, also, were understood not to apply to unions. In the mid-1890s the Ontario government had provided for voluntary mediation which was meant to bring employers and employees to agreement more quickly and more peaceably. In 1900 the dominion set up its own Labour Department, with the twenty-six-year-old William Lyon Mackenzie King, six years from his Toronto BA and fresh from graduate work in the United States, as deputy minister. King and his new department also set to work on the task of conciliation and mediation. Strikes might be uncommon, but they were disruptive and gave a bad impression. King himself was active in mediating a cotton strike at Valleyfield, a miners' dispute at Rossland, strikes of coal miners in Fernie and of steel workers in Sydney, and, in 1910, a major stoppage on the Grand Trunk Railway.

The legal framework for conciliation was developing quite quickly. Dominion legislation of 1900 provided for it. Although it was apparently assumed that in industries where dominion jurisdiction was unquestioned, as on the railways, it was the dominion Labour Department which should bring disputants together, in other industries disputants effectively had a choice between dominion and provincial conciliation and mediation, except where no provincial system had been created. Thus, in Ontario, some disputes were mediated by Ottawa, some by Queen's Park – and some by nobody at all, in that mediation and conciliation were entirely voluntary.

The period between 1900 and 1914 was momentous in the history of Canadian labour organization. Two significant appointments marked the new century: the first minister of labour, Sir William Mulock, chose Mackenzie King as the first dominion deputy minister of labour; and Samuel Gompers, the president of the American Federation of Labor, appointed John Flett of Hamilton, Ontario, as AFL organizer in Canada. Both were deeply committed to their tasks, and both were remarkably talented. King's views on labour's place were not yet fully developed, but his appointment and the formation of the Labour Department indicated the awareness of the Laurier government that labour issues – and the labour vote – were legitimate concerns. Flett's views were more fully developed: he believed that Canadian unionism could best expand through affiliation with American unionism, specifically the AFL. Like Gompers, Flett believed that labour's concern should be good legislation, not independent political action. He even voted against the seating of a representative of the Canadian Socialist League at the 1900 Trades and Labor Congress convention. In this respect, Flett and King coincided in their aims. Flett's remarkable success in organizing union locals – over one hundred in 1901 and 1902 – also made King's position in Ottawa's tiny bureaucracy a more important one.

Between 1900 and 1903 there was a remarkable expansion of unionism in Canada, and this expansion was based mostly on the efforts of Flett and other international organizers. There were roughly three times as many union locals in Ontario in 1902 as there were in 1897, and roughly five times as many in British Columbia.[6] Representatives of these many new unionists as well as of older locals and union movements gathered in Berlin, Ontario (now Kitchener), in September 1902. This meeting of the Trades and Labor Congress has been termed by Robert Babcock 'the most fateful trade-union session in Canada labour history.' Two decisions taken by the congress made it so. The first prevented the congress from organizing and chartering locals in trades where an international or national union was already present; no national union was to exist where an international union existed. The other decision required that there be no more than 'one Central Body in any City or Town, said Central Body to be chartered by the Trades and Labor Congress of Canada.' In effect, this was meant to mean a monopoly for the TLC and the end to unionism it did not control. The TLC interpreted this decision as enabling it to give pre-eminence to American Federation of Labor Councils. This interpretation was not surprising given that John Flett was elected as the new president of the TLC at the Berlin meeting. The meeting delighted Samuel Gompers who, in a letter of congratulations to his employee Flett, rejoiced that 'The policy declared and the officers elected demonstrate beyond question that the spirit of the labor movement is growing toward the recognition that our interests are identical regarding the arbitrary geographical lines.'

What the Canadian unionists got was the economic support of the Americans; what they lost was a distinctly national labour movement. That at least was true for the TLC where the international craft unions had won unquestioned sway. Others, however, now stood outside: 2287 unionists were expelled at the Berlin congress, most of them supporters of the Knights of

6 For more detailed accounts see Robert Babcock, *Gompers in Canada: A Study in American Continentalism before the First World War* (Toronto 1974), chapter 4, and Bryan Palmer, *A Culture in Conflict: Skilled Workers and Industrial Capitalism in Hamilton, Ontario, 1860-1914* (Montreal 1979), 201-2.

Labour in Quebec. Others, especially in western Canada, also rejected the TLC, and the implied embrace of the American Federation of Labor, because they thought Gompers's approach too moderate. As a result, after 1902 most of Quebec and much of the west stood outside the TLC, and the Canadian labour movement lacked the stature and strength which would have come from national solidarity. It was indeed a fateful meeting and a fateful year.

In the west, the reaction to the events in Berlin was particularly hostile. Even before the 1902 congress convention, Nanaimo miners had refused to issue convention credentials to TLC president Ralph Smith whom the socialists in charge of the Nanaimo local derisively termed the 'Gompers of Canada.' After the Berlin decisions, the TLC rapidly lost ground in the west to the Western Federation of Miners and its affiliated American Labor Union. Obviously, the western objection to the Berlin decision rested upon the lack of militancy, not upon nationalism. In 1903 this militancy swept British Columbia and had a drastic effect on the province's economy. A strike organized by the United Brotherhood of Railway Employees, a strongly socialist union, won the sympathetic support of the militant locals affiliated with he American Labor Union and the Western Federation of Miners. The Canadian Pacific Railway, the focus of the initial strike action, used threats, intimidation, and even violence to break the strike. The federal government responded to the troubles with the establishment of a royal commission. The commission came down strongly against the American affiliations of the union locals which had organized the strike, the militancy of the strikers, and the use of sympathetic strikes. These syndicalist techniques were 'really nothing more than conspiracies against society in general and employers in particular.' It recommended that the American Federation of Labor and its affiliates should be declared illegal.

This declaration was unnecessary; the strikes petered out. The American parent unions exhausted their funds in strikes in the United States, and the TLC fought hard to recover lost ground in the west. TLC officers denounced the influence of the so-called 'new unionism' which rejected the traditional craft orientation of unions. At first, progress was slow, but by 1907 the TLC had recaptured control of most western locals and councils. Nevertheless, they remained considerably more radical than their eastern counterparts. The memories of 1903 endured and gave strength to later radical movements in the west.[7]

---

7   The best account of these British Columbia events is found in A. Ross McCormack, *Reformers, Rebels, and Revolutionaries: The Western Canadian Radical Movement 1899-1919* (Toronto 1977), chapter 3.

The organizational division in labour and the end of the crisis of 1903 in the west gave the Laurier government some breathing space in its dealings with organized labour. The rapid growth of union strength between 1898 and 1903 did not continue. In his study of Hamilton workers, Bryan Palmer attributes this decline in the growth rate to an employer offensive to wrest control of the workplace from the craft workers. In Hamilton, this offensive took the form of an open-shop drive which attacked traditional limitations imposed by the craft unions on employee control at the place of work. Certainly, many employers did take the offensive against the unions, and their efforts had some effect.[8] But there were also other factors.

Labour spoke with too many voices, and its arguments frequently lacked logical consistency. There was, for example, no agreement on what political role labour should play. Some, even within the TLC, favoured Marxist socialist parties, as in British Columbia where the Socialist party of Canada had some electoral success. Others wanted a labour party similar to the model of the emerging Labour party of Great Britain, while still others supported independent labour candidates whose parliamentary job was to prod the government. Endless hours were spent by labour reformers splitting the thinnest doctrinal hairs. In their brief moments in the voting booth, however, the overwhelming majority of Canadian workers and Canadian unionists cast their ballots for the Liberals and the Conservatives. Implicitly they expressed their lack of interest in and probably their boredom with the anxious political harangues of the trade union leaders.

The unions also tended to be haphazard in their recruitment. Too many workers meant lower wages. Employers favoured immigration, but unionized workers did not. Throughout Canada, the new workers were often immigrants, especially after 1903. Even though many of the non-British immigrants were ready to join trade unions, the trade unions of Canada nearly always did not want them.

No contradiction in the Canadian trade union movement was more obvious than the constant rhetoric about the brotherhood of workers and racist denunciation of 'foreigners.' Trade unionists were among the most vocal opponents of immigration, and some of the virulent denunciations of non-British immigrants by labour leaders, who were often British immigrants themselves, were decidedly vulgar. A Lethbridge labour leader, for instance, charged that Clifford Sifton was destroying trade unions by bringing in 'hordes of half-civilized people who can live on ... a crust and an onion.'[9] In British Columbia, the violence which employers directed towards trade un-

8   Palmer, *A Culture in Conflict*, 222-33
9   Terry Copp, *The Anatomy of Poverty: The Condition of the Working Class in Montreal, 1897-1929* (Toronto 1974)

ionists was often exceeded by the violence directed towards Asian immigrants by workers. Indeed, union growth in British Columbia may be attributable as much to racism as to effective organization. Very few trade unionists shared Charles Gordon's belief that 'Out of breeds diverse in traditions, in ideals, in speech, and in manner of life' would come one great breed and a great nation. The difference in vision perhaps explains the reluctance of many Social Gospellers to embrace labour's aims.

The leading figure in the development of government policy towards labour, Mackenzie King, also seemed reluctant to embrace all of labour's aims. The reason for this reluctance was not so much King's dishonesty and his desire to be all things to all men, as some critics have charged, as the contradictions within labour itself. King wanted to be the champion of labour. He also wanted stability within society. How to achieve both goals was never clear. The much-criticized Industrial Disputes Investigation Act must be understood in this context. The act, which was passed in 1907, reflected King's prewar faith in the efficacy of public opinion in achieving social peace. An underlying assumption of the act was the unity of purpose within capitalist society. The act of 1907 provided for general conciliation, while prohibiting strikes or lockouts if a conciliation board was at work. Any party to a dispute could apply for conciliation, thereby preventing either strike or lockout until after the board had reported.[10] Recommendations, however, were binding on neither party. Although there were amendments from time to time, the IDI Act remained in force until 1925, when the courts declared it *ultra vires* (beyond the powers) of the dominion. King himself regarded it as one of his most profound achievements, although its only element of novelty was the provision for suspending strikes and lockouts during the conciliation process. Later Marxist critics have ridiculed this assumption and declared King's 'corporatist' vision naïve. What has been too often ignored is the initial reception which the bill received.

In the House of Commons, the president of the Trades and Labor Congress, the Labour MP Alphonse Verville, energetically supported the bill. At the Toronto District Labor Council in February 1907 there was little opposition to the bill, and, after the act was passed, the TLC annual congress in Winnipeg endorsed it by a vote of 81 to 19. Opposition came not from Canada's leading trade unionists but from Samuel Gompers, who deeply disliked some aspects of the bill which he wrongly believed might lead to compulsory arbitration. Although his Canadian agent James Flett initially approved of the bill, Gompers's intense hostility persuaded Flett to alter his stand; ultimately, the TLC followed.

10 H.D. Woods and Sylvia Ostry, *Labour Policy and Labour Economics in Canada* (Toronto 1962), 50-1

In truth, the Canadian unionists were never sure what they wanted. Many had been influenced by the effects of compulsory arbitration upon the wages of Australian and New Zealand workers, but the imperial example did not impress Gompers. The Canadians gave way because Gompers at least had strong convictions, whereas they were often confused. This confusion created the atmosphere for weak legislation, intermittent gains, rhetorical flourish, and a search for scapegoats in the thousands of new Canadians who could do little to respond to the taunts directed towards them. Like Leacock's famous horse, labour rode off in too many directions at once.

While governments tried to ensure social peace by managing labour-employer relations, unions of all sorts organized, fought among themselves, and tried to attract members. There is no doubt that this internecine warfare was involved with important issues. Should organized labour overthrow the capitalist system, or work within it? Should the principle of labour organization be the craft, such as locomotive driving, shoemaking, and typography, or the industry, such as mining or car-building? Were there some peculiarly national ends or goals that a union should keep in mind? Or should it simply represent 'labour interests' before government and fight for better wages and working conditions? Certainly, these wages and working conditions were often appalling, especially in the logging and mining districts. Nevertheless, we must ask whether the sound and fury signified anything in particular.

Consider the example of mining, one of the most strike-prone activities during these years. The industry was not profoundly important in Laurier's Canada. In 1911, after a decade of rapid expansion, coal mining employed only 1 per cent of Canada's workforce, and other mining absorbed only another 1.1 per cent. Government, underdeveloped though it was, employed substantially more workers; construction employed more than three times as many. Nor was mining crucial to the nation's economic life; central Canada ran on imported coal and processed few of its own minerals. Yet mining was emotive and very dangerous. Most of the workers were isolated, living and working in 'one-task towns' that were sometimes 'one-mine towns' as well. The work itself was hard, dirty, dangerous, and isolated. Mine-owners had great power over the miners and their families, especially if they ran the stores and offered the houses for rent, as was frequently the case. It is no wonder that miners often struck, that miners' strikes were sometimes violent, or that miners opted for union structures that sought to attack the established order, the government, capitalism – or all of the above. Yet it is absolutely certain that the small groups of isolated miners, whether in Sydney, Nova Scotia, or Rossland, British Columbia, could not possibly have changed Canada's socio-economic order. They were too few, too scattered, too weak.

Now consider the more politically conservative unions, those which organized the craft workers in the towns. It is far from clear that unity gave them any particular strength. The heads of the more respectable national federations, such as the TLC and the Canadian Federation of Labour, regularly put the 'views of labour' before the dominion government and the provincial authorities. Would their representations have been more effective if there had been one national federation instead of two, or if that federation had consisted only of 'national' unions? Probably not. The unions could not deliver the vote. They contained only a tiny minority of Canada's non-agricultural labour force. They were neither willing nor able to organize any sort of co-ordinated general strike action. What sort of strength, then, did 'union' give? At the workplace, or in a single craft or industry, it might give a great deal; even here, however, technological change and employer resistance would weaken the power of the craft unions, such as the iron molders, while in many lines of work the immigrants could swamp the locals, no matter how organized they might be. And in the nation as a whole, 'union' meant little or nothing.

It is not surprising that few middle-class reformers were willing to mount the saddle and ride with labour. Leacock was one who refused, with respect not only to labour but to other reform as well. He thus took small part in the effort to clean up the worst of urban ills, even though he himself maintained a social conservatism which implicitly was suspicious of urban life. The urban reform movement fought its bitterest battles in Leacock's Montreal, where utility franchises and corrupt politicians inflamed the reformer's soul. In this cause, French Canadians and English Canadians united in a way that they never did on prohibition, suffrage, and some other Social Gospel crusades. The French-Canadian nationalist, Olivar Asselin, for example, was a frequent critic of urban ills, as was Henri Bourassa. Unlike most English-Canadian urban reformers, however, Bourassa always believed that the city itself was the source of most of the ills within it. In the cities, the faith and the culture of the French Canadian faced their greatest threat, he argued, and in a sense this was so, not least because of the strongly collectivist thrust of the urban reform doctrines advanced by English-Canadian reformers.

In the prewar years, urban reform meant greater uniformity in urban life and the sacrifice of individual interest to the public good. Reformers showed remarkably little doubt about what that good might be. Urban reform took several shapes. There was, first of all, the quest for moral purity. The middle-class men and women who dominated urban reform movements took their first shots at the bars and pubs which abounded in working-class areas, and they also sought to extinguish the prostitution which flourished in and around the pubs. Before Mackenzie King embarked on his career to reform

Canada's labour laws, he had personally sought out some prostitutes and begged them to stop their 'wicked life and turn to Christ.'

These scattered efforts for reform were institutionalized with the creation of urban missions in the 1890s and settlement houses in the early 1900s. The Methodist church, using money provided by the Massey family, established the Fred Victor Mission in Toronto in 1894 to provide moral and physical sustenance for the urban poor. In 1902 Sara Libby Carson of the Presbyterian church introduced the settlement house to Canada, after successful experiments in the United States and Britain. These houses not only cared for the destitute; they also offered an opportunity to study them. Settlement houses in Toronto and Montreal were associated with the universities and were instrumental in creating a new profession, the social worker, in Canada. By 1914, the notion that moral reform would greatly relieve the distress of the destitute and poor had given way to a belief that more fundamental changes were required in the structure of society before poverty could disappear.

Moral purity thus took second place to a broader concern for purity in urban life. In particular, this concern reflected a belief that sanitary and health conditions in the modern city should and could be much improved. Herbert Ames's 1897 study of the conditions of poverty in working-class Montreal expressed outrage that 'that relic of rural conditions, that insanitary abomination, the out-of-door-pit-in-the-ground privy' was still used by half the households in the area which he surveyed. Considering the dense housing conditions of the area, it is not surprising that Montreal's public health was in a truly desperate state in the 'city below the hill.' In 1898 Ames, as a newly elected alderman, became chairman of the municipal Board of Health and introduced practical reforms which significantly enhanced public health conditions. Animated by the claims of contemporary medical researchers that improvements in sanitary conditions, water supplies, and food quality could wipe out parasitic disease, reformers in other Canadian cities fought for sewage treatment plants and more efficient regulation of food supplies.

Canadian municipalities in the 1880s and the 1890s recognized their community responsibilities in the area of health by creating municipal waterworks. In the 1900s the conception of municipal responsibility broadened to include other utilities which had developed under private auspices. Angered by the excessive power and pricing policies of private utilities, Mayor O.A. Howland of Toronto called a convention of municipalities for Toronto in 1901. The Union of Canadian Municipalities thereupon fought the private monopolies which controlled the streets of many Canadian cities. This battle often took the form of a call for public ownership of utilities. Cities in prairie Canada, where public ownership took hold at an early date, bragged about their achievements, as well as the profits which the municipally owned street railways and gasworks and the provincially owned telephones brought to the cities. Before 1914, many other Canadian cities followed the public ownership path.

As John Weaver has pointed out, the public ownership movement often served specific private interests. Municipally owned street railways could perhaps offer better service than privately owned companies (although this was not necessarily so), but they also brought considerable benefit to real-estate interests in developing the city's new suburbs. In the case of publicly owned power distribution, this same benefit to private interests can be discerned. H.V. Nelles has shown how the movement to obtain public power for Winnipeg was, in essence, 'a cabal of leading businessmen' who were determined to break a private monopoly in order to bring down costs for Winnipeg's manufacturers. In contrast, the public power movement in Ontario had much broader support and appeal. In Nelles's words, 'the power question successfully fused an otherwise disparate group of progressive businessmen and manufacturers, Board of Trade activists, social gospellers and temperance men, municipal reformers, local politicians and workers into an indomitable and enduring non-partisan mass movement.'[11] Nor surprisingly, it was Ontario Hydro which lasted, although for decades it co-existed with private electrical utilities of various kinds.

One of the strongest arguments made for public ownership of utilities was the corrupting influence of private ownership upon municipal politics. All Canadians were familiar with the supposed horrors of Tammany Hall and were proud that, on the whole, Canada had avoided the worst ills of civic government. S. Morley Wickett, Canada's leading authority on city government, boasted that the government of Canadian cities was not at all the 'conspicuous failure' which British political scientist James Bryce deemed American civic government to be. Still, there were problems, notably in Montreal, and there were reformers who had solutions to these problems.

As Leacock showed, the 'solution' sometimes meant little more than exchanging old rascals for new ones. For some reformers, however, ambitions were greater. In general, these reformers wanted to make civic government more a matter of administration than of politics. The ward system was the first target for such reformers because they regarded the ward as dividing the natural community which must exist within an urban setting. City-wide

11 H.V. Nelles, 'Public Ownership of Electrical Utilities in Manitoba and Ontario, 1906-1930,' *Canadian Historical Review* 57 (Dec. 1976): 460-84. Also, John Weaver, '"Tomorrow's Metropolis" Revisited: A Critical Assessment of Urban Reform in Canada, 1890-1920,' in Gilbert Stelter and Alan Artibise, eds., *The Canadian City* (Toronto 1977), 393-418

elections and smaller councils were strongly recommended to give the cities the centralization which efficient planning required. With the 'ward-heeler' eliminated, the opportunities for 'parochial' influence on civic action would be much reduced. That at least was the theory. In the minds of the reformers, these changes would have little effect without an improvement in the quality of the civic administrators. Wickett thus argued that 'municipal administration' was 'mainly a technical task,' a task which required technicians. The future of the city belonged to the expert, not the politician.[12]

Laurier's establishment of a Commission of Conservation, with a broad mandate under the chairmanship of Clifford Sifton, spurred the advance of town planning in Canada. The commission explicitly upheld the belief that the 'ordinary capable amateur' could do the 'work which ought to be done by a trained scientific man.' The British town planner Thomas Adams was brought to Canada to bring order and beauty to the chaos of Canadian civic life. After 1910, many Canadian towns and cities experimented with plans which were clearly influenced by experiments in Europe or the United States. The 'City Beautiful' movement had a powerful impact, directing planners towards the monumental and, in some cases, the imaginary. Indeed, the impact on reality was always weaker than the lines and whorls on drafting boards might indicate. The outbreak of war punctured the lofty visions, and postwar planners gazed less into the heavens and more at the sewers for new suburbs.

The spirit of the clean government movement also affected the reformers' attitude towards federal and provincial politics. Leacock and other imperialists believed that endemic corruption, federal, provincial, and municipal, prevented politicians from serving the highest aims of the nation. Mired in Ottawa's mud, ministers and MPs could not see that Canada's interest lay in participating in the grandeur and high purpose of the British empire. In Sara Jeannette Duncan's 1904 novel *The Imperialist,* her politician hero fails because 'his mind accepted the old working formulas for dealing with an average electorate, but to his eager apprehending heart it seemed unbelievable that the great imperial possibility, the dramatic chance for the race than hung even now, in the history of the world, between the rising and the setting of the sun, should fail to be perceived and acknowledged as the paramount issue.'

Other reformers might not have agreed with the 'imperial possibility,' but they would have accepted that 'the dramatic chance for the race' was at hand. Their time was an historic moment, an opportunity that could not be

---

12 A good selection of readings may be found in Paul Rutherford, ed., *Saving the Canadian City: The First Phase 1880-1920* (Toronto 1974). A wealth of information on Canadian cities may be found in the *Urban History Review.*

allowed to pass. Whatever their beliefs, whatever their class, whatever their nationality, reformers shared this perception. This was the 'great wave' which swept over Leacock and other Canadians in the early twentieth century. They believed they had to take the tide at the flood or, in an image they knew well, the voyage of their lives would be bound in shallows and miseries. There was, then, a sense of urgency.

There was also a sense of power. Carl Berger's brilliant study of Canadian imperialists[13] describes the sense of power his subjects felt. As we have seen, the imperialists were not alone among reformers in this regard. The Social Gospellers also possessed the spirit in abundance. The belief that a heavenly kingdom could be erected on earth empowered the Social Gospellers to seek fundamental changes in the ways human beings organized their affairs. It was no longer enough to trust that good would conquer ill; the Social Gospellers would assure that it did so.

Since man was a creature who lived in society, they shared the belief with other and more radical reformers – Social Gospellers, urban reformers, Marxists – that, in Marx's words, human life was 'more fundamental' than political life. The angry tirades directed against politicians came from a sense that political structure blocked the needs both of humans and of society. Some prewar Canadians, like other Western peoples, were entranced with the possibilities for the rational management of human affairs, based on the success which modern science had achieved in the world of nature. These reformers accepted, in effect, Max Weber's contemporary argument that 'the choice' was only between bureaucracy and dilettantism in administration. Rational decision, efficiency, and order were possible; political dilettantism prevented their realization. Many elements of this vision of rationality and order were romantic, unreasonable, and, to our age, profoundly dangerous. In its own time, however, the vision created much of the vitality described above.

Contemporary scholars often delight in poking fun at the reformers – at their pomposity, enthusiasm, false hopes, and naïvete. Indeed, we must recognize that the reforms which they espoused would not and could not make much difference to any large socio-economic developments. For instance, although they were worried by some of the side effects which flowed from the Great Boom described in Chapter 4, they would never have thought of trying to stop it, nor did they know how to. They were not nationalizers, regulators, collectivizers, or socialists, as later generations would understand these slippery terms; indeed, they often showed a touching faith in Victorian virtues and techniques: taking thought; considering responsibilities; making

13 *The Sense of Power: Studies in the Ideas of Canadian Imperialism, 1867-1914* (Toronto 1970)

the facts known. Having shed traditional Christian dogma, they had lost the sense of human fallibility and greed; operating nonetheless in a post-Victorian environment and using vaguely post-Christian ideas, they were quite unable to think about socio-economic processes in anything other than personal terms. Self-interest also motivated many reformers – and not only in the middle class. But the perception of the Social Gospel or urban reform movements as simply expressions of class interest is far too limited and reductionist. It denies the passion and variety of reform, and the different courses taken by reformers ranging from Woodsworth, through Mackenzie King and Stephen Leacock, to Charles Gordon. It also leads to the distortion which arises when historians lavish more attention on reformers or revolutionaries who were obscure in their own times than upon major figures of the age. A Marxist miner may fit more easily into the familiar boxes of modern historiography, but the result is misrepresentation for the age and over-inflation for the Marxist miner.

In the age of reform it seemed that the string had become untuned. As discord appeared, reformers scrambled for harmony and for opportunity. Much of what they sought now seems chimerical – prohibition, for example. In its time, however, that movement had more meaning than others which appear to be the antecedents to the various nostrums for the ills of a later period. Its glory in its own time must be recognized; only then can we see the monuments which remain.

6

Canada, the World, and the Empire

If the world of pre-1914 reform seems distant to modern readers, Canada's position in the world must seem equally unusual. Canada in prewar days had no diplomats. To be Canadian was to be a British subject, whether English, Irish, French, or German in origin. Canada's Britishness was of fundamental importance in understanding the political, economic, and even social history of the period.

Victoria Regina, 'VR,' reigned over Canada and sundry other parts of the globe from 1837 to 1901. Her birth made such an impression that it became an annual holiday in Canada, and in English Canada at least is still celebrated as such, on the Monday closest to the actual date of birth, the 24th of May. (French Canadians have renamed Victoria Day in honour of Dollard des Ormeaux, a semi-mythic hero of the wars against the Iroquois in the seventeenth century.) By 1900, very few Canadians could remember any other reign. Victoria's image – remote, rotund, and vaguely benign – stared out from classroom walls, post offices, and postage stamps. Her statues squatted in squares around the world, giving substance to the loyal poem penned by a Canadian would-be laureate:

Here's to Queen Victoria,
Dressed in all her regalia,
With one foot in Canada,
And the other in Australia.

But while the peoples of the empire gazed on their queen, she had never gazed on them. England, Scotland, and occasionally Ireland saw their queen, and so did a couple of European capitals, generally those ruled by her relatives. But India, whose empress she had been since 1877, Canada, the Australasian colonies, and Africa were too distant in those days of slow and laborious travel for a royal visit to be considered. Indeed, few Canadians had ever met their queen. Prime ministers did, if they visited England; one of them, Sir John Thompson, even expired at Windsor Castle shortly after leaving the royal presence. The queen held her Canadian subjects in distant regard, since Canada seldom intruded on daily conversation or life. In 1891, when Sir John A. Macdonald and his Conservatives won a general election on what appeared to be the issue of loyalty to the British empire, the queen was moved to express 'her great gratification' at the results, which would keep Canada safe, reliable, and out of the news.

Well-informed Canadians had to take an interest in Britain, because British imperial entanglements would necessarily involve Canada. In 1900 the Boer War in South Africa was clear evidence of such involvement. Even if the British showed little direct interest in Canada, the empire, including Canada, was something that the average Briton was proud of, and it contained spots that he or she might move to. It supplied wool, wheat, and cheese, in return absorbing British products and British investment. It sent colourful contingents to parade London's streets when the queen held her Golden and Diamond jubilees in 1887 and 1897. Canada had snow, police in red coats, buffalo, and Indians. But the British government spent little money in Canada, and that little was connected to two tiny coastal garrisons 4000 miles apart at Halifax and Esquimalt. The most penny-pinching political economist would find it difficult to be concerned about that.

Nevertheless, even in 1900 there were issues arising that would eventually affect both Britain and Canada. Most of them were far from the public eye, the stuff of official studies and royal commissions, but they were beginning to spill over into the consciousness of the careful, educated reader. Britain's unique industrial mastery, for long a constant around which international trade revolved, had become an increasingly distant memory. Although the British economy still gave every indication of rude health, other countries, and particularly the United States and Germany, were matching and surpassing British industry in a disturbingly large number of areas. Government studies, learned articles, and alarmist reports from threatened industries gradually penetrated public consciousness. 'Free trade,' the doctrine that had revolutionized politics in the 1830s and 1840s, was coming under attack from the proponents of 'fair trade' and 'protectionism.' The latter, in its National Policy garb, was firmly ensconced in the policies of Canada and other self-governing colonies. In 1897 the Laurier government took its first imperial excursion by cutting the duties on British and empire goods – 'imperial preference' in tariffs.

But free trade was too firmly entrenched in Britain's political folklore to be overturned at this first gust of colonial wind. Although some British politicians favoured Canadian-style imperial preference, and even made efforts to enlist colonial (including Canadian) spokesmen on their side, the majority were resistant. Because Britain taxed few imports, she could grant a useful 'preference' only by imposing new duties on non-empire goods, especially wheat, meat, and dairy products. No such policy could be popular. Moreover, there was greater urgency elsewhere.

The deterioration in Britain's relative economic position was matched by a perception of a decline in its diplomatic status. For many years Britain had held itself aloof from formal alliances with other states. Britain's international associations were matters of convenience rather than habit or principle. Secure behind the iron wall of the Royal Navy, whom should the British fear? The answer to that, it appeared, was manifold. First, there was the French navy, reconstructed in a burst of republican enthusiasm in the 1880s. Then there was Russia, Britain's rival in the Balkans and the Middle East and antagonist on the borders of India. Germany, the industrial giant of Europe, co-operated only fitfully with Britain, as did Italy and Austria-Hungary. Germany's official attitude stopped well short of friendship, and the Americans made belligerent noises from time to time.

Taken separately, these strains and antagonisms were hardly serious. The French obligingly laid up most of their navy in order to pursue a ruinously eccentric naval policy devised by one of their naval ministers. The Russians had internal problems which would soon bulk very large. The Germans were ruled by Queen Victoria's grandson, Wilhelm II, and it was hoped that family ties might help to keep his empire within bounds. In any case, France and Germany were bitterly at odds, and their alliance systems (France with Russia, Germany with Italy and Austria-Hungary) were competitive and mutually exclusive. Yet occasionally Europe seemed to speak with one voice, and when it did, the British found the circumstances peculiarly uncomfortable. Britain had boasted of its 'splendid isolation.' It was isolation, truly enough, but as the events surrounding the South African War showed, it was anything but splendid.

In October 1899 the armies of the Orange Free State and the Transvaal, two autonomous Dutch-speaking states at the tip of Africa, invaded the British South African colonies. The inhabitants of these two countries called themselves Boers, and the war they began was called the Boer War. From the British side it looked like straightforward aggression, but the reality was somewhat more complicated. The British had been provocative towards the Boers, the situation in South Africa had been unstable for decades, and Briton and Boer had not demonstrated a facility for good neighbourhood. In Europe (and French Canada) the Boer War was easily interpreted as barefaced aggression by Britain rather than by the Boers. Unofficial support was readily forthcoming, and warning growls were voiced by politicians of widely differing stripes. Outside the empire, few if any countries sustained the British cause.

It did not help that the Boer War dragged on for two-and-a-half years, and that the British had to dispatch hundreds of thousands of soldiers (including 30,000 colonials) to the conflict. Support from the empire was the only cheerful sign; a dragged-out guerrilla war, which was finally won only with the help of concentration camps into which the Boer population was herded, did not contribute to the glory of British arms. Nor did the initially inept performance of British generals reassure an anxious public that the British army had retained the laurels of Waterloo. Eventually, competent generals were selected and sent; and one of them, H.H. Kitchener, gained prominence in the First World War.

A blundering army; an absence of friends; what else could go wrong in British foreign policy? The answer to that question lay across the North Sea, where Wilhelm II and his ministers were falling under the spell of seapower – the root of Britain's greatness and the link with her empire. Germany had a few colonies too, but the colonies were hostage to Britain's navy. The British were commercial and diplomatic rivals. Germany's army, the most modern and powerful in Europe, could have no effect on Britain as long as the Royal Navy lay between the continent and England. The answer to this dilemma, obviously, was to build a navy; as Bertrand Russell once put it, 'to have a fleet as big as grand-mama's.'

Starting in 1898, the German navy began to increase in size and power. There was some question at the time, and much controversy since, as to what it was intended to do. There is little doubt that its real purpose was the obvious one: to rival the British navy, and to seize control of the narrow seas that lay between Europe and the British Isles. British attempts to secure a political accommodation with Germany at the turn of the century were rebuffed, and as the new century dawned it was only a matter of time until a naval race began. The stakes were high and very real; only the counters seem, in retrospect, to have been misplaced.

Naval power was measured, as it had been since the eighteenth century, in battleships, ships of the line, the modern equivalents of Nelson's *Victory* at Trafalgar. Battleships were, obviously, bigger than other ships, more heavily armoured with bigger guns. They were expensive, but they were necessary. Soon, thanks to a revolution in naval technology, they would be more expensive. The revolution came from Britain, where a super-battleship, the *Dreadnought,* was launched in 1906. With heavier armour and 'all big guns,' the *Dreadnought* immediately set a new standard in naval construction. All other battleships would soon be obsolete, and the future belonged to the country that could build the most in the fastest possible time. The naval race would be denominated in dreadnoughts. In the event, few dreadnoughts ever fired a shot in anger. The fact that they existed tended to deter attack from other dreadnoughts until sufficient force could be assembled. They were, to quote a useful phrase, truly 'yesterday's deterrent.' Like other deterrents, they were costly and apparently illimitable.

During the nineteenth century, the Royal Navy was scattered the world around. There were West Indian and North American squadrons, ships off the China coast, ships in the Indian Ocean and Mediterranean, and a world-wide complex of dockyards and coaling stations to maintain them. One effect of the disasters of the Boer War was to call this network, or parts of it, into question. A new army general staff, with its counterparts in the navy, began studying the whole question of colonial and imperial defence. These staffs had to consider, first, against whom they were most likely to be employed, and second, against whom they could not hope to defend. The answer to the first question lay in Europe, with the finger pointing at Germany; the most obvious candidate in the second category was the United States.

It had been clear for some time that the defence of Canada against the United States posed special problems for Great Britain. The cost of a North American garrison was heavy, and its utility doubtful. The American Civil War, and the decades of population and industrial growth since, indicated to the British government that the United States could, if it wished, easily out-build even the Royal Navy, without mentioning what it could do on land. It became obvious that the answer to the problem of defending Canada was not to have to do it. British troops were withdrawn from central Canada in 1871; in 1905-6 they were withdrawn from Halifax and Esquimalt, the only remaining 'imperial fortresses.' Indefensible against the Americans (it was estimated that the Royal Navy could not even get to Halifax in the event of war), but defensible against the likely scale of attack that any other power could mount, the two fortresses were handed over to the Canadian government to preserve and defend – or so it was hoped.

CANADA AND THE LIBERAL EMPIRE

Great Britain's relations with its colonial empire were conducted through a variety of channels. The War Office (army) and Admiralty (navy) defended the empire. They had bases and stations around the world, often together, sometimes apart. The India Office ran the Indian empire, and the Foreign Office also had responsibilities for certain territories. The bulk of the colonial empire came under the Colonial Office, a department of great seniority but little prestige, whose ministers (properly styled secretaries of state for the colonies) were often selected as an afterthought. The Treasury, although it administered no colonial lands and collected no colonial taxes, did allocate some funds to colonial purposes. Such outlays, naturally, were controlled by the chancellor of the exchequer and his officials. But after the winding-up of the imperial fortresses at Nanaimo and Esquimalt in 1905-6, there was no reason to spend money in Canada. It could, of course, be argued that Canada enjoyed incidental protection from the Royal Navy and the British army, blocking the access of Wilhelm II's war machine to the open sea; but it was no longer seriously contended that either navy or army would or could do anything to protect Canada from the United States.[1]

The consequences of this situation were sometimes painful for Canada. In 1903, when Canada and the United States disagreed over exactly where the boundary of the Alaska panhandle should be sited, the problem was referred to an 'impartial' commission of two Canadians, one Briton, and three Americans. It has been convincingly argued that on the important points of the case the Americans had the facts on their side;[2] nevertheless, the Alaska Boundary tribunal's final decision favouring the American cause bore every sign of haste and political pressure. Perhaps a diplomatic retirement in the face of overwhelming odds was indeed the better part of valour, for the Americans would doubtless have proceeded to take by force what they considered to be rightfully theirs. But it left a bad taste and encouraged scepticism about an empire that would so blatantly abandon the interests of its colony.

The party in power in Canada at the time was the Liberal party; the prime minister, Sir Wilfrid Laurier. Sir Wilfrid was, as he described himself, a good English-style Liberal. He admired British liberalism, with its emphasis on individual rights and freedoms. He liked the British, on the whole, and was prepared to make certain gestures towards them, such as the preferential tariff. Laurier was not schooled in international affairs. Despite occasional irruptions, the Canadian prime minister was content with things as they were, conscious that public opinion in English Canada liked it that way. There was no point in needless controversy over the forms of Canada's association with the British empire. During most of Laurier's political lifetime – and it was a long one – the burden of that association had sat lightly on the dominion. There had been occasional complications, the Boer War being one, when the empire had been a little too rich for Canada's political

---

1 Two books are of special value here: John Kendle, *The Colonial and Imperial Conferences, 1887-1911* (London 1967), and Max Beloff, *Imperial Sunset*, I: *Britain's Liberal Empire, 1897-1921* (London 1969).

2 Norman Penlington, *The Alaska Boundary Dispute: A Critical Reappraisal* (Toronto 1972)

digestion. Laurier was not anxious to recreate the divisions that arose between English- and French-Canadian Liberals over the question of sending troops to South Africa, but in the end both sides appeared satisfied. Some 8200 Canadian soldiers, all volunteers, had gone to South Africa, where they performed very creditably on the battlefield. Those who wanted to had stayed home. In the middle of the war, in 1900, Laurier's Liberals swept to an easy election victory.

The most direct embodiment of the empire in Laurier's Ottawa was the office and person of the governor general sent from England to preside in the queen's name. The position was described in 1893 as 'the first of Colonial Governors' in prestige and importance, and there was consequently some competition among British aristocrats for the job. Canadians, as yet, could not aspire to it. Laurier's governors general, Lords Aberdeen, Minto, and Grey, were all men of some distinction, though with varying qualities and interests. To succeed Lord Grey came no less than a son of Queen Victoria, Prince Arthur of Connaught, whose royal blood and field marshal's rank compensated for what he lacked in tact and brains. Obviously, Ottawa held some real attractions. Of the major colonies it was the closest to Britain. Unlike her Irish viceroy, the queen's Canadian representative was not liable to be shot, or shot at. Transatlantic mail and steamer connections were reliable, and, indeed, sea-mail took less time than airmail usually does today.

The governor general was the queen's representative, and for Canada's domestic purposes fulfilled the same royal functions. He could listen to his ministers' advice, and follow it when required. He could advise his ministers, if he chose. As commander-in-chief he could take an interest in the Canada's part-time, amateur militia and in its tiny permanent force of professional soldiers. He acted as a bond of union, not merely between Canada and Britain, but between the French and English and among the nine provinces.

The governor general had a more practical and utilitarian function. He was the official link between London and Ottawa, the channel through which messages passed to and from the Colonial Office. The governor general was, in this sense, the Canadian government's department of external affairs. To him came messages from British government departments, as well as communications from foreign powers which had made their way through the Foreign and Colonial offices to arrive in Ottawa, where no foreign diplomats were stationed. The governor general, or his office, would then pass such messages to the appropriate authority in Ottawa for action. The trouble was that there was no single authority to receive them. The prime minister was empowered to handle such messages, but his duties were many and heavy. His cabinet members had problems of their own. There were no civil servants with a specifically diplomatic function, although by default and design the undersecretary of state, Joseph Pope, came to handle much of Canada's business with the outside world.

The confusion engendered by this lack of system was frustrating to those who, by nature of their office, were obliged to communicate with Canada. The British ambassador in Washington discovered that Canada was Britain's longest land frontier, and that many problems, from duck hunting without a licence to smuggling, could arise along that border. The Americans, not unreasonably, wanted answers to specific questions and solutions to problems. Answers were often not forthcoming, even when the ambassador travelled to Ottawa in search of them. One ambassador estimated that no less than two-thirds of the British embassy's business in Washington derived from Canada. He did not claim that it was the most important two-thirds, but, great or small, business was business.

Here again the British Liberal government of 1906 produced a sea change. As ambassador to Washington they sent the distinguished historian James Bryce, renowned in the United States for an earlier study of American democracy. Bryce's prestige and personality appealed to Americans. These same qualities were not without impact in Ottawa, where Laurier and his Liberals were prepared to admire a fellow Liberal with scholarly attributes. Bryce wanted to 'clean the slate' of bothersome Canadian-American disputes, and this, with co-operation in Washington and Ottawa, he succeeded in doing.

Bryce made possible, though he did not negotiate, the Boundary Waters Treaty of 1909, which established facilities for dealing with transborder water problems – pollution, water diversion, and navigation – in an International Joint Commission boasting three Canadian and three American members. The treaty also made provision for the assignment of any and every kind of Canadian-American question to the commission, which, it was assumed, would sit as a kind of North American high court. There is some evidence that the United States government regarded it as just such a tribunal: President Taft (1909-13) even invited the commission's members to his annual dinner for the judiciary. Romantic though the gesture may have been, it was a good sign. If Canadian-American relations were placed on the footing of law and, possibly, justice too, there was less likelihood of force and pressure in North American diplomacy.

Bryce's next task was both simpler and more delicate. It was simpler because only Canada was involved, and more delicate because it implied a criticism of how matters were handled in Ottawa. It was high time that Canada acquired some bureau for handling external matters. Laurier procrastinated. Lord Grey enlisted in the cause, as did Joseph Pope. Finally, in September 1908, Laurier gave in. The cabinet agreed to establish a Department of External Affairs. When legislation was introduced into the House of Commons, the new department was attached to the Department of the Secretary of State, an insignificant office, instead of the entourage of the prime minister, as Pope had originally intended. The new department was justified to Parliament on the grounds of efficiency, which was true enough, rather than as a new beginning of a future Canadian foreign policy. In October 1909 the new department finally settled into its offices, considerately vacated by the Ottawa school board, just above a barber shop on Bank Street. Pope, soon to be Sir Joseph, became the department's first undersecretary.

Laurier had been a reluctant housekeeper, but at least boundary waters and the Department of External Affairs counted as positive acts, however limited in scope. In the larger sphere of imperial affairs Laurier preferred to leave well enough alone, to the extent that British and Canadian public opinion would let him. Fortunately, imperial affairs were a sometime thing, recurring like a periodic nightmare every fifth year to complicate Canada's politics and annoy its government. The focus of imperial negotiations was the colonial (later imperial) conference, a gathering of the prime ministers of the empire's self-governing colonies meeting under the presidency of the colonial secretary.

Joseph Chamberlain, colonial secretary from 1895 to 1903, summoned his first colonial conference to coincide with Queen Victoria's Diamond Jubilee in 1897. Chamberlain was a Liberal who had deserted the British Liberal party on the issue of Irish autonomy and had allied himself with the Conservatives, thus becoming a Liberal Unionist. His standing was high and his influence considerable, something that could not normally be said of colonial secretaries. A unionist at home, Chamberlain was an imperial unionist as well. Imperial federation, a term which could mean as much as a legislative union among the various parts of the empire or as little as some machinery for enhanced co-operation, was on the colonial secretary's mind. This proposition did not get far with Laurier and the majority of the colonial prime ministers. They passed a resolution expressing satisfaction with the existing order of things, resisted attempts to make them contemplate imperial defence, wined, dined, and went home.

Many things had happened before the next imperial conference met: the Boer War had been fought and won; the Australian colonies had federated; the Anglo-Japanese alliance had ended Britain's splendid isolation; Queen Victoria had died, and her successor, Edward VII, had to be crowned. The pace of the meetings, held between the end of June and the middle of August 1902, was leisurely. The conference's ten sessions mulled over problems of trade and defence; for the first time the assembled premiers were treated to an exposé of Britain's problems so as to encourage them to contribute materially to their solution. In addressing the colonial conference, Chamberlain laid down an agenda which would dominate imperial, and particularly Anglo-Canadian, relations for the next fifty years. 'The Weary Titan,' Chamberlain told the prime ministers, 'staggers under the too vast orb of its fate. We have borne the burden for many years. We think it is time our children should assist us to support it, and whenever you make the request to us, be very sure we shall hasten gladly to call you to our Councils.' Chamberlain's oratory has often been taken at face value. It was intended to spur the self-governing colonies into support for some kind of imperial executive or imperial legislature, or both, and it promised to swap consultation over policy for material aid; in effect, Chamberlain offered taxation *with* representation.

Could he make such an offer? Perhaps he could, and with impunity, only because nobody expected it to be taken seriously. How British politicians and civil servants would have reacted to the injection of colonials into the business of the United Kingdom can only be imagined. Even members of the British cabinet were kept in the dark about the extent of British contacts with the French between 1905 and 1911. If the basis of foreign policy was kept out of the cabinet and the British Parliament, would the dominions have been admitted into the secret? That the colonials should contribute to Britain's defence was desirable and laudable. That they should understand why was quite another matter.

The question of 'how' was not as controversial. The Laurier government's minister of militia and defence, Sir Frederick Borden, enjoyed a moderate success in reforming the structure of Canada's tiny professional army. He consulted readily with his British counterparts in London and returned to Canada with his head stuffed with good ideas about how best to get an army in fighting trim. Orders for munitions flowed from Canada to England. Many of the orders remained just that, since British industry failed to produce the goods on time. A Canadian general staff was created and assigned the task of producing proper plans for emergencies. One such plan was commissioned by Borden just before he and the Liberals were turned out of office in 1911: it was for an expeditionary force of one division, to be sent to 'a civilized country.' Not all of Borden's efforts were successful, but on balance he left his mark on Canada's military; as a result, mobilization for war in 1914 was not quite as chaotic as it might otherwise have been.

Defence policy was one subject that the Canadian public could seize with enthusiasm – too much enthusiasm in the eyes of those who worried about militaristic displays and martial airs. Militia regiments, cadet corps, patronage for supplies and officers' commissions: all these were part of the stuff of Canadian politics. Less attention was given to why or where the men and implements of war would be used. Foreign affairs were not much studied in Canada. Parliament seldom debated them, and when it did it was concerned with form, as in the debate over the establishment of the Department of External Affairs in 1909, or with local matters of special interest to Canada, such as the Alaska Boundary dispute. Canadian papers seldom carried much foreign news, although the Toronto *Globe* made a valiant effort to interest its readers in the subject. Newspaper opinion on foreign policy was less informative than reflexive: Britain was best, and Britain's enemies were beastly.

By 1900, Canada was developing a sufficient number of educated and well-informed citizens for whom the future of the empire was becoming a subject of real concern. British and American periodicals naturally circulated in Canada. British debates were scrutinized, reproduced, and sometimes amplified in university common rooms and at businessmen's clubs. Canadians travelling in the United States and Great Britain brought back their impressions and, if they happened to have friends abroad, collected impressions and disseminated their concerns.

For the first time there were friends abroad who took an active, professional concern in the shaping of Canada's external policy. On the fringes of the British government a group of bright youngish men undertook to secure what the British government could not: an empire united around a definition of its true common interests, united against its external foes and rivals. The empire, they told themselves, was a 'practical' achievement. Most recently, the Boer colonies of South Africa had been encouraged to join with the British colonies in that region in a Union of South Africa whose leadership included men who had a decade before fought the British rifle in hand. South Africa was held to be a triumph of broad-minded, liberal statesmanship, which inside ten years had reconciled the irreconcilables. Surely much the same could be done elsewhere in the empire.

The young Britons who felt this way sent a reconnaissance to Canada in 1909. The expedition did more than talk to politicians in Ottawa. Travelling across the country, it interviewed bank managers, railway executives, lawyers, and editors. Laurier told Philip Kerr, one of the expeditionaries, that without being isolationist, he did not want Canada dragged into the 'turmoil' of Europe. Another Canadian minister predictably denounced Chamberlain and his works. Kerr also saw the most junior of Laurier's ministers, and his account of their meeting makes interesting reading. Mackenzie King, the minister of labour, struck Kerr as 'sensible – [with] rather the Laurier point of view.' King preached a gospel of social internationalism: the empire, in his opinion, would 'grow as an association for civilisation & peace.'

Next came Robert Borden, leader of the opposition, a Conservative from

Nova Scotia. Borden had just returned from England, which had left him 'rather pessimistic.' Borden spoke from a somewhat unusual perspective, since while in England he had conferred with Lord Milner, Britain's former high commissioner in South Africa and latterly the inspiration of the young men who had decided, like Kerr, to investigate the possibilities of the empire. Closely examined, Borden's approach to the empire had much in common with Laurier's. It was wrong to force the growth of imperial institutions, as Kerr and his master Milner were proposing. 'The institutions of the Empire will point themselves as they are needed. The sentiment is universal today. If a crisis arose, the response of Canada would be overwhelming.'

Kerr took his observations back to England, where he and his friends scrutinized them for hopeful signs. The empire, they concluded, had reached a turning point. It was necessary to direct the empire's energies to the task of collecting its strength 'under one intelligent control,' thereby 'securing the interests and performing the duties, which are common to all the States of the Empire alike.' To achieve this goal, Milner's collection of young imperialists constituted themselves as a movement, the Round Table, implying both rational discussion and the romantic knight errantry of King Arthur's Camelot. Lionel Curtis, who played pope in the Round Table religion to Milner's godhead, embodied this conclusion in a lengthy memorandum. Curtis stressed the debt owed by the countries of the empire to Britain, which defended them at great cost to itself and with relatively slight contributions from the self-governing colonies. This debt furnished leverage in future negotiations between the mother country and its children; in the final analysis the British could stress that the dominions (South Africa, New Zealand, and Australia as well as Canada) owed more to them than the British owed to their colonies.

But politicians, British and Canadian, had scant time for the Round Tablers and their fanciful schemes, all of which seemed to demand a considerable expenditure of political capital for no very quick return. The Round Tablers consoled themselves that this was precisely the trouble with politicians. The imperial conferences – there were two more, in 1907 and 1911 – held out no hope of progress. What was needed was some great cause, some overwhelming event, which could concentrate men's minds on what really needed to be done. And that event, although they did not know it, would soon arrive in the form of the First World War.

7

The Politics of War

Robert Borden had much to care about during his late July vacation at Port Carling on Lake Muskoka, but European turmoil bothered him little. The parliamentary session had been long, and he had heard rumours of war many times before. He knew on 28 July 1914, the day Austria sent a declaration of war to Serbia, that it would be almost impossible for Canada to stay out of a general European war, but this did not keep him from the golf course on that day, or the next, or the day following. On Friday, 1 August, the situation finally seemed serious enough to return to Ottawa. Even so, he told his wife Laura to stay in Muskoka just in case he might be able to return 'in a few days.' He did not: on 4 August 1914 the colonial secretary cabled Prime Minister Borden that the empire was at war. Borden had already promised that Canada would 'put forth every effort' and make whatever sacrifice was necessary 'to ensure the integrity and maintain the honour of our Empire.' And so in midsummer Canada went to war.

Compared to Britain, Canada entered war with little open dissent and remarkably few fears. Indeed, minister of militia Sam Hughes feared that the war would end before his Canadian 'boys' had fired a shot in anger. To a modern generation which associates war with horror, Hughes's attitude and the exuberant celebrations at the outbreak of war seem, at the very least, peculiar. One must consider, however, how remote war had been for Canadians living in 1914 and how romantic the image of war had become in the latter part of the nineteenth century. Young Canadians had grown up reading the stirring tales of the Khyber Pass and of valiant imperial servants bringing new and better ways to barbarian people. The children's novelist G.A. Henty and, on a more enduring level, Rudyard Kipling provided the script for thousands of Canadians' fantasies of patriotism, duty, and war. In the streets of Calgary, Halifax, and many other Canadian towns, imaginary whirling dervishes were driven off and the empire's honour was saved.

These images remained etched in the minds of many older Canadians who believed that war was the test of national honour. Regaled by tales of dastardly foes vanquished, and inspired by acts of individuals who rose to greatness in battle, many Canadians – and Germans, Britons, and French – believed that war would call forth the best that their traditions represented. In doing so, it would sweep away the sloth, inertia, and baseness of prewar society. The prominent Canadian writer and physician Andrew Macphail put it bluntly in 1914: 'A nation which is good in war is good in peace; and a nation which is no good in war is good for nothing.'[1] War had not meant the destruction of civilization; in the memory of Canadians in 1914 it had usually meant the transferral of 'civilization' to 'lesser breeds without the law' in Asia, Africa, and elsewhere. It had meant, in the Boer War in which Canadians fought so valiantly, that the democratic rights of British subjects would never more be denied. And in 1914, when former Boer generals committed South Africa to fight for the British cause, the usefulness of that earlier war seemed justified.

Yet even the militaristic did not consider all wars and warring nations worthy. Shakespeare had provided the standard when he had Prince Hal declare that arms were fair only when the intent of bearing them was just. The justice of the British and the Canadian cause was firmly established when imperial Germany's army smashed through neutral Belgium. It was not Borden but Sir Wilfrid Laurier who expressed most eloquently the outrage that Canadians felt in those first days of war. The war, Laurier declared in the special session of Parliament in August 1914, 'is for as noble a cause as ever impelled a nation to risk her all upon the arbitrament of the sword. That question is no longer at issue – the judgment of the world has already pronounced upon it.' Britain had not sought the war. For that reason it would 'go down on a still nobler page of history that England could have averted this war if she had been willing to forego the position which she had maintained for many centuries at the head of European civilization; if she had been willing to desert her allies, to sacrifice her obligations, to allow the German Emperor to bully heroic Belgium, to trample upon defenceless Luxembourg, to rush upon isolated France, and to put down his booted heel upon continental Europe.' No, England had refused to do that. For that reason, 'there is not today ... a single man whose admiration for England is not greater by reason of this firm and noble attitude.'[2]

1 Quoted in Carl Berger, *The Sense of Power: Studies in the Ideas of Canadian Imperialism* (Toronto 1970), 239. Chapter 10 of this book is an excellent summary of the influence of militarism in Canada.
2 Quoted in O.D. Skelton, *Life and Letters of Sir Wilfrid Laurier,* volume 2 (Toronto 1921), 432-4

In fact, there were a few dissenters, but their voices were drowned out or, more often, silenced in August 1914. Others did not share Laurier's full-blown enthusiasm. Certainly that was true of many of his French-Canadian compatriots, who were generally willing to admit the justice of the cause but reluctant to accept that the war demanded a new commitment in their lives. For German Canadians, so many of them new arrivals to Canada, the war brought considerable fear, which was not much relieved by the assurances of Borden and Laurier in those early days. There were others, such as Finns, Mennonites, Doukhobours, and pacifists, who found it either difficult to understand or impossible to accept the war enthusiasm of many English Canadians. In their addresses in August 1914, Laurier and Borden spoke of these persons, and both called for a spirit of generosity and tolerance. Such sentiments came easily then. So did political actions which became impossible later.

With the agreement of the opposition, the Conservative government introduced an Emergency War Measures Bill. The bill quickly became an act – the War Measures Act – which allowed the government to do whatever it deemed necessary for the prosecution of the war, enormously widening the government's power to issue orders-in-council. These could now fundamentally affect the lives of Canadians, without any parliamentary scrutiny. That was the bill's intention, and in the short term the act proved both effective and relatively uncontroversial. As the war became dreary and long, however, the act became a dangerous temptation for a government facing political troubles. For those opposed to the government's policies, the existence of this act which bestowed dictatorial powers on the government was thoroughly frightening.

When Laurier uttered his passionate approval of the war, he did so not only because he believed deeply in the British cause but also because he knew that the Liberal party and its leader had to be seen as unquestionably patriotic. He worried that the Conservatives could successfully argue that the Liberal refusal to support the prewar Naval Bill was irresponsible and anti-British. Laurier therefore sought to remove all suspicions by promising in August 1914 that he and his party would 'offer no criticism so long as there is danger at the front.' In fact, the promise was easily kept so long as Canadians were not in danger at the front. When the dangers appeared and the inevitable blunders occurred, this unique mood of political truce became much more difficult to maintain.

The political truce began to fall apart soon after it was declared. Many Conservatives urged Borden to call an election to take advantage of the vindication which they believed the war gave to prewar government policies. Such an election might have been useful in cleansing the political air, thereby permitting the nation to see more clearly what it faced and what it wanted to do. In view of Laurier's pledge, however, election talk struck many as close to sacrilege. When rumours of an impending election began to circulate, the Liberals reacted with calculated outrage: how dare the Tories plot an election when Canadian boys were dying in France? The Liberals had laid down their politics for their country; the Tories could not. This stance was of course politically shrewd, especially when abundant evidence of Tory favouritism in the Canadian war effort appeared in 1915.

Most of the problems came from Sam Hughes. The minister of militia had received much publicity and praise in August and September 1914 for his boundless energy and the rapid preparation of the Canadian Expeditionary Force. Energetic Hughes certainly was, but unfortunately much of that energy was spent in getting special positions for his friends and contracts for party supporters. Outrage focused on the Shell Committee, a typical Hughes device which was intended to circumvent normal channels, draw further power and attention to himself, and reward his friends. The committee proved most inexpert at producing shells but adept at creating political explosions. In the summer of 1915 the British army faced a serious shortage of artillery, caused in part by the fact that of $170 million of orders placed in Canada, only $5.5 million had been delivered on time under Shell Committee contracts. The opposition angrily charged that Hughes was playing with the lives of British and Canadian soldiers as he played his political game.

In the spring of 1915, as the first of many Canadians fell fighting for small patches of French soil, Hughes's eccentricities became much less tolerable. The Ross rifle, which had been Hughes's pride, failed the test of battle. And there were other scandals. In April 1915 Borden had to read two Conservative MPs out of the party because of their involvement in contract scandals. Laurier's Liberals and their party press sniped away at the faltering government, all the time professing their continued adherence to the political truce. An infuriated Borden once again thought of an election in which his party would confront the Grits directly on the question of where they stood on the war. But in the spring of 1915 an election had become unthinkable to most Tories: even calling one would hand the Liberals a powerful war-related issue. Once again, an election was postponed until times were better. All the while, better times moved farther away.

In assessing party strength for a spring or summer 1915 election, Borden thought that he could 'give' the Liberals fifty-five Quebec seats and still have a Conservative working majority. He had seen in 1911 how effective an appeal to British-Canadian sentiment could be. In a wartime election, however, the Conservatives could not ally with Quebec nationalists as they had in 1911. The Tories were in very bad shape in Quebec in mid-1915, and Bor-

I wish Sam were here. He says there is nothing in these shells, but I ha'e ma doots!'
Borden confronts the 'Shell committee' scandal, 1915
Arch Dale, *Winnipeg Free Press*

den's view of Liberal strength in the province might have been an underestimate. Since Monk's resignation, no figure of comparable stature had emerged to represent French Canada in the Conservative cabinet. Borden himself remained aloof from his French-Canadian colleagues, for whom in any case he had little respect. The situation improved somewhat with the outbreak of war. After all, the naval emergency had been genuine, as Borden had warned in 1912. Moreover, Borden assured the Catholic hierarchy in the province that there would be no conscription, and this pledge was widely circulated and accepted by French Canadians. The provincial Liberal government assured Borden of its full-fledged co-operation, pledged a gift to Britain as other British provinces had done, and offered full salary to Quebec government employees who enlisted. Combined with Laurier's pledges in Ottawa and Henri Bourassa's decision not to oppose the war, these provincial actions seemed to bode well for the future of the war effort in the province of Quebec. But then things went badly wrong.

Sam Hughes was a large part of the problem. The boisterous Orangeman would not trust French Canadians in senior positions and would not agree readily to French-speaking battalions. In one notorious instance of insensitivity, Hughes used a Methodist clergyman to recruit in Quebec. When French Canadians did not seem to be enlisting as rapidly as those from other parts of Canada, Hughes quickly made public the fact. By 1915 Hughes had become, to French Canada, a caricature of the blustering militarist who represented all that was anathema. In the eyes of French Canada in 1915, the war may still have been theirs, but the Canadian army under Sam Hughes could never be.

A more important factor in alienating French Canadians may have been the move by the Ontario government to limit French-language education in that province. Regulation XVII, which restricted French as a language of instruction to the first two primary grades, passed from being a directive into law in 1915. It was exquisitely bad timing – at least from the point of view of national unity. Politically, in Ontario, the move to limit French-language rights was irresistible. Both the Liberal party and the ruling Conservative party supported Regulation XVII. Their support became more intense as Nationalists from Quebec angrily demanded justice for francophones in Ontario and denounced the 'Prussians' of Ontario. Laurier felt himself trapped. The Nationalists in Quebec had found another popular cause that could only weaken war sentiment in that province. Laurier pleaded with the Ontario Liberal leader Newton Rowell to support the rights of French Canadians in the province. To an Ontario Liberal he complained: 'We, French Liberals of Quebec, are fighting Bourassa and Lavergne; will the English Liberals in Ontario fight Howard Ferguson and the extreme Orange element?' They would not.

Nor did Borden contribute much to the resolution of the dispute. He refused a request by his French-Canadian ministers to have the matter referred to the Imperial Privy Council, a tactic which might have bought some time. In the view of his French-Canadian ministers, Borden had 'proposed no alternative plan, made no suggestion or offered no advice as to the manner in which the controversy might be ended.' He stood firm on the rock of provincial authority in education at a time when provincial authority was being limited in other realms in the interests of war. When Ernest Lapointe, a young Liberal MP from Kamouraska, introduced a mildly worded resolution which called upon Ontario to continue to recognize 'the privilege of the children of French parentage being taught in their mother tongue,' Borden warned that the resolution might cause much mischief because it would 'intensify feelings already sufficiently aroused.' So it did. In Ontario and elsewhere, the antagonism created by the Regulation XVII controversy passed easily into a general resentment directed towards the attitude of French Canada on the war. In Quebec, the Nationalist case was reinforced. Now more people could agree with the Nationalists' rhetorical question:

Suicide?

Laurier plays Russian roulette, 1916
Forrester, 1916

Why fight the Boche in Europe when they ruled in Ontario?

In the vote on the Lapointe Resolution, which was decisively defeated, party lines disintegrated as French-Canadian Tories voted for the resolution and several English-Canadian Liberals defied Laurier and voted against. The disarray of the Liberals brought some contentment to Tory ranks, but in 1916 the Conservative position had weakened and Laurier was unprepared to agree to a further extension of the parliamentary term. A new series of scandals tarnished the government's reputation, and even government supporters lamented the weakness of national leadership. At the provincial level, the Conservatives had lost much of the strength which had helped the federal party in 1911. In Ontario, the death of premier Sir James Whitney had removed an influential voice in national and provincial affairs. The British Columbia Conservative party, like Ontario's, also showed signs of age, and in 1916 the Liberals gained power on the Pacific coast, as they had already in Manitoba. These victories gave scant comfort to Laurier. The western Canadian Liberal governments were strongly pro-war and generally reformist in tone. Their outlook appealed to Conservatives who were discouraged by the apparent floundering and favouritism in Ottawa.

To nationalists and imperialists, to westerners and easterners, the government seemed unable to do what was necessary. The demands of the war outran the capacity of government to deal with them. Borden's frustration in this situation is understandable. On the one hand, there were so many groups demanding so many new things from government. The demands often conflicted and, as in the case of the bilingual school controversy, there was no action which would not have outraged a significant interest. Canadians were not used to having government influence their lives as it was doing in wartime. Much of this new influence they demanded; much of it they resented. On the other hand, Borden did make some difficult decisions in 1916, but decisions in the national interest did not always or even often coincide with his party's interest. The result of his decisiveness was sometimes a weaker political position. His political world was filled with paradox. The greatest dilemma, and the most difficult, lay in the strident demands for a greater Canadian war effort and the failure of Canadians to respond by joining the Canadian Expeditionary Force.

On New Year's Day, 1916, Borden announced that the Canadian commitment through the Canadian Expeditionary Force would be 500,000 men. His announcement was greeted with public acclaim in most of English Canada. Patriotic organizations vowed that they would stir young men to join the force, and the voices demanding enlistment by all those who could go rose in a crescendo throughout 1916.

Some of Borden's colleagues had feared that the commitment of 500,000 men was too much, as it proved to be. Nevertheless, once it was made it had to be met. By the end of 1916 the difficulties in meeting this pledge became the dominant issue in Canadian politics. Borden refused to reiterate his earlier promise that he would not bring in conscription. Privately, he told friends that he would resort to compulsion if necessary, whatever French Canada thought of it. There was little sympathy for French Canada's attitude. 'The vision of the French Canadian,' Borden wrote, 'is very limited. He is not well informed and he is in a condition of extreme exasperation by reason of fancied wrongs supposed to be inflicted upon his compatriots in other provinces, especially Ontario.' On his side, Bourassa now spoke openly against the war, against 'Anglo-Saxon civilization,' and against Borden and even Laurier, 'the warmongers' who had decided 'to ruin Canada to save Europe.'

For Bourassa and for many other French Canadians, the war was only a British war and Canada had already spent too much blood in a dubious cause. For Borden and many more Canadians, the blood that had flowed had made the war a Canadian war, a struggle where national honour was at stake and in which national greatness could be attained. The war had become a great national opportunity. If that opportunity were not realized, it would be the greatest national tragedy.

The crisis came in early 1917. There had been peace rumours in late 1916, but they soon passed and it became clear that the fight would be to the finish. France's morale was slipping, Russia was lurching towards chaos, and British politicians and generals were quarrelling over who should run the war. This was the troubling situation Borden learned of when he arrived in Britain in late February 1917. He had left Canada without making a clear decision on conscription or on the reorganization of his government. Both questions were to await his return from his participation in the Imperial War Cabinet chaired by the new British prime minister, David Lloyd George. Lloyd George's fervent demands for a fuller war effort, combined with support for a new relationship among the dominions and Britain, won Borden's approval. Entranced with the excitement of London in the heat of wartime, Borden told the British that Canada would not fail. Proof of Canada's commitment and of its soldiers' valour came in most dramatic fashion at Easter when the Canadian Corps won its greatest victory at Vimy Ridge. To Borden, the glory of that bloody battle made the ultimate triumph even more important. He returned to Canada a more determined man.

On 17 May 1917 Borden took the fateful step, telling his cabinet that conscription must come to Canada. The cabinet agreed, but his French-Canadian ministers warned him that conscription would 'kill them politically and the party for 25 years.' Not only Quebec ministers were concerned. Others saw that many Canadian workers would be reluctant to leave the booming factories and that many farmers would resent leaving untended harvests. Could conscription succeed if the country was so divided? That question troubled Borden far more than did the future of his party. He was, therefore, driven towards an attempt to forge a coalition to carry conscription through. On 25 May he proposed to Laurier that they form a coalition government made up of an equal number of Conservatives and Liberals, apart from the office of the prime minister. As an opening offer, Borden's terms were generous.

Laurier, however, could never accept conscription; coalition was impossible for him. If he agreed to join a government committed to conscription, he knew that his influence in Quebec would be lost and that the Nationalists would have solid evidence for their arguments against Laurier Liberalism. At the same time, Laurier faced great pressure from prominent English-Canadian Liberals who had, in some cases, called for a coalition before Borden. Seeing how his party was divided, Laurier scrambled to find a compromise. By the first week of June he thought he had found one. He rejected coalition, but offered those Liberals who favoured conscription the right to run as 'Official Liberals' if they agreed to a referendum on conscription. It was a clever stroke which cut down the momentum for coalition and conscription.

Borden was nonetheless determined that conscription must become the law of the land and that the widest support for it must be found. He kept open his offer of coalition, hoping that leading Liberals and independents could be attracted into the government. Despite strong support for conscription among Liberals such as Ontario leader Newton Rowell and *Manitoba Free Press* editor John W. Dafoe, Borden found surprisingly little interest in his offer. Several reasons for this apathy can be suggested. Any breakdown in strong party ties required virtually a leap of faith. Moreover, such a leap was made more difficult by the deep animosity between the parties, especially the Liberals' great distrust of Borden and his government for their actions since 1911. Most important, perhaps, was the discovery by leading English-Canadian Liberals that conscription was not so generally popular as they had originally believed.

The pressure for conscription in English Canada came from the most articulate – the urban middle class and their spokesmen in the media and the professions. The opposition came from the more inarticulate – farmers, immigrants from non-British cultures, and workers. By 25 May the Borden cabinet was already worrying that an election on the conscription issue would be lost to a combination of farmers, French Canadians, 'foreigners,' and 'slackers.' When, in the summer of 1917, Borden tried to strengthen the government by wooing some of the twenty-six (out of thirty-eight) English-Canadian Liberals who voted for the Military Service Act on final reading, there was little response. Both Ontario Liberals and western Canadian Liberals had well-publicized meetings in mid-summer at which attempts to get Liberals from these areas to abandon Laurier failed dismally. With an election nearing and with Laurier's hold on his party apparently strengthening, the supporters of conscription and the Conservative government became frightened.

This extraordinary situation produced unusual measures. After coalition talks failed in August, the government came forward with two acts which have provoked criticism ever since. The first, the Military Voters' Act, allowed a soldier in a wartime election to choose a constituency if he claimed he had no close links with any particular constituency. This meant, of course, that the soldier who so declared acquired a 'floating vote' which he could bestow upon whichever constituency he chose. Although soldiers voted for either the government or the opposition, this irregular ballot seemed likely to help the Conservatives. This act upset the Liberals but the second act introduced by the government, the War-time Elections Act, enraged them. It gave the vote to the wives, mothers, and sisters of soldiers and withheld it from women who were unrelated. While granting a vote in this questionable manner, the act took away votes in an even more dubious fashion: it disfranchised Canadians of enemy origin who had been naturalized after 1902. The act, Laurier bitterly declaimed, was 'a blot upon every instinct of justice, honesty and fair play.' Historians have usually agreed.

To Borden and his supporters, however, the needs of justice in Europe were paramount. To make his point that it was the demands of the war, not mere party considerations, which motivated him to reshape the electorate in such a blatant manner, Borden reiterated his willingness to form a coalition. The effect of the two acts was to shake loose enough Liberals to make a coalition possible. Western Liberals, no longer worried about carrying the west in a conscriptionist coalition government, hastened to Ottawa. In Ontario, Newton Rowell finally made up his mind to join, as did Frank Carvell, a senior Liberal from New Brunswick. On 12 October Borden presented the new Union government to the people. Premier Arthur Sifton of Alberta became the minister of customs. The prominent Saskatchewan Liberal, James Calder, took the important immigration and colonization portfolio, and Thomas Crerar, the leading spokesman of western agriculture, and probably the most important acquisition, became minister of agriculture. Rowell and Carvell were appointed president of the Privy Council and minister of public works, respectively. Gideon Robertson, a representative of labour, and A.K. Maclean, a designate of Nova Scotia Liberal premier George Murray, obtained posts as ministers without portfolio. In the end, there were twelve Conservatives and nine Liberals, in addition to Robertson, in the new cabinet. It was not the government 'based upon the support of all elements of the population' which Borden had said he wanted. It was, nevertheless, a much stronger national government than the one that preceded it.

Several months before he announced the Union government's formation, Borden had written privately to a friend that the war would lead to 'new party alignments, reconstruction of past political formulas and a new political outlook.' His actions in October and afterwards ensured that these changes occurred. The traditional Canadian party system did not survive the shocks it received in 1917. Party loyalties were shed in solemn anger, and the institutions which were the foundation of the old party system lost their effectiveness. The Union government election program, which was announced on 18 October 1917, indicated how much the nation and its politics had changed since the first days of August 1914.

The Unionist platform was interventionist, and it proclaimed the right, indeed the duty, of the state to assume more control over the lives of individ-

A SQUARE SHAKE

The country: 'I back you, Sir Robert, you're backing my boys.'
McConnell, 1917. Courtesy Public Archives of Canada

uals. Conscription was of course an example of this tendency, but there were several others, notably in the realm of economic affairs. The Unionists proposed to control the economy much more completely than Canadian governments had ever done before. The assertion of power was justified by the needs of the war; but in foreshadowing the more activist state in the future, it was portentous. Politically, all women were to be given the vote – for the next federal election, not the one in 1917. The issue that the women's movement had promoted so fervently, prohibition, was also a plank in the Unionist platform. Patronage was to be eliminated as well, and future appointments would be made on merit, not political affiliation. This final item was made necessary by the very fact of coalition: Liberals and Conservatives had to share the appointments. Since patronage had been such a powerful glue holding together the prewar parties, its abolition caused all manner of people and things to come unstuck.

The election was set for 17 December. The issue was the war, and the tone of the campaign was therefore especially bitter. Laurier knew he could not win; he ran a dignified campaign knowing that the war and the anger it produced would pass. What would be remembered were the wounds inflicted upon French Canadians and 'foreigners' whose allegiance his party would command in the future. For the Unionists, the campaign was a crusade. Their campaign rhetoric borrowed from the language of religion, at times adopting an almost millenarian tone. Borden saw what was happening as the birthpangs of a 'truer and nobler civilization.' Heretics were condemned with a fury that grew with each passing day of the campaign. Unionist cartoonists showed a bloody-handed Laurier cavorting with the Kaiser. The *Toronto News* printed a map of Canada with all parts British imperial red except Quebec, which was black. A Conservative Unionist MP called Quebec 'the spoiled child of Confederation,' while George Allan, a Liberal supporting the Unionists, described the province as 'the plague-spot of the whole Dominion.' The major charge against Quebec was that made by Anglican Archdeacon H.J. Cody, a future president of the University of Toronto: 'Henri Bourassa is the real leader of Quebec, and I ask if that Province, led by him, shall have the domination of the rest of this free Dominion which has sacrificed and suffered.'

Bourassa was an easy target, and never had his language been so intemperate: the Unionists were mad for blood; the war was the product of naked British imperialism; and Union government was 'the synthesis of all we detest, of all we despise.' By late November the Unionist campaign had become centred on Quebec and Bourassa's malign influence. Other opponents of conscription, such as labour groups and farmers, were appealed to on a racial basis. In the case of the farmers, the appeal was enhanced by an announcement on 3 December that agricultural workers would be exempt from conscription. Opposition from farm groups melted away, and rural constituencies throughout Ontario fell behind the campaign against Quebec.[3] Organized labour in eastern Canada also found the pressure to back conscription too strong, and eastern labour leaders came out in support of Union government, thereby widening the gap between the easterners and their more radical western comrades.

As election day neared, the Unionists spurred on their supporters, emphasizing the seriousness of the task at hand. The Rev. S.D. Chown, general superintendant of the Methodist church, reflected the spirit of the campaign in an impassioned last-minute appeal: 'We shall fail, and fail lamentably, as Christian people unless we catch the martyr spirit of true Christianity and do our sacrificial duty between now and the 17th of December.' Not to be outdone, Anglican Bishop J.C. Farthing of Montreal called upon all Anglicans to 'close up our ranks and unite the country behind our Union Government for God and country.' Neither Chown nor Farthing, of course, would be sent to the trenches. 'Our Union Government' – by election day the campaign had become a clash between nationalisms: British-Canadian nationalism on the one side, French-Canadian nationalism on the other. In such a contest, the former had by far the largest legions. On 17 December it triumphed decisively. (See Appendix 1.)

The vote had divided largely on ethnic lines, except in Nova Scotia and Prince Edward Island. The Liberals carried the French-Canadian vote overwhelmingly, not only in Quebec but also in New Brunswick, Ontario, and Manitoba. They also won the support of German Canadians. The best example of this support was in the constituency of North Waterloo, Canada's most 'German' constituency, where an incumbent Conservative Unionist was defeated almost two to one by an outspoken opponent of conscription. In the surrounding 'British' constituencies, however, polls that had been traditionally Liberal went by margins of as much as eight to one for the Unionists. As Borden had predicted, the war had brought a new kind of politics and, it seemed, a new political system. But what kind of politics and what kind of system? On New Year's Day, 1918, no one was sure.

The Union government's primary mandate was to maintain the Canadian war effort. It never wavered in this regard. Conscription was enforced, and in March 1918 Borden cancelled the exemption to farmers which he had promised the previous December. His actions caused riots in the streets of Quebec and strong protests from farmers. Workers too became angrier as they discovered that their economic gains made during 1915 and 1916 were

---

3   Not all rural Liberals fell into line. J.K. Galbraith's father was one such exception; see his *A Life in Our Times* (Boston 1981), 1.

being eroded quickly by inflation. The government did bring in a labour code which increased workers' bargaining and organizational rights, but workers did not see any tangible benefit because the government also banned strikes. When workers defied the ban, the government realized that the ban was unenforceable. It did, however, seek to stamp out 'sedition' through censorship. In general, then, the hand of government was hard and its fears great. As Sir George Foster, a Unionist cabinet minister and veteran of political wars since the days of Macdonald, noted, the 'public nerves' were on edge as never before. They could 'respond to every critical or querulous touch.'

The Union government reflected the nation in its own nervousness. The grand hopes for a more efficient government evaporated, as many of the old problems would not go away. The confidence in the ability of the state to direct the economy and to enter new areas of social concern weakened. Borden's frustration grew, as he discovered that partisanship and personal rivalry abounded in his new cabinet. He found the atmosphere overseas much more to his liking, and began to believe that his European tasks were his major obligation.

Borden played a large role in planning the strategy for war in 1918 and, after 11 November 1918, shaping the peace. Between the spring of 1918 and his retirement in July 1920 he was outside of Ottawa approximately three-quarters of the time, mostly in Europe. His accomplishments there were considerable, and they are described elsewhere in this book. What is significant here is the extent to which these activities, praiseworthy as they may have been, were harmful politically. Borden tried to convince Canadians that the major political question they faced was Canada's relationship with Europe. After all, the war which had been the election issue in 1917 and had so profoundly transformed Canadian society was the product of Canada's relationship with Great Britain. A lasting peace was therefore pre-eminently in the Canadian interest. In Borden's view, too, Canada could get nothing out of the victory except recognition. His work in London and Paris was to ensure that recognition was given. Unfortunately, neither the Canadian people nor even the Unionist cabinet were convinced by his arguments.

By the end of 1918, Canadians were impatient of authority in general and Union government in particular. Borden and his government were frustrated by their inability to act and the apparent unwillingness of Canadians to follow their lead. Unionists interpreted the vote of December 1917 as a mandate for a strong government. In respect to war needs, the mandate was strong, but when peace arrived the government lost its legitimacy. Even before the armistice was signed, the Union government's strength began to ebb away.

The first prop to fall away was the farmer, especially in Ontario and the west. Even before 1914 rural Canada sensed that its position in the Canadian political and economic system was weakening and, as we have seen, the evidence supporting this belief became stronger with each succeeding census. The results of the 1911 election were rude confirmation of the loss or agrarian power. The defeat of reciprocity, W.L. Morton has written, 'was the first act in the agrarian revolt of Western Canada.' The stage chosen for the second act was the provincial governments of the prairie provinces. By 1916 the governments of these provinces had become very much the reflections of strong agrarian movements.[4] The abolition of the farmers' exemption from conscription and the end of the bonanza which war represented for many Canadian farmers were two new and major causes of agrarian disaffection.

In 1917 many farm leaders opposed conscription until the Union government appealed to the British background of most western and Ontario farmers and to the reform sentiments which those groups had long held. The entry of the powerful western agrarian spokesman, T.A. Crerar, into the Union government and the enlistment of several others active in farm movements assuaged the doubts of the farmers about the domination of Union government by central Canadian economic interests. Still, Borden was sufficiently frightened by the possibility of a rural defection to promise exemption to farmers' sons in the last month of the 1917 campaign.

In March 1918 the government cancelled the exemption. This occurred as the farmers were beginning to fear for their prosperity in the postwar years. Many had done well during the war, but they knew that the circumstances were exceptional. Unwilling to accept a return to prewar uncertainties, and increasingly distrustful of the Conservative majority within Unionist ranks, farm leaders were ready for action as soon as the war ended. On 29 November 1918 the Canadian Council of Agriculture adopted a new 'Farmers' Platform,' which soon became 'A New National Policy.' What the council proposed was a repudiation of the National Policy of 1879; it urged a different direction for Canada which would lead away from a protective tariff and from policies which had created the urban and industrial nation Canada had become by 1918. To carry out the platform, political action was essential.

Although there was little talk in early 1919 about an independent political party, the farmers, in truth, had no political home. Tom Crerar found the pressures too much to bear and, on 29 May just as workers and government were approaching the final confrontation in the Winnipeg General

---

4 See W.L. Morton, *The Progressive Party in Canada* (Toronto 1950), 26-7.

Strike, he told his Union government colleagues that he was resigning. The Unionists had lowered the tariff, but not enough. He quickly cut his Unionist ties, and eight western Unionists followed. By the summer of 1919 the farmers were organizing throughout western Canada and rural Ontario. Rumours of their political power were confirmed as they won by-elections and as political leaders scurried for cover. These eight western Unionists joined Crerar in voting against the budget on final division, and they moved to the 'crossbenches' of the House of Commons. The embryo of the Progressive party was formed. Thereafter, the support for independent farmers' political action spread like wildfire in midsummer.

The rapid progress of farm groups in the west was surprising; their election victory in Ontario in October 1919 was stunning. In June 1919 a former Unionist from Ontario, E.C. Drury, predicted that the western agrarian leaders and the United Farmers of Ontario would form a new party which would force the traditional parties into union. The new party would stand for 'wisdom, justice and honesty in public affairs.' It would be a party untainted by campaign funds and would 'cleanse the whole public life of Canada.' He ended with an appropriate metaphor: 'We intend to hoe our own row.' In October, in a stunning election victory, Drury was called upon to lead a farmers' government in Ontario.

The results showed 43 seats for the United Farmers of Ontario, 28 seats for the Liberals, 26 for the Conservatives who had held power, and 12 Labour seats. The Farmers had little organization but a great deal of enthusiasm. Their platform seemed more innovative than it really was. It called for help for co-operative movements but less assistance to business, for better rural roads and less extensive main highways, for abolition of patronage but greater recognition of farmers. Prohibition was, of course, a central plank, as was proportional representation. Little thought was given to priorities or to the adaption of their proposals to the traditions of cabinet government. In those heady days of October such problems were suffused in the great excitement which accompanied the first farmers' government in Canada's largest and most industrialized province.

In Ontario, Drury became premier in a minority government which also had the support of the Labour group. Now he had his chance to hoe his own row. His approach to government was traditional in most respects, though initially he had flirted rhetorically with different approaches. In Alberta, however, the United Farmers under the leadership of Henry Wise Wood were adopting a theory of group government whereby individual constituency representation would give way to representation by economic interests. This idea frightened Arthur Meighen, who succeeded Borden as prime minister in July 1920 and who immediately turned his oratorical skills to the destruction of the farmers' movement. Wood's ideas, Meighen claimed, were akin to 'Socialistic, Bolshevistic and Soviet nonsense.' Meighen's former colleague T.A. Crerar attacked Meighen for the use of smear tactics, but privately he shared some of the fears. Crerar, who had become the leader of the Progressive party in the House of Commons, was not inclined to follow radical paths.

In 1921 the triumph of the United Farmers in Alberta and the success of the Progressives in the Canadian general election seemed to indicate the continuing power of the agrarian movement – in the same year that the census was showing Canada to be, statistically, an urban nation. The Progressives under Crerar took sixty-five seats in 1921, and in 1922 a United Farmers government gained power in Manitoba. Nevertheless, the momentum had slipped away from the farmers' movement. In Ontario, Drury's government failed to transform the province; indeed, it found it difficult to maintain those wartime reforms such as prohibition which it had inherited. In the west, the farmers' programs had been presented as a miraculous panacea, but the miracles failed to occur. The result was the radicalization of some farm leaders and the disenchantment of others. The New National Policy had been a clever but unconvincing blend of democratic rhetoric and interest-group appeal. It had paraded its political novelty while seeking to maintain traditional values – the values of the land, the rural community, and Protestant religion. These values circumscribed the appeal of the Progressives. The French-Canadian farmers, for example, could never make common cause. Organized labour could join in rhetorical denunciation of plutocrats, but it too had a fundamentally different perception of Canadian development. Like so many reform movements in Canada and elsewhere, the Progressives idealized the past and feared the future. Living the present was too difficult, and thus they died.

Yet in Ottawa the death had still to occur. By the beginnning of 1920 the farmers' group in Parliament was made up of eleven members, and in late February 1920 it dubbed itself the 'National Progressive Party.' The new party proved virtually invincible in by-elections in rural constituencies west of the Ottawa River. Together with the strength of labour, the farm movement threatened the foundations of Canadian political tradition. In fact, however, more was left of that tradition than most imagined.

On 17 February 1919 Sir Wilfrid Laurier died. With his death much of the anger concerning current events passed and there was nostalgia for the simpler times when the hard edges of politics had not cut so deeply. His successor as Liberal leader was William Lyon Mackenzie King, the minister of labour in Laurier's last government. Perhaps the leading labour mediator in North America, King seemed a man of the new age; but those who knew him well saw how much the past was with him (although we now know that King's seances with mediums had not yet begun). When Borden retired in July 1920, his successor was the young westerner Arthur Meighen. Meighen had not been Borden's choice: Borden thought him too rigid and too much a Conservative partisan. It was the backbenchers who supported Meighen; they did so because they wanted a Conservative. Meighen's first action was to bury and dispose of Union government.

Union government left few monuments. Historians today pay more attention to the sudden explosion in influence of the farmers and labour in 1919 because these movements seem to have had more enduring effects. In a sense that is so. The election of 1917 could never be duplicated. As Craig Brown and Ramsay Cook have observed, that election was the greatest victory for British-Canadian nationalism, but it was also its last.[5] Nevertheless, there were many Canadians who could not forget that victory; ironically, they were those who were defeated. After 1917, the Conservative party, which was the heir of Unionism, could not convince francophones and, to a large extent, non-British groups in Canadian society to support their cause. United by what they opposed, these groups landed in the Liberal camp where Mackenzie King was a genial and undemanding host. So too did most of the farmers and many of the workers who found that their own sectional movements were too narrow in a land of very broad tastes. In postwar as in prewar Canada, Canadians wanted a party system where compromise was cherished and consensus a major goal. Although the structure of the postwar party system may have looked the same, the foundations were different and the house had several new rooms. And in many corners, one could easily find the remnants of what the war had done to Canadian political life.

---

5 R.C. Brown and Ramsay Cook, *Canada 1896-1921: A Nation Transformed* (Toronto 1974), chapter 13

8

Canada's Army

The outbreak of war on 4 August 1914 caught Canadians unprepared. The unfolding of the map of Europe, the mobilization of armies, even the first movements of troops seemed immensely distant. In the east and west, army reservists from various countries packed their bags and prepared to entrain for Europe. This was reported as a natural curiosity in the press. 'Expected that two thousand Ruthenians will leave this city for the Seat of War,' the Moose Jaw *Evening Times* headlined on 30 July. On 31 July the Regina *Leader* published a list of Austrian reservists who had responded to the ca of the fatherland to join its armies. It was all rather natural, quite exciting, but still very far away.

The news on 4 August lagged behind the cadence of events in Europe. Great Britain declared war on Germany at 11 PM, British time, too late to catch the relevant papers in Canada. It was from bulletins published outside newspaper offices that Canadians learned that their country was at war, and thousands gathered on the streets outside the local *Globe, Star, Leader, Sun,* or *Times* to learn what had occurred.[1]

By the time the declarations of war were complete, on 23 August, 'the Allies' consisted of the British empire, France, the Russian empire, Serbia, Belgium (a late and very unwilling recruit), and Japan. They faced the 'Central Powers,' Germany and Austria-Hungary, on two broad European fronts, the eastern along the Russian frontier, and the western. The Western Front, in August, was in continuous motion backwards towards Paris, as the German army ground up the opposing French in a vast flanking movement that took it across the plains of Belgium into the heart of France.

The British army, renamed the British Expeditionary Force [BEF], took up position on the left or northern flank of the allied armies. Small by com-

---

1   J.L. McWilliams and R.J. Steel, *The Suicide Battalion* (Edmonton

parison with the conscript armies of the continent, the British army consisted entirely of professional soldiers – volunteers – who made up in quality what they lacked in number. The German army was halted before Paris, early in September 1914, in the battle of the Marne and forced to retreat some distance. Then, in a series of flanking movements, the Allies and the Germans raced for the French ports along the English Channel (a manoeuvre called, appropriately enough, the 'Race to the Sea'). By November the allied line was anchored on the North Sea just in front of the old Belgian cloth town of Ypres (a name which did not come trippingly to Anglo-Saxon tongues; soldiers of the First World War rendered it as 'Wipers'). The battle front wended its way southeastwards in an irregular pattern until it arrived at the Swiss border. The Belgians and the British held the northern end of this line; the French were in the centre and south.

The Germans remained in possession of a large and economically valuable part of France, including an important section of the iron and steel industry. The Allies intended to dislodge the enemy from the area; the Germans vowed to resist. There was little doubt in the mind of commanders on both sides that the Western Front was the crucial one. There the largest armies were encamped or entrenched, and good military doctrine dictated that wars were won by the destruction of the enemy army in the field.

To destroy an army, however, required more than the tiny force that Great Britain had fielded in August 1914. Lord Kitchener, the hero of the South African war, was brought into the British cabinet and placed in charge of the creation of an army for a war which he believed would be long and bloody. Kitchener gave more than his talents to the task; he contributed his face as well, to a poster which informed male civilians of appropriate age that their country wanted 'YOU.' By and large, what the country wanted, it got. Kitchener raised a 'New Army' in volunteer batches of 100,000, totalling 600,000 men. From these volunteers were created five 'new armies' of six divisions each. It was this army that Canada's soldiers would join.[2]

The BEF was the largest army Britain had ever raised and, in the opinion of historians since, it was one of the best. Its morale was high and its equipment good. British staff work usually got the troops trained, clothed, and transported on time. As the war continued – though not always near the beginning – it kept them adequately supplied with arms and ammunition.

---

2   The unmilitary reader will doubtless wish for an explanation of military terminology. The basic fighting unit in the First World War was the battalion, consisting of about 1000 men and commanded by a lieutenant-colonel. Four battalions made up a brigade, commanded by a brigadier-general, and three brigades equalled a division, which was commanded by a major-general. A varying number of divisions were combined in a corps (lieutenant-general), and several corps made up an army, which was confided, usually, to a full general.

Though there was much criticism at the time and since of the 'staff' – officers with red tabs and conspicuously clean uniforms – there cannot now be much doubt that the staff knew what it was doing and, within limits, did it well, perhaps too well, as military historians have also pointed out.

The Canadian army replicated its elder British cousin. Canadian uniforms were cut on British lines; indeed, British military suppliers found Canada a lucrative market for their wares, when they were able to produce them on time. A British officer, Willoughby Gwatkin, was Canada's able chief of the general staff in Ottawa. Admittedly, there were some differences. Canadian infantry were equipped not with the British standard issue Lee-Enfield rifle but with the Canadian-made and Scottish designed Ross rifle. Unfortunately for the infantry, and for Canada, the Ross was a particular favourite of the minister of militia and defence, Sir Sam Hughes.

Hughes was a Conservative warhorse from central Ontario, but unlike the majority of warhorses, who are content to graze in the lush fields of political patronage, he was also a man with a mission. Few Canadians conformed so completely to the satiric image of the militarist. In pursuit of military glory, Hughes joined the militia, consigned himself to South Africa, trumpeted his own merits, and was amply rewarded for his faith in himself when Borden made him minister of militia and defence in 1911. Hughes, active and vigorous, and with a decisive impression of his own superior military wisdom, was a soldier in motion. In 1913 he carried off thirty members of the staff, with hangers-on, on an inspection of several European military establishments. Impressed by an ingenious Swiss entrenching tool, a shovel with a four-inch handle and a hole in the centre of the shovel to permit its lucky owner to sight his rifle through it, Hughes had his secretary patent the thing, ordered 25,000 of them, and issued them to the troops. Only then was it discovered that the 'MacAdam shovel,' as it was called, could neither dig properly nor offer protection from bullets. Hughes's preference for ingenuity over intelligence could not have been more markedly displayed.

The minister could also be stubborn. The Ross rifle was, he knew, a remarkable hunting weapon, a marksman's delight. He had tried it himself. What better weapon to equip Canada's soldiers, the collateral descendants of Hawkeye and Chingachgook and Cuthbert Grant? But the Ross had problems. It worked well under ideal conditions, on a firing range or in a hunt. However, if fired too quickly, it jammed, and was unsuited to dirt. In the dirty trench warfare the Ross was often good only as a club.[3]

3   On this and other military details see John Swettenham, *To Seize the Victory: The Canadian Corps in World War I* (Toronto 1965); on the British army and trench warfare see John Keegan, *The Face of Battle* (London 1976).

Still, Canada's army was not totally unprepared. A mobilization plan existed for the dispatch of a division-sized expeditionary force to fight in a civilized country, presumably Europe. When Hughes took over, this plan was
the first task he confronted. Characteristically, he cancelled it. Instead of
relying on existing militia units and established command structures,
Hughes made up his own. He telegraphed to militia colonels across Canada
a list of qualifications that volunteers for Canada's expeditionary force must
have. Confusion followed. Canada's soldiers would be formed into numbered
battalions, discarding their traditional regimental labels. They would assemble at a new camp at Valcartier, outside Quebec City, to prepare for embar-
kation. Fortunately, Hughes's frenetic energy made up for some of the
disorder that ensued as he personally supervised the construction of the new
camp and dispensed commands and commissions to the troops who inhabit-
ed it. Soon rumours flew, most of them probably unfounded but all too plau-
sible, as with the story of the railway waiter who served the minister so
adeptly that he was rewarded with a commission in lieu of tip.

Hughes wanted 25,000 volunteers; he got 34,500. Of these, 65 per cent
were born in the United Kingdom and only 30 per cent in Canada. Seventeen battalions were formed, instead of the twelve that made up a full division. No fewer than eight battalions hailed from western Canada, six from
Ontario, and two from English Quebec. The remaining battalion was formed
of French Canadians and Maritimers. This 'first contingent' sailed from
Quebec City on 1 October and arrived in England on 14 October, after an
uneventful voyage.

Further training followed, on Salisbury Plain near Stonehenge. Formed
into the 1st Canadian Division, Canada's expeditionary force entered the
British line in France for the first time in February 1915. Their commanding
general, E.A.H. Alderson, was British; so were most of their staff officers,
since no Canadian had the kind of experience that would justify assuming
either the command of a division or detailed staff work. When Canadian
generals were appointed eventually, it was widely rumoured among the
troops that the real commander of a Canadian division was not the general
but the staff officer standing at his side.

The year 1915 would prove a disappointment to the allied cause. On the
Western Front the Germans stood on the defensive, concentrating their forces to defeat the Russians in the east. Both British and French commanders
believed that a breakthrough was possible on the Western Front and decided
to attack. In practice, this meant that the infantry, supported by artillery,
were to storm the German positions. Once the Hun was put to flight, the
cavalry would charge through into open country, and the German line would
be rolled up.

Even in 1915 this was a difficult proposition. Once the Race to the Sea was over, both armies looked to their own protection. Trenches were dug in the earth, shelters constructed, and gradually a line of earthworks snaked 500 miles from the North Sea down to Switzerland. Trenches, at first shallow, were constructed to allow regular movement sheltered from enemy rifle fire; to get in and out of trenches required regular scaling ladders. An attacker, having decided to go 'over the top,' would form his men in long lines facing the enemy positions. Wave after wave was launched at the opposing trenches which, it was hoped, the artillery would have pulverized into sand or, in the waterlogged areas of northern France and Flanders, into mud.

The trouble with this tactic was twofold. Often the artillery did not do its job, simply because its guns and shells were not powerful enough to have the desired effect. That being so, a second fatal factor entered the equation. The German army was plentifully equipped with machine guns. If the British artillery was imperfect, the machine gun was not. Its effect was to tear apart anything that strayed into its line of fire. The lines of British soldiers surging over their trench tops were, therefore, made to order for the conscientious machine gunner, and the result, in terms of casualties, could be horrendous.

There were, of course, variations in battles. Some, such as the battle of the St Eloi Craters in April 1916, seem to have involved incompetence on the part of senior Canadian commanders. Others reflected the stubbornness of the British High Command in believing that a breakthrough could be effected against what were, in fact, insuperable odds. The troops, despite deficiencies in training, could be relied on to fight bravely, generally against very heavy opposition.

This proposition was demonstrated within months of the Canadians' arrival on the Western Front. In April 1915 the 1st Canadian Division was stationed at the north end of the allied line near Ypres. The Germans attacked, using poison gas to demoralize and destroy their opponents. Despite confusion and the flight of neighbouring formations, the Canadians stood their ground and the German attack was repulsed.

The number of Canadians in Europe was steadily growing. In May 1915 a 2nd Division was constituted (it entered the line in September) and in December, a 3rd. A Canadian Corps was now established, with Alderson in command, and two Canadian officers, Arthur Currie and Richard Turner, took over the divisional commands. The Canadian military establishment in England, which supported the troops across the Channel, was growing too. It received the brunt of Hughes's attention during 1915 and 1916, and consequently became the focus of anxious contemplation by Borden and his resident minister in England, Sir George Perley.

There was also a change of command in the British army in 1915. After the failure of the allied offensives, Sir John French, the commander of the BEF, was replaced by Sir Douglas Haig in December 1915. Haig was soon hard at work on the plans for the next year. There would be another attack on the German lines along the river Somme, in co-ordination with the French. Before these plans had a chance to mature, the Germans launched an attack of their own on the French fortress of Verdun. Its object was only partly the capture of Verdun; it was also to force the French to bleed their army to death defending it. The French obliged. To relieve the pressure they begged the British to launch their Somme offensive sooner rather than later, on 1 July 1916. No Canadian troops took part in the battle that day, although the Newfoundland Regiment was involved. It was wiped out near the hamlet of Beaumont Hamel, but its fate was not unique. Some 60,000 British troops were killed, wounded, or reported missing on that single day, the worst toll of casualties in British history.

The Canadian Corps entered the latter stages of the Somme battle, in which the newly established 4th Division was engaged for the first time. Casualties were heavy and gains small. The best that can be said is that the Canadian Corps gained in self-confidence and learned valuable lessons in the preparation of attacks against well-defended positions. The corps had not, however, achieved the desired breakthrough, and as fighting slowed for the winter the Allies were no farther ahead than they had been in the spring.

For the Germans the record for 1916 was mixed. The war in the east continued to go well. Russian attacks were beaten back and Romania, which had joined the Allies in August 1916, was defeated and overrun. The situation elsewhere in the Balkans was not unfavourable, and Germany's allies, Turkey (which entered the war in November 1914) and Bulgaria (which joined in October 1915), kept the Allies busy in the Middle East. Submarine warfare, mounting in intensity, frightened the Allies and constricted their seaborne supplies, but irritated the neutral United States. For the moment the German government felt constrained to deal gently with the Americans, but that situation might well not last forever. The British offensive on the Somme had been repulsed, but the cost to Germany was also high. The British, it was estimated, suffered 419,654 losses in that battle, and the French 204,253, for a combined total of 623,907 (24,029 casualties were Canadian). But the Germans, according to a later British estimate, had lost between 660,000 and 680,000 men.

The name for this phenomenon was attrition, soaking off casualties in the hope of so weakening the enemy's force that the army would eventually disintegrate or suffer defeat in the field. It was not without effect. The British army would never be quite the same again after the Somme; but then neither would the German. The question was, which would last the longer?

The termination of the Somme battle coincided with a political change in Great Britain. In December 1916, in a complicated series of manoeuvres, Prime Minister Asquith was toppled and David Lloyd George replaced him. One of his first actions was to summon the leaders of the British dominions to his councils, a summons that was not unconnected to the diminishing reserves of British money and manpower after the Somme.

Lloyd George's summons came as a pleasant surprise to the Canadian government. From their point of view, the years 1915 and 1916 were spent sending successive drafts of Canadian troops – all volunteers – overseas to expand and support the Canadian Expeditionary Force. Seventy-one infantry battalions were authorized between November 1914 and September 1915, and again the response was enthusiastic. Thirty-four of the seventy-one sent their full quota and more besides. Once again the largest single grouping came from the west, closely followed by Ontario. English Quebec raised six battalions and French Quebec, four. There was a tendency for recruits to come mainly from urban areas. Interestingly, as two historians have recently shown, the cost of the recruiting campaigns was by no means small and frequently beyond the capacity of local militia organizations.[4] Some noticed that the rhetoric that accompanied recruiting drives was becoming more fervent – and strident.

The war became a great crusade – an experience that transcended the ·dreary round of selfish politics which had, some believed, characterized prewar Canada. Addressing a group of American lawyers, Borden explained that Canadians had 'learned that self sacrifice in a just cause is at once a duty and a blessing, and this lesson has both inspired and ennobled the men and women of Canada.' It was appropriate for Borden to announce triumphantly on New Year's Day, 1916, that the authorized level of the CEF had been raised to 500,000 men – a tremendous figure, and an inspiring one.

But where were the men going to come from? Recruiting in 1915 had kept pace with demand, and levels remained high in the first six months of 1916. From July 1916 until October 1917, however, only 2810 men were sent overseas to serve in the infantry. The total number of battalions authorized was impressive, but the numbers they contained were far less so. Worse still, the common fate of a battalion on arriving in England was to be broken up as reinforcements to existing units. The 46th Battalion (South Saskatchewan) was typical. Training in England, and hoping to join the 4th Division, it became a distant casualty of the battle of Mount Sorrel in June 1916. No fewer than 800 men were removed from the 46th Battalion, some to join the

4 R.C. Brown and D. Loveridge, 'Unrequited Faith: Recruiting the CEF, 1914-1918,' *Revue internationale d'histoire militaire* 51 (1982): 53-79

58th Ontario Battalion, some the 13th Royal Highlanders, and others the 16th Canadian Scottish. Replacements arrived from Edmonton, Woodstock, Prince Albert, and Saskatoon.[5] Any sense of locality still existing crumbled under these heavy administrative blows. Moreover, what was needed was privates and non-commissioned officers. Officers, often prominent men in their communities, were left behind, eventually to creep back to Canada without ever seeing the shores of France. (For some, a kind of Cook's tour of the front was arranged so they could say that they had been 'over there.')

It was this situation that Borden attempted to master in the spring of 1917 through the one remaining method – conscription. The British government had already been forced to this expedient, despite a long tradition of voluntary military enlistment, and the American government adopted it right from the start, when the United States declared war on Germany in April 1917. The American adoption of conscription removed more than one powerful argument against Canadian conscription; in addition to the good example, it ensured that draft dodgers would not slip over the border to a neutral or voluntary neighbour.

What could reasonably have been expected from the conscription policy? A glance at the 1911 census indicated that there had been 1,888,825 men of military age in Canada. The strength of the army was 300,000, as of early 1917. A national registration scheme turned up the information that 475,363 men could be regarded as likely military prospects. Obviously, these men were not volunteering; moreover, potential soldiers were not equally distributed across the country.

The reasons for the reluctance of roughly half a million men to serve in the armed forces were complex. Some opposed war out of conviction. Some had well-paying jobs for the first time in their lives or at least for the first time in years. The economic depression which had struck in 1913 was at an end, drying up the pool of unemployed. Many of the British-born, who felt a stronger attachment to the empire and its cause, had already gone. Regionally, 15.52 per cent of the relevant age group (fifteen to forty-four in the 1911 census) had joined up in western Canada; 14.42 per cent in Ontario; 4.69 per cent in Quebec; and 9.96 per cent in the Maritimes. Many of the Quebeckers who went spoke English and, although there was some French-Canadian recruitment, it obviously did not match Quebec's proportion of the population. Plainly, many English Canadians expected the burden of conscription to fall on Quebec, and hoped that compulsion would finally force French-speaking Quebeckers to 'do their duty.'

5   McWilliams and Steel, *Suicide Battalion,* 26

Their hopes were to be disappointed. In the most eligible category, single males aged twenty to thirty-two, there were 401,882 men willing to register their vital statistics. There were also, of course, thousands or tens of thousands who would not. Across Canada, 93.7 per cent of those eligible immediately applied for an exemption. The rate of exemption applications was higher in Quebec (98 per cent), but not by much. Eventually, the Military Service Act produced 105,016 men available for service, of whom 96,379 served in the CEF. The recruiters concentrated on men in urban areas; farmers were less severely affected, perhaps because their protests were stronger and better organized. And despite the generous acceptance by appeal tribunals of requests for exemption, some 19,050 Quebeckers were numbered among the draftees sent to join the troops overseas, a number proportionate to the number of Quebec males who fell into the appropriate age bracket. The result was, roughly, equitable, although it could hardly have satisfied those who wished Quebec to make up for three years of low recruitment.

There was much need, as Borden perceived, for the draftees. The year 1917, which had begun so dismally, continued on its downward path as far as the Allies were concerned. The entry of the United States into the war in April was counterbalanced by the collapse of the Russian tsarist government in March and the increasing disruption of that country's army. When, in November, the Bolsheviks, a revolutionary socialist party pledged to remove Russia from the war altogether, took power, the Allies faced the very real prospect of seeing the Eastern Front vanish, with the consequent concentration of the German army in the west. A disastrous French offensive in May 1917 produced high casualties and, worse, a mutiny. The mutiny was brought under control, but the French army needed time to recuperate. The time was bought by a renewed British offensive in Flanders.

The Canadian army faced two enemies in 1917; the German army and the mud of Flanders. The German army came first, in April 1917, when the Canadian Corps under General Sir Julian Byng swept across the German trenches on Vimy Ridge overlooking the Flanders plain. The Canadians had learned a great deal about attacking in the previous couple of years, with the result that their artillery fire was more intense and effective than previously. Vimy Ridge had defied allied attempts to capture it, and when it fell it yielded 4000 prisoners, fifty-four guns, and quantities of trench mortars and machine guns. The Canadian Corps suffered 3598 killed.

In October came the mud. The British army had been battering at the German lines east of Ypres since July, slowly moving towards the Belgian village of Passchendaele in the hope of capturing Belgium's Channel ports. British attacks were blunted by bad weather which, beginning in August, saturated low-lying land that was daily being churned into soup by artillery fire. In four weeks in August the British suffered 68,000 casualties and, even though the Germans were suffering too, the effect on the army's morale and organization was disheartening. Despite advice from his commanders in the field, Field-Marshal Haig (as he now was) persisted in order to keep the pressure off the French. By October, any hope for a distant or significant objective had been lost; it would be enough to occupy Passchendaele, or what was left of it.

To perform this task Haig called on the Canadian Corps, now under General Arthur Currie, its first Canadian commander. Between 26 October and 10 November the Corps conquered about two square miles, including Passchendaele, terrain which Lieutenant E.L.M. Burns of the Canadian artillery described as 'primeval bog.' Boardwalks crossed the mud, and to leave them was to invite death by drowning. 'As far as the eye could see,' Burns wrote, 'through rain or generally misty autumn air, there were shell craters, great and small, in patterns which so many have compared to the moonscape. But these craters were full to the brim with water.'[6] For the privilege of occupying this swamp, the Canadian Corps expended 8134 killed, wounded, and missing.

The new year, 1918, brought two developments. The Germans concluded peace with the new Bolshevik government in March, and succeeded in moving large numbers of troops from east to west. The Americans, meanwhile, were sending their army overseas as fast as it could be raised; unlike the Germans, however, they were untrained and inexperienced, and their equipment lagged even further behind: using French guns, British tanks and even uniforms, they could be introduced to trench warfare only gradually. Towards the end of 1918 the weight of American numbers would begin to tell; the trick for the Allies was to last that long.

The Germans were determined that they should not. On 21 March 1918 the German army opened an offensive along a fifty-mile front facing the British army. They broke through, and only with extreme difficulty did the British succeed in reforming a line. In a few days all the territory so painfully won in 1916 and 1917 was lost; Haig scrambled to find as many troops as he could to plug the gap. Among the formations that caught his eye was the Canadian Corps. It was strong, relative to other British corps, and its men had a formidable fighting reputation. Haig did not want the corps as a whole; rather, he wanted it division by division, as required, since divisions were quicker and easier to move than a whole cumbersome corps. To Haig's fury, Currie balked, and secured political backing from the Canadian minister resident in London. Had the situation been only slightly more urgent,

6   E.L.M. Burns, *General Mud* (Toronto 1970), 57

Currie would not have been justified in objecting, but in terms of the fighting effectiveness of his troops the Canadian general had a point. His corps was unusually homogeneous. It had been raised as a Canadian army and it had always fought as such, together, rather than piecemeal. It even differed in its organization from other British formations, for while a British division had been reduced from twelve battalions to nine, the Canadians remained at the original number.

The first German offensive petered out, but Germany was not through yet. The pressure point was shifted north, to Flanders, and then south, towards Paris. Finally, exhausted, the Germans ground to a halt along the Marne, where they had been four years before. The Allies, who had been frightened into a formal unity of command by the gravity of the German threat, now prepared to reply, and in their response the Canadian Corps had a part.

On 8 August, outside the French city of Amiens, Canadian, Australian, and French troops attacked the German positions. Once again, Currie had carefully studied the terrain and prepared his men for the exact circumstances they would be facing. On this occasion he had two additional, and indispensable, advantages. The ground was covered in thick fog, so that the Germans literally could not see their attackers, and those attackers were supported by a heavy concentration of tanks, which could roll over the German barbed wire. This they did, and as the infantry cleared the Germans from their positions, they looked back to see something almost unknown since 1914: cavalry were passing through their lines to pursue the enemy. At the end of the day green trees and grass were visible, a far cry from the mud and slime of the previous year. Although results on succeeding days were disappointing, the initiative had passed decisively to the Allies. By early September the Germans were back where they had been in March, and the Allies began to assemble troops for an attack on the principal German fortifications, the Hindenburg Line.

Behind the line, German morale was beginning to crack. The German High Command panicked, and demanded that their government arrange an end to hostilities. At the end of September Bulgaria collapsed, and in October, Turkey. Austria-Hungary was now threatened with invasion from the south. Instead, that ancient monarchy dissolved into civil chaos and broke into its constituent parts. The German army, still resisting, was being driven from one position to another. The Belgian ports were lost, the Hindenburg Line crossed, and in early November the Canadian Corps found itself on the road to Mons, site of a battle between the Germans and the British in 1914.

As the corps moved into the outskirts of that Belgian city, frantic negotiations were taking place between the German government and the allied supreme commander, Marshal Foch. Just as Mons fell, an armistice was signed, stipulating that at 11 AM on 11 November fighting would stop.

Allied terms were severe. In return for a cease-fire, or armistice (not to be confused with a peace treaty), the German army would return to Germany. It was to keep going until it was east of the Rhine. There the Allies would follow it, occupying three bridgeheads over the river, ready to resume the attack if necessary. Alsace-Lorraine, which Germany had annexed from the French in 1871, returned immediately to its former owner. The German navy was interned by the British pending a peace treaty. The allied naval blockade of Germany would continue, despite protests to Foch from the German plenipotentiaries.

Two Canadian divisions, the 1st and 2nd, joined the occupation of Germany, and on 13 December paraded over the Rhine, with bands playing. Then they settled down for Christmas, and to prepare for the long trip home.

The story of that return is not an entirely happy one. Transport governed the rate of repatriation, and there were not enough suitable ships (British officials sniffed that Canadian standards were too high) and, on the other side, not enough trains to take the troops home from Canada's two ice-free Atlantic ports, Halifax and Saint John. There was confusion over who should be sent home first; it took some time to sort out priorities, and even then they were not uniform across the whole of the Canadian army overseas. Soldiers putting in time at transit camps in England rioted, something which damaged Canada's reputation in the British press but which proved effective in accelerating their departure across the Atlantic.

What the soldiers had experienced while abroad changed them and changed Canada. They had entered a world very far from the one they had grown up in. Boys from temperance households learned how to smoke and drink; some learned how to make use of the services of camp followers or of the delights that European city life had to offer. But back at home Canada had been sacrificing demon rum in the cause of efficiency and virtue; somewhere, somehow, the old and the new streams of Canadian life would meet and clash.

These changes, though profound, did not pose an acute, immediate problem to society. Other changes, which could be expressed in statistics, did: 56,634 Canadian troops were killed in the First World War; 6347 officers and 143,385 other ranks were wounded. As a result, the government was dispensing, by 1921, 188,263 pensions for disabilities incurred in war service, or to soldiers' dependants. The dominion found itself running thirty-one military hospitals, which were jammed with 6264 invalids, of whom 889 were mental patients. This number declined over time, as was to be expected, but in 1927 the number of permanent inhabitants of the eight remaining veterans' hospitals was 2805. As well, the Department of Soldiers' Civil Reestablishment created and operated workshops providing 'sheltered employment' for those incapable of working at regular jobs.

That was not all. The government viewed the return of the Canadian corps with an understandable mixture of relief and apprehension. If the corps returned too soon, or under unfavourable conditions, the veterans might become a menace to public order. A belated attempt, utilizing questionnaires, was made to match soldiers with jobs at home. When unemployment nevertheless resulted, the government gave emergency unemployment relief in 1919-20. Loans were provided to those who wished to secure suitable training for new jobs – to a maximum of $500 per individual, and secured, if possible, by chattel mortgages. A War Service Gratuity, based on length of service, was also paid, to furnish the veterans with some ready cash. It too became the subject of controversy between veterans and politicians, as the government struggled to strike a balance between the claims of gratitude and financial rectitude. Rectitude won.

Finally, since Canada still thought of itself as an agricultural country, assistance was offered to those who wished to settle on the land. Almost 20,000 settlement loans had been granted by 1921, and more were to follow. If a veteran wished for a more sedentary life, he received a veteran's preference for government employment. For security, the government also offered life insurance at lower than commercial rates. But there assistance stopped.[7]

The public controversy over war service gratuities established a lasting impression that Canada had not treated its veterans with abounding generosity or even, in some cases, common sense. A generation of veterans, and of politicians (increasingly veterans themselves), pondered the lessons to be derived from the experience. Should Canada ever face a similar situation in the future, it would not make the same mistakes again.

The lessons of war, or rather the perceived lessons of this war, were long lasting. The Canadian Corps had a proud fighting record. Its major fiascos were few, its victories many. Its separateness from the British army was a matter of pride. For many veterans, the lesson learned from the war was nationalism and pride in Canada, her distinctive identity and capacity. But these feelings were not universally shared. Many veterans, if not most, continued to identify with the empire. War crises in the years ahead regularly called forth a flood of patriotic rhetoric and even offers of service from veterans' organizations across the country. Although there is no reliable way of quantifying how veterans thought of the world on their return to Canada, it

7 On repatriation, see D. Morton, *A Peculiar Kind of Politics: Canada's Overseas Ministry in the First World War* (Toronto 1982), chapters 9 and 10.

is reasonably certain that they were not inclined to turn their backs on it.

Certainly, the confidence of some returned soldiers in the way they had been handled while in service was greatly shaken. There was a natural animosity during the war towards staff officers behind the line, and occasionally the feeling was justified. There was also a sentiment that the generals who threw hundreds of thousands of troops onto German machine guns were themselves too unconcerned or too cowardly to visit the front to discover what they were really doing. This feeling, though undoubtedly authentic, was also exaggerated in retrospect. The problem with the generals, as E.L.M. Burns has pointed out, was not that they were too timid but that they were too brave. With distinguished war records in past – and very different – wars, they tended to discount the feelings of those less brave than themselves, and sometimes imagined that bravery had some magic quality which would permit it to conquer all – even machine guns.

Jitters over generals were sometimes transferred to the institution of empire itself. *British* generals were bad; *Canadian* generals, with the exception of Sam Hughes, were good. Such a criticism was too broad to stand close examination. Some British generals were very capable; some Canadian generals were not. Some Canadian divisions were well run because of the staff work done by unsung British officers working at divisional headquarters; and some of these staff officers were later to become major military figures in their own right.

Nevertheless, some of the criticism stuck. War was not a glorious adventure, as pre-1914 romanticism taught. For some it might be an ennobling experience, but Canada as a whole was certainly no more pure on Armistice Day, 1918, than it had been in 1914. No Canadian government could approach the possibility of war without greater trepidation than Borden had shown in 1914. But the demands made of Borden were to be made again; they would receive the same answer.

9

The War at Home

War never leaves a nation as it found it. The two world wars of this century have refashioned the globe, shattered old visions, given birth to new universalist dreams, ended abruptly tens of millions of lives, and ensured that many others would not live as their forefathers did. The most brutal and lasting effects of the First World War were felt in central and eastern Europe where probably eleven million died and where the patterns of centuries were permanently broken. Even where fewer died, the mark was deep. In Britain, where civilian casualties were almost unknown, daily life changed greatly. The American scholar of that war, Paul Fussell, still finds that the 'whole texture' of British life 'could be said to commemorate the war.' The wristwatch, pub closing hours, cigarette smoking, and that English staple, fish and chips, are all reminders of the war. So is the language and the way it is used: the directness, the obscenity, and the battlefield images that mark modern English were shaped by the British war experience. The origins of what Britons have become can be recognized in scenes from the war of 1914-18.[1]

Other nations were also deeply affected, although the kind and the degree of the impact varied greatly. This was true within nations as well. In Canada, for example, some parts of the country were only slightly touched by the war. In postwar censuses, some constituencies in rural Quebec showed only a handful of war veterans in a population of tens of thousands. In those areas, there was mainly a memory of resisting the war's impact. This was not true elsewhere in Canada. Visitors to Canada's older universities, such as McGill and the University of Toronto, will view long lists of those who served and on those lists many asterisks indicating the many young men who never returned. Recently, Grace Morris Craig has reminded

---

1   See Paul Fussell, *The Great War and Modern Memory* (New York 1975).

us in her ninetieth year how much the war meant to people of her background and generation in Canada. The First World War was, in retrospect, the most important event in her life. Her book makes the argument convincingly.[2]

From the lovely summer morning in early August when her brother Basil hurried up the steps announcing that war was declared until the death of her fiancé in the early 1920s from a heart defect he had contracted in the trenches in 1916, the war enveloped the young Grace Morris's life. On the verandah that August morning were Alf Bastedo, Grace's suitor, and her brother Ramsey. Alf's name stood at the top of the casualty list which appeared in Canadian papers after the Battle of Ypres in April 1915. Basil's plane was shot down in March 1917. Ramsey fought at Vimy Ridge, after which a relative spirited him off to Scotland to save the Morris's last son from his likely fate if he were to stay in France. Eventually Grace married another soldier who went off in 1939 to fight in another war. Surely Mrs Craig must have wondered when younger Canadians in the 1960s called their land the peaceable kingdom. It had not been so for her.

Grace Morris Craig and her brothers came from a prosperous English-Canadian family. When war came, her brothers rushed forward to enlist. Grace worked in soldiers' canteens at nearby Camp Petawawa, dishing out apple pie and ice cream. In Pembroke, she sewed scarves and gloves, acted as hostess to the young soldiers who stayed with her parents, and organized concerts for the soldiers at which she sang 'Keep the Home Fires Burning' and 'It's a Long Way to Tipperary.' Other women took up the jobs men had left, in the banks as clerks, in the factories a labourers, in the fields as farmers. To Nellie McClung, this was the heroic front army. The opportunity for heroism was rare and glorious. 'It took a war to show how heroic our people are,' McClung boasted. In the realm of heroes, women took high ranks.

The enthusiasm for war reflected in the attitude of the Craigs and McClung derived in part from what they believed the war would do to society. As we have seen earlier, the strongest support for the war and for the government which prosecuted it so energetically came from urban and middle-class English Canada. The emotional link with Britain was obviously responsible for the attitude of this group, but only in part. Perhaps equally important in explaining their sometimes frenzied support for the war was the belief that the war would be the midwife to a new kind of society. Those like McClung who had called most loudly for changes in prewar Canada raised their voices even louder as they saw the opportunity for prohibition, political purity, women's suffrage, and many other causes come nearer with the war.

2   Grace Morris Craig, *But This is Our War* (Toronto 1981)

Rhetoric billowed. The war would end all wars; justice would reign; truth would triumph; and wrongs would be avenged. The limits on what humans could do seemed to roll away.

These sensations were deeply felt in much of English Canada, but not everywhere. Canadian historians have, in recent years, emphasized how rural areas did not share the sentiment of the cities. What has not been noted, however, is that this pattern obtained not only in Canada but throughout the world. Recent European studies have shown how urban Europe, in contrast to rural Europe, reacted to war with an orgy of patriotism in 1914. In this interpretation, war enthusiasm was a release for psychological adjustments required by the shift from the country to the city.[3] In the country, traditions were cherished. In the early twentieth-century city, in Canada as elsewhere, the new technology and the unprecedented crowding of urban life created a profound sense of disorder and need for change. War brought the justification for order that so many craved while simultaneously promising dramatic change. It is small wonder that cheering crowds thronged city squares in August 1914.

For the farmer, it seems to have been different. Robert Stead, a Canadian writer who shared the urban enthusiasm during wartime, described rural feelings well in his postwar novel *Grain*. His hero, Gander Stake, would not serve: 'For Gander the furrow was that unending routine which encircled his father's farm. It was a routine from which he had no desire to be disturbed. Several times the war threatened to shoulder him out of his furrow and he made the war his enemy on that account.'[4] By the end of the war, many other farmers had joined Gander in making the war their enemy. So had many French Canadians and other Canadians of non-British stock. These Canadians had cheered little, if at all, in 1914; by 1918, many of them were openly booing. In 1914, the reformers were those who did the cheering; by war's end, the hitherto silent were those who called for changes.

The Protestant churches which had promoted 'moral reform' most vociferously were in the vanguard of war enthusiasm. In a sense, this was surprising because those same churches had often espoused pacifist beliefs in the pre-1914 period. The influence of peace activists such as Norman Angell was often evident in the writings of Canadian Protestant ministers. Yet all but a few abandoned pacifism in August 1914. When they did so, their earlier beliefs made them more eager to make the war into a moral crusade. The Germans became Huns, murderers of women and children, brutal beyond civilized imagination. The Reverend C.W. Gordon (Ralph Connor) responded typically and poetically to the outbreak of war:

3 See William McNeill, *The Pursuit of Power* (Chicago 1982), 307.
4 Robert Stead, *Grain* (Toronto 1963), 141. Originally published in 1926.

O Canada, What answer make to calling voice and beating drum,
To sword gleam and to pleading prayer of God
For right? What answer makes my soul?
'Mother, to thee! God, to thy help! Quick! My sword.'

The sword was drawn not only against the Germans but also against those foes at home who threatened the war effort. Liquor was an easy target. The prohibition movement had laid the grounds for the debate in prewar days. The war gave new and enormous force to the prohibitionist's arguments. Just as the Kaiser's armies must be defeated because they destroyed innocents, so must liquor also be vanquished. Using the language of war, Winnipeg reformer the Rev. J.E. Hughson urged Manitobans to 'use ballots for bullets and shoot straight and strong in order that the demon of drink might be driven from the haunts of men.'[5] Each battle death strengthened the prohibitionist cause. Those at home must sacrifice as those at the front were so obviously doing. The manufacture of liquor used up resources that could be used for war purposes. Liquor robbed young men of the vitality that might be necessary to preserve their lives on the battlefield. Arguments such as these became increasingly difficult to answer.

In July 1915 Alberta voted strongly for prohibition; seven months later Manitoba followed. The prohibitionist tide swept over every province except Quebec. In the fall of 1917 the Union government made prohibition on a national basis a major campaign plank. Protestant clergymen rallied to the Unionist cause more enthusiastically because of this commitment to reform. True to its word, the Union government brought in federal prohibition effective April Fool's Day, 1918. Except for supposed medicinal and sacramental needs, Canada was officially dry.

Prohibition was effective. As James Gray has argued, prohibition did bring a remarkable drop in criminal activity, and it probably aided Canadian society in adjusting to the social strains of the war years. Crime rates dropped from 2299 per 100,000 in 1913 and 2369 per 100,000 in 1914 to 1431 per 100,000 in 1918. In Calgary, arrests for drunkenness dropped from 1743 in 1914 to 183 in 1917, with the result that the police patrol of city streets was reduced from sixty-three to only twenty-eight constables. Jails were closed down, and industrial observers noted the end of the Monday morning absenteeism that had marked prewar days. These results were what prohibitionists had promised: in the lives of tens of thousands of Canadians, prohibition brought a social revolution.

5   Quoted in John Thompson, *The Harvest of War: The Prairie West, 1914-1918* (Toronto 1978), 98

By 1919, however, prohibition's hold was weakening as the postwar state proved unable and unwilling to maintain the supports for it. The order-in-council establishing prohibition was based upon wartime emergency powers. When those powers lapsed in November 1919, they were replaced by a new Canada Temperance Act, which was weaker than the order-in-council. There were new loopholes which shrewd Canadians with a taste for alcohol or dollars effectively exploited. Moreover, sentiment in favour of prohibition weakened. In October 1920 British Columbians voted in favour of allowing liquor sold through a government monopoly. In that same month, the three prairie provinces voted 'dry,' but the dry majority was considerably lower than it had been in the wartime plebiscites. Gradually other provinces, including Ontario which had supported prohibition in 1919, adopted the British Columbia precedent. Liquor came back to Canada, only this time the governments clasped much more of liquor's profits to their capacious bosoms. In all, it was a very Canadian solution.

In their arguments for prohibition, both male and female prohibitionists saw women's suffrage as a key to the successful imposition of prohibition. Like prohibition, women's suffrage acquired new and potent arguments with the coming of war. In a war being fought for liberty and democracy, the exclusion of over half the population from the ballot box became more difficult to justify. Suffragettes argued that in wartime, women were taking on tasks previously carried out by men. Moreover, they were making sacrifices which the state should honour just as it honoured the heroes in Europe. Some, like Nellie McClung, went farther, claiming that the war was the product of male rule: 'The hand that rocks the cradle does not rule the world. If it did, human life would be held dearer and the world would be a sweeter, cleaner, safer place than it is now.'[6] Excited by such a prospect, many Canadians took up the cause of female suffrage.

The war had brought together women in organizations outside the home. Knitting groups, social welfare organizations, patriotic organizations, and prohibitionist lobbies represented a way in which women could 'serve' as men did; they also provided a basis for organization. Many of these apolitical organizations were excellent training for future political action. The Woman's Christian Temperance Association supported suffrage more enthusiastically than ever, linking it with the need to ban alcohol. Other voluntary associations such as associations of farm women in the west also spoke out more loudly in defence of women's rights. The most vocal suffragists were

6   Nellie McClung, *In Times Like These* (Toronto 1972), 22. Originally published in 1915.

middle class and British in background – the same group which was most deeply committed to the war.

In January 1916, Manitoba, where Nellie McClung and her followers had led the suffragists' campaign, became the first Canadian province to give women the vote. Women had proven to be a powerful political force in defeating the Roblin government in Manitoba, and the new Liberal premier, T.C. Norris, was quick to reward them. No one in the Manitoba legislature opposed his action. Alberta, Saskatchewan, and British Columbia followed in early 1916. In 1917, Premier Hearst of Ontario was the first Conservative premier to grant women the right to vote. Nova Scotia, New Brunswick, and Prince Edward Island followed in 1918, 1919, and 1922, respectively. Quebec women, however, had to wait until 1940. Even then there were important voices in the province, such as Cardinal Villeneuve, who opposed female suffrage because 'it exposes women to all the passions and intrigues of electoralism.' So it did.

The grant of a limited federal franchise to women in 1917 was very much caught up in the 'passions and intrigues' of wartime electioneering. In order to strengthen what Arthur Meighen termed the 'patriotic vote,' the Borden government granted the vote to those who they thought would vote for a government which supported conscription. In August 1917 the Military Voters Act enfranchised female members of the armed forces, and in September 1917 the War-time Elections Act enfranchised all female relatives (wives, mothers, daughters, and sisters) of Canadian servicemen. Even some of the leaders of the suffrage movement were outraged by the blatant political use of the women's vote. Borden promised that this was only a temporary expedient and that all women would vote in future federal elections. He kept his promise in 1918.

The war was of fundamental importance in the changes in the political role of women. Women's suffrage would have come to Canada, as it eventually did to all Western democratic societies, but war made denial of suffrage much more difficult for Canadian political leaders in all provinces except Quebec. The changes in the political status of Canadian women reflected in part changes in their cultural and economic roles as well. Women took over groups like the Red Cross where men had previously predominated. Working women were much less often domestic servants and much more likely to be clerks. The war accelerated trends that had been observed in prewar Canada, but in many areas of the country the changes must have been dramatic. Between 1911 and 1921 the percentage of working women in clerical positions increased from 9.4 per cent to 18.7 per cent, and the number in professional areas increased from 12.7 per cent to 19.1 per cent. Some scholars have minimized this last figure, which was not reached again until the

1970s.[7] They charge that these professional jobs were 'women's jobs,' and thus the term professional is less meaningful. This argument seems unhistorical. These profesional jobs were mainly in the fields of teaching and nursing, and they did give women a mobility, economic and geographical, which they had lacked in the nineteenth century. Teachers can move. They also must think, and Emerson told us that they can affect eternity. That over 50 per cent of all teachers of Canadian boys and girls were women in 1921 (this proportion had been reached in Ontario by 1870) surely left a mark on those children. To deny the impact of women in the classroom is to overlook the basic insights of modern psychology and, of course, common sense.

Both prohibition and women's suffrage occurred through actions of the state. Similarly, the state had intervened in myriad other areas of Canadian life where it had not acted in prewar times. In 1916 and 1917, supporters of the war effort became strong critics of voluntarism and advocates of compulsion and more extensive state direction of Canadian social and economic life. Conscription of manpower was the central demand, but it was not the only one. In the preface to a 1917 book aptly entitled *The New Era in Canada,* the editor, J.O. Miller, principal of Ontario's elite Ridley College, argued that 'the final triumph of Democracy can only be assured by the willing subordination of the individual to the State, for the common good.' That, Miller claimed, was the 'lesson' Canadians had learned in wartime. Other authors in the book, such as Stephen Leacock and Clifford Sifton, echoed Miller's demand that the state actively shape the 'new era.'

Several of the book's authors testified that they had personally been transformed by the experience of war. The most remarkable testimonial came from Sifton, who was widely considered to be a political manipulator of consummate skill and whose fortune seemed to have dubious origins and uses. Surely, Sifton exclaimed, 'we may hope that a young nation whose sons have sprung to arms at the call of the oppressed, and who have made the supreme sacrifice for human liberty, will not fail to scrutinize closely the principles of its polity and strive to cast out everything that threatens its moral health.' Sifton's vision was of a land without poverty, extremes of wealth, political corruption, and old prejudices. His vision, like most of his contemporaries, was a work of emotion, not reason; its hues were vivid but its details vague. Nevertheless, its impact on the political system was significant.

For decades, political reformers had blamed patronage for corrupting the Canadian political system. A civil service based on merit was a key reform plank throughout the Anglo-American democracies. In 1917 the Union

7 See Ceta Ramkhalawansingh, 'Women during the Great War,' in *Women and Work* (Toronto 1974), 261-303.

War may come and war may go,
but we'll go on for ever – if we can
Racey, 1918. Courtesy *Montreal Daily Star*

government promised that it would introduce this reform, and in 1918 it did so, much to the chagrin of some backbenchers. Some but not all provincial governments followed with more limited reforms. Even the income tax was regarded in some circles as a major reform since its rates rose with income; those who had more, paid more. The Union government, in theory, and provincial governments, in fact, also encouraged the development of co-operative movements. In most cases, however, co-operative movements sprang from local initiatives, whether in Quebec, where the Roman Catholic church was active, or in western Canada, where farmers took independent action. As with prohibition and women's suffrage, wartime brought to sudden maturity movements which already had well established bases. The limits of possibility were quickly expanded.

The expansion of limits came first for the governors and then for the governed. Various individuals, such as Nellie McClung and Charles Gordon, carried their war enthusiasm over into the reform causes. Hence, the first reforms were those long favoured by Anglo-Saxons, Protestants, and the middle class: prohibition and women's suffrage, for example. They had broader support than the middle class (a troublesome term), but their most earnest and identifiable promoters came from that sector. Before mid-1917 the agenda for reform was set by those who possessed political and economic power. In 1918 the agenda was set by those who lacked such power, notably labour and farmers.

The depression of 1913-14 hit the Canadian labour movement very hard. Membership in unions fell as unemployment grew. Although there was some discontent with the war among radical labour, Canadian workers generally accepted the war and looked for some benefits from war contracts. Responding to the patriotic mood, workers became reluctant to strike. In 1913 there had been 113 industrial disputes which had resulted in 1,287,678 lost working days. In 1914 these figures dropped to 44 disputes and 430,054 lost days, and in 1915, to 43 disputes and only 106,149 lost days. This last figure was the lowest since records were first kept in 1901. In 1915 workers began to receive the first benefits from the war as the labour surplus created by the depression gave way to a labour shortage in most parts of Canada. Union membership increased quickly, and so did strikes.

Wartime demand offered unions and workers generally an opportunity to make gains in the workplace which had been denied to them in peacetime. The manner in which the federal government intervened in the economy to direct war production led workers to believe that the government could and should intervene to improve their lot. The Borden government, however, was reluctant to act in response to labour's demands. Although business was unusually good as far as the owners were concerned, working conditions remained largely the same for the workers. The union organizing drives of 1915 and 1916 played upon the workers' fears that they were being ignored and that they were the main victims of wartime profiteering. By this time, there was much evidence which seemed to support these fears. In Canada, unlike Great Britain, labour was not invited to participate in government; indeed, the Borden government was rather cavalier in the fashion in which it treated labour leaders in the early war years. Since most labour leaders had expressed strong support for the war effort, their obvious lack of influence rankled with them and their followers.

Discontent over labour's exclusion from government circles grew as it appeared that the government would do little to protect the gains which labour had made in the early war years. In 1914 and 1915 workers did well as companies competed for their skills at a time when prices remained stable. Real wages rose. After the summer of 1916, prices rose rapidly, and workers suddenly feared that their gains would be eroded. In 1917 the inflation rate was 18 per cent and in 1918, 13.5 per cent. Effects of this inflation varied and, in some cases, wages managed to keep pace with prices. For most Canadian workers, however, it is probably correct to suggest that real wages declined after the summer of 1916. Workers became angry and much more willing to protest. As David Bercuson has written, 'the belief that dark forces were at work to rob consumers through illegal or unfair practices was buttressed by a general feeling that measures could have been taken to end inflation except for government reluctance.'[8]

In 1916 munitions workers seeking higher wages and better working conditions walked out of plants in Toronto and Hamilton. The owners responded by lockouts and the use of strikebreakers. Even though a royal commission supported the workers' case, the companies would not bend and the government did nothing to make them do so. The strike was broken but bitter memories lingered. This bitterness increased when the Imperial Munitions Board refused to insert a fair-wage clause in munitions contracts, even though the Canadian government was willing to support this clause. This refusal was especially galling because the chairman of the Imperial Munitions Board was Sir Joseph Flavelle, a wealthy Toronto businessman whose own businesses had clearly prospered through wartime orders. It seemed that patriotism had brought profits for the businessman but only more suffering for the workers.

Union membership and militancy rose in 1917. There were 148 work stoppages which resulted in 1,134,970 working days lost, a figure over ten times that of 1915. Owners denounced strikers as the Kaiser's friends, but

8   David Bercuson, *Confrontation at Winnipeg* (Montreal and London 1974), 35

by this point many workers agreed with Dr Johnson that patriotism was merely a convenient refuge for a scoundrel. The debate about patriotism crystallized around the issue of conscription. In 1916 the federal government adopted a national registration scheme which labour suspected might be the prelude to conscription. The Trades and Labor Congress grumbled, but went along with the scheme after Borden assured them it was not related to a plan for conscription. Radical labour leaders, especially in western Canada, were unhappy with the acquiescence of the TLC leadership. The radical fears became reality with Borden's May 1917 announcement of conscription. Coming at a moment when inflation's sting was sharp and when revelations of large business profits were appearing daily beside the casualty lists in newspapers, conscription outraged most Canadian labour leaders.

Western leaders called for a general strike. Joe Naylor, the socialist president of the British Columbia Federation of Labour, called his 'fellow slaves' to arms: 'if our masters force us to fight let us fight for our own liberty and cast from our limbs the chains of bondage.'[9] In the east more moderate voices, such as James Watters, called for direct political action by labour and for conscription of wealth. If the poor were required to give their blood, the rich must give up their wealth. The Borden government made a few gestures in this direction through the imposition of special war taxes, including the income tax, but these actions satisfied few. The new Union government also promised to consult more fully with labour for the remainder of the war, and a Conservative trade unionist, Gideon Robertson, was appointed minister without portfolio in the new government. A more important factor in the weakening of labour resistance in eastern Canada was the strong support of the American Federation of Labor for the war effort now that the United States had entered the war. Samuel Gompers of the AFL was Borden's most useful platform speaker among labour groups in the 1917 campaign. In the east, Gompers and the Unionists generally had receptive audiences because, outside of Quebec, many wage-earners were of Anglo-Saxon background and most shared the government's emotional attachment to the war. As a result, the labour candidates in the 1917 general election failed dismally to attract votes. The anger of the more radical western labour leaders erupted into open condemnation of their eastern counterparts.

In the fall of 1917 the Bolshevik Revolution in Russia gave the militants a model for action and, it seemed, for a state that workers controlled. In Canada, calls for Canadian soviets came quickly from western unionists who contrasted the pitiful showing of labour in the 1917 election with what Russian workers had done in a so-called backward country. There was also

9 Quoted in A. Ross McCormack, *Reformers, Rebels, and Revolutionaries: The Western Canadian Radical Movement, 1899-1919* (Toronto 1977), 128

evidence that direct action helped in Canada. Despite strong disapproval of strikes by the government and the press, workers in early 1918 did win higher wages by striking in several areas. The most noticeable gain came in Winnipeg, where a strike by civic employees, followed by sympathetic strikes by many other unionists, resulted in a victory for the workers. Such general strikes appeared to be devices of enormous potency, which would cause authority to tremble. Following this Winnipeg strike and the rapid growth in union membership in 1918, the Union government presented a new war labour policy in July 1918. It promised a great deal: the right of employees to organize in unions without interference; the right to decent wages; equal pay for equal work for women; and the right of workers to negotiate with employers about their work, pay, and safety. The order-in-council enunciating this policy, however, contained no provision for enforcing these promises. Employers were requested to comply with the provisions. Of course, very few did.

While attempting to be conciliatory on some occasions, at other times the government used a stick. A so-called 'anti-loafing law' (actually an order-in-council) was issued and a national manpower registration begun. These moves seemed to many workers the first step towards conscription of labour. Conscription itself was applied unequally. At first farmers had been exempted, but workers had not. In some areas, evaders were vigorously pursued and exemptions denied, while in other places officials were more lenient. The same type of inequalities seemed to apply to the government's policy on food and fuel control. In certain districts the government's attempt to control waste and luxury had a real effect, but in other areas high life went on apparently unimpaired. In this setting, labour's complaints were understood by Sir George Foster, a veteran Conservative politician and member of the Union government. On 6 February 1918 he wrote in his diary: 'Yet how little we sacrifice! Of nine women more or less prominent in the (Canadian) Club here, it transpired during a conversation that only one was observing meatless days. Other Red Cross workers use coal to keep their motorcars warm. I often ask if in Britain and Canada class and labor upheavals could result in murder and [revolution]. Dare one say "impossible"?'[10] By February 1919 many were saying that it was possible.

In the fall of 1918, just as the war was coming to an end, the government banned strikes in war-related industries and proscribed associations and political parties which it regarded as seditious. Although the ban on strikes was lifted after the armistice, the government's harsh policies only served to engender a strong response, especially in the west. At the TLC convention in

10 Public Archives of Canada, Foster Papers, Foster Diary, 6 Feb. 1918

Quebec, western radicalism was defeated by eastern moderation. The election of the moderate Tom Moore as TLC president was the harshest blow, and it led directly to the decision to organize a regional labour convention in Calgary in early 1919. The winter of 1918-19 witnessed unprecedented labour union growth; it also brought new fears for the future on the part of both the authorities and the workers. The return of the soldiers and the end of war orders threatened to bring large-scale unemployment. Prices continued their dramatic rise, and the real wages of workers declined. All the rhetoric of wartime about a richer democracy and a new era came back to haunt those political leaders who had uttered it. They could not deliver on their promises at the very moment when others in Russia, Britain, and even defeated Germany were proclaiming airy visions of equality.

On 16 March 1919 the Western Labour Conference opened at Calgary, and very quickly its radical direction was obvious. Fraternal greetings were extended to workers in the Soviet Union, and the government's attacks on radicalism were roundly condemned. The western unionists committed themselves to secession from the Trades and Labor Congress of Canada and endorsed the policies of the One Big Union. The most significant OBU policy was the general strike. In the spring of 1919 the general strike became, for many western unionists, a magical device which would suddenly right all wrongs and make the state respond to labour's needs. These people saw the possibility of a new heaven in the streets of Russia's Petrograd; others in Ottawa and elsewhere saw the makings of a new hell. In the spring of 1919 these visions clashed during the Winnipeg General Strike, Canada's greatest industrial confrontation.

The strike began with a walkout by Winnipeg's metal and building trades workers who initially demanded no more than union recognition and better wages and working conditions. The setting, however, was crucial: both labour and business were spoiling for a confrontation. The Trades and Labor Council endorsed a general strike in sympathy with the metal workers and, on 15 May, Winnipeg's economy closed down as most of the city's workers left their jobs. Moderates joined radicals on the Strike Committee which, in those first days of the strike, directed most of civic life. Ten thousand unorganized workers walked off their job in support of the strikers' aims. What those aims were was often vague, but the stirring events and the fiery eloquence of diverse strike leaders like J.S. Woodsworth and Robert Russell kept the embers burning. Woodsworth's passion came from the Old Testament, Russell's from the Manifesto, but both blended in the solidarity which strikers had in late May in Winnipeg.

The chords the Winnipeggers struck created a sympathetic reaction among workers elsewhere in Canada, from Vancouver through Toronto to

Sydney, Nova Scotia. There were over 370,000 union members in Canada in 1919 – still barely 17 per cent of the nonagricultural work force, yet a remarkable increase from the 205,000 in 1917. Their expectations were higher because their union affiliation was so new. What was happening in Winnipeg seemed a fulfilment of the promises the new unionists had heard when they were recruited. Moreover, the Canadian events fitted into the larger pattern whereby workers in Germany, Britain, the United States, and elsewhere were refusing to return to prewar conditions. In seeing the strike as part of a broader radical wave sweeping over western civilization, the strikers and federal government both believed that urgency was essential.

The strikers wanted gains quickly. The federal government sent Senator Gideon Robertson and Arthur Meighen immediately to Winnipeg to report on how the strike could be broken. The two cabinet ministers were frightened by what they saw in the streets and were soon convinced by the Citizens' Committee of One Thousand, a business group opposed to the strike, that there was a revolution in Winnipeg. Meighen and Robertson were most disturbed by the evidence that the normal civic institutions had given way to a civic order controlled by the Strike Committee. Delivery wagons with placards announcing they were operating with the permission of the Strike Committee, coupled with an uncertain police force, seemed to be adequate confirmation of the weakness of the traditional structure of government in Winnipeg. Acting on the recommendations of Meighen and Robertson, the federal cabinet refused to intervene to establish collective bargaining rights in Winnipeg or to deal with the conditions of work. This was not a normal strike; the response must be different. The forces of order were strengthened as additional militia and Mounted Police were moved to Winnipeg. Striking postal workers received an ultimatum: return to work or lose your jobs. On 6 June the Immigration Act was amended to permit the immediate deportation of anyone advocating social change through the use of force.

Winnipeg's mayor, Charles F. Gray, banned public demonstrations, and the city council and the Citizens' Committee recruited a Special Police Force to maintain order. On 17 June several strike leaders were jailed early in the morning. The action left the remaining strike leaders and their followers angry and confused. On 20 June a crowd gathered in Winnipeg's market square to protest the arrests and the federal government's refusal to meet their demands. If the government would not listen to them, they would not heed the government: they resolved to march to city hall the next day in defiance of Mayor Gray's proclamation banning demonstrations.

The strikers did not change their mind overnight. The next morning came, and the returned veterans who had swollen the strikers' ranks were not intimidated by Gray's warning that he would not tolerate a demonstration. The mayor asked for the help of the Mounted Police as the crowd gathered along Main Street. The Mounties came and moved through the crowd on horseback three times; each time the crowd parted but did not leave. A Mountie fell. A striker beat him. Guns fired; many strikers fell but most fled. The militia moved in and the strikers gave up. On Monday, 23 June, the tattered Strike Committee agreed to end the strike officially if a royal commission would examine the causes of the strike.

The strikers salvaged little in the short run. In the longer run, however, their demands received recognition. The royal commission reported that the strikers' central aim was the establishment of collective bargaining, and it supported that aim. It further emphasized that the strike's fundamental cause was inequality. The contrast between poverty and affluence inevitably bred discontent, and this discontent could take many forms, too many forms. The Winnipeg strikers were united by their discontent, but they were too excited in that heady spring to present a coherent image of what new society they wanted. Canadian labour, too, was ineffective because of the divisions within its ranks, between east and west, British and non-British, and radical and reformers. In this regard, it is often forgotten that the reformers on the Trades and Labor Council executive were consulted before the government brought in the notorious changes in the Immigration Act. Executive members generally approved of the change which they believed would get rid of the revolutionary troublemakers who were giving traditional unionism a bad name.

After Black Saturday in Winnipeg, union membership tumbled as unemployment rose and the postwar slump deepened. The One Big Union flared briefly, but it too succumbed to strong opposition from governments and employers and to divisions within its own ranks. In Quebec, the church took the lead in forming unions, and, in 1920, the Canadian and Catholic Confederation of Labour was formed. Its emphasis was upon social harmony, not class conflict, a view in accord with that of the various Canadian governments after 1919. In this respect, the governments reflected an increasing disposition on the part of Canadians to suspect grand promises and lofty visions. The year 1919 had shown that passion alone brought not change but reaction. The lesson took, but memories remained which, as reflected in voting booths, profoundly changed Canadian politics.

The events of Winnipeg flared brightly in the summer of 1919, but the flames died out quickly. It was not the urban working class which appeared to threaten the Canadian political system; rather, the Canadian farmer seemed to represent a greater challenge to Canadian governments.

Wartime reform began as an adjunct of the emotional commitment of urban English Canadians to the war. It built upon the strong tradition of the

Social Gospel which had so much affected many Protestant churches. The crusade for prohibition united the countryside with the middle-class Protestants in the city. It also raised expectations that a new era had dawned and that heaven could come to earth borne by good people and good will. The mood was infectious, and it spread. In the last years of the war, those who had not been caught up in the reform enthusiasm of the early war years also began to believe in the possibility of sudden change. Others, especially in Quebec, began to fear what these changes would take away. Still others who had most energetically promoted reform now hesitated to follow the path on which they had begun. Confusion and vision, disappointment and anger swirled about in 1919 as reform and rebellion exhausted themselves. There would be a new age, but it would not be what reformers had expected.

10

Slump and Boom and Slump Again, 1913-22

The years 1913-22 saw a dramatic economic upheaval, only partly because of the strain which the war placed on the economy. Indeed, compared with what happened in the 1939-45 war, that strain was relatively slight: at the peak of its First World War effort the dominion government consumed roughly 10 per cent of national output, as against 50 per cent in the Second, although in relation to the nation's population both army and casualties were far larger in the 1914-18 war. In human terms the First World War was an immense effort for the young dominion; economically, the government's effort was far less demanding. In measuring what the war meant for Canada's economy, however, we must also remember the flow of exports from Canadian factories and farms, a flow which prevented starvation in Britain and which, at its peak, provided 25 per cent of the shells which the Allies were firing on the Western Front. Although slow to get under way, these exports in due course would provide a hectic prosperity for many Canadian producers, and would propel the government towards economic control and central planning.

CYCLICAL MOVEMENTS

The first two years of war were marked by a flaccid economy. Business investment had collapsed from the peak levels of 1912-13, government expenditure was slow to rise, and, in order to compensate, much developmental spending was cut back. In many districts it was easy to raise recruits for Canada's volunteer army. The pressure of demand was not great enough, however, to raise the price level, in spite of monetary expansion and the unbalanced national budget. Some prices, such as transatlantic shipping space, increased quickly and markedly: in 1913 it cost 8 cents to ship a bushel of wheat from Montreal to Liverpool, but in 1915, 26.4 cents.[1] Foodstuffs, too, rose in price, as British and French demand pulled prices up. The Canadian government was eager to find orders for Canadian manufacturers – partly to help with the war effort, of course, but also to absorb the capacity left underemployed because of the collapse in investment. Such ordering could not be expected to revive the building trades, which by 1915 were sunk in a long-lasting and deep depression.

As time passed there was more pressure from overseas demand, while Canada's productive capacity was reduced as the army drained off more of the young and energetic. The war had ended immigration from Europe. Fortunately, with the completion of the new transcontinental railways, the elaboration of the prairie branch-line network, and the expansion of settlement in the wheat belt, in some important respects the economy's productive capacity increased. Also, the nation's producers were gradually learning how best to serve the war machine. So far as manufacturing was concerned, the advance was especially noticeable in the food industries and in some of the heavy industries, such as iron and steel, which had been hammered most severely in the recession of 1913-15.

Data on construction and steelmaking reveal the cyclical fluctuations most clearly. The output of clay bricks fell from 894 million in 1912 to 205 million in 1918. Cement production fell from 8.6 million barrels in 1913 to 3.6 million in 1918, while the output of steel rails fell from 567,500 tons in 1913 to 46,300 in 1917. At first, pig iron and steel production also declined, but less dramatically – some 30 per cent between 1913 and 1914. Thereafter, stimulated by war demands, iron and steel production began to climb. In 1916, outputs were larger than in 1913; pig iron outputs in 1916-18 were sustained just above the 1913 levels, while steel output grew very rapidly indeed, so that in 1918 Canada produced 1.87 million tons of steel – almost 90 per cent more than in 1913, and considerably more than in any later year until 1940. But from 1918 to 1922 pig iron production fell 64 per cent, and steel output declined by 71 per cent. Nor was the demand for rails sustained. Between 1921 and 1922 rail output fell by 53 per cent, so that it was only one-quarter of what it had been in 1913. In 1918-20 production of softwoods, bricks, and cement all recovered considerably but remained far below 1913 levels. In 1921 these industries slumped again, so that brick output was barely one-third of what it had been in 1912, cement output stood at two-thirds of the 1913 level, and the softwood cut was only 58 per cent of what it had been in 1911.

1   Except where noted, statistics derive from *Historical Statistics of Canada*, 1st edition (Toronto 1965), and 2nd edition (Ottawa 1983).

Meanwhile, some 'new industries,' not closely linked to the volume of domestic investment, were growing steadily. Woodpulp production rose from 855,000 tons in 1913 to 1,960,000 in 1920. In 1921, when only 1,549,000 tons were produced, output was still much larger than in 1913. As for newsprint, in 1913-14 the Canadian industry produced 436,000 tons per year, in 1917 output was already 690,000 tons, and in 1920, 876,000 tons. The 1921 slump reduced the output of newsprint by barely 8 per cent.

Similarly, the refining of crude petroleum suffered only a very small pause in 1915, then resumed an expansion which pushed output in 1919 to 250 per cent of the 1913 figure. Not surprisingly, the output of cars and trucks increased dramatically. In 1920 the dominion produced 79,369 cars and 10,174 commercial vehicles. Distressingly, however, this new 'consumer durable industry' proved to be cyclically unstable: in 1921, output was 30 per cent lower than in 1920.

Some mining also did well. Nickel, zinc, and copper, all prime materials of war, expanded rapidly through 1918, but slumped spectacularly thereafter. Nickel, in particular, benefited from the wartime demand for nickelsteel alloy. Salt production doubled between 1913 and 1920, apparently because salt was an important input for the chemical industries.

It was only in 1917 that Ottawa began a regular annual census of manufacturing, and data before that date is scattered and discontinuous. regular annual census of manufacturing. All we can safely say is that by 1917, manufacturing employment was considerably larger than in 1910. The raw data suggest a growth of 15 per cent, or less than 2 per cent per year, which we know masks the slump of 1913-15 and the recovery of 1915-17. Real output presumably grew more, because the productivity of the typical worker must have been on the increase. But the difference does not seem to have been great. From 1910 to 1917 the relevant price level doubled, while the gross value of manufacturing production in 1917 was 240 per cent of what it had been in 1910. Adjusting for price change, we get 'real growth' of 20 per cent, or rather less than 3 per cent per year, between 1910 and 1917.

Thereafter things went less well. Total manufacturing employment fell in 1918 and again in 1919. In 1920 there was a slight recovery, but in 1921, manufacturing employment fell by 134,629 – a 23 per cent decline from 1917-20. From 1917 through 1920 the value of manufacturing output rose 32 per cent. But the relevant price level rose 36 per cent, so that the real output of manufactures was drifting downward from 1917 through 1920. In the 1921 slump the price level fell 28 per cent in a single year. The value of manufacturing output, however, fell almost one-third. For Canadian manufacturing the end of the war meant first stagnation, and then deep depression.

THE FATE OF THE FARMER

In 1921 there were 711,090 occupied farms, 86 per cent of which were operated by their owners. Ten years before there had been only 682,329 farms.
In 1921, 157,022 farms possessed motor cars, and 26,842 possessed electric
or gas power. There were also 47,455 tractors. The age of the motor had arrived, and gradually it was penetrating the life and work of Canada's farms.
But although farmers must have been accumulating cars and equipment
throughout the First World War, the penetration had really just begun: the
nation's farms still contained 3,452,000 horses – 22 per cent more than in
1913. More than half of the horsepower on Canada's farms was still horse
power. And there were roughly three horses for every four rural residents, or
almost five horses per farm.

Between 1911 and 1921 the total of 'improved farm land' went up from
48.3 million acres to 70.8 million. There were small decreases in Ontario and
the Maritimes, small increases in British Columbia and Quebec, and a very
large increase – almost 100 per cent of the national total – on the prairies,
where the increase in acreage and occupied farms continued through the
War.

Although the number of farms was rising, the advance of wheat production and exportation was much more irregular and uncertain, partly because
of the weather. The First World War was anything but a bonanza for prairie
wheat farmers. Wheat prices increased, but so did farm costs. At first the
price of wheat rose precipitously, but then it slipped downward, so that in
1922-3 it was lower than in 1914. Thus the first years were good years, the
later years much less good, and the early 1920s almost disastrous. Since in
1921 there were 114 per cent more prairie farmers than in 1911, and 17 per
cent more than in 1916, the real income per farm family fell sharply.

Farmers had worked hard, opened new acreage, set up new farms in great
number, and bought horses and tractors. But outputs did not respond, and
prices – determined in world markets – often moved most inconveniently.
Throughout 1920 the cost of doing business, and the cost of living, inexora-
bly moved upward. No wonder farmers came to believe they were the victims of mysterious malign forces.

The western wheat economy had become very important, yet Canada –
especially eastern Canada – produced enormous amounts of coarse grains,
including oats, barley, rye, and flaxseed. Indeed, the nation's transport system was still largely 'oat-burning,' so that in 1921, as in 1913, the dominion
had to produce far more oats than wheat. Taken together, the three main
coarse grains were worth more than the wheat crops, yet for all three there

were inconvenient fluctuations in yields and prices, with no upward trend. For coarse grains, as for wheat, the war years brought higher prices – but also higher costs. Production, meanwhile, continued its awkward and distressing fluctuations in spite of the upward trend in sown acreage.

Yields, in other words, fluctuated dramatically. In the bumper crop year of 1916, each acre of wheat yielded twenty-six bushels; in 1920, the average yield was only ten bushels per acre. Similarly, oat lands yielded forty bushels per acre in 1916 and twenty-six bushels per acre in 1920. These were the uncontrollable fluctuations with which Canada's grain growers had to live.

In livestock raising there are almost no natural fluctuations, except when disease breaks out. Farmers can and do change the sizes of their herds, responding to costs and expected prices, but that is another story. During the years 1913-22 there were plentiful incentives to expand, and the number of horses, cows, and other cattle rose considerably. The increase in the number of sheep, lambs, and hogs, though not consistent, was substantial.

This expansion was to be expected. The increase in the horse population was entirely on the prairies, where the animals were needed to cultivate the growing acreage. In other livestock products, between 1913 and 1919 market prices in Ontario and Quebec, where production was concentrated, rose more rapidly than farm costs. The terms of trade were turning in favour of the livestock producer.

Wartime demand from Britain and Europe accounted for much of this expansion. From 1913 to 1916 the export of cattle and calves rose from 44,000 head to 421,000; after some decline in 1917-18, the outflow increased further in 1919-20, when over 315,000 head were exported. This figure was next reached only in 1937. Beef exports rose from insignificant levels in 1911-13 to 127 million pounds in 1919. Pork exports increased almost tenfold between 1913 and 1919, while export of sheep and lambs increased more rapidly still. Cheese exports, which had been declining for some years before the war, continued downward until 1915, then increased substantially in 1917-19.

As most of the marketable surplus of livestock products came from Ontario, the stimulus to production and farm profits was especially strong there. Perhaps it is not surprising that between 1914 and 1921 Ontario's horse population declined steadily, or that by 1921, 25 per cent of the motor cars in the province belonged to farmers. The impact on Ontario business was considerable. The William Davies Company, which specialized in packing pork for the British market, found that its bacon exports doubled between 1913-14 and 1914-15. Corned beef also moved overseas. Profits rose sharply – so sharply that in 1917 there were outcries against the 'profiteering' of the packing houses.[2] Ontario farmers were also doing quite well, but naturally no one said so.

GOVERNMENT AND THE WAR ECONOMY

Canada's governments had no idea how to manage a war economy. Ottawa was confused and the provinces were mindless. The wartime motto, in Canada as in Britain, was 'business as usual.' For some years Canada's agricultural products moved to Britain and Europe through the ordinary channels of private trade. Indeed, it was industrial output which was first mobilized for wartime needs in an organized way.[3]

When war broke out, the Dominion Arsenal in Quebec City could produce limited amounts of heavy ammunition. There were also a few private firms, such as Sir Charles Ross's rifle manufacturing plant. Before the end of 1914 Britain asked if Canada could produce shells, so Ottawa constituted a Shell Committee to handle and allocate orders. As J.M. Bliss writes, 'Only ten manufacturers could start work on the contract in October [1914] because there were only ten sets of gauges suitable for the job in the country.'[4] Shell orders poured in, but few shells were produced. By May 1915 less than 3 per cent of the orders had actually been shipped. Yet in the summer of 1915 the Canadian government continued to press for more British shell orders, despite its failure to equip the dominion's own troops. In November 1915, therefore, the British government set up the Imperial Munitions Board, under Canadian management, to purchase munitions in Canada on its behalf. Its chairman, the Toronto pork packer and financier Joseph Flavelle, had to deal not only with an inherited mess of administrative disorder and incompetence but also with new requests from Britain, which now wanted fuzes as well as shell casings. Components happily trundled back and forth across the dominion, from Ontario to British Columbia and back again, so that work could be distributed among the hungry manufacturers in various regions. Flavelle successfully brought order into chaos, set up his own plant to load the shells, and arranged for the Canadian banks to finance a large part of Britain's Canadian purchases.

By the winter of 1916-17 the board also operated seven 'national factories.' More would follow. In July 1916 the board had an Ottawa staff of 500; in 1911 the entire central governmental apparatus of the dominion had employed no more than 3000 men and women. The seventh national factory

---

2   J.M. Bliss, *A Canadian Millionaire: The Life and Business Times of Sir Joseph Flavelle, Bart. 1858-1939* (Toronto 1978), 237, 337
3   Ibid., 238ff
4   Ibid., 249

was Canadian Aeroplanes Ltd, whose Toronto plant was able to produce fifteen planes a week. Other national factories produced explosives, chemicals, and acetone. In April 1917 the board began to buy the entire steel-vessel capacity of Canada's shipyards and to organize the production of aircraft spruce in British Columbia. When the United States entered the war in 1917, the board became an agency for American munitions purchases in the dominion. In Toronto, as arranged by the board, Willys-Overland of Canada was trying to manufacture aero engines. The firm finally succeeded just after the Armistice.[5]

Although the Imperial Munitions Board was staffed, managed, directed, and largely financed by Canadians, it was not a Canadian government agency. In Canada, as in other belligerent countries, government was reluctant to recognize that the war would be a long one, and Ottawa was slow to make the administrative changes which would allow it to mobilize the nation's economic power for war purposes. In any event, Ottawa could not readily have done much, at least at first, because the central administrative apparatus of the dominion was both small and inexperienced. As and when it found itself obliged to do new things, Ottawa normally reached outside, recruiting businessmen and other members of the groups which would be most directly affected.

One problem area was grain. Canadian wheat output was on the rise, so that throughout the war the dominion produced more than in any previous year except 1910. However, there were trying fluctuations; 1916 produced a bumper crop, but output was lower in 1917 and in 1918 lower still. By 1917, unemployment having been absorbed partly by the army and partly by the revival of urban industry, the dominion was facing serious shortages of farm labour. Various attempts were made to attract labour and to raise production in other ways. Meanwhile, because of German submarine activity, Britain and France found it hard to draw supplies from the Southern Hemisphere. European production was not well sustained, in spite of efforts to raise it. By late 1916 Great Britain, which had already arranged for the bulk purchase of Indian, Australian, and Egyptian wheat, proposed to buy all of Canada's surplus.

There followed an unseemly row about the appropriate price. Canada's farmers were holding out for higher prices than Ottawa thought proper. In the absence of agreement, British purchasing agents began to buy heavily on the Winnipeg market, where prices rose impressively. Ottawa responded, on 11 June 1917, by establishing a Board of Grain Supervisors, with power to fix prices and make bulk sales to Britain and the Allies. Farmers were de-

5   Ibid., 316, 369, 377

lighted with the board's pricing policies, which produced returns far in excess of what Ottawa had thought proper in the spring of 1917 – $2.40 per bushel, as opposed to $1.30.

In June 1917 the government also appointed a food controller, W.J. Hanna, giving him power to control the prices, utilization, allocation, manufacture, and storage of 'any article of food.' Hanna was willing to control prices, but in fact he did not do so, nor did he ration supplies to households; instead, he preferred to rely on exhortation. The Canada Food Board, which replaced Hanna in February 1918, had essentially the same powers. The board concentrated its efforts on the encouragement of production and avoidance of waste, eschewing both consumer price control and consumer rationing. Price control it thought ineffective, and rationing administratively impossible in a far flung agrarian country such as Canada. The Food Board wound up its affairs in December 1918.

Food prices continued to spiral during 1919, so that at the end of May the House of Commons established a committee to look into prices and profits. The committee reported in July that there had been little profiteering, but went on to recommend the creation of a Board of Commerce which could carry on the good work done during the war. In the summer of 1919 Parliament actually established the board, giving it wide powers of investigation and regulation with an eye to the prevention of profiteering. But it was worldwide demand-pull inflation, not profiteering, which had raised consumer prices in Canada. The board therefore had little to do, and its impact was even less than its activities. Ruled unconstitutional by the courts, it expired. Regrettably, with the board went a series of powers regarding trusts, mergers, and monopolies which a more vigorous or interested administration might have put to better use.

In fuels, as in agriculture, June 1917 was a month of great change. On 11 June Ottawa appointed a fuel controller, who worked with American authorities to increase and allocate coal supplies in Canada and achieve more economy in the use of all fuels. In the spring of 1918 steps were taken to ration anthracite, which was imported from the United States and used by Canadians mostly for home heating. Prices were not regulated, but traders' margins were controlled. Much thought was given to the production of lignite and peat fuel, but little was done. All these arrangements ended with the Armistice, or soon afterward, and owing to the end of the war and the mildness of the 1918-19 winter season, serious shortages did not appear. But it was a near thing, especially for a cold country.

For Canada's wheat farmers, the end of the war posed difficult problems of adjustment. For two years they had enjoyed a guaranteed outlet at a fixed price. In the winter of 1918-19 there was pressure for a price guarantee on the 1919 crop. Following discussions among the British authorities, farm organizations, railways, and government, on 30 June 1919 the government announced that it would set up a Canadian Wheat Board to buy and market the 1919 crop. A minimum price was guaranteed, but the final returns to the farmers would depend on the board's success in selling the wheat. Advances were to be paid on delivery. The board ceased to accept wheat in August 1920, although it was given some time to wind up its business. As wheat prices fell, farmers pressed for the re-establishment of the board. The law officers of the crown opined, however, that except in time of war the dominion government did not have the constitutional power to market wheat.

Although these wartime changes in economic arrangements had echoes later, especially in the hopes and dreams of the farmers and various reformers' movements to whom guaranteed prices and regulated trades of the later war years looked quite attractive, the new devices could not be anything but temporary, if only for constitutional reasons. In addition, no major Canadian party had the stomach for such comprehensive economic regulations in peacetime. However, the war also saw one important structural change – the nationalization of three large railways – which proved very permanent indeed.

THE RAILWAY MESS

It will be remembered that in the great wheat boom the Laurier government made arrangements with the Grand Trunk and Canadian Northern managements for the creation of new transcontinental and western rail networks. The dominion itself was to build a new line through trackless and unremunerative country, from Winnipeg via Quebec to Moncton; the Grand Trunk was to guarantee the obligations of the Grand Trunk Pacific and lease the dominion's new National Transcontinental; the Bank of Commerce was to be heavily involved in the interim financing of the Canadian Northern, but everyone thought that it would be easy to raise the long-term finance by selling bonds in London.

Even before the outbreak of war, these arrangements were coming unstuck. Because all the lines were costing far more than had been foreseen, early in 1914 the London market was already proving anything but responsive, and Ottawa had to find money for the Canadian Northern. The National Transcontinental, which was supposed to cost about $61 million, actually cost over $161 million. Thus, when Ottawa asked the Grand Trunk Pacific to take over the line, as arranged, in 1913, the GTP refused, arguing that it could not afford the lease payments. Following a further refusal in 1915,

Ottawa began to operate the National Transcontinental itself. In 1916 the dominion had to provide temporary financial assistance to the Canadian Northern and also to the Grand Trunk Pacific, both for current obligations and interest. Another worrying problem was the network of provincial guarantees for Canadian railway bonds. Suppose the provinces had to pay up? Further, the Bank of Commerce had lent immense sums to the Canadian Northern. If the railways collapsed, so might the bank. What was to be done?

The dominion's immediate answer was a royal commission – the Smith-Drayton-Acworth Commission – which was appointed in July 1916 and reported in May 1917. Drayton and Acworth thought that the dominion should take over the Canadian Northern, Grand Trunk, and Grand Trunk Pacific, operating them in combination with the National Transcontinental and the Intercolonial as one enormous integrated dominion-owned railway company. Their report suggested that there were too many railway lines in Canada, but hoped that the new 'Dominion Railway' might eventually be able to meet its overhead charges as well as its operating expenses. Smith, who was president of the New York Central, wanted the Canadian Northern to take over the Grand Trunk Pacific, and the Grand Trunk to take over the Canadian Northern's eastern lines, with the dominion operating or subsidizing the two 'land bridge' lines through northern Ontario.

The government proceeded to acquire the Canadian Northern, for a price which was eventually fixed by arbitration at $10.8 million – just over 10 per cent of the par value of the capital stock. It also provided interim aid to the Grand Trunk Pacific, which the minister of finance shortly announced would have to 'come in' also. Negotiations began in 1918 and were well advanced in March 1919, when the Grand Trunk Pacific announced it would shut down. The government arranged for the minister of railways and canals to become receiver for the bankrupt railway. By the autumn of 1919 the arrangements for the takeover of the Grand Trunk and Grand Trunk Pacific were completed.

Grand Trunk shareholders were to get a sum set by arbitration, but two arbitrators decided in due course that the common and preferred shares of the Grand Trunk had no value; therefore, no compensation was paid. Meanwhile, railway administrators were working to integrate these various lines and companies into the new Canadian National system – a Crown corporation which began with heavy overhead charges, too much trackage, and very uncertain prospects.

Could the debacle have been prevented? A.W. Currie[6] suggests that if

6   A.W. Currie, *Canadian Transportation Economics* (Toronto 1967), 413

the Canadian government had controlled railway costs as well as railway rates during the First World War, 'the railway history of Canada might have been very different.' There is no doubt that government rate-fixing did squeeze all the railways, especially during the later years of the war. But the overcapacity was the result of prewar decisions, and both the Canadian Northern and the Grand Trunk Pacific were in difficulties even before war broke out. The war did cause London loans to dry up, but here too there had been serious problems even before 1914. Also, the cyclical fluctuation of 1913-15 created temporary but painful overcapacity, especially for the Grand Trunk, while the railway system did not have enough rolling stock to seize the traffic opportunities which the war later created.

Fortunately, the dominion's experience with new levels of wartime taxing and spending enabled Ottawa to accept levels of railway subsidy which the Laurier government probably could not have imagined. In human and engineering terms, of course, the new transcontinentals were immensely impressive achievements, even if in economic terms their worth was less certain. Thanks to the Borden government's actions, the Bank of Commerce and the provinces escaped with their loans intact and their guarantees uncalled, while the Toronto promoters Sir William MacKenzie and Sir Donald Mann escaped with $10.8 million untaxed dollars.

FINANCING THE WAR EFFORT

Even before the completion of nationalization in 1919, the railways involved Ottawa in heavy financial burdens. For instance, in 1914 the dominion had to lend the Canadian Northern $40 million so that construction could be continued. However, the war itself involved very much larger outlays. The dominion found the money by borrowing not only in London but also in Canada and New York, where dominion securities had not previously been seen. Up to 30 November 1918 the dominion spent $1,068,606,527 on the war. Net debt increased by $971,429,661. Almost all of the war was financed by borrowing.

Some borrowing was informal, and there was informal lending too. Although the London new-issue market was closed to Canada after the loan of March 1915, the imperial government advanced hundreds of millions of pounds to pay for the overseas costs of Canada's armies. Similarly, Canada advanced hundreds of millions to Britain, and in the settlement of the accounts, although there was some perplexity as to the rate of exchange which should be used in the calculations, no one doubted that so far as Britain was concerned, the Canadian government had become a net lender.

Ottawa had also to concern itself with the balance-of-payments patterns in which its war effort was embedded. Before 1914, Canada had blithely bought far more in the United States than she had sold there, paying the excess by converting the proceeds from exports to Britain and from borrowings on the British market. After 1914 this was no longer possible: Britain could not lend convertible currency to Canada, which now, in addition, found itself financing a large part of Britain's Canadian purchases. Canada's New York loans, therefore, helped to pay for Canada's imports from the United States. Life became more difficult in 1918 when the United States, having entered the war, placed an embargo on new foreign borrowings. In May 1918 the minister of finance, Sir Thomas White, was obliged to visit Washington, where he sought an exception from this rule – perhaps the first instance of Canadian 'exemptionalism.' The result, in June 1918, was a New York loan for $65 million which pushed the dominion's American borrowings to $285 million. But Sir Thomas had borrowed far larger sums in Canada.

The government's principle was to treat war outlays as 'extraordinary' items, borrow for them, and raise taxes enough to cover the resulting debt-service charges. In 1914-15, therefore, Sir Thomas decreed many increases in customs and excise duties and in taxes on bank note circulation, non-life insurance premiums, and the gross income of trust and loan companies. As the dominion already had full information about these matters, such new taxes had the additional advantage of requiring no new administrative apparatus. In 1916, however, Ottawa had to move into new fields, imposing a 'business war profits tax' on profits taken in 1915-17, inclusive. In 1917 the rates were raised. In addition, the dominion introduced its first income tax. This applied both to individuals and corporations. The rates were not high. Corporations paid 4 per cent; individuals who earned less than $2000 – the great mass of the Canadian nation – were exempt; there were further exemptions for married persons; for the unmarried, rates progressed from 1 per cent on the first $2000 to 8 per cent on an income of $25,000. Not very much, it would seem. Nor were the revenues great, even though rates were raised in 1918 and again in 1919.

Revenues from the new income taxes did not materialize until the fiscal year 1919, because at that time, and indeed until the Second World War, dominion income taxes were never deducted at source, but were paid only after the year to which they applied. Thus in the fiscal year 1919, the dominion's total revenues were $312.9 million, of which almost every dollar came from customs, excise, the post office, and dominion lands; only 3 per cent came from personal income tax, 0.4 per cent from the corporation tax, and 11 per cent from the excess profits tax. In the Second World War things would be very different.

The idea was to repeal such new taxes once the war had passed. But the income tax is with us still. Furthermore, these wartime tax changes are important because they mark the dominion's entry into the field of 'direct taxation,' a field which Ottawa has constitutional power to use but where the provinces had previously browsed as they wished. The provinces had been taxing corporations since the 1890s, and by 1907 there was some form of corporation tax, usually on capital value in every province; British Columbia first taxed personal incomes in 1876, and Prince Edward Island in 1894, although other provinces did not do so until the 1930s. The dominion had also left the provinces the field of succession duties, another tax where collection costs were low and which the provinces had been collecting since the 1890s. The dominion did not levy succession duties until the Second World War.

Sir Thomas White was proud that he had not 'financed the War through inflation,' by which he meant that he had not printed money to pay the government's bills. Nevertheless, during the war, Canadian price levels rose quite dramatically. The general wholesale price index, whose base is 100 for 1935-9, rose from 85.4 in 1914 to 166 in 1918, and then went on up to 203.2 in 1920, falling back to 126.8 in 1922. The Department of Labour's family budget index went from 100 in 1913 to 98.7 in 1915, then rose to 147.2 in 1918 and to 184.7 in 1920. These price increases, whose causes were not well understood, provided much of the fuel for two successive fires: the attack on 'corporate profiteering' and the wave of labour unrest which swept the entire dominion in 1917-20.

Why were prices rising? The causes were partly domestic and partly international, but neither cause had anything much to do with 'profiteering.' Nor were they exclusively Canadian. From the outbreak of war until 1920 the entire Western world experienced an inflation the like of which had last been seen during the Napoleonic Wars. The rate varied among the various countries. There was more inflation in France than in Britain, and more in Britain than in the United States. But the phenomenon was universal, and so was the basic cause: the pressure of war demand on economies whose productive possibilities were declining, as in France and Russia, or not growing proportionately, as in Britain and the United States.

In principle, by following a really stringent policy of high taxation and tight money, Canada could have financed her war effort without importing this inflation. The value of the Canadian dollar, which was freed from its link with gold in 1914, would then have floated up, offsetting the effect of inflation abroad. In practice, of course, nobody in Ottawa ever thought of any such thing. The dominion had long been accustomed to finance 'extraordinary' outlays, such as railway building, by loans. Surely the war was an 'extraordinary' event? Surely it was natural to finance the war by borrowing?

Although some provinces and many municipalities and corporations were accustomed to borrow within Canada before 1914, the dominion had not floated a domestic bond issue for many years, and its informal or automatic borrowings from the public through the post-office savings system had for some years been falling. But because the London market, on which the Canadian government had chiefly depended in peacetime, was no longer readily available, Ottawa was obliged to explore the resources of the domestic market. White was surprised to find how much he could raise, and how easily. The great chartered banks were a natural channel through which the public could subscribe. As Sir Thomas later explained, nothing could be easier than to float a new dominion issue. One telephone call to the Canadian Bankers Association sufficed.

If the Canadian financial system had not already become accustomed to various kinds of government and corporate bonds, the solution might not have been so easy. If the chartered banks had not been so helpful, matters would have been very much worse. For the banks did not act merely as conduits and distributing centres. Although they did not often subscribe themselves, they were delighted to lend money to would-be subscribers. After all, what better pledge than the new dominion bond which the borrower would purchase?

The banks made such loans in the usual way, by creating additional deposits. Further increases came from the banks' continuing willingness to finance the 'legitimate needs of trade.' As prices began to rise, so did the costs of doing business, as well as the advances which businesses would need to pay for inventories, raw materials, supplies or labour, and so on. The loans would appear perfectly sound, and *were* sound, in that the eventual selling price would cover the full amount borrowed. But the process was circular: by financing the 'needs of trade' in this way, the banks allowed businesses to compete against one another for the limited supplies of labour and raw materials, just as through financing the bond borrowers the banks allowed the government to compete with private business. As competition bid up the prices of inputs, at the next round a higher level of borrowing would be 'justified by the legitimate needs of trade.' In this process the money supply increased very rapidly indeed – from $1108 million in 1914 to $1828 million in autumn 1918, and to $2091 million in 1920. Most of this supply was extra bank deposits, not extra paper currency.

There were no legal limits on the amount of deposit liabilities which the banking system could create. However, before 1914 the gold standard provided an automatic control, in that too rapid an expansion of the banks' lending would produce a rise in the domestic price level and a tendency to demand dominion notes or gold in inconvenient amounts. With the end of gold convertibility in 1914, and with the arrangements by which banks could borrow newly printed dominion notes on demand, this restraint was removed. If the banks found they were paying out too many notes they could borrow some, cheaply, from the government; if they wanted to preserve some sort of 'window-dressing,' maintaining some target ratio between their deposit liabilities and their holdings of gold and dominion notes, they could borrow new notes for that purpose too. In either case, the dominion government would be happy to print some.

THE GOLD STANDARD, THE FINANCE ACT, AND THE BANKS

The war caused Canada to leave the gold standard almost at once, first through an order-in-council and then through the terms of the 1914 Finance Act. The nation was not driven off the gold standard in any sense. But the chartered banks were afraid that there would be panic and an 'internal drain': that is, the public might present too many chartered-bank notes for payment in gold. Naturally, the value of outstanding bank notes was far larger than the quantity of gold reserves. Accordingly, the dominion government decided that bank notes and dominion notes should no longer be convertible into gold on demand. Further, it arranged to print new dominion notes for lending to any chartered bank which might apply for such an advance. Before 1914 there had been no such provision; Canadian banks were accustomed to hold funds in New York and London, from which centres they could obtain help in case of need. Under wartime conditions there was no guarantee that this would be possible. Hence the need for some domestic 'lender of last resort.' The dominion Department of Finance charged interest on these advances, which could be secured in any way the department thought suitable. The department followed current financial practice, deducting the interest at the beginning of the loan period and crediting the borrower with the amount of the loan minus the interest. For obvious reasons, this practice was known as 'discounting.' Hence, such dominion advances were known as 'discounts under the Finance Act,' or, for short, as 'Finance Act discounting.' Through this provision, the dominion could and did create large additional quantities of dominion notes, without having to provide any 'gold backing.' Ottawa also took power to expand the 'unbacked' dominion note issue for other reasons – chiefly for advances to railways and war expenses. In two respects, therefore, Canada had left the gold standard: paper money was no longer convertible into gold at a fixed price, and the quantity of the dominion's own paper money was no longer related in any simple or mechanical way to the quantity of gold reserves in Ottawa's possession.

Exchange rates, therefore, moved away from the 'par rates' which before 1914 had been fixed by the comparative gold contents of the various national monies. The price of the United States dollar changed little until 1919-20, when it rose from $1.0138 to $1.19 Canadian. The pound, however, fell sharply. In 1913, on average, a pound cost $4.853 Canadian; by 1920 the price of a pound was only $4.0757 Canadian and, although there was recovery thereafter, the 1913 sterling-dollar rate was not restored until 1925, when Britain returned to the gold standard at the 1914 'par.'

Although the dominion did not leave gold for the sake of financing the war effort, it came to welcome its new freedom to manipulate the money supply. Nor was the Ottawa exchequer the only beneficiary: thanks to the new provisions of the Finance Act, the British government was able to borrow large sums from the Canadian chartered banks, who at once presented the British short-term obligations to the Canadian Department of Finance for 'discounting.' In later years, Sir Thomas White would heatedly deny that Canada's war finance had been inflationary. Certainly Canada did not deliberately finance the war by printing money – at least, not to any great extent. Nor did Ottawa itself borrow much from the banks. It merely continued the tradition of borrowing from the public for extraordinary outlays. Indirectly, however, government deficit spending had an immense although unintentional inflationary effect, even though the banks themselves hardly bought any of the new dominion bonds.

By 1920 the chartered banks were devoted to the 'Finance Act system.' It provided them with an assured, low-cost source of paper currency – an alternative to the central banking mechanism which, in more developed economies, functioned as a 'lender of last resort' for banks. They did not really like to borrow, lest they appear weak; nevertheless, they valued the chance to do so. The banks, therefore, resisted suggestions that Canada should set up its own central bank. What, they asked, did the dominion need with such a thing? Only the Royal Bank showed some interest. Nothing was done.[7] And when the economy contracted in 1920-2, several banks found that they had overextended themselves in the inflationary atmosphere of 1916-20. For that sort of difficulty the mechanism of the Finance Act was no solution, and the banks resorted to a much older medicine – merger. The weaker banks, such as Molson's and Merchant's, were absorbed by stronger institutions such as the Bank of Montreal.

7 See R. Craig McIvor, *Canadian Monetary, Banking, and Fiscal Development* (Toronto 1958), 109ff.

RECONSTRUCTION WITHOUT MUCH REFORM

The Borden government knew that it would have to plan for the return of servicemen into the civilian economy. The dominion began, in co-operation with the provinces, to lend money for municipally sponsored public housing and to operate a system of labour exchanges. But the plans for postwar reconstruction did not involve much new social engineering. For instance, although Britain and other European states had long provided old-age pensions, unemployment benefit, and medical insurance, the government had no such plans for Canada. The Liberal opposition said in 1919 that it wanted national health insurance, but only in the 1960s did a Liberal government produce such a plan. There were plans to settle ex-soldiers on farms, though, as events unfolded, it was not the best time to be setting up as a farmer. The government, however, could not have foreseen the slump of 1920-2. And, during that slump, life in the cities would be no easier, and no more secure, than life on the land.

11

Literacy, Literature, and Education

Economic change had a great impact on all aspects of Canadian life. The relationship between economic change and political, intellectual, and social change is difficult to trace. What is clear, however, is the influence of Canadian industrialization and urbanization upon the way Canadians educated themselves and, indeed, thought about themselves. The transformation can best be seen if we look at what the earlier situation had been.

In 1893 John Bourinot addressed the Royal Society of Canada, which had been founded to honour and promote Canadian intellectual advance. His earnest tone and traditional attitudes no doubt reflected the view of most of his distinguished audience:

> I do not for one moment deprecate the influence of good fiction on the minds of a reading community like ours; it is inevitable that a busy people, and especially women distracted with household cares, should always find that relief in this branch of literature which no other reading can give them; and if the novel has then become a necessity of the times in which we live, at all events I hope Canadians, who may soon venture into this field, will study the better models ... and not bring the Canadian fiction of the future to that low level to which the school of Realism in France, and in a minor degree in England and the United States, would degrade the novel and story of every-day life.[1]

Thus did Bourinot dismiss most of the contemporary works which we now consider classics. Madame Bovary, Tess, and Colette had a rough passage to Canadian shores.

This moral earnestness, combined with an aggressive capitalism, convinced many visitors that Canada offered little fertile ground for artistic or

1 Sir John Bourinot, *Our Intellectual Strength and Weakness* (Toronto 1973), 30

intellectual achievement. George Bernard Shaw, for example, thought Canada was an agglomeration of primitive barbarians whose romantic colonialism offered little scope for the growth of the 'higher civilization' found in the great European cities, or even in New York and Boston. Such an impression could easily develop from a tour of the major Canadian cities at the turn of the century. The few bookstores carried mostly books from abroad, with a strong emphasis on the practical and the sentimental. The theatres hosted mainly American touring companies which featured melodramas with dashing heroes and especially roguish villains. The plays and the songs of English Canada were those which titillated the American mid-west, and the endings were invariably happy and morally instructive. Nevertheless, a perceptive and persistent visitor to prewar Canada would have noticed how the native products, whether plays or books, exhibited a robust patriotic spirit, one that celebrated the Canadian landscape and people. Moreover, if the turn-of-the-century visitor had returned after the war, he would have noticed how many more books, newspapers, and theatres there were.

The fact was that many more Canadians could read and those basic skills of literacy were rising in both quantity and quality. In 1901, 82.88 per cent of Canadians over the age of five could both read and write. Younger Canadians were more often and more fully literate than their parents and, especially, than their grandparents.[2] There were also distinct regional differences, with Ontario being 89.78 per cent literate in 1901 and Quebec only 77.92 per cent literate. In Saskatchewan that same year only 63.88 per cent were literate in either English or French. In the next two decades the effect of almost universal elementary education, along with the death of the older illiterates, combined to raise literacy rates – dramatically in some areas – as Table 3 indicates.

More Canadians could read, and there was much more available for them to read. The price of paper fell considerably in the 1890s, and new typesetting and typewriting machines greatly increased the speed and efficiency of production. The result was an intense competition among newspapers, and the development of newspapers, dailies as well as weeklies, for all classes and for different tastes. In 1899 Toronto alone had approximately 150 publications, and even smaller communities of 10,000-15,000 people supported their daily paper. Between 1891 and 1900 the circulation of daily and weekly newspapers rose from 879,000 to 1,237,000, the latter figure being considerably above the number of families in Canada.[3] The number of newspapers was to increase until the First World War, when a permanent decline set in.

2   See Paul Rutherford, *A Victorian Authority: The Daily Press in Late Nineteenth Century Canada* (Toronto 1982), 24ff.
3   These figures are taken from Rutherford, *A Victorian Authority,* 3 and 5.

TABLE 3
Literary Rates in Canada, 1901-11 (per cent literate)

	Nova Scotia	Quebec	Ontario	Saskatch- ewan	British Columbia	Canada
1901	81.30	77.92	89.78	63.88	74.56	82.88
1911	88.66	86.51	93.11	86.08	88.11	88.98
1921	89.32	88.79	92.99	87.85	90.01	90.0

Source: *Census of Canada 1921*

In the two decades before the war the newspaper flourished, swollen by advertising revenues from new department stores and consumer products and by an urban population that seemed to hunger for 'news.' Sometimes the 'news' was of grisly murders or scandal, but, thanks to telegraph and other communication improvements, there was far more coverage of national and world affairs than had earlier been true. *La Presse,* the Montreal *Star,* and similar papers in Toronto all sought to appeal to broad markets, and a scent of scandal and outrage imbued the pages of these popular dailies. Yet there was much serious content, and the need for moral instruction was as fully recognized in these new popular dailies as in more staid and traditional newspapers. In forming popular culture before the war the newspaper was pre-eminent. It took the first place in the system of mass communication that Canadian society was developing.

This modern system emerged simultaneously with the urbanization of Canada, a process which fundamentally affected the values of Canadians. The percentage of Canadians who lived in urban areas and who had access to the new popular press, to the proliferating libraries, and to the abundant newsstands grew from roughly 23 per cent in 1881 to 35 per cent in 1901, to 41.8 per cent in 1911, and to 47.4 per cent in 1921. Despite an enduring distrust of the city among rural Canadians, the city nonetheless continued to exert ever greater influence over the countryside as communications and transportation improved.

If Canadians read more in the first decade of the twentieth century, it probably means that they read more by non-Canadian authors. In the public libraries, which became much more common because of the Scottish-American millionaire Andrew Carnegie's generosity, fiction titles were the most popular. The same was no doubt true of book purchases, and the market for romance seemed insatiable. The best evidence for this abundance was the regularity with which educators, religious leaders, and politicians

'Home, Sweet Home'   Bengough, 1897

deplored the 'flood of trash' from below the forty-ninth parallel. Libraries censored the works upon their shelves, and Canadian Customs and Post Office officials forbade the circulation of other undesirable works ranging from the notorious *Police Gazette* to the seemingly innocuous *American Farmer.*[4] In French Canada the church exerted an even more zealous scrutiny over offending publications from France, placing on its index many of the greatest French writers of the age. The Montreal City Council reflected this mood in 1903 when it decided not to accept the offer of a Carnegie library.

What Canadians read in the first two decades of the century can perhaps best be understood through a visit to an unselective retailer of old books. In the mustiest corners of such stores, books can be found organized into patterns very unlike those in a modern bookstore. Although Canadians did read the popular works by American and British authors, there were numerous Canadian writers who acquired a popular audience. Usually these authors, such as Charles Gordon (Ralph Connor), Gilbert Parker, and Stephen Leacock, saw their works published in Canada as reprints of work published elsewhere. Gordon's adventure stories and moralistic tales acquired an especially broad audience in Canada and beyond. His *Man from Glengarry*

4 See Neil Sutherland, *Children in English-Canadian Society 1880-1920* (Toronto 1976), 19-20, where a report of the National Council of Women is cited which listed fifty-two banned publications.

(1901) sold 25,000 copies within ten months of its Canadian publication. It sold far more elsewhere.

In 1902 Gordon published *Glengarry School Days,* which also attracted much attention. In the *Canadian Annual Review* of that year, J. Castell Hopkins published a list of Canadian books which he said 'naturally fall into works of romance, poetry, history and politics, biography and works of reference.' That most fiction was indeed romance is clear from the list of titles:

TITLE	AUTHOR
Glengarry School Days	Ralph Connor
Why Not, Sweetheart?	Mrs Julia N. Henshaw
Where the Sugar Maple Grows	Adelaide M. Teskey
Donelbane of Darien	J. Macdonald Oxley
A Maid of Many Moods	Mrs Verna Sheard
Tilda Jane	Margaret Marshall Saunders
With Rogers on the Frontier	J. Macdonald Oxley
Heralds of Empire	Agnes C. Laut
The Kindred of the Wild	Charles G.D. Roberts
Barbara Ladd	Charles G.D. Roberts
Donovan Pasha and Some People of Egypt	Sir Gilbert Parker
Thoroughbreds	W.A. Fraser
Those Delightful Americans	Mrs Everard Cotes (Sara Jeannette Duncan)
Beautiful Joe's Paradise	Margaret Marshall Saunders

Many of these authors had a commercial success that modern Canadian authors might envy. Saunders's *Beautiful Joe,* the story of a dog, reportedly sold over one million copies internationally. Sentimental animal stories, or suspenseful nature studies such as Roberts's *The Kindred of the Wild,* were, perhaps, Canada's major contribution to world literature in the first three decades of the century. Gordon's tales with their simple and moralistic tone also captured many readers in Britain and elsewhere. Sara Jeannette Duncan's work reflects a broader mentality and considerable skill in understanding manners and probing personality. In 1904, after ten years away from southern Ontario, Duncan, in Calcutta, wrote her only novel with an exclusively Canadian setting and her most successful work: *The Imperialist* gently mocked Canadians for their political corruption, materialism, and inability to seek broader political visions. Although the novel abounds in personal insight, it is not psychologically subtle as European and American novels were increasingly becoming at that time.

There were, however, many Canadians who feared that modern currents would sweep away those traditions which seemed all the more essential in a new North American nation. In 1904 the archbishop and bishops of the Anglican church issued a pastoral which included prohibition of remarriage of either party to a divorce, a warning against 'race suicide,' and a denunciation not only of the 'vagaries and follies of modern society' but even of new music and similar innovations in churches. In the same month, Archbishop Bruchési of Montreal issued a pastoral letter which condemned some 'Parisian' plays in Montreal, including some in which the great Sarah Bernhardt was then performing. 'We have,' the bishop declaimed, 'no need in this Catholic city of such literature and of such plays brought from a country where morality and modesty are only vain words.' When Bernhardt complained about the philistinism of such an attitude, Laval students gave her a rough reception in Quebec City, so rough that Laurier himself was moved to apologize to the famous actress for the rude reception Canada gave her. Nevertheless, when she returned to Montreal in 1911 she was more circumspect in what she chose to perform.

Canadians today may know Bernhardt's name but to turn-of-the-century Canadians the Marks brothers from Christie Lake, Ontario, were likely far better known. Their staple was melodrama, and the titles were suspiciously familiar though the plays were declared to be original works. Virtue was always threatened but never vanquished. When the Marks brothers and their troupe arrived in town, they paraded down the main street to the hearty blasts of a brass band. They never missed a Sunday in church after a Saturday night performance, and if there were several congregations they dispersed their religious fidelity equally. Touring American companies, who sometimes left town in disgrace just before dawn, took greater liberties with conventional beliefs. As Americans bought up Canadian opera and vaudeville houses, touring American companies came to dominate the Canadian stage. Canadians responded by turning to Britain for help, but the efforts of the British and Canadian Theatre Organization Society were unsuccessful. The war intervened, and so did Hollywood. By 1919 the opera house had given way to the movie house, and the era of the touring company had almost ended. The market for theatre narrowed to the highly literate on the one hand and the connoisseurs of burlesque on the other. For most Canadians in the 1920s, movies were the rage. Ontario, which had one theatre in 1871, had only two by 1930.

For Canadians, the spirit of modernism in art, literature, and religion was sipped in small doses, and often surreptitiously, through the war. The literary culture remained traditional, one where the honours fell upon those like Sir Gilbert Parker and Senator Thomas Chapais who reflected the patriotic and civic values of the ordinary society. Those, such as Frances Beynon, who questioned established values and flirted with literary realism, found their Canadian outlets few and the temptations of the United States or Europe great. Official comment continued to condemn realism for its degrading qualities, as in the *Manitoba Free Press* drama critic's review of Ibsen's *Ghosts* which an American touring company injudiciously put on in Winnipeg in 1904: 'High art they called it! Perhaps it is – perhaps in this wild and wooly [sic] west we lack the intelligence to discern high art. To me it is dirt – just dirt! The audacious daring with which sex questions are discussed in this play has no stage precedent ... while the utter depravity of the character is astounding ... But why write of the ghastly thing. Let's forget it if we can. The Ibsen cult may be all right but in this morally healthy western community we want none of his gruesome dissections.' Nor did the gruesome dissections of society performed by George Bernard Shaw fare much better with most Canadian critics.[5]

Not all shared these critics' views; the audiences for *Ghosts* and *Mrs Warren's Profession* confirm the existence of different viewpoints. Nevertheless, it is clear that the 'Ibsen cult' was that of a small minority. Indeed, few Canadians gave much thought to the matters which preoccupied Freud, Weber, James, and others who seem to us today to have been the giants of the age. Some Canadians knew about Freud, but most lacked the educational background to understand what he said even if they had heard his name. The universities did have some notable thinkers who engaged in lively debate about subjects such as idealism and empiricism. University intellectuals such as Adam Shortt of Queen's University, Maurice Hutton of the University of Toronto, and Sir Andrew Macphail acquired an audience among middle-class Canadians for their strong views about Canadian public life. Undoubtedly they left their mark on their students as well.[6] But students were few.

Universities continued to be insignificant, except to their members. In 1901, fewer than 7000 Canadians attended the country's thirteen universities, at a time when over a million were enrolled in the nation's schools. Most university teachers taught 'practical' subjects such as medicine, which trained students for a specific career. Even within arts faculties, the teaching of subjects such as philosophy was often directed towards the student's vocational aims – the ministry, for example. Only a minority of students attended 'secular' institutions, such as the University of Toronto, and even

5 Quotation is from Murray Edwards, *A Stage in Our Past: English-Language Theatre in Eastern Canada from the 1790s to 1914* (Toronto 1968), 67. For the reception of Shaw see ibid., 73ff. See also Jean Beraud, *350 ans de Théâtre au Canada Français* (Ottawa 1958). Other plays presented in the 1903-4 season in Winnipeg were *Sherlock Holmes, The New Dominion, Human Hearts, Katherine and Petruchio, Twelfth Night, Hamlet, The Merchant of Venice, Living Canada,* and *East Lynne.*

6 A good study of intellectuals of the time is S.E.D. Shortt, *The Search for an Ideal: Six Canadian Intellectuals and Their Convictions in an Age of Transition 1890-1930* (Toronto 1976).

Toronto incorporated five semi-autonomous church-related colleges in its federal structure.

When the brilliant young French sociologist André Siegfried evaluated Canada's educational system in 1906, he concluded that 'disinterested study for study's sake can scarcely exist in Canada, not because Canadians are incapable of it but because they cannot afford to devote several years of their life to the acquisition of a culture which can be of no immediate use to them.' In French Canada, the university was essentially a part of the Roman Catholic church and thus devoted to its purposes. Siegfried found Laval University an institution of great charm, but one whose charm lay in its isolation from modern society. To understand Laval and its purpose, he wrote: 'You must have made your way along its dark interminable corridors, lit up here and there by narrow windows. You must have seen passing through its ante-chambers and sombre, old world classrooms the long processions of clerical-looking students, in their curious old-fashioned uniforms – long blue frock-coats with emerald-green scarves. Above all, you must have conversed in their neat and cosy little cell-like studies with the clerical masters themselves, so French in their utterance and yet so far removed from the Catholicity of our present-day France.'[7] Siegfried's account is, of course, almost unrecognizable in terms of the institution still called Laval today.

The English-Canadian universities were also deeply influenced by religious tradition and practice, certainly far more so than the rapidly developing university system in the United States. Sports and the sports hero had already taken a large place on the campuses of Toronto and McGill, and 'college life' with its fraternities, parties, social rituals, and experimentation did exist for a few young Canadians in the early years of the century. Nevertheless, the Canadian student who left Dalhousie, Toronto, McGill, or Western University for Oxford, Cambridge, or Harvard was most often overwhelmed by the size, breadth, and intellectual scope of such institutions. This remained so through the First World War. In the academic year 1918-19, for example, Dalhousie had only twenty-seven staff members in the faculty of arts and science (compared to thirty-one full and part-time teachers in medicine and thirteen in dentistry); Toronto had only 213 in arts and science (compared to 193 in medicine), and the relatively new University of Alberta had thirty-two in arts and science (compared to twelve in medicine, twenty-six in engineering, and nineteen in household science).[8] The bent remained practical.

7 André Siegfried, *The Race Question in Canada* (New York 1907), 92
8 Statistics from Census of Canada, 1901-21, and from *The Canada Year Book 1919* (Ottawa 1920), 150-1

Nevertheless, the conditions for change had become firmly established. Between 1900 and 1920 more Canadians spent more time in school. In 1901 there were 18,472 schools in the dominion, a figure which increased to 24,883 in 1911 and 31,814 in 1920. The number of students increased from 1,062,527 in 1901 to 1,350,821 in 1911, and to 1,804,680 by 1920. Urban Canadian children tended to stay longer in school, and the school was called upon to serve more purposes. In these two decades, the training of teachers had become much more sophisticated. Indeed, teacher education had become a discipline in itself, one influenced by the ideas of Froebel about the growth of a child and the impact of environment, and by the concepts of John Dewey about the necessary link between democratic citizenship and education. Education became increasingly standardized, and the curriculum at the elementary and secondary level was directed towards the needs of a modern society: industrial arts, household science, health studies, and social studies all made their ways into the curriculum. Not all Canadian schools experienced these changes – in Quebec and rural Canada there were notable exceptions – but generally the conception of a child as a special being to be nurtured and tended had taken solid root. Most Canadian children in 1920 lived and learned in a different way from their parents. The modern child, with all its hopes and flaws, had come to Canada.[9]

Yet in spite of such changes, few observers at the end of the First World War would have claimed that Canada's schools were places of joy and liberation – much less that they should be or even could be. Admittedly, in some provinces the high school curricula contained carefully metered doses of such new and practical subjects as 'manual training,' health, and civics. There were the beginnings of parallel secondary school streams which aimed to produce skilled technicians, secretaries, and commercial clerks – fodder for growing service occupations and the repair shops of the automobile age. Here and there could be found the beginnings of specialized secondary education in such areas as agriculture, mining, and household management. But for most of Canada's pupils, most of the time, the subject matter was traditional and solid, while the pedagogical methods were equally so. Things could hardly have been different: most teachers had been sketchily trained, and it was still common for woman teachers to abandon teaching for marriage after only a few years. Teaching was a path not only towards marriage but higher social status, yet it was far from being a high-status occupation. Furthermore, in all parts of Canada the schools, whether 'public' or 'separate,' 'Catholic' or 'Protestant,' were still seen as extensions and reinforcers of traditional values and folkways. If joy and liberation were to be

9   Much of this discussion is based upon Neil Sutherland's *Children in English-Canadian Society.*

sought at all – a matter about which most Canadians were still highly uncertain – they would have to be found elsewhere, and in the all-too-limited spare time.

There was not much spare time but more than for the previous generation – at least in peacetime. This growth in leisure time, along with lengthened school years, was one of many reasons for the growth of spectator sports. Another important reason was the increase in the number of sports pages in Canadian newspapers. The latest hockey games in Ottawa, Montreal, Toronto, or New York were breathlessly reported in the daily newspapers. Baseball had far overwhelmed lacrosse and cricket as Canada's summer sport, and a few Canadians even made it to the 'big leagues' in the United States. In schools, 'physical education' was much encouraged, and a 'sound body' came to mean more than moral purity. Every small town had its teams which were loudly cheered. Local businesses provided jobs with free time so that local athletes could exhibit their prowess often and widely. Professional sports in Canada were in their infancy, although in hockey, professionalism was arriving quickly. Some Canadians, while demonstrating their great athletic talents, were also showing that sports brought acclaim and financial rewards. A Canadian, Tommy Burns, was briefly the heavyweight champion of the world. The black Maritimer, Sam Langford, was toasted throughout North America as 'the best fighter pound for pound' in history. Tom Longboat, the outstanding runner, reaped few financial rewards, but he was one of the best-known Canadians of the age. And Canadian hockey players like Cyclone Taylor and Frank Nighbor were commonly agreed to be the world's best. As in so many other Canadian affairs, the local interest was giving way to national and even international sporting interests.

In the 1920s and thereafter, Canadian society changed much more quickly, and more dramatically, than in the preceding twenty years. Education produced a definite effect not only on skill levels and literacy but on attitudes and values, perhaps speeding that secularization of culture which had made little headway by 1920. After all, in prewar cultural life the influence of religion in the countryside, as in cities and towns, had been profound. The churches, for adult Canadians, continued and reinforced what the schools had begun; Bible classes, Sunday schools, chatecetical and devotional exercises, volunteer welfare work, church socials, and unbelievably lengthy sermons filled the leisure hours of most Canadians before 1914. This pattern did not vanish all at once, even though by 1920 it was visibly retreating. Before 1914, few doubted that the churches could properly censor other forms of culture, and their efforts at information control were successful to a degree that later generations would find surprising. Few observers thought it odd that clergymen like Gordon would write sermons in novel form – and that such novelized sermons would be best sellers.

These patterns and habits would not long survive the end of the Great War. The new secularizing ideas may have affected those few thousand Canadians who read at all widely; surely they cannot have affected the masses. The old patterns broke down after the war for many reasons, and these are only dimly understood. One possibility, of course, is that, at least in English Canada, people increasingly came to find the old ways boring. Certainly after 1920 more leisure, more individualism, and new competition from movies, radio, and popular sport would all change the ways in which Canadians lived and learned. Hand in hand with the new secularism would come a new hedonism, even though neither would triumph fully for many decades.

12

The Politics of the 1920s

For many, 1919 is the beginning of our times, a year that contains many familiar scenes for modern Canadians. John Alcock and Arthur Brown made the first transatlantic flight from Newfoundland to Galway. Ernest Rutherford, once a McGill physicist, achieved the first artificial transmutation of an element, an important step towards splitting the atom. In Paris at the Peace Conference, there were buoyant hopes for a new world order based upon liberal democracy. Yet the world was to lurch into the international uncertainty and conflict that has marked it since that time. That uncertainty was assured by Lenin's success in consolidating his revolution in Russia, a revolution which was the ultimate repudiation of liberal democracy and which, in Winston Churchill's shrewd judgment, was a spectre looming over statesmen's deliberations to create a more ordered world. Lenin's anger had found its echoes at Winnipeg's Portage and Main streets. But by the end of the year, that intersection which had been filled with revolutionaries in June, and with horse-drawn vehicles a decade earlier, bustled with automobile traffic. There had been only 69,598 cars in 1914; there were 341,316 in 1919.[1] Far away on a south sea island, scientists proved Einstein's theory of relativity. In Toronto, Ernest Hemingway, aged twenty, was about to join the Toronto *Star*. In the United States the first translation of Freud's lectures on psychoanalysis was being prepared, and a young writer, Scott Fitzgerald, was completing his first novel, *This Side of Paradise,* which, on its appearance in 1920, made him the muse of the Jazz Age: 'Here was a new generation, shouting the old cries, learning the old creeds, through a revery of long days and nights; destined finally to go out into that dirty gray turmoil to follow love and pride; a new generation dedicated more than the last to the fear of poverty and the worship of success; grown up to find all Gods

1 *Canada Year Book 1919* (Ottawa 1920), 438

dead, all wars fought, all faiths in man shaken.'[2] There were, however, other voices.

In 1919 William Lyon Mackenzie King became the leader of Canada's Liberal party. On that occasion in 1919, he wrote: 'The majority was better than I had anticipated. I was too heavy of heart and soul to appreciate the tumult of applause, my thoughts were of dear mother & father & little Bell all of whom I felt to be very close to me, of grandfather & and Sir Wilfrid also. I thought: it is right, it is the call of duty. I have sought nothing, it has come. It has come from God. The dear loved ones know and are about, they are alive and with me in this great everlasting Now and Here. It is to His work I am called, and to it I dedicate my life.'[3] Honouring his father and mother, worshipping his God, believing in life after death, conscious of civic duty, Victorian in his sentimentality and his prose, King is thoroughly pre-Freudian in tone and seemingly distant from those currents that flowed strongly through the war years and created the modern temper. The three decades after 1919 were, in Canada, the age of Mackenzie King.

In fact, King had early reached a compromise with a secular and techno-logical age, and he would live through his age much more easily than those who followed Fitzgerald's siren in the 1920s or those who harkened to Mos-cow in 1919 or later. While many others believed that the war had destroyed a civilization and set off a political and cultural revolution – such a belief came easily in 1919 both to those who supported and those who opposed such a revolution – King saw that there was much that had endured the del-uge. In a sense King represented to Canada what 'Silent Cal' (Calvin Cool-idge) was to the United States, an opportunity, in Walter Lippmann's words, 'to praise the classic virtues, while continuing to enjoy all the modern con-veniences.' Thus as Canadians bought Model-T Fords and all kinds of new consumer goods, and went to the latest Mary Pickford movie, they gained security from the dull, plump, balding, and Godfearing Mackenzie King. It was, as Lippmann said, a Puritanism deluxe.

King could be many things to different people because he was many dif-ferent things. He was deeply religious; in his lifetime he probably read more books on religion than on any other subject. He prayed and read the Bible daily in the fashion of the Victorian middle class. He shunned movies in fav-our of the reading aloud of the classics, usually with a female friend whose first name he used only after months of acquaintance. He treated his staff as Mr Scrooge treated Bob Cratchit, and his parsimony kept him from enjoy-ing the consumer delights which the twenties offered in abundance. But then

2 F. Scott Fitzgerald, *This Side of Paradise* (New York 1920), 282
3 King Diary, as quoted in C.P. Stacey, *A Very Double Life* (Toronto 1976), 157. King, in fact, read Freud on the interpretation of dreams in 1920.

King had a car, a chauffeur, and a cook. Towards the end of his life he installed a private elevator in his house. He owned a radio, even if his preferred use for it was to listen to election results. Like his father, he read widely – more so than any other Canadian prime minister. Still, he knew and cared little about the ideologies which infected so many Europeans and North Americans in the postwar period. Yet in many ways he was more 'modern' than nearly all of his contemporary Canadians. In an age which valued education, his credentials were impeccable: law and political economy at the universities of Toronto, Chicago, and Harvard. His range of acquaintance was extraordinary, and he had a knack for finding those who would count most in the future: Ramsay Macdonald, the first Labour prime minister of Britain, John D. Rockefeller Jr, and Ernest Lapointe of Quebec are a few of many examples which could be given. At university he chose a field of study which looked to the future, industrial relations, and in this area he was soon acknowledged as an international expert. Unlike most Canadians who undertook academic graduate work, King chose the United States rather than the customary precincts of Oxford and Cambridge. This choice was also wise because the twentieth century was to be Canada's American century. King fitted in well, and he moved easily over the forty-ninth parallel. Indeed, his work for American corporations probably makes him the Canadian who has had the greatest influence upon the United States. That would have been true if he had never become Canada's prime minister; in fact, the influence would probably have been much greater. King had weight in Cambridge, Massachusetts, and in America's boardrooms. Both places contained many people who were, like King, a blend of the modern and the Victorian, that blend which later critics of King find difficult to understand and easy to ridicule. Harvard's greatest president and King's mentor, Charles Eliot, became president of the American Association for the Advancement of Science in the same year (1914) that he published a book on modern Christianity in which he looked forward to the Christianization of the world and the rapid conversion of all heathen. King's great friend, the business leader John D. Rockefeller Jr, spent a large amount from his considerable fortune erecting a Gothic skyscraper in New York, Riverside Church, into whose portals were carved the images of Darwin and Einstein. The church endures as a monument to the paradox and confusion of the times. King's constructions were more modest – pseudo-Gothic ruins on the lawns of his estate at Kingsmere. But he was a part of these times, as was his sentimental, Victorian puritanism, his spiritualism, and his intellectual confusion. They were all as much a part of the 1920s as flappers, movies, and bathtub gin; for most North Americans they were the stuff of daily life.

The three youngish Canadians who led their parties in the 1921 general election, Tom Crerar of the Progressives, Arthur Meighen of the Conservatives, and Mackenzie King of the Liberals, were similar in many respects. They were all Presbyterians born in Ontario and, despite their relative youth (Crerar was born in 1867, King and Meighen in 1874), none had served in the First World War. Meighen and Crerar had supported conscription and been colleagues in the Union government which, it seems probable, King would have joined at one point had anyone asked. The fact that he did not join the Unionists and that he ran as a Laurier Liberal in the 1917 election was the most important factor in King's victory at the Liberal convention in 1919. All three were deeply affected by the events of 1919, a year in which King and Crerar became party leaders and in which Meighen made clear his leadership intentions which were fulfilled the following summer. Their response to the labour troubles and political turmoil of 1919 differed in many ways, but once again they had significant similarities.

Building upon his work in labour relations and reflecting the social reform currents which were becoming strong in pre-1917 English-Canadian Liberalism, King used the 1919 Liberal convention as a platform for a reformist Liberal program. This program promised health insurance, old-age pensions, and other social insurance schemes. In an attempt to regain western Canadian support, the Liberals promised tariff reform. King was careful, however, to avoid any commitment to some of the political reforms such as referenda and proportional representation which the west favoured but he feared. Tom Crerar, too, was suspicious of some of the schemes of his fellow Progressives. For that reason, he tended to focus upon the tariff once he became Progressive leader in 1920. To Arthur Meighen, the tariff was the Conservatives' strongest issue: the Liberals and Progressives, Meighen charged, were threatening the bases of Canadian nationhood by attacking the protective tariff. As a campaign issue, the tariff had worked very well for Borden and Macdonald. Meighen hoped it could be the political elixir for a tired government once again.

The tariff became the major issue in the general election on 6 December 1921 because the three party leaders preferred the safety which that familiar issue provided. The campaign showed that after the helter-skelter war years, Canadians wanted security and calm. It is fashionable to emphasize how much the war changed Canada, but it must not be forgotten how much remained the same and how much the war reinforced tendencies and beliefs which obtained in prewar days. Laurier, for example, had established a Liberal pre-eminence in French Canada. The war strengthened this affinity, and in 1921 the Progressives and the Tories put forward almost no challenge to the Liberals in French Canada. The result was an overwhelming Liberal vote in French Canadian constituencies and an election victory for Mackenzie King. (See Appendix 1.)

Laurier's legacy to King had been of immeasurable value to the Liberals as French Canadians not only in Quebec but also in New Brunswick, Ontario, and Manitoba cast their ballots. The strong Liberal vote in the Maritimes came from that region's sense that the benefits of the war which it had supported had flowed mostly to other areas. The Union government and its Conservative successor got the blame. In Ontario the 'British' vote tended to remain with the Conservatives, but the Progressives made strong inroads in rural areas. The fact that the United Farmers of Ontario had shown that farm governments did not lead to miraculous transformations probably hurt the Progressive cause. The western results are deceptive. Overall, they reveal that the war had its greatest political impact on the west and that the traditional two-party system had been shattered. The labour vote was high, and it is hardly surprising that the west was the birthplace of Canadian socialism and its area of most consistent support. The Conservatives continued to do well among the British in British Columbia and elsewhere. The Progressives received weak support in western cities, but they swept through rural areas. They also did surprisingly well in ethnic areas, an indication that ethnic westerners blamed the Liberal Unionists as much as the Conservatives for the War-time Elections Act and sundry other wrongs done to them. The Liberals, however, might have done better in ethnic areas and in the west generally had they made a more intense effort. King's strategy was to leave the attack on the Progressives to the Tories and to emphasize those things that the Progressives shared with the Liberals. The Liberals thus did poorly in the west in 1921, but in the long run they did better than either the Tories and the Progressives. It was the right strategy.

Even before the election results were announced, King had begun to woo the Progressives. Some were very susceptible to his entreaties. Crerar himself seemed to be attracted by the thought of sharing power. He had been in office; he knew the charms of cabinet position. Nevertheless, the Progressives had fought a hard campaign against the traditional parties and their ways. To accept office so quickly would have been a shock to many supporters and would probably have caused a revolt within the party. The Progressives thus maintained their post-election purity, but King had seen the Liberal twinkle in Crerar's eyes and set out to seduce him and those who thought like him.

Crerar was wise in resisting King in the winter of 1921, but King was also fortunate that Crerar did not join his government. The admission of Crerar would have frightened some Liberals, especially Quebec Liberals, who strongly opposed Progressive policy in the area of the tariff and economic reform. The former premier of Quebec, Sir Lomer Gouin, and the former Quebec treasurer, Walter Mitchell, were strongly opposed to tariff changes and alteration of economic policy. Gouin was a member of King's cabinet as was another protectionist, W.S. Fielding, King's major opponent at the 1919 leadership convention. Both were old men, and King could afford to wait. In December 1923 Fielding had a stroke, and Gouin left the government because of poor health. Having lost an important by-election in Nova Scotia the same month, King saw that he had both the need and the opportunity to woo the Progressives more openly and to choose his own leaders in Quebec.

To fill Gouin's Justice portfolio, King turned to Ernest Lapointe, who, unlike Gouin, had few ties to Montreal business interests but possessed a reputation as a solid defender of French-Canadian rights. Lapointe simultaneously became King's Quebec lieutenant. The choice was probably the most important and the best of King's career. Lapointe combined loyalty, political savoir faire, and oratorical flair in equal measure. Until his lieutenant's death in 1941, King's Quebec flank was secure.

Lapointe supported King's attempt to concoct stronger links with the Progressives, and in early 1924 King tried once more to lure Crerar, who had given up the leadership of his fractious party to Robert Forke. Crerar, however, asked too much. King instead took the advice of the Liberal premier of Saskatchewan, Charles Dunning, who advocated the wooing of the Progressives through policy rather than personnel. In the 1924 Speech from the Throne King announced tax reductions and a lower tariff on many items, in particular on implements of production in primary industries. The Progressives voted with the Liberals on the Address. It was, King noted in his diary, 'a great victory a splendid beginning.' He was celebrating too soon.

The Progressives began to fall apart too rapidly for any leader to control. The budget debate revealed how deeply split the party was between the moderates who wanted to align more closely with the Liberals and the radicals who were anxious to maintain a separate identity. In 1924 ten of the radical Progressives joined with the two-member Labour group led by J.S. Woodsworth to form the so-called Ginger Group. The remaining Progressives, with the parliamentary term beyond the half-way point, hesitated to act at all. King's Liberals also lost ground when King failed to move beyond the tariff reforms of 1924. Those reforms were not enough to satisfy the farmers. At the same time, King's concentration upon the western Progressives led him to ignore the complaints about discrimination which emanated from the Maritimes, complaints which the Conservative party was effectively exploiting in provincial politics. The choices seemed too difficult to make, and the result was inaction. King's biographer Blair Neatby describes the situation in early 1925: 'The Cabinet marked time on the Hudson Bay Railway and its immigration policy. It moved slowly towards an agreement with Alberta on the return of natural resources. It took no steps to cope with the serious problem of mounting railway deficits, except to make them larger through its action on freight rates. It did show a sort of negative virtue in refusing to bring about railway amalgamation ... There was nothing in all this to compensate for the blunders of the session.'[4] There was nothing to save the government.

In the summer of 1925 the Nova Scotia Conservatives under E.N. Rhodes broke the forty-three-year-old Liberal hold on the province. Rhodes had taken an outspoken Maritime Rights stand, and the federal Conservatives adopted the stand for the election campaign in the fall. In Ontario, the Liberals' attention to the west had lost some support as had the tariff reforms which the Liberals had undertaken or seemed likely to undertake. The Ontario Liberals, like their Nova Scotian counterparts, had suffered a drubbing at the hands of the local Conservatives, who replaced the United Farmers in government in 1923. The Progressives, as we have seen, had not gelled as a party. The results reflected the national confusion. The Conservatives had a decisive lead in the popular vote, but the Liberals still had power. The Progressives had lost much support, but they controlled the balance of power. They were better disposed towards the Liberals than towards the Tories who, in the campaign, had upheld the importance of the tariff. Thus Mackenzie King clung to office.

The Liberals scrambled to find security in their minority position. They quickly moved to win back Maritime support with the appointment of the Royal Commission on Maritimes Claims (The Duncan Commission). King continued to push the remaining Progressives towards affiliation with the Liberals, and the election results had made some Progressives, although not the Ginger Group, sympathetic to King's entreaties. At first, all went well. The first major blunder was Arthur Meighen's. Seeking to improve his standing among French Canadians and English-Canadian nationalists, Meighen gave a speech in Hamilton in which he said he believed that the Canadian people must approve of any entry into a British war through a general election. Compared to Meighen's declaration at the time of the Chanak Crisis – 'Ready, aye ready' – this statement was both confusing and contradictory. His remarks outraged some Ontario Tories including Premier Howard Ferguson. King had won some time thanks to his opponent's blunder.

When the session met in January 1926, King had the support of enough Progressives to sustain his government. He had won over the two Labour

4 H.B. Neatby, *William Lyon Mackenzie King, 1923-1932: The Lonely Heights* (Toronto 1963), 58-9

members, J.S. Woodsworth and Abraham Heaps, with a promise that he would introduce an old-age pension. By early May, the government's majority on votes was regularly over ten in number. In mid-June, however, the situation suddenly changed with the report of the Special Committee on the Department of Customs and Excise.

The department reeked of alcoholic fumes. The report was full of tales of smuggled cars stuffed with liquor and of politicians and officials benefiting from these hijinks. The carefully constructed alliance with some of the Progressives began to come apart. Facing the possibility of a defeat in the House of Commons, a defeat that would have meant a Meighen government, King asked Governor General Lord Byng for a dissolution of Parliament. Byng refused. Byng's decision led to one of the greatest controversies in Canadian political history, one where right and wrong are still unclear to constitutional scholars and historians. Byng's refusal angered King, who argued that a democratically elected leader had the right to a dissolution. In the circumstances, however, King had to resign. Byng asked Meighen to form a government, and he eagerly accepted the request.

Meighen was too eager. He took power at a time when many Canadians were disgusted by the chicanery of the Liberals as revealed in the customs scandal. Meighen's ability to use this mood for his party's benefit was seriously hurt by his decision to appoint seven ministers without portfolio in order that these ministers would not have to resign their seats and seek re-election as new ministers then ordinarily did – a custom dating from the eighteenth century. As acting ministers of departments, however, these men were normal ministers in fact if not in name, and the device seemed cheap and most unconvincing. It made an easy target for King who, by constant repetition, managed to divert attention from the customs problems of the Liberals. Meighen himself could probably have handled King, who was terrified of his rival's sarcasm and oratorical skills, but Meighen was not in the House because he had to resign as soon as he became prime minister. The result was a leaderless Conservative party, thoroughly confused Progressives, and a reinvigorated Liberal party.

Meighen believed he could sway enough Progressives to win votes until he could bring the session to the end. But he had not asked the Progressives; neither had Lord Byng.[5] Meighen's government lasted only three days. The

---

5 Current debate on the subject seems to revolve around the question of whether Byng should have ascertained the views of leading Progressives before asking Meighen to form a government. The traditional interpretation which supports Byng's approach is Eugene Forsey, *The Royal Power of Dissolution of Parliament in the British Commonwealth* (Toronto 1968), chapters 5 and 6. See also Neatby, *William Lyon Mackenzie King, 1923-1932*, chapter 8;

House dissolved, and an election was called for 14 September 1926. Mackenzie King was delighted by the extraordinary turn of events. His diary recorded the joy which he carried into the campaign: 'Like Saul I need to see the light. The light has come, has come around me in this crisis. "The God of our fathers hath chosen me" – as he did Saul in the midst of Saul's persecution of the "Just One." I see it all so clearly. From now on, I go forward in the strength of God & his Might and Right to battle as my forefathers battled for the rights of the people – and God's will on earth "even as it is done in Heaven."' The light King saw shone forth from the legacy of William Lyon Mackenzie. He had found an issue that was his own – the suppression of the rights of free-born Canadians by a British governor general. The issue was almost entirely rubbish and rhetoric, but it was effective.

In the 1920s the constitutional advances which had begun with the Paris Peace Conference had made relatively little impression on the public until they were packaged by King and others in nationalistic wrapping. In a period of growing affluence, education, and self-confidence, Canadians were satisfied with the wrappings and did not bother much with the contents of the box, so difficult to understand. For the 1926 campaign King produced the most colourful wrappings for the constitutional package. He denounced the dictatorship of Lord Byng, excoriated the British attempt to dominate Canada's independent political life, and promised to complete the battle his grandfather had begun in 1837. Never had King spoken so forcefully on the hustings. For his part, Meighen found it impossible to skewer King as he had hoped to do. The customs scandal was often forgotten, and the campaign was fought mainly on the ground of King's choosing.

In Ontario and Manitoba, Liberals and the Progressives, who had been frightened by the prospect of a Conservative government which they believed would be unsympathetic to their interests, co-operated in the election. In general, the two parties agreed in those provinces that they would fight Tories, not each other. Liberal-Progressives were nominated in many constituencies, and these members indicated that they would sit with the Liberals. On 26 September, God's will, according to Mackenzie King, was done.

King's strategy of chipping away at the Progressives' unity had paid off. Although the Conservative vote had declined only slightly (from 46.5 per cent to 45.3 per cent), the party had lost seats and the possibility of government because the Progressive vote moved in large part to the Liberals. In Ontario, the Progressives had virtually disappeared, as had the United Farmers of Ontario in provincial politics. The Progressives remained strong in Alberta, where John Brownlee's effective leadership of the United Farm-

and John Thompson with Allan Seager, *Canada 1922-1939: Decades of Discord* (Toronto 1985), 123ff

ers of Alberta was confirmed in the provincial election of 1926. In Manitoba, too, John Bracken's provincial government maintained independence
from the Liberals. Nevertheless, the Progressives were a spent force nationally. The biographer of the party, W.L. Morton, explained well what the
general election of 1926 meant: 'The disruption of the classic parties, begun
by the denial of the sectional demands of the West in 1911, and completed
by the election of 1917, was ended. Two composite, national parties, one in
power and one in opposition, dominated the House. Government once more
rested on the sure foundation of a disciplined party majority. Canadian unity, so severely tried by economic sectionalism and communal hostility, was
renewed on the old basis of sectional compromise, the denial of class differences, and the sovereignty of caucus.'[6] The renewal, however, was temporary, for in the 1930s the ghost of western revolt returned to haunt Canadian
politics once more.

Women's participation in electoral politics, which both opponents and
proponents in prewar days had claimed would transform Canadian political
life, had less impact than was expected. In July 1920 women gained the
right to vote and be elected in federal elections. Many did vote but in a pattern which reflected how men voted. Very few were elected, although Agnes
Macphail, a thirty-one-year-old teacher of remarkable intelligence and political skill, did enter the House of Commons as a Progressive in 1921. It was
fourteen years before she had a female counterpart in the House. Nellie
McClung was elected to the Alberta legislature in 1921, but little of her
wartime feminist agenda was fulfilled. Ironically, mothers' allowances were
the major advance of the 1920s but, as feminist historians have reminded us,
these were a reflection of a maternalist approach to social reform. In the
1920s, Canadian women turned away from public causes towards their private concerns. So did Canadian men.

It was easy to govern Canada between 1926 and 1929. People seemed
bored with politics; there had been too much excitement for too long. Now
there were other opportunities and interests which shunted politics to the
side: movies, automobiles, songs of the jazz age, the stock market, and, now
that prohibition had faded in most areas, the bottle. Affluence bred contentment, and pride in what Canada had accomplished was reflected in the celebrations of Canada's Diamond Jubilee in 1927. The contrast was marked
with the sombre days a decade before, when casualties in Europe and the
conscription crisis at home ended all celebrations of the nation's Golden Jubilee. In 1927, old-age pensions, a product of the political bargaining of
1925-6, began. They were only a first step in building a national social secur-

6   W.L. Morton, *The Progressive Party in Canada* (Toronto 1950), 265

ity system; at the time, however, there was little demand for further steps, although some provinces had already introduced mothers' allowances. Most rejoiced at the apparent recognition that the country was receiving in the British Commonwealth and at the League of Nations. There seemed to be little risk attached to involvement in international affairs, and Ernest Lapointe, who had become King's most trusted political adviser, persuaded King to let Canada become a member of the League Council in 1928. The bitter divisions of the past over foreign policy disappeared in this era of good international feelings.

The feelings would not last, but for those who had them in the late 1920s they were a memory which would endure through the hard times which followed.

13

The Economy in the 1920s

In the shorthand with which the popular mind replaces thought and evidence, the 1920s are usually called 'roaring.' In Canada, 'roaring' does not seem very apposite, at least with respect to the economy. By 1921 the heroic days of Canadian economic development seemed to be over. The west was settled, more or less. The railways were built – all too many of them. In central Canada the economic balance had already shifted decisively from countryside to town, and from agriculture to industry; the nation's cities and towns now possessed a wide range of sophisticated industries, serving households, other domestic manufacturers, and foreign markets, and exploiting the remarkable technological development which had been so marked a feature of Western civilization since the 1870s. This is not to say that nothing interesting happened in Canada during the 1920s. Agriculture continued to grow and change. A few new industries appeared, and some others grew with remarkable speed, especially during the prosperous years of the middle and late 1920s. Retailing was transformed, as Eaton's became a chain and Loblaws, Dominion, A&P, Safeway, and Piggly Wiggly scattered chain grocery stores across the land. Movies and radio spread apace. But compared with the years from the mid-1890s to 1914, the industrial economy grew more slowly and more predictably, with far fewer surprises. As for agriculture, the 1920s saw no renewal of the mass immigration and extensive settlement which had marked the Great Boom. The decade saw the introduction of Canada's first old-age pensions, a good deal of industrial consolidation, and extensive American direct investment, especially in mining and manufacturing. One bank collapsed. The nation re-established the gold standard, then abandoned it. The labour movement tried, with little success, to unionize Canada's wage earners and to raise their political consciousness.

MIGRATION IN THE 1920s

The First World War interrupted the transatlantic flow of migrants, but once the war was over the influx began again. The annual numbers were much smaller during the 1920s than in the immediate prewar years. Even so, from 1919 through 1930 1.2 million immigrants arrived at Canada's ocean ports, and total immigration, including movement from the United States, was 1.5 million. As before, of course, many of these immigrants were 'in transit' to the United States, and many native-born Canadians were emigrating at the same time. Net migration, or immigration minus emigration, was quite small – only 229,000 from 1921 to 1931. From 1919 to 1930 Canada's population grew from 8.3 million to 10.2 million, and from 1921 to 1931, by 1.6 million. Thus, net immigration accounted for only 14 per cent of the population growth during the Roaring Twenties – far less than in the years between 1900 and 1914.

The composition of the immigrants was much the same as before 1914, and their patterns of settlement had changed little. Some Ukrainians, however, were now turning up in the cities, and there were more temporary migrants who spent some months or years in industrial work, then went home again. Altogether, between 1919 and 1930, 711,000 immigrants came from the British Isles (including 'other' British before 1926); but only 26,000 arrived from France, and 53,000 were identified as Jewish. There were 76,000 immigrants from the USSR, and 52,000 from Poland. As the Ukrainians were now partly in the Soviet Union and partly in the new Republic of Poland, these figures include the renewed Ukrainian immigration of the 1920s, but they also include Russian-speakers, Poles, and perhaps some Jews as well. There were only 30,000 Italian immigrants, and 7000 from elsewhere in southern Europe and the Mediterranean basin. As for immigrants from Africa and Asia, these were proportionately even fewer than before 1914 – 13,000 from China and Japan, and 7000 from elsewhere in Asia, Africa, the Caribbean, and Latin America.[1]

But the arrivals of the earlier years were now reproducing, and the ethnic composition of the population continued its drift away from 'Anglo-Saxon dominance.' The reduction in net immigration did little to revive francophone hopes and anglophone fears with respect to a 'revenge of the cradle.' In 1931, 52 per cent of Canada's population came from the British Isles – a decline of 2.5 percentage points in a decade. But the proportion of ethnic French had only risen from 27.9 per cent to 28.2 per cent, and the propor-

1   All the figures in this paragraph include arrivals by land and sea in and after 1926. American immigrants are allocated by ethnic origin, and do not appear separately.

tion of 'others' had gone up from 16.7 per cent to 19.9 per cent. In 1931, as in 1921 and 1911, 78 per cent of Canada's population had been born in the dominion.

Throughout the 1920s the Canadian government preference was clear: would-be farmers, agricultural workers, and domestic servants were welcome, but other kinds of workers much less so; migrants from Britain, France, and northern and north-western Europe were far more welcome than those from elsewhere in Europe; would-be migrants from Asia and Africa were not welcome at all. With respect to ethnic origin, the figures clearly reflect these preferences. The occupational mix, however, does not. Only half a million immigrants – just one-third of the total – said they were farmers or farm labourers. Naturally, many of these people did not stay on the farms, and many of them probably never arrived on farms. As for female domestic servants, from 1919 through 1930 Canada received 136,000 such persons – less than 10 per cent of total immigration. In all, then, slightly under 40 per cent of the immigrants even claimed to be members of the 'preferred occupations.'

From 1918 until 1923 the dominion government made little active effort to encourage immigration, even from the 'preferred areas,' but from 1923 until early 1930 there was active recruitment and encouragement not only in Britain but in continental Europe as well. Even though there were no formal quotas, and nothing like the 'point system' of the 1970s and 1980s, there is little doubt that the immigration was 'managed' to some extent. However, throughout these years, immigration from Britain, the United States, and the white dominions was essentially unregulated and uncontrolled. As for other immigrants, in 1921 a new rule was devised: they would all need visas, which they would have to obtain overseas. Little is known about the bases on which these visas were awarded or denied.

There were new rules from time to time. In 1919 the landing money was raised to $250, although for farm workers, domestic servants, and close relatives of Canadian residents it was not compulsory. Enemy aliens were excluded from 1918 until 1923, and Mennonites, Hutterites, and Doukhobors, from 1918 to 1922. From 1919 to 1928 alien strike leaders were subject to deportation. After 1919, alcoholics, conspirators, and illiterates were denied entry. In 1923 a new Chinese Immigration Act cut off such migration almost completely. The Japanese government, meanwhile, continued to restrict emigration to Canada, in accord with the agreement of 1908. By 1927 the list of 'prohibited classes' had grown to include the tubercular, feebleminded, imbecilic, epileptic, insane, alcoholic, female prostitute or male pimp, beggar, vagrant, dumb, blind, or physically defective, anarchist, spy, treasonous, most of the adult illiterate, and the 'charity-aided immigrants and persons who are likely to become public charges.'[2]

Besides the new rules, there were new initiatives. These followed on developments in the United Kingdom, where the government was now eager to encourage emigration, especially to white dominions such as Canada. Thus Ottawa was able to experiment with new means by which the 'right sort of migrant' could be assisted. And London, for the first time in almost a hundred years, was willing to pay through an assisted emigration plan which brought some agricultural immigrants to Canada.[3]

FARMS AND FACTORIES

The 1920s were years of declining prices and rising real wage rates. Having fallen by one-third between 1920 and 1922, the wholesale price index rose about 3 per cent in 1922-5, only to drift downward once again, so that in 1929 almost all wholesale prices were very much lower than they had been in 1921. Cost-of-living indices fell less dramatically, but they showed the same general tendency. Except in coal-mining, wage rates either rose a little or remained more or less stable, so that real wage rates must have risen for the vast majority of Canada's wage earners. For some consumer durable goods, such as cars and electrical appliances, the price declines were dramatic, helping to explain the rapid growth of production in such industries. Among farmers, however, because so many had incurred debts on the basis of high prices during 1916-19, price declines could mean trouble, even when the costs of farm operation fell more or less in step with farm-gate prices. As prices went down, so the real burden of the debt went up. For some farmers, the net result left them better off in 1929 than in 1921; for others, the reverse was true.

It is not surprising that farmers asked for cheap or subsidized credit, that the dominion responded, and that many provincial governments did the same. In 1921, for instance, Ontario set up a network of government savings offices to garner funds from the public, and arranged to lend farmers whatever the public deposited. Other provinces were less ingenious but equally forthcoming.

The failure of the Home Bank in 1923 was of little economic significance to the nation as a whole. But Home Bank shares and deposits were especially widespread on the prairies. The collapse, Canada's last bank failure until 1985, increased the pressure on western farmers.

2 *Canada Year Book 1927-8* (Ottawa 1928), 198
3 For more detail see Ian Drummond, *British Economic Policy and the Empire, 1919-1939* (London 1972), and *Imperial Economic Policy, 1917-1939* (London 1974).

Uncertain though agriculture's circumstances might be, the agricultural population was still rising. In 1911, 934,000 people had been engaged in agricultural pursuits; in 1921 there were just over one million, and in 1931, 1,127,682 – 29 per cent of the nation's gainful workers, as against 40 per cent in 1901. The number of occupied farms was increasing as well: in 1931 there were 728,623, an increase of 2.5 per cent since 1921, and of 6.9 per cent since 1911. Only in Ontario and the Maritime provinces was the number of farms going down, while on the prairies the number of occupied farms went up by 13 per cent during the 1920s. By 1931 almost one-third of Canada's farm population lived on the prairies, another 25 per cent in Ontario, and 24 per cent in Quebec. In spite of its increasing industrialization, and in spite of Ontario's rural depopulation, central Canada remained as it had always been – much the most populous and productive agricultural region in the dominion. On the prairies, however, the cultivated area was still increasing quite rapidly – by 24 per cent during the 1920s – while in Ontario and Quebec the area under crops increased by only 2.3 per cent during that decade, and the area of improved pasture in central Canada actually decreased.

No important agricultural product would match the prices of 1918-20 until the Second World War, or afterwards. The price of wheat rose almost 50 per cent between 1923 and 1925, but then it dribbled downward once more, ending the decade, in 1929, below the 1921 level. However, wheat production rose so far and so fast that total receipts increased from 1921-2 to 1928-9 even though prices were not buoyant. As farm costs drifted downward, the real incomes of wheat farmers rose quite considerably during the decade. Although there was a crop failure in 1924-5, when yields fell to 11.9 bushels per acre, the general tendency was strongly upward. Gross revenue from wheat production rose 80 per cent; because farm costs were falling gently, the purchasing power of the wheat crop rose 91.5 per cent, largely because yields were moving perceptibly higher. The average real income per occupied wheat farm was a good deal higher in 1928-9 than it had been in 1921-2; debts, presumably, became easier to manage. It is not surprising, therefore, that on the prairies the number of horses began to decrease, while the number of tractors rose from 38,400 in 1921 to 85,100 in 1930 and the number of prairie motor vehicles went up from 141,400 to 307,100.

Prairie farmers were annoyed when wheat prices drifted downward. In the price decline of 1921-2, farmers pressed for the re-establishment of the Canadian Wheat Board, which had marketed their crops at the end of the war. Regrettably for them, it appeared that in peacetime the dominion had no power to market prairie wheat. Therefore, in 1922-3 Ottawa sponsored a project for a dominion-provincial wheat marketing board in which the two levels of government would co-operate. These efforts came to naught. During 1923 the farmers of each wheat province set up a 'voluntary contract pool organized on a provincial basis, with one central selling agency.'[4] Farmers were invited to sign contracts with their pools, delivering all their crops to the pools in exchange for cash advances, with the final proceeds to be divided among farmers in proportion to their imput. The private grain trade also continued, vilified though it generally was.

The pool plan was simple. Speculation and private profit would be eliminated from wheat marketing and farmers would gain the full return from their crops, whether sold in Canada or abroad. Supported by credits from the banks, the pools would be able to hold inventories and manage sales so as to maximize the returns to the farmers. No more would temporary wheat gluts force prices down.

There was a limit to what the pools could do, as their managers discovered in the crop year 1929-30. Export prices were then falling fast, and the Canadian pools did not have enough power over the international market to support the export price by holding grain off the market. Having borrowed from the banks so as to make advance payments to farmers, by February 1930 the pools found that the market value of the wheat they held did not equal the amount they owed the banks. They were obliged to ask the provincial governments to guarantee their borrowings.

Thus the Depression came to the prairies. Farmers bought less. Tractor sales fell from 17,100 in 1928 to 9000 in 1930, and to 787 in 1931. Few new autos were bought. Farmers battened down the hatches, preparing for storm. Neither they nor anyone else realized that the storm would be a hurricane.

Important though prairie agriculture had become, the agriculture of central Canada remained almost as important. In 1929 prairie farmers earned $250 million from their farming operations, while the farmers of Ontario and Quebec earned $240 million, even though the farm area was far larger on the prairies – in 1931, 40 million acres of improved land as against 16 million. The difference was that in central Canada farmers concentrated on higher-value products, especially livestock, fruit, vegetables, and such special-purpose crops as tobacco. During the 1920s, Quebec farms increased their holdings of most sorts of livestock. In Ontario there was a parallel development, although it was less general, and in both provinces the number of horses was falling steadily, reducing the demand for oats and hay. By 1929 central Canada contained many more milk cows and other cattle, hogs, sheep, lambs, and chickens than the Prairie provinces, which, however, still had more horses. The agriculture of central Canada was continuing the transformation which had begun before 1913, by which it converted itself

4   D.A. Macgibbon, *The Canadian Grain Trade* (Toronto 1932), 69

into a supplier for the region's cities and towns. As for price movements, farm costs were falling relative to the values of meat and dairy products, which were holding steady or even rising a little. Ontario and Quebec farmers, without increasing their holdings of livestock very much, were able to share in the national prosperity, largely because their urban markets were growing.

The development of the manufacturing industry fuelled that urban growth. From 1921 through 1923 manufacturing employment rose 16 per cent, while value added in manufacturing went up by 9 per cent. After a small recession in 1924, expansion was renewed, so that in 1929 there were 666,181 workers in Canada's manufacturing industry as against 441,788 in 1921; value added in manufacturing had risen to $1.7 billion, 64 per cent higher than it had been in 1921. Furthermore, the prices of manufactures almost all fell. The overall fall between 1921 and 1929 may have been as much as 20 per cent. Thus, the real value added in manufacturing may have gone up by as much as 84 per cent, or more, in eight years. And, in 1929, Ontario contributed 51.9 per cent of the value added in manufacturing, while another 29.2 per cent was produced in Quebec; moreover, the two central provinces contained 79.7 per cent of the employment in manufacturing. Admittedly, there was growth and development elsewhere in Canada – iron and steel on Cape Breton; underwear in Truro; sawmilling, smelting, pulp and paper in British Columbia. Nevertheless, overwhelmingly and increasingly, manufacturing was a matter for central Canada, because it was in that region that the great new industries – pulp, paper, cars, rubber, aluminum, electrical equipment and appliances – were concentrated.

Some dramatic changes took place. Canada's output of cars rose from 69,801 in 1918 to 188,721 in 1929, of trucks and buses, from 7,319 to 50,293, and output of rubber tires went from 1,840,000 in 1920 to 4,766,000 in 1929. Canada became an important exporter of cars and parts, second only to the United States. Canadian cars went everywhere in the British Commonwealth, especially to India and to Australia, New Zealand, and South Africa. Output of wood pulp rose from 1,464,000 tons to 4,021,000 tons, while output of newsprint paper rose from 690,000 tons in 1917 to 2,725,000 tons in 1929. The United States was now a really important market for Canadian newsprint, and many Canadian mills were owned by American newspaper publishers. Gasoline output, which came almost entirely from American crude oil, sextupled in a decade. In 1920 Canada produced twenty-one locomotives and 5084 railroad cars, while in 1929 the respective figures were ninety-eight and 13,242. Between 1925 and 1929 the output of radios tripled, and in the period 1921-8 the value of washing-machine production increased more than ten-fold.

From 1921 to 1929 value added in Canadian manufacturing grew by just over 6 per cent per year, while annual employment grew by just over 5 per cent. These were good but not remarkable figures, given that 1921 was a year of deep depression. Comparing the more prosperous year of 1917 with 1929, we find that employment grew very slowly indeed – barely 1 per cent per year – while value added grew at less than 4 per cent per year. In the 1920s, with the exception of knitting mills, the rapidly growing sectors within manufacturing were all connected with the exploitation of the new technologies – rubber products, iron and steel products, transportation equipment, electrical apparatus, non-metallic mineral products, and chemicals. The paper products industries did well, but not quite well enough to match the figures for manufactures as a whole, while the older industries, many of which served the more traditional needs of households, grew much more slowly.

During the 1920s some mining industries did very well indeed. Admittedly there were some disappointments. Iron-ore production fell steadily from 1915 to 1923, when it ended, not to return until 1939. Petroleum production also was falling, having peaked in 1894; only in 1929, thanks to new discoveries in Alberta, did output surpass the levels which the old fields of Ontario had yielded in the 1890s. And the Alberta fields were as yet very small: Canada in 1929 was importing almost thirty times as much crude oil as it produced. Natural gas was as yet of little importance, either in value or in the national energy balance. In 1929 the value of its output was less than $10 million – one-sixth of the value of Canada's coal production and about one-sixth of 1 per cent of the dominion's gross national product. The non-ferrous metals, not including oil and gas, excited the national imagination during the 1920s. Ontario, Quebec, and British Columbia all saw dramatic new developments. The mining developments stimulated the cities – Montreal, Vancouver, and particularly Toronto – all of which gained from the development of mining-related business in finance, stockbroking, and the service industries generally.

Certainly, mining was important during the 1920s, and attractive to foreign investors. In domestic investment, however, during 1926-9 only 3 per cent of the nation's gross fixed capital formation occurred in 'mines, quarries, and oil wells.' Investment by public utilities was more than twice as important; manufacturing investment was several times as large. The export of non-ferrous metals and minerals earned large amounts of foreign currency – $147.9 million in 1929 – but this was only 13 per cent of the dominion's total export earnings. It was less than half of what forest products earned, and only a quarter of what came from agricultural exports. Perhaps the glamour of the mining camps and the new northern towns made the industry look more important than it really was; perhaps the shady dealings of some mining promoters drew attention to it.

Unlike economists of the 1920s, who lacked both data and interpretative framework, historians and economists of the 1980s are able to sketch the course of recovery and renewed growth from the slump of 1921-2 to the peak of 1929. Much of the push came from housing investment, which in 1922-6 recovered quite smartly from its 1921 low point. Railway investment operated in the opposite direction, increasing the depressionary forces from 1921 through 1925. Exports, however, moved strongly upward, both in terms of volume and value, from their 1922 trough to their 1928 peak. Assisted by preferential tariff arrangements in Britain, Australia, New Zealand, the West Indies, and some other empire countries, and by what would now be called 'world product mandating' inside such firms as Ford, automobile exports increased sharply. But so did the exports of pulp and paper and non-ferrous metals. From a low point in the fiscal year 1921-2, the value of Canada's exports rose 67 per cent to the 1928 peak. Although the value of exports of agricultural and animal products rose only 17 per cent, that of forest products rose 38 per cent, of iron and steel products, 150 per cent, and of non-ferrous metals and products, 233 per cent.

The expansion of exports was paralleled, and very much exceeded, by the expansion of domestic investment. Kenneth Buckley's annual estimates of construction work rise from $692 million in 1924 to a peak of $1046 million in 1929. Splicing his estimates onto the official income and expenditure figures which begin in 1926, we find that spending on new machinery and equipment rose from something like $200 million in the 1925 trough to $464 million in 1929. Inventory accumulation went up from an average of $32 million in 1921-5 to an average of $120 million per year in 1925-30. But from 1924/5 to 1929, exports rose only $12 million in current prices, and in constant prices they actually declined. Obviously, in the recovery and expansion of 1925-9 it was domestic capital formation, not export growth, which was propelling Canada's economy upward.

Was the Canadian economy really prosperous in the late 1920s? Official GNP data are available for 1926 and thereafter; they show that real GNP rose by 20 per cent in three years – a very creditable performance. Moreover, prices tended to fall in this decade. Regrettably for the historian, in the 1920s and 1930s the unemployed were not counted regularly. Since 1919 there had been a system of dominion-provincial labour exchanges, but registration was not compulsory and there was no system of unemployment insurance to generate administrative data on 'claimants.' By arcane methods of calculation, the Dominion Bureau of Statistics later produced annual estimates of the labour force and the number of unemployed, starting in 1926.

If we relate the estimated number of unemployed to the estimated non-agricultural labour force, we find that in 1927-8 something very close to full employment must have existed: only 2.7 per cent of the non-agricultural labour force seems to have been out of work. In 1929, however, economic growth failed to keep pace with the growth of the labour force, so that non-agricultural employment stagnated, throwing 4.6 per cent of that group into unemployment. Thus began the slide into depression. The investment-propelled boom was over, export volumes were already falling, and in 1930 investment would decline too, joining with the fall in exports to pull the whole economy into the Great Depression.

The Great Boom of 1900-13 was in part the product of government policy, which frantically stimulated the construction of transcontinental railways. During the 1920s, government policy played no such significant role. Government spending was quite small – in 1929, barely 11 per cent of national output. In 1926-9 all levels of government collectively ran a small surplus. Government spending was not providing any expansionary force, but rather the reverse, although the surplus was too small to matter much. Nor was there anything which later generations would call a 'monetary policy.'

MONEY AND THE EXCHANGES

No one in the 1920s reported or meditated on the quantity of money, although all the materials for measuring it were published from time to time. The Canadian dollar was freely convertible into gold at the 1914 price of $20.67 per Troy ounce from 1 July 1926 until the winter of 1928-9. Canada was thus, formally and for a short time, on the gold standard, the exchange rate for its dollar firmly fixed to the pound and the American dollar at the same exchange rates as in 1914. When gold flowed into the Department of Finance, new dominion notes flowed out into the vaults of the banks and, to a limited extent, into the hands of the public. This same public, however, chiefly used the notes of the chartered banks. Owing to the mechanism of the 1914 Finance Act, which was renewed and made permanent in 1923, the dominion did not control the quantity of its own note circulation: new dominion notes could be, and were, issued at the request of the chartered banks even when no gold was flowing into the coffers of the dominion. Before returning to gold in 1926, the minister of finance sought the advice of an academic economist – almost the first time that any Canadian politician had done so. The advice was unequivocal – the gold standard and the Finance Act were incompatible. The minister of finance paid no attention.

Meanwhile, the quantity of money rose very gently indeed – certainly more slowly than the volume of national output. One measure reports $1926 million in 1921 and $2271 million at the end of 1929 – an 18 per cent increase, barely 2 per cent per year. Hence, perhaps, the downward pressure on prices? Or, since government had no monetary policy of its own, did the money supply merely respond to movements in prices and physical outputs? Economists and historians are still unsure of the answer.

Most of the money consisted of bank deposits; in 1929 only 8 per cent of the money supply was paper currency, and another 1 per cent was coin. Banks, therefore, were at the centre of the financial system. There were not very many of them – eighteen in 1921, and, after one failure and several mergers, eleven in 1929. But branches were everywhere – 4069 of them in 1929. The one failure was that of the Home Bank. Although inconvenient to its depositors and note-holders, the collapse of the Home Bank, because the institution was so small, mattered little to the national financial system – it had less than 5 per cent of the assets and liabilities of the banks as a whole.

In the popular consciousness of North America, the great event of the late 1920s is the boom and crash of the Wall Street stock market. In Canada, too, there was a boom and a slump on the stock exchange. The same forces were present in both countries – buoyant profits in many firms, credit that was easy and cheap in relation to expected capital gains, and a feeling that things would go on getting better, indefinitely, perhaps at a faster pace than before. In fact, as we saw above, well before the stock market break in the autumn of 1929, export earnings had turned downward, and by then the wheat economy of the prairies was anything but healthy. But business investment strode on upward, so that for many firms 1929 really was a banner year. Hence, perhaps, the exuberance which gave rise to the splendid stock market performance. From 1921 to the break in autumn 1929, the year-to-year trend was consistently upward, and in eight years the level of stock prices increased more than three-fold. When it is remembered that the prices of ordinary goods and services were tending to fall, this performance is even more extraordinary: in real terms, enormous gains were made by those who bought stocks early in the game – and who sold out in time.

In general, most of Canada's corporations gained nothing from the stock market boom; the main gainers were those few ordinary citizens who held common stock. Nevertheless, on a rising market a company generally finds it comparatively easy to sell new common stocks, whether to finance a new plant or buy some other company, and Canada's businesses, especially in 1928, acted accordingly. They took advantage of the Great Bull Market to float unprecedentedly large issues of new common stocks.

The American stock market boom was fuelled in part by easy credit, and by the fact that people could buy stocks 'on margin' – that is, by putting up only a small fraction of the price, borrowing the balance from an accommodating banker. The same was true in Canada, but the dominion's banks and brokers were more cautious than their American brethren. In the mid-1920s the normal margin requirement in Canada was 10 per cent. In 1927 it had already risen to 20 per cent. In 1928, fearing that speculation was becoming excessive, the banks and brokers took joint action to raise the margin requirement to 35 per cent, and in 1929, to around 40 per cent. Therefore the banks' domestic 'call loans,' which were secured on stocks and bonds, rose slowly – from $242 million at the end of 1927 to $266 million at the end of 1928, and to only $280 million at the peak, in September 1929. Relative to the market values of Canadian stocks, these call loans were quite small – less than 5 per cent in mid-1929. The Canadian stock market, therefore, was a good deal more stable than the American, and much less exposed to the risk of cumulative collapse as banks sold their customers' securities to protect their advances to the same customers. Nevertheless, when the downward spiral began, it was as painful in Canada as in the United States.

Black Friday, 25 October 1929, was a day of panic in Toronto and Montreal as well as in New York. The newspapers, perhaps, bear some of the blame for transmitting the panic, but once selling got well under way there seemed for some time to be no bottom. When the exchanges reopened the following Monday, things were equally black. Then after some days of rally, the markets crashed again on 13 November. The banks responded by lowering the margin requirements on the more expensive stocks to 15 per cent, and to $10 per share on those which traded for less than $30. These steps had some steadying effect, but things did not improve for long. Soon after, a University of Toronto economist pointed out that in the Great Bull Market prices had become ridiculously high in relation to dividends, prospective yields, or anything else. Calling the collapse a 'return to sanity,' he foresaw that general business would emerge unscathed; there would be no return to the general business depressions which followed similar collapses in 1893-4 and 1907-8. So much for the prophecies of economists. But in a way Professor Gilbert Jackson proved to be right: if only because the coming slump would be far deeper and far longer than those earlier economic misadventures, it would indeed be unlike them.

The government of Mackenzie King had no policy to combat the slump. Indeed, King's biographer has suggested that because the prime minister's own private income consisted of bond interest, he may not have noticed just what was happening.[5] There was no central bank through which an expansionary monetary policy might have been introduced; in the Department of Finance there were some able officials and many incompetent ones, none of

5   H.B. Neatby, *William Lyon Mackenzie King, 1923-1932: The Lonely Heights* (Toronto 1963), 344

whom seems to have thought that the Finance Act mechanism might be used to expand bank credit. Nor would anyone have thought of cutting taxes or raising dominion spending for the sake of the economy. In any event, the dominion budget was small in relation to the economy, and both revenues and outlays were hard to adjust. In 1929 dominion revenue was 6 per cent of GNP, and 79 per cent of that revenue came from customs duties, excise taxes, and other indirect taxes. Indeed, almost half of the dominion's revenues came from the tariff. The Depression would soon reduce these and other receipts, producing unplanned and very embarrassing deficits. But that outcome was neither planned nor desired. As for outlays, in 1929, 31 per cent of dominion revenue was spent in debt service, and another 11 per cent on First World War pensions and allowances, while 4 per cent was paid over to the provinces; only 14 per cent of government revenue, or 1 per cent of GNP, consisted of spending on new buildings and structures. In other words, the dominion government apparatus was simply not set up to undertake counter-cyclical public works, even if anyone in Ottawa had thought of doing so. In the coming slump, as in the whole decade of the 1920s, 'fiscal policy' would mean little more than the customs tariff.

CANADA, THE IMPERIAL ECONOMY, AND THE TARIFF

In an earlier chapter we saw something of the currents of imperial thought which drifted between Britain and Canada before 1914. We also saw how the Great War produced a new intimacy between the dominion and the 'Mother Country.' Besides its costs in terms of Canadian money, men, and morale, the war had some unexpected payoffs for Canada's export trades. Ever since Canada herself had begun, in 1897, to charge lower duties on British goods, the dominion had pressed the United Kingdom to reciprocate by imposing duties on 'foreign' foodstuffs so that empire foodstuffs would command the immense British market. Although Lord Milner and Joseph Chamberlain had been willing – indeed, eager – to agree, the British electorate thought otherwise. Thus, at the outbreak of war, Britain still imposed no duties on wheat, cheese, butter, bacon, or any of the other goods which Canadians sent eastward across the Atlantic. In the stress of war, however, things changed, although not to the extent that Canada wished. Lord Milner joined Britain's War Cabinet and some of his followers entered Parliament, where they and their ilk enjoyed unwonted influence. When the Imperial War Cabinet was convened in 1917, the southern dominions renewed their demands for 'imperial preference.' Their wartime sacrifices had been great; surely, it was suggested, they deserved some sort of recompense. Further, in 1917-18 it was expected that after hostilities had ended, the allied powers, including the dominions, would co-operate in trade so as to discriminate against Germany. In the 'world fit for heroes' that would follow the peace, Britain would buy her grain from Canada, her meat from Australia, and her sugar from the West Indies.

After the war, events developed rather differently. The Allies did not proceed with their plans for trade discrimination against the defeated Central Powers. Although they exacted reparations from Germany, by 1924 they were trying with increasing desperation not to discriminate in one another's favour but to help Central Europe recover. Nor did Britain enact any general measure of 'imperial preference.' Foreign wheat, cheese, and meat still entered Britain duty free, as did fresh fruit from temperate-zone countries. However, in 1919 Britain honoured the pledges of 1917 so far as she could, by providing a general scheme of preferential concessions on those of her imports which were already dutiable. Given the limited coverage of these duties, the main benefit went to Britain's tropical connections – the West Indies, India, and some parts of Africa. But in the middle of the war, in an effort to save shipping space and foreign exchange, Britain had imposed new duties on a few manufactures, including cars, tires, and optical goods. In 1919, when British officials and politicians were meditating on imperial preference, it was decided that there would be preferential concessions on these 'McKenna duties' too. The normal level of the McKenna duties was 33-1/3 per cent; empire goods would pay only two-thirds as much, or just over 22 per cent. Among those who pressed for this concession was the publicist-politician Leo Amery. Reporting the deliberations many years later, he said that Britain's chancellor of the exchequer had not resisted because he did not think the concessions mattered; he did not know, Amery said, that Canada possessed a car industry.

In the event, these concessions were of great value. Together with similar concessions in many other parts of the British empire, they account for the fact that by 1928, Canada was the world's second largest producer and second largest exporter of cars.

Throughout the decade of the 1920s, although more and more of Canada's imports were coming from the United States, the dominion's tariff policy was largely shaped by and in the imperial context. With the increasingly protectionist United States, tariff bargaining was believed to be impossible. In 1923 the government received authority to negotiate with the United States, but no agreement was concluded. Nor had Prime Minister King forgotten the reciprocity election of 1911. In the empire, however, various concessions could be sought. When dealing with the United Kingdom, Ottawa argued that preferential concessions should be unilateral and unrequited. Nevertheless, whenever Whitehall showed signs of an interest in 'tariff reform,' as in 1923, Canada was anxious to obtain whatever might be on offer. And when, in 1924, Britain temporarily suspended the McKenna duties and the concessions that accompanied them, Canada's high commissioner became very agitated indeed. As for relations with other empire countries, the prohibition on tariff-bargaining somehow did not apply: at various times Canada negotiated trade agreements with the West Indies, New Zealand, and Australia.

Within Canada itself, the seesaw battle between free traders and protectionists continued apace, deriving new force from the rise of the prairie agricultural interest. There were, however, no dramatic changes. The three-column tariff structure of 1907 remained in place. In 1922 Ottawa cut the duties on sugar, agricultural implements, textiles, boots, and shoes. Next year there were some reductions in British preferential rates. In 1924 there were some additional reductions, and, in 1926, substantial further reductions on coffee, spices, pineapples, raw sugar, automobiles, and tin plate – hardly the stuff of life. In 1928 Ottawa reduced its levies on machinery and other inputs for mining and fishing, on textiles, yarns, and textile machinery; in 1929 there were further, although minor, tariff changes. Thus, while the United States moved ever more deeply into protectionism, Canada appeared to be moving, slowly but perceptibly, in the other direction. Yet the effect was not very noticeable. In 1922 customs duties were 14 per cent of the value of imports; for 1929, the figure was 15 per cent. It would seem that the dominion was importing relatively more of the highly taxed imports, and relatively less of the imports on which levies were being reduced.

Throughout the decade, therefore, the prairie and west-coast producers of primary products complained that the tariff was mulcting them: obliged to sell their goods on world markets, they had to buy many of their inputs, and most of their consumer manufactures, from tariff-protected Canadian sources. Some latter-day commentators have argued that the tariff, because it made all Canadians turn to Ottawa for favours, has been a unifying influence in Canadian history. But in the 1920s it was already clear that the protective tariff exacerbated Canada's interregional tensions: central Canada supplied manufactures to the west at inflated prices, while the west had to sell its wheat and timber on world markets, at unprotected prices. No better recipe for interregional friction could have been devised.

In the spring of 1930 the sharp increase in American duties, embodied in the new Hawley-Smoot tariff, could not be allowed to pass without retaliation. Some Canadian rates, therefore, were raised, and in the process an effort was made to increase British preferential margins. The departing Liberals thus might be said to have set the stage for the dramatic increases in tariffs and preferences which the Conservatives were shortly to effect.

Meanwhile, as Ottawa elaborated neither fiscal nor monetary policy, provincial spending was raising fast. By 1930 the provinces were spending a great deal more than the dominion. The dominion was spending more than 50 per cent of its revenues on the war debt and on veterans' pensions. In May 1920 Ottawa imposed its own sales tax. 'Wartime' levies, such as the income and corporation taxes, lingered on. The dominion began to make grants to the provinces for technical education, employment exchanges, highways, and old-age pensions. But the provinces themselves had to raise most of the money which the infrastructure of a modern economy would require. In particular, with the motor car came enormous new outlays on highways. Before the war, the provinces had spent little in this way. Indeed, only in 1914 had Ontario decided to build its first intercity paved highway – a two-lane concrete ribbon between Toronto and Hamilton. And only in 1917 did that province decide to set up a 'provincial highway system.' At first, that 'system' consisted of old earth roads which local authorities had built but not maintained. Furthermore, at first the province's plans were limited in scope. Early Highways Department reports spoke of a single provincial highway from east to west, and these reports were loud in their praise of 'well-maintained gravel.' Within two years, however, the single stem was acquiring branches, and paving had begun. In all provinces, governments began to tax gasoline, and to collect licence fees from the vehicles themselves. Liquor, furthermore, provided immense new revenues in almost all provinces, as monopoly distribution replaced partial prohibition. 'Liquor control' became a synonym for 'taxation.' By 1929, revenues from liquor constituted by far the largest item in the revenues of Nova Scotia, Quebec, Ontario, Manitoba, Alberta, and British Columbia. All provinces were taxing estates and corporations; Prince Edward Island, Manitoba, and British Columbia were taxing personal incomes; but, as yet, no provinces were taxing retail sales. Still, provincial revenues could not keep pace with expenditure, and very large borrowings occurred. In most provinces, the main justification was road-building; in Ontario, furthermore, the province was borrowing large amounts to finance the provincially owned hydro system.

A WELFARE STATE FOR CANADA?

In the 1920s some provinces took the first tentative steps towards the welfare state. At first, not much help could be expected from Ottawa. In 1919 the Liberal party, out of office, was an advocate of national health insurance; 'insurance against unemployment, sickness and dependence in old age and other disability, which would include old age pensions and maternity benefits.' Back in office after 1921, it did nothing about these campaign planks. The provinces, meanwhile, continued to finance mental hospitals, and to give grants for hospitals, schools, and various other institutions. Some, such as Ontario, introduced mothers' allowances. But neither dominion nor provincial governments devised any scheme of unemployment insurance, and the principal responsibility for aiding the needy still rested with the municipalities. Unfortunately, in the coming time of stress, as the economy slumped from its 1929 peak, they could not fulfil that responsibility.

Thanks to the divided parliaments and minority governments of the mid-1920s, Ottawa at length was induced to move on the pension front. On 7 January 1926 J.S. Woodsworth and Abe Heaps, two Labour MPs, asked Meighen and King if they were proposing to introduce unemployment insurance or old-age pensions. Meighen did not respond encouragingly, but King asked Heaps and Woodsworth to discuss the matter with him. On 14 January the two Labour members voted with the Liberals; on 26 January the cabinet discussed the pension question with Woodsworth and Heaps, agreeing on an arrangement by which the dominion would provide half the money for non-contributory, means-tested pensions at age seventy. Provinces could opt in as they wished. The resultant bill passed the Commons without division, but was defeated in the Senate. In the election campaign of 1926 the pension question was a major issue, and on his return to power King quickly reintroduced the 1926 bill, which passed into law in March.

The Old Age Pension Act of 1927 was not a particularly generous measure. The basic pension was fixed at $240 per year, and the pensioner could enjoy a total income of $365 per year including the pension; any excess income produced an equal reduction in pension. Provincial authorities were allowed to recover the values of pensions actually paid, plus 5 per cent compound interest, from the estates of pensioners. The provinces had to pay half the cost, but they could recover some or all of their share from the municipalities if they wished, and several of them did so. At first, the amounts were small – $2 million in 1928, $3 million in 1929, $11 million in 1930. But the first steps had been taken along the road towards the welfare state.

14

Defining Canada and her New Empire, 1917-31

Prior to 1914, few Canadians had much doubt as to their country's constitutional status. It was a colony, a senior colony to be sure, of the British empire. This fact satisfied some, and perturbed others, but the vast majority of Canadians gave the question only occasional thought, perhaps around election day or on festive public holidays when abundant patriotic spirits bubbled over into song and sermon. Many Canadians would have agreed that a colony like Canada had 'no concern with the outside world,' as a Canadian civil servant was to write in 1917, and certainly 'no responsibility.' But few would have followed the line of argument to add, as the civil servant did, 'and consequently ... neither reason for self-respect nor claim to the respect of others.'

That had changed by 1917. In the election of that year the Union government strove to persuade Canadians, among other things, that they indeed had a 'responsibility' for what happened outside, a responsibility that had been ratified in tens of thousands of deaths on the battlefields of Europe. These deaths were more than sacrifices for a distant empire in an irrelevant holocaust. As Sir Robert Borden's principal foreign affairs adviser, Loring Christie, wrote in 1917, they showed that 'Canada has a separate individuality, a will and power of her own, a self-respecting national consciousness – all manifested in a determination to recognize and shoulder her responsibility in the affairs of the world as a member of the family of nations which constitute the British Commonwealth.'

The empire was not what it had been. In fulfilling their duty as British subjects, Canadians and other colonials had ceased to be mere colonists, and the empire was no longer an empire but a commonwealth. Commonwealth had a ring to it, a more liberal and democratic sound, but that, after all, was what the troops had been fighting for, a mass goal for the mass armies of 1914-18. The relationship of the components of the British empire to one another was defined in Resolution IX of the Imperial War Conference in 1917, and an attempt to work it out in practice was made at the Paris Peace Conference in 1919. This new practice had yet to find a legal expression, and that, in the minds of some, meant that nothing had really changed after all.

In daily speech, 'empire' prevailed over the more unwieldy common-wealth. When the Canadian political scientist R. MacGregor Dawson wrote about Canada's constitutional development in 1936, he knew where his read-ers would look for enlightenment, as his index proclaimed. Under the entry 'Commonwealth, British' there followed the brief advice to the reader, 'see Empire, British.'

And, legally, there could be no question in 1920 that this was so. The empire still stood, as it had before the war. George V was king of Great Brit-ain, Ireland, and the British dominions beyond the seas, and emperor of In-dia. Parliament in Westminster was the supreme legislature of the empire. The Judicial Committee of the Privy Council was the court of last resort for imperial subjects. Most important of all, if the king-emperor decided to go to war or to make peace, he could constitutionally do so only on the advice of his British ministers. In such matters they acted for the whole empire, and no one else could contradict them or seek exemption from their actions. When Canadian ministers signed the Treaty of Versailles in 1919, they did so as members of the British Empire Delegation, and their individual coun-try, Canada, was indented under the heading of the British empire. Canada had not signed on its own, but as part of an imperial package.

Where did this leave the 'separate individuality' and 'self respecting na-tional consciousness' that Christie laid claim to in 1917? What would be-come of the 'responsibility in the affairs of the world' that attached to them? That was a paradox. The 'separate individuality' was in fine fettle in the years after 1919, and there were even glimmerings of a 'national conscious-ness,' though whether it was 'self respecting' may be a matter for debate. A Progressive MP from Alberta, Michael Clark, may have come close to the dead centre of public opinion when he told the House of Commons in 1921 that 'My own feeling is that this country and the world have had all the for-eign policy they want for a number of years.' The war, with its heavy casual-ties and the social disruption it brought in its train, had not convinced Clark, and many other Canadians, that virtue was its own reward.

The Union government, which had fought the war for the principle of sacrifice and responsibility, was naturally not inclined to follow Clark's ad-vice. Canada, these politicians knew, was bound by British foreign policy whether it wished to be or not. They hoped, in return, to be able to help de-termine that policy, while preserving what had been gained for Canada in war and its immediate aftermath.

The first and most tangible gain from the war was separate membership for Canada in the League of Nations, set up under the Treaty of Versailles in 1919, and its affiliate, the International Labour Organization. Membership in both organizations presumed a separate identity and a willingness to assume obligations imposed by the majority of state members of either entity. In the Department of External Affairs, Loring Christie early on ensured that all communications from the League were properly addressed to Ottawa, rather than London, thereby affirming Canada's separate identity; but he and his ministerial superiors could do little about those voices in Canada that claimed exemption from further formal responsibility for the affairs of the world.

Luckily for Canada's early relations with the League, the great powers did not initially treat that organization very seriously. War, rebellion, and revolution flickered and flashed around the edges of the great battlefields of the First World War. Civil war in Russia lasted until 1922, and was paralleled by a horrifying famine which took millions of lives. There were riots and disturbances in China. Hungary and Bavaria had their own civil conflicts and Germany teetered on the edge of rebellion and coup d'état. In Italy, continuing political disorder led in 1922 to the establishment of a fascist dictatorship under a new kind of leader, Benito Mussolini; we shall hear more of him later. In the Middle East, Turkey had refused to accept the expansion of Greek hegemony, as embodied in the Treaty of Sèvres. Consequently, fighting broke out between Greeks and Turks in Asia Minor. Inside the British empire, British forces struggled with Irish rebels, Iraqi tribesmen, and Indian agitators.

None of these problems was referred to the League of Nations. Those with an international dimension were discussed at conferences of great powers, to which only the former Allies were invited. The United States remained ostentatiously aloof, leaving Lloyd George and a kaleidoscope of French and Italian leaders to negotiate the future of Europe on their own. The British told Canadian leaders what was going on, but Ottawa's own internal preoccupations precluded much intelligent study of foreign affairs.

The most consistent actor in Canada's international affairs was Loring Christie, the legal adviser of the Department of External Affairs and the confidential adviser to Prime Ministers Borden and Meighen. Meighen, who reached the prime ministership innocent of diplomacy, placed special trust and confidence in Christie. Christie's perceptions and preoccupations found an echo in the pronouncements of his master, though it should be stressed that the two men had essentially similar views. Meighen was fond of the empire, and preferred to think of Canada as an active partner in a great imperial enterprise. Christie, with his memories of the smoothly running Imperial War Cabinets and the British Empire Delegation at Paris, believed that it was truly possible to work out a mechanism whereby the empire would enjoy a single, workable foreign policy which would reflect the informed consent and natural interests of all its members. In his view, Canada had moved from subordination to responsibility in the empire; now it was up to the British to respect that fact.

The opportunity came at the Imperial Conference of 1921. The prime ministers of the empire had not met since 1919 because of pressures at home, but most of the participants summoned to London in the summer of 1921 were familiar. Lloyd George, still British prime minister, presided. W.M. Hughes of Australia made up in noise and excitability for what he lacked in stature and judgment. W.F. Massey of New Zealand could be relied on to support most imperial schemes, but while his conclusions were certain, the means whereby he reached them remained a mystery to his fellow prime ministers. Jan Smuts of South Africa was a familiar figure too; he had spent a great part of the war in London and had become a favourite of Lloyd George and his ministers. In 1921 he would help the British 'solve' the Irish problem by granting dominion status to the southern, Catholic part of Ireland, a partial solution which would work, partially, for the next fifty years.

Arthur Meighen was a mystery to most of the men who would face him around the conference table, but Christie was not. A well-known figure in London, a friend and colleague to British civil servants, Christie had late in 1920 discovered what the major course at the forthcoming imperial lovefeast was to be, and he did not much like what he heard. The Anglo-Japanese Alliance, originally concluded in 1902 and most recently renewed in 1911, was, because of a technicality in the League Covenant, on the point of expiring. It was essential, from the British point of view, to decide what to do next, and a discussion on this subject raged up and down the Foreign Office and the military services for the first six months of 1921.

If the alliance were not renewed or renegotiated, Anglo-Japanese relations would suffer. But if it were, the Americans would begin to wonder against whom this alliance was directed. The Germans were banished from the Pacific by the Treaty of Versailles, and the German High Seas Fleet rested on the bottom of a Scottish loch. The French and Italians were allies, and the Russian Revolution had not left much of the tsar's fleet intact. Where, then, was the enemy?

Christie learned that prominent Americans took the possibility of a new Anglo-Japanese Alliance very seriously. Such an event could well start a new naval race, with the Americans fully capable of outbuilding and outclassing the Royal Navy. The British, as everyone knew, were in poor financial shape, more inclined to lay up ships than to build them. But Lloyd George and his foreign secretary, Lord Curzon, took comfort and refuge in assurances from their Washington embassy that American displeasure over the alliance was more rhetorical than real. Christie, who believed he knew better from his own American contacts, became concerned. If Anglo-American relations deteriorated, as they were bound to should the alliance be perpetuated, Canada would be caught in the middle. The North Atlantic Triangle would become a shooting gallery, with Canada cast in the role of duck.

It followed that Canada had a strong interest in being consulted during the preliminaries to the Imperial Conference. Foreign Office opinion actually supported Canadian misgivings; a committee studying the question of renewing the alliance produced conclusions that were 'in the main in harmony with those now advanced by the Canadian Government,' as a British diplomat pointed out in April 1921. Moreover, there could be little if any doubt that 'the policy of Anglo-American co-operation advocated by Canada is the right one.' Perhaps someone could tell the Canadians so.

That was not Lloyd George's idea of imperial co-operation. The dominions, and especially Canada, should not be admitted to the internal debate over the alliance. Once the British position was properly formulated, in conformity with Lloyd George's own desires, it could be discussed with others. The proper forum for such discussions would be the Imperial Conference in June, where time would be short and urgency great. Under those circumstances, what Lloyd George wanted he would almost certainly get.

And so it happened that two of the strongest proponents of Canadian participation in a common imperial foreign policy, Meighen and Christie, found themselves on a collision course with the imperial government on an issue of policy and a matter of principle. In April the British were firmly told that if they went ahead and renewed the alliance, Canada would not be bound by it. If the British could not be persuaded that terminating the alliance was in their own self-interest, then Canada would have to strike out on its own. Christie hoped that this would not prove necessary, since in his view there were no fundamental differences between American interests and those of the British empire. A tacit alliance with the United States should be the supreme objective of British policy, and if the British failed to grasp that elementary fact, Canada could not afford to take the consequences.

Equally important, however, was the question of consultation. If there were to be a true imperial foreign policy, then the information and services of the British government could not be monopolized by the British cabinet alone. Canadian perceptions should be injected into bureaucratic debate and, in return, Canada should have access to the policy proposals and documents of the Foreign Office. Without such an exchange, Canada and any other dominion would be at a permanent disadvantage in conferences held in London where Lloyd George and his platoon of experts could sweep away objections on the ground of experience and superior information. That was what Lloyd George intended.

The meeting of the dominion and British prime ministers acquired an element of high drama, but as so often in high policy the drama slid easily into farce. Meighen performed as the British knew he would, reciting a carefully prepared denunciation of the alliance. The Australians responded by stressing the advantages to the empire of retaining Japanese friendship. The Australian position was logical, given that country's closeness to Japan; but then so was Canada's, given this country's proximity to the United States. Between these two opposing views, Lloyd George insinuated himself. At first the British prime minister was perfectly prepared to support the Australians, and to let the Canadians go where they might. But at the last moment he received news from Washington that the Canadians were right after all. The United States government would take a renewed alliance as a hostile act; previous information to the contrary was erroneous. Lloyd George now discovered that the renewal of the alliance was not urgent at all. The alliance was not about to expire, as he had wrongly believed; fortunately, his legal advisers were flexible enough to produce an opinion to that effect on a moment's notice. Instead of a renewed alliance there would be a great international conference in Washington, to which all concerned powers would be invited, to discuss the security of the Pacific region. Empire solidarity was saved.

It used to be believed that Meighen and Christie had a hand in saving it. Sadly, this was not the case. What persuaded Lloyd George to change his mind was American pressure, not Canadian. Canadian threats to go it alone were of no avail, and of only marginal concern to the British government. The fact that the Canadian assessment of the international situation was superior to the one Lloyd George relied on was of no consequence.

These facts were not immediately apparent. There was a public display of harmony, and a chorus of 'all's well that ends well.' There was still an imperial foreign policy, the same one for all parts of the empire. The empire went to Washington in the fall of 1921, and it emerged in the spring of 1922 with a naval disarmament treaty that would save money for the British, American, and Japanese taxpayers by limiting naval construction. There was a security pact for the Pacific, and good wishes all round. In Canada, Conservatives continued to believe that they were the party of 'the empire,' a belief that the Liberals encouraged because they found it electorally useful in Quebec. Meighen had no time to apply the lessons, it any, of the Imperial Conference, which turned out to be the only one he would ever attend. In December 1921 he and his tattered government were swept out of office, and the Liberals under William Lyon Mackenzie King replaced them.

It would be an understatement to say that King approached foreign and imperial affairs cautiously. Not for him the stirring sounds of 'responsibility' and duty. His duty was to keep his party together and to avoid contentious issues. The chief prophet of 'responsibility,' Christie, was in King's eyes the chief wasp in a 'Tory hive' that Meighen left behind him. By his deeds if not his words, King set about to encourage Christie to leave, and in May 1923 he did. In leaving King's service, Christie quoted a current witticism about the new prime minister: 'He is such a pompous ass that an orang-outang that would flatter him could choose its own reward.'

The years between 1921 and 1923 represent a watershed not only in Canadian foreign policy but also in Canada's constitutional development. A constitution, ideally, should be consistent with current conceptions of reality. In the aftermath of the First World War there was a possibility that the constitutional relations of the British empire would be adapted to meet the requirements of a single imperial foreign policy, along the lines envisioned by Borden and the other imperial statesmen of 1917. But a single imperial foreign policy had been impossible to achieve in 1921. Just in case anybody missed the point, however, Lloyd George and his successors would now repeat the lesson.

In the summer of 1922 the Turks finally overcame the Greeks in Asia Minor and drove them into the Aegean Sea. The Turkish armies advanced towards a zone occupied by the British army on the Dardanelles at Chanak. Lloyd George and some of his closest colleagues (including Winston Churchill) became excited, and began to draft messages to the dominions calling for support. Churchill then informed the press of what had been done.

Inevitably, the press report reached Canada before the actual message did. Mackenzie King received the news from a *Toronto Star* reporter while speechifying north of Toronto. The prime minister knew he faced a ticklish problem. However untoward the message, or however unconventional its manner of delivery, English Canadians might react emotionally to the British plea for help. The headline in the Toronto *Globe,* a Liberal paper, on 16 September 1922, caught the atmosphere beautifully: 'DIM AND UNCERTAIN ROLLING OF DRUMS OF WAR QUICKLY AWAKENS IN HEARTS OF TORONTONIANS FULL BEAT OF KINSHIP WITH "OLD GREY MOTHER."' Significantly, another headline proclaimed that 'Veterans of Last War Are Ready To Go If Needed'; and files of telegrams in the archives in Ottawa confirm the fact that volunteers were available. Arthur Meighen expressed more than a personal sentiment when he argued, on 22 September, that Canada's reaction should have been 'Ready, aye ready; we stand by you.' Meighen should have known better and, as events unravelled, so should Lloyd George's government.

Mackenzie King, whose cabinet was divided on the issue, procrastinated. He needed time, he needed information. The British, as it turned out, had neither. A storm of political protest swept Lloyd George away. In his place there arrived the Conservative Andrew Bonar Law, and peace. There would be no more hysterical demands for an imperial expeditionary force to the Middle East. Instead, there would be another conference in the summer of 1923 to regulate matters between Turkey and its erstwhile enemies. It was a conference to which Canada would not be invited.

This development concerned Christie, who was by then off in London making money, but it did not bother Mackenzie King. The failure to invite Canada to this last of the postwar peacemaking conferences, or seriously to seek Canadian views on the process, expressed the Foreign Office conviction that whatever Canada had to say would be irrelevant at best. King did not protest: as his biographer put it, 'he was relieved rather than affronted.'[1] Arthur Meighen was right when he pointed out that the Liberals had 'acquiesced, apparently cheerfully, in the old imperial situation,' and King's concession that Canada was bound by Britain's signature on the Turkish peace treaty confirms this analysis. But for King it would be a case of 'reculer pour mieux sauter.' One step back preceded a rather large march forward.

King now enlisted the aid of a new expert. O.D. Skelton, dean of arts at Queen's University, had attracted King's attention long before. He had written an admiring, as well as exceedingly competent, biography of Sir Wilfrid Laurier. Skelton had strong views on the subject of a common imperial foreign policy. The developments of the past generation did not point, as Christie, Borden, and Meighen wrongly believed, in the direction of such a policy; rather, they indicated an autonomous Canadian policy, guided by Canadian needs alone. King approved. He recruited Skelton to be a special adviser for the next Imperial Conference in 1923, and then hired him to be 'counsellor' and undersecretary in the Department of External Affairs, thus making him the prime minister's own deputy minister, since that was King's own department. Together the two men would chart Canada's constitutional development for the next twenty years.

1   H.B. Neatby, *William Lyon Mackenzie King, 1923-1932: The Lonely Heights* (Toronto 1963), 33

The first task was to lay that awkward ghost, an imperial foreign policy. At the Imperial Conference of 1923, at which yet another British prime minister, Stanley Baldwin, presided, King and the Foreign Office unwittingly laid the foundations of a mutually satisfactory compromise. Lord Curzon, still foreign secretary, treated the assembled prime ministers to a grand tour of British foreign policy. Curzon's principal adviser, Eyre Crowe, had already privately argued that 'it is ... not possible to delay all action until ... the Dominions have been consulted and have agreed upon a common decision.' Crowe accurately represented his department's position over the Turkish peace treaties; and not for the last time the British argued that some decisions were too important to be left to the leisurely workings of an overseas courier service.[2]

Mackenzie King heartily agreed. 'If it is not possible,' he told the conference, 'or desirable that Great Britain or other Dominions should control these foreign affairs which are distinctly of primary concern to one Dominion, so it is equally impossible or undesirable for the Dominions to seek to control those foreign affairs which primarily affect Great Britain.' S.M. Bruce, the Australian prime minister, protested, but his misgivings cut no ice with Curzon. The British cabinet rallied behind Curzon's position that there should be no alteration in the existing way of doing business as between the dominions and the Foreign Office.

Mackenzie King and Curzon nevertheless clashed over what was implied by the mere fact of discussion of British foreign policy at the conference. Curzon naturally hoped that the dominions would fall in behind the principles and policies he had enunciated; King wanted no such thing. Curzon made no specific demands for dominion action. For him, solidarity would be enough. For King, solidarity was too much, and in this case, as so often in the future, King eventually had his own way. The published conclusions of the conference were watered down to the point of being meaningless, and when King was satisfied that no positive commitments could be derived from them, he gave Canada's concurrence.

Almost unnoticed in the brouhaha was a casual comment King made in explaining his government's position at the time of Chanak. C.P. Stacey has rightly called attention to King's remark, that 'If a great and clear call of duty comes, Canada will respond, whether or not the United States responds, as she did in 1914, but it is a most important consideration against intervention in other issues.' King was warning against more Chanaks, and in the generally peaceful state of the world in 1923 it might have seemed that his invocation of the 'great and clear call of duty' was little more than a

2 See Philip Wigley, *Canada and the Transition to Commonwealth* (Cambridge 1977), 185-99, for the best account of the conference.

rhetorical flourish. But as Stacey has shown, it was much more than that.[3] It was a perceptive reading of Canadian public opinion, and it represented King's own inner inclination. Naturally he hoped that the great call would never come, but when it did, in the late 1930s, King would respond.

A satisfied Canadian delegation sailed back across the Atlantic in 1923. Commitments had been avoided. The most fervent Canadian autonomist could not reproach King with knuckling under to the British; at the same time, the mossbacks in King's cabinet could not claim that the diplomatic unity of the empire was any less real than it had been before the conference. Soon the mossbacks – principally the minister of finance, W.S. Fielding – would be gone. When they were, King could embark on a bolder policy.

Between 1923 and 1926 King had a number of occasions to lay down foreign policy initiatives. In 1923 Canada signed a treaty on halibut with the United States entirely on its own, without any intervention by a British representative. In 1924 and 1925 King evaded making any further commitments to the League of Nations beyond what was already in the Covenant, another nail in the coffin of 'responsibility.' These actions established, in a practical way, Canadian autonomy in certain aspects of foreign affairs. King also planned to post Canada's first diplomat outside the British empire, by establishing a legation in Washington, and he designated a Liberal millionaire from Toronto, Vincent Massey, for the job. But before Massey took up his duties he accompanied King across the ocean for yet another Imperial Conference in the fall of 1926.

The conference faced a serious constitutional crisis. The South African prime minister, General J.B.M. Hertzog, demanded that the constitutional links between Great Britain and the dominions be clarified in a manner satisfactory to himself. What that meant was free and full autonomy, failing which, he implied, South Africa would leave the empire. The Imperial Conference struck a committee of prime ministers, presided over by Lord Balfour, a former prime minister and the empire's ranking statesman. The definition that resulted was inevitably known as the Balfour Report; in substance, though not in wording, it conceded everything Hertzog could have wanted. Great Britain and its dominions were described as 'autonomous Communities within the British Empire, equal in status, in no way subordinate one to another in any aspect of their domestic or external affairs, though united by a common allegiance to the Crown, and freely associated as members of the British Commonwealth of Nations.' To give effect to this pleasing principle, the conference provided for a later, more technical gathering to work out whatever legal implications there might be.

3   See C.P. Stacey, *Canada and the Age of Conflict,* volume 2 (Toronto 1981), 70-2.

And so, in the space of five years, the idea of imperial co-operation which had attracted Borden and the Round Tablers vanished as though it had never been. The 'inevitable' evolution which the proponents of 'responsible' diplomacy had discerned – a great, mutually co-operative empire wielding a unified and powerful influence in the affairs of the world – had been replaced by another 'inevitable' trend sketched out by King and Skelton in which the First World War was treated as a way station on the road to the great perpetual objective of autonomy. In principle, Canada was becoming completely emancipated, although still within the British empire, as the project of a common imperial foreign policy began to dissolve. Furthermore, in constitutional evolution as in diplomatic matters, Canada was more and more on its own. What did Canadians make of their autonomy, and how did the constitutional balance inside the country shift during the 1920s?

THE CONSTITUTIONAL BALANCE

Under Section 132 of the British North America Act, the Parliament and government of Canada were empowered to perform any and all obligations that the dominion or any province might have under imperial treaties with foreign countries. As we have seen, the Treaty of Versailles listed Canada as part of the British empire, and there was no legal doubt that the dominion Parliament had the power to enact legislation in response to that treaty. The very scope of the Treaty of Versailles, however, proved the undoing of Section 132. Besides its numerous clauses regulating German boundaries, war guilt, and armaments, the treaty included the Covenant of the new League of Nations and an agreement establishing an International Labour Organization. The new ILO, at its founding convention in Washington in 1919, promptly passed a convention establishing the principles of the eight-hour working day, the reasonable minimum wage, and the abolition of child labour.

Most Canadians applauded those principles, at least in public. Under ordinary circumstances, it was up to the provinces to enact them, since they fell under what was generally conceded to be the provincial powers regulating property and civil rights. Yet the ILO convention opened up enticing possibilities. According to the dominion's deputy minister of labour in 1922, it could now be 'taken for granted that the Dominion had the right, if it pleased, to carry out this eight-hour law or any of these other matters under its treaty-making powers.'[4]

---

4 Quoted in Christopher Armstrong, *The Politics of Federalism: Ontario's Relations with the Federal Government, 1867-1942* (Toronto 1979), 136

'If it pleased.' But did the dominion government really want the jurisdiction so unexpectedly proffered it at the hand of the empire? Did any government, faced with heavy expenditures, industrial unrest, and insufficient funds, want to assume unqualified responsibility for the most volatile political subject in the country? The answer, naturally, was 'no.'

When Newton Rowell, minister of health and Canada's representative to the ILO's Washington conference, promised that the dominion would get busy on implementing draft labour conventions, he found that he could not carry his colleagues' assent. The government discovered that provincial rights stood in the way, and ministers so informed Parliament. The incoming Liberals were no more enthusiastic, and a reference to the Supreme Court in 1925 produced the opinion that the government had done no more, in accepting the ILO conventions, than agree to recommend them to the competent authorities. Those authorities were the provinces.

The question soon became moot. The King government's determination to extract Canada from the treaty obligations of the British empire created a situation in which all new treaties were signed by and for Canada only. Section 132 no longer applied. Hence it became impossible for the Parliament or government of Canada to invoke any over-arching power to implement treaty commitments.[5] In the 1920s, at least, the government had no desire to do so. Nor could the government make binding international commitments with respect to such things as labour standards, except for the small section of the economy that was in dominion jurisdiction – banking and railways, for instance. At the same time, the provinces did not and could not have the power to conduct their own separate foreign policies. Matters affecting their rights and responsibilities could only be discussed internationally by a complicated process of careful consultation among several watertight authorities, none of which had any formal political or legal control over the other. Without concurrence there could be no general implementation, a situation which junior governments would learn they could turn to their advantage.

That did not mean that the 1920s were devoid of dominion-provincial controversy. It was, in fact, a lively decade constitutionally as the federal government fought off, or accommodated itself to, challenges from east, west, and centre.

Part of the liveliness derived from the eternal question of money. No level of government was ever prepared to admit it had enough, but during that decade, the federal slice of the revenue pie showed a tendency to shrink, in contrast to those of the provinces and municipalities. As the historian of

5   The question arose once more in 1930-6, and, after some judicial confusion, was settled in the same way. See below, page 267.

Canadian taxation, Harvey Perry, has shown, dominion revenues actually declined during the decade (1921-30) by 5.7 per cent. Those of municipalities, however, went up by 37.8 per cent, and those of the provinces by a whopping 105 per cent.[6] The proceeds were spent on new public buildings, such as hospitals and universities, and on such utilitarian items as highways, streetcars, and schools. Fortunately for provincial revenue, vehicles and gasoline could readily be taxed, and prohibition was losing its appeal for the electorate at the same time that liquor taxes were increasing. Relying on the principle that vice should be heavily taxed, Canada's provinces, or most of them (Prince Edward Island kept its drinking illegal), soon transformed their fiscal circumstances for the better. Vice, obviously, was its own reward.

What the dominion government had, however, it held. The BNA Act was explicit – Ottawa could impose whatever taxes it liked. The income war tax remained to pay for the continuing cost of war debt as well as the new pensions. A sales tax, introduced in 1920, also became a permanent part of Ottawa's taxation arsenal. Although several provinces urged Ottawa to vacate the income-tax field in view of their greater current needs, the dominion government steadfastly refused.

The two great provincial issues of the 1920s involved claims from the west and the east. The three prairie provinces coveted their public lands, which had been left under dominion administration – for the national purpose of immigration and settlement – when they entered Confederation. Now they wanted the lands, or what was left of them, and they wanted compensation for those that Canada had granted away. Mackenzie King's government bent to their demands, and at a dominion-provincial conference in 1927 gave Alberta, Saskatchewan, and Manitoba control over their public domain, effective in 1930.

The prairies were not the only section of Canada with a grievance against Ottawa. The Maritime provinces regarded with alarm their growing unimportance in the federal scheme of things. As Prince Edward Island, New Brunswick, and Nova Scotia failed to grow and even lost population, they also lost representation in the House of Commons. Economically, business was moving west. And when, as part of the establishment of the Canadian National Railway system, the old Intercolonial Railway headquarters in Moncton were wound up, resentment spilled over into rage. Conservative and Liberal governments suffered equally from the anger of Maritime voters during the 1920s, but in the end the King government was more successful in coping with the three eastern provinces.

6   J. Harvey Perry, *Taxes, Tariffs, and Subsidies,* volume 2 (Toronto 1955), 619

King achieved this politically happy result in two ways. He appointed a royal commission to investigate the question of Maritime grievances (or 'rights'), and he recruited a number of exceptionally able Maritime politicians to his cabinet and caucus. A great deal of rhetoric came the commission's way. Many of the local arguments were logically or factually unsound, while some of the remedies proposed – a regional tariff, for example – were so vaguely described as not to bear examination. One Maritime claim, however, was irrefutable. The three lower provinces had insufficient revenues to maintain an adequate structure of government, in addition to what were by then regarded as essential services. Responding to this claim, the commission recommended that Ottawa immediately increase its subsidies to the Maritimes pending a complete re-examination of the subsidy issue. Railway freight rates, another deeply felt grievance, also received attention. Rate reductions, improvements in the administration of Maritime ports, and additional subsidized coal facilities were also recommended.[7]

J.L. Ralston, minister of national defence in the King government, defended the recommendations, and most passed into law in 1927: harbour boards for the ports; rate reductions on the railways; special subsidies to Maritime governments; and even encouragement for new coking facilities. Despite the feeling on the part of some of the Maritime Rights advocates that symptoms, rather than causes, had been addressed, most Maritimers were pleased. The Maritime Rights agitation vanished as a political force.

Soon afterwards, Mackenzie King and his minister of justice Ernest Lapointe convened the nine provinces to a dominion-provincial conference in Ottawa to celebrate the sixtieth anniversary of Confederation. Ontario and Quebec, which might have been expected to object to the Maritime subsidies, did not; they wanted Maritime support for their claims to jurisdiction over waterpower on navigable rivers. An attempt to discover where the boundaries of federal and provincial jurisdiction lay in the area of social policy was barely mentioned. Some grumbling over federal levying of direct taxation (income tax being the most prominent instance) occurred, but in that area provincial demands were firmly squelched.

The last, and most lasting, item before the conference was the question of amending the constitution. Premier Howard Ferguson of Ontario immediately took a rigid position. Confederation was a compact among the provinces, he believed, and no aspect of the Confederation bargain could be altered without the consent of all. The federal government, in contrast, argued that unanimous consent ought to apply only to a few sensitive subjects, such as

7 See E.R. Forbes, *The Maritime Rights Movement, 1919-1927: A Study in Canadian Regionalism* (Montreal 1978), chapters 8 and 9, for a discussion of the Maritime Rights agitation.

language and religion. Otherwise, a two-thirds majority of the provinces should suffice for an amendment.

The federal government was unwilling to press its point, and the provinces were unwilling to concede the federal position without some substantial quid pro quo. The amending proposal was therefore shelved, and not for the last time. The significance of the discussion was that it had occurred; the federal government seemed to be conceding that the provinces had a right to be consulted. The shelving of the proposal might also, to some, seem tacitly to concede Ferguson's point: consent, as well as consultation, was needed. And while the idea that the Canadian constitution should be amended in Canada might be high on the federal agenda, it ranked very low on those of the provinces.

The failure to reach agreement on an amending formula had an effect on Canada's international position as well. As we have seen, the 1926 Imperial Conference looked to a formal readjustment of the existing links among the nations of the British empire. A Conference on the Operation of Dominion Legislation was scheduled to be held (it would be called, inevitably, ODL or CODL), although it did not meet until 1929. Its purpose was to sort out those areas where the Parliament and government of the United Kingdom still retained jurisdiction over the dominions, and to propose ways and means of abolishing that jurisdiction.

For Canada, the issue might have appeared academic. It was many decades since Whitehall had disallowed a dominion statute, nor was the Imperial Parliament likely to pass measures that applied to Canada. Yet the Canadian delegation to ODL went prepared for battle. They were determined to extract full jurisdiction over any and all aspects of government that might affect Canada, with two exceptions: the status of the Crown and legislation that might affect it, and the amendment of the British North America Act. A Canadian delegate later observed that Canadians had got everything they could want at the ODL meetings. But the discussions were anything but tame, especially as between the Irish and the British. Indeed, the British government had serious misgivings about the final report of the conference, but in the end they signed it, partly in the hope that a forthcoming Imperial Conference would produce a better result.

Between ODL and the 1930 Imperial Conference, a new, Conservative government was elected in Canada. It was natural to expect that R.B. Bennett, the new prime minister, would reverse the course his nationalist Liberal predecessors had charted. In fact he did not. The Imperial Conference of 1930, which Bennett attended, did little more than ratify the results of ODL; although it is the 1930 conference which usually receives more attention, it was the 1929 meeting that held the greater significance. Bennett's most serious qualm, in discussing the results of ODL, was to reserve the position of Canada's provinces. Although there was some disposition in the federal Department of Justice to reject any provincial claim to a say in the adjustment of the dominion's relations with the empire (Canada would be 'saddled with an absolutely rigid and stereotyped constitution,' one official argued), Bennett referred the matter to a dominion-provincial conference in April 1931.[8]

This 1931 conference was in some senses the high-water mark of provincial influence in and over the Canadian constitution. Lapointe had sketched the general direction four years earlier, and Bennett now travelled further down the road. The dominion government got what it wanted – provincial consent to the embodiment of the results of ODL in an imperial law, the Statute of Westminster. This abolished imperial review of dominion legislation, conferred diplomatic powers on dominion governments, and straightened out certain other technical matters. A special Canadian codicil to the statute, however, disclaimed any devolution to Canada of the power to amend the British North America Act. That power remained with the British Parliament, a testimony to the fact that the provinces of Canada did not wish the current constitutional status quo to be altered. That was reasonable enough, from their point of view, because Bennett also agreed, under pressure from Ontario and Quebec, that 'in the future no amendments to the British North America Act would be made by the present government until an opportunity had been given the Provinces to discuss the amendment, and the practice that has heretofore prevailed would not be relied upon.'

The Statute of Westminster was formally approved and enacted on 11 December 1931. For most purposes Canada's formal status changed from that of a British colony or possession to that of an independent monarchy, albeit a country which shared its monarch and its citizenship with the United Kingdom and which could not agree on how to amend its own constitution. It was a country divided into watertight constitutional compartments, whose government had the power only to speak on and negotiate for those compartments which belonged to the federal side of the British North America Act.

Not everyone received the news with joy. Sir Thomas Chapais, a Quebec Conservative, is reported to have lamented to a gathering of Canadian students in Paris, 'Messieurs, où allons-nous?' But nationalists, including the radical French-Canadian nationalist Abbé Lionel Groulx, received the news with varying degrees of joy and satisfaction. It was, J.S. Ewart wrote, the advent of 'true Canadianism.' It only remained to define what that was.

8   Norman Hillmer, 'Anglo-Canadian Relations, 1926-1937' (PhD thesis, Cambridge University, 1974), provides the best analysis of these developments; also useful is Armstrong, *The Politics of Federalism,* chapter 7, from which the quotation is taken.

15

The Social and Economic Impact of the Depression

The Great Depression, Canadians are apt to believe, started with the crash of the New York Stock Exchange in October 1929, and ended with the outbreak of the Second World War in September 1939. In between were what the popular historian Barry Broadfoot has titled 'Ten Lost Years,' a decade of desperation, anger, and broken dreams.

For many Canadians the picture is accurate enough. The urban unemployed, the rural poor, the farmers driven by drought and dust from an unforgiving land, not to mention the unpaid schoolteachers, harassed social workers, as well as the embittered victims of business failure, all considered it a time of struggle. But on a more general level it was a time of failure as well. The 1930s were years of unremitting federal-provincial warfare. Federal politicians and provincial statesmen battled an economic problem they barely understood with remedies left behind by earlier generations. When these failed, there was little short of voodoo in the government's medicine chest, and Canada's political physicians shrank from prescribing it.

In terms of social, economic, and political images, then, the Depression has been seen, and is still seen, in powerfully negative terms. The 'chaos,' 'lowness,' and 'dishonesty' of politics can easily be stressed, and no fair picture of the Depression decade is complete without them. Other politicians, however, with allies among journalists, the socially concerned, the adventurous, and the desperate, have reacted against this stereotype. Their perceptions and analysis often bore fruit in the years that followed. If we look at their activities, it is easy to see the 1930s as a 'red decade,' when discontent bubbled over into every section of society, Communists led welfare marches, socialists surged into action, and intellectuals and academics banded together, in print and in lecture halls, to demand revolutionary change. These pictures are true; but they are incomplete. We must clarify and reunite the scattered pieces of the past in order to represent more precisely what happened in Canada between 1929 and 1939. To do that we should begin with the population and the economy.

THE POPULATION IN DEPRESSION

In 1931 Canada contained 10.4 million people. Between 1931 and 1941 natural increase was less than in the 1920s: deaths were more numerous than in the 1920s, but so were births, so that natural increase was the lowest since 1901-11, when the population was a great deal smaller. The Great Demographic Transition, plus the Great Depression, were at work: death rates had fallen since the end of the Great War, but birth rates had fallen still more. Immigration and emigration almost ceased.[1]

The proportion of native-born went up slightly in the 1930s, and the proportion of French origin went up perceptibly. For the first time since well before 1867, however, those from the British Isles made up less than 50 per cent of the population. The reasons are obvious enough: although British migration continued throughout the Depression, the levels were far lower than in the 1920s. Given the relatively low birth rate among anglophone Canadians, the proportion of British origin had to decline: there were no longer enough British immigrants to offset the difference between the two reproduction rates. Perhaps the revenge of the cradle was in sight once more.

The Depression changed everything. Britain's Empire Settlement subsidies were quickly dismantled. For Asians, regulations became even more stringent. In 1930 the government decided that only prospective farm owners, residents' wives and minor children, American citizens, and British subjects from the United Kingdom and the white dominions were to be admissible. All recruitment and promotion were stopped. Even British subjects from the United Kingdom, theoretically admissible if they had the necessary landing money, were generally told that they could not expect to find work in Canada. Only those who were going to join close relatives, or those who had really substantial capital, were allowed to cross the Atlantic or the Pacific. Refugees from Nazism and fascism were admitted reluctantly or not at all. The responsible bureaucrats were especially reluctant to admit Jews. With the outbreak of war in 1939, immigration ended completely, except for such special categories as the wives and children of Canadian servicemen.

It should be noted that although Canadian immigration arrangements

---

1 Canadian Immigration and Population Study, *Immigration and Population Statistics* (Ottawa 1974); Warren E. Kalbach and Wayne McVey, *The Demographic Bases of Canadian Society*, 2nd edition (Toronto 1979), table 6:1

had long been anti-Asian, anti-African, and pro-agricultural, they had not been in any explicit way anti-Semitic, at least until 1938. It is true that many politicians and officials wanted immigrants to settle on the land, and thought ill of the Jewish migrants because they drifted quickly into trade, commerce, and urban life, especially in Toronto, Montreal, and Winnipeg. No doubt many of these people disliked Jews as such, yet Asians and Africans were far more completely excluded than Jews. This statement, of course, does not exonerate Canada from the charge that little was done to welcome Jewish fugitives from Nazi bestiality.[2]

Birth rates, meanwhile, continued to drift downward, as they had done in the 1920s. Until 1921 the crude birth rate had changed remarkably little, hovering between 29 and 32 per thousand. Then began a striking decline, so that the crude birth rate was 23.5 in 1929 and 20.6 in 1939 – a decline of one-third in less than twenty years. The decline was so sharp that although the population was rising, the number of live births declined as well. In 1900 there were 146,000 live births; in 1921, the peak year, more than 265,000; and in 1938-9 only 237,000. When we examine 'age-specific fertility rates,' which group mothers and babies according to the mothers' age, the same pattern appears in every age group. In other words, during the 1920s and 1930s every female, regardless of age, was less likely to have a baby, and each would tend to have fewer babies during her lifetime.

Crude death rates fell too, but like birth rates they had moved little until the 1920s: the crude death rates were 14.1 per thousand in 1901 and 13.3 in 1920; the rates of natural increase were therefore 17.1 in 1901 and 15.9 in 1920; on the average, the rate of natural increase was 17.8 per thousand in 1901-5, and 15 in 1919-20. Thereafter, in the 1920s and 1930s, there was a perceptible downward drift both in crude death rates and in the 'standardized' rates which are calculated by adjusting for changes in the age composition of the population. In 1921 the crude death rate was 11.6 per thousand; in 1939 it was 9.7. And since the death rate was falling less rapidly than the birth rate, the rate of natural increase fell dramatically – from 17.7 per thousand in 1921 to 12.1 in 1929, and on down to 9.7 in 1937. It was slightly higher in 1938-9, but even in those years it was only 62 per cent of what it had been in 1921 – and barely half of what it would be in the 'baby boom' of the later 1950s.

Since immigration had declined and rates of natural increase had fallen less in Quebec than elsewhere in the dominion, it is not surprising that in the 1930s, Quebec's population was rising in relation to Canada's. In 1941, 29

2 See I. Abella and H. Troper, *None is Too Many: Canada and the Jews of Europe, 1933-1948* (Toronto 1982).

per cent of all Canadians lived in Quebec. As for Canada's first peoples, they were few in number and increasing slowly. Indeed, so slow was their increase that by 1941 the people of Jewish origin outnumbered them. In 1901, 16,131 Canadians identified themselves as Jewish, while in 1941, 170,241 did so. In 1901 the census reported 93,460 Indians and 34,481 Métis; the figures for 1941 were 118,316 and 35,416, respectively. The 1901 census did not report Inuit or Eskimo as such, but in 1941 they numbered only 7205. Indeed, it is likely that few of Canada's Inuit were actually enumerated. In the relevant territories of the dominion there were, in 1901, 16,763 people of 'unspecified origin,' and this figure must include those Inuit whom the census-takers reached, because there is no other category in which they could have been placed. Canada's first peoples were increasing in number, but the growth was extraordinarily slow because of a high rate of infant mortality and short life expectancy.

THE ECONOMY IN DEPRESSION

The Depression stung its victims most ferociously in its early years. Canadian newspapers carried news of collapsing wheat prices, shrinking pulp and paper markets, bankrupt businesses, closed factories, and building projects abandoned. Workers joined farmers on relief. Young men and women, just out of school, found themselves out of work as well. Older Canadians, caught short by the Depression, moved from job to job, and often from town to town or city to city, looking for work. Often they did not find it.

Economically the Depression can be measured in terms of real national output. By 1971 prices, output fell by 30 per cent between 1929 and 1933. The year 1933 was 'the trough.' Thereafter, things got better, slowly, but by 1938 real national output was still smaller than it had been in 1929. Since there were 1.2 million more Canadians in 1938 compared to 1929, it is obvious that real per capita income fell, from $1680 to $1480. Unemployment, meanwhile, rose. The available estimates are probably not very reliable, but they suggest that the number of unemployed was 116,000 in 1929, 826,000 in 1933, and more than 522,000 in 1938. Translated into percentages of the non-agricultural labour force, these figures mean that under 5 per cent of Canadians were unemployed in 1929, 27 per cent (or more) in 1933, and 16 per cent in 1938. And the unemployment figures do not take into account underemployment, which was unmeasured but also great. Furthermore, because of low prices and crop failures the agricultural population suffered great impoverishment even though, in the statisticians' sense, it was not unemployed. Eager to work for no more than room and board, farm girls poured into the cities to work as maids and nannies. If they found jobs they were happy exceptions to those without disposable income, who posed problems of 'relief' – what later generations called 'welfare' – with which governments were ill-equipped to cope.

One striking feature of the crisis was the collapse in the price level. The decline in prices was dramatic and almost universal; the United States was hit as severely as Canada, and price recovery there was equally slow. In the dominion, the best general price index declined by 18 per cent between 1929 and 1933, but many individual prices fell much more steeply. Export prices, for instance, fell by 31 per cent in those four years, nor was recovery very rapid. From 1933 to 1939 the general price index rose less than 7 per cent and export prices rose 16 per cent, so that, on the outbreak of war, export prices were in general some 20 per cent lower than they had been in 1929, and the general price level was 13 per cent lower.

In Great Britain, the United States, and Canada, it was widely believed in the early 1930s that the fall in prices had caused the Depression, or at least helped to make it worse. Prices fell, so goods and services fetched less. People had less money to spend, and they looked around for a cause. The search became more intense, more desperate as the decade wore on and conditions failed to improve. The more thoughtful asked whether overproduction had caused prices to fall. Had money become scarce? Were both forces at work? Or was there some other, more sinister explanation?

There is little doubt that overproduction and overcapacity did have an effect in bringing down prices, especially once demand started to fall in Canada's major export markets – the United States, Great Britain, and the rest of the British empire. Producers reacted by attempting to control prices by agreement. An International Wheat Agreement in 1933 tried to confront the problem by controlling both acreage and sales. It failed, and once its failure was clear, wheat producers lurched to the other end of the spectrum. If prices were low, let farmers produce more; and they did. They did not, however, earn more money as a result, for the consequence was simply more unsold wheat.

As for the scarcity of money, there was some truth to that, too. In the United States the money supply shrank by one-third in the four years between 1929 and 1933. This phenomenon contributed massively not only to the price fall but also to the contraction in physical output and employment. Canada did not follow the American lead in this instance. The money dropped, but only by 13 per cent in the three years 1929-32 (1932 was Canada's low point in money supply). Many American banks failed, but no Canadian bank. What happened? Economic historians now tend to agree that Canadian banks reduced their lending because prices and production were falling, thus reducing the demand for bank credit; the fall in Canada's money supply was consequently an effect, not a cause, of the Canadian slump.

In 1929-33 there was no national monetary management. Indeed, until the Bank of Canada began to operate in 1935, there was no central bank, and no other agency which could try to manage the money supply and the exchange rate. R.B. Bennett inherited a system in which the chartered banks could borrow newly printed dominion notes from the Department of Finance, on request, and in which the foreign exchange rate was fixed by supply and demand. When the Depression began, the Canadian dollar was theoretically convertible into gold at a fixed price, but the King government had quietly suspended that arrangement in the winter of 1928-9, and in autumn 1931 the Bennett government made the suspension public and permanent. Bennett himself was anxious to manage the money supply and the exchange rate; his officials convinced him that this could best be done by creating a central bank – an innovation which almost all Canada's bankers strongly opposed. Having come into existence, the Bank worked to hold the Canadian dollar at par with the American; it also exerted a gentle pressure for monetary expansion. But this pressure began only after recovery had already got under way.

Why did Canada's economy contract so far and so fast and revive so slowly? Most economists have seen the Canadian experience as a classic example of the 'multiple-accelerator' process working its way downward into the slump, and then upwards again. What they mean by this opaque terminology is that the contraction in output, production, and employment was induced by declines in what we might call 'autonomous forces' – business spending on new plant and equipment, residential construction, inventories, and exports. Recovery, in turn, followed on the revival in such spending; it was slow and incomplete because Canada's export markets did not revive, and, even more, because business spending on investment remained unduly and painfully low through most of the 1930s. To understand why exports behaved as they did we would have to pursue the causes of the Depression into an analysis of the British, American, and other world economies, and into a discussion of the protectionist measures adopted by those countries between 1929 and 1933, and afterwards; for once launched, the protectionist trend was difficult to reverse. The behaviour of business investment is even more curious and mysterious, depending as it did on the balance between sales and existing capacity, on the pace of technological change, and on the 'animal spirits of the business community,' as John Maynard Keynes, the British economist, wrote in 1936.

To return to the Canadian case, we find that between 1929 and 1933 the volume of new business investment fell by 79 per cent. From 1932 through 1936, net investment was negative. In other words, for five years the value of new investment fell short of the value of the equipment that was wearing out, so that the country was consuming its capital. Even in 1938 the volume of new business investment was only 61 per cent of what it had been in 1929.

The results were depressingly impressive. In many of the nation's capital goods industries, and in almost all of Canada's consumer durables industries, production all but collapsed. The output of railway cars fell to thirty-one in 1933-4, and, in the same year, Canada, one of the world's great railway nations, produced no locomotives at all. Rail production fell by 88 per cent. Washing-machines and stoves, the consumer miracles of the 1920s, lost 42 per cent and 61 per cent of their production, respectively. Not everything suffered, but those few areas where production was sustained or increased, such as radios and refrigerators, were not especially important in the economy.

The most striking example of decline, and one of the most important, was in Canada's motor-car industry. The motor industry and its suppliers suffered dramatically, and their sufferings may be taken as a symbol and summary of the troubles which afflicted Canada's heavy industries. In Ontario, the industry's centre, car production fell from 128,496 units in 1929 to 30,606 in 1933, and trucks and buses dropped from 25,762 to 6062. But once the slump had started to wane, automobile production rebounded until, by 1937, it was well above even the record levels of the late 1920s. And related industries, such as tires and steel, rebounded too.

Interestingly, government stimulus and assistance had relatively little to do with the revival. Government spending dropped so far and so fast between 1930 and 1933 that even by the end of the decade its transfer payments to individuals or its spending on investment were still lagging behind the levels achieved in 1930. What did help? One encouragement was lower interest costs, which by reducing the price of credit encouraged business investment. The dominion government helped by easing the rules on mortgages for residential housing in 1935 and again in 1938, but the statistics on house construction (half in the late 1930s of what it had been in 1926-9) show that this initiative had little impact. The same was true of non-residential construction.

In these circumstances, it was quite clearly impossible for the capital goods industries, or for heavy industry generally, to revive. Personal consumer spending did in fact stand up rather better, both in the early 1930s and thereafter. After 1933 it certainly rose farther and faster than investment spending. Personal spending fell only 18 per cent between 1929 and 1933, and then it rose steadily, back to 1929 levels in 1937. It fell slightly in 1938, when there was a short recession, and then resumed its upward trend until, in the early years of the war, it was some 16 per cent above 1929. Consumer goods industries and many consumer durables industries (stoves and the like) therefore recovered much faster than other sectors of the economy.

How could this happen? Why was consumer demand so strong in the 1930s? Obviously, Canadian households did not cut back their spending in step with the shrinkage in their earnings. They must have saved less, or consumed past savings, and, as recovery proceeded in the late 1930s, they must have tried to spend themselves back to the living standards of the late 1920s. And, of course, not everybody was worse off. Wages fell and salaries fell, but not, generally, as far as prices were falling, and so for many Canadians who had jobs real incomes actually rose, even if we allow for the heavier income taxes which were also a feature of the period. Furthermore, in many industries real output per worker was rising, and so were average real annual earnings. The gains from this growth in productivity were not as striking as they might have been because many firms were working below capacity. Nevertheless, in spite of mass unemployment, when gains were realized they must often have been passed on to the workers.

For Canada's exports, the story of the 1930s is less dismal than for business investment. Between 1928 and 1933, export volumes went down by 32 per cent. Thereafter there was a sharp increase, so that by 1937 the volume of Canada's exports was larger than in 1928. Unfortunately, because price levels had fallen so far, these higher volumes earned less money. In spite of this decline, non-ferrous metals did well, relatively speaking, and so did forest products, although overcapacity in pulp and paper helped keep prices low. The great paper producing firms, such as Abitibi or Price Brothers, found themselves in trouble, and there they stayed. Appeals to Ottawa or to the provincial governments were pointless. Canada by itself could not raise the price of paper in export markets.

As we have suggested, developments in these markets contributed to Canada's slump. Australia and New Zealand were afflicted by many of the same troubles as Canada, and so they bought fewer Canadian cars and trucks. They raised their tariffs too, as the Americans had already done. But sometimes the contraction in Canadian exports was assisted by purely domestic developments. The great crop failures that occurred between 1934 and 1938 were disastrous for prairie wheat production. In Saskatchewan the worst year was 1937, when the total value of agricultural production sank to a pitiful $52 million, compared to $255 million in the not very prosperous year of 1929. True, the disaster of 1937 was not repeated, but it would take years for Saskatchewan to recover, and not until the mid-1940s was the income achieved in 1925 surpassed.

Because the British market contracted much less than the American, the United Kingdom did little to discourage Canadian sales in its domestic market, and Canada's exports to Britain were basic foodstuffs rather than industrial raw materials, the early 1930s saw a paradoxical redirection of Canada's export trade away from the American market and into Britain. This picture is in some respects misleading. Whereas the American slump and new and higher American tariffs shut out Canadian timber and metals from the American market, the British market was chiefly interested in Canadian foodstuffs. Britain, however, did buy wood products and metals in Canada.

AGRICULTURE AND THE SLUMP

The nation's farms were also in serious trouble. Even before the world slump began, wheat prices were falling as export markets turned sour. As the slump deepened, foreign governments tried to shut out the crisis by protecting their domestic markets, further worsening the prospects for Canada's wheat. Finally, drought and dustbowl conditions swept many parts of the prairies. The result was a regional disaster on a scale that caught farmers and governments alike unprepared.

In the years before the slump, about half of prairie wheat was marketed by the Wheat Pool. The pool, and its various provincial components, was accounted to be a success. It owned country and terminal elevators from railway sidings in the interior to the head of navigation at Port Arthur and Fort William on Lake Superior. The pools looked solid, and in 1928 they marketed a record crop. The price was not very satisfactory – $1.18 a bushel, down from $1.42 the year before – but it was acceptable, and the farmers hoped for better things the next year.

They did not get them. Despite a record for seeded (planted) acreage, the crop was barely half what it had been in the fall of 1928. By 1931 local governments were having to provide relief to devastated areas, where the crops had been destroyed by natural calamities. The crop yield, measured in terms of bushels of wheat per acre, dwindled; from 23.5 in the fall of 1928 it fell to 11.5 in 1929, to 8.1 in 1936, and finally to 6.4 in 1937. In terms of farm income, for all three prairie provinces, it fell from nearly $450 million in calendar 1928 to under $100 million in 1931. It would never be so bad again for the prairies as a whole, although in 1937 it would be worse in Saskatchewan.

Farm relief was essential. It had to come from government, but just as government, local and provincial, was dispensing individual relief payments, a larger customer came along. The wheat pools were in financial trouble. Overextended, they asked the three provinces to guarantee their borrowings from the banks. The borrowings had gone to pay advances on the 1929 crop and the banks had become sceptical of the pools' ability to cover those advances. But the provinces themselves were strapped for funds; they could not, and dared not, provide enough to save the pools. And so the problem was promoted to Ottawa, where it lay on the federal cabinet table. The federal government did what the Prairie provinces could not do, and guaranteed the bank loans, first temporarily and then, in January 1931, permanently. The pools' problems now merged in the larger problems of Canada's central government. And as government became the pools' standby, so politics became central to Canada's Depression experience.

The central government was, by 1931, in the hands of the Conservative party led by Prime Minister R.B. Bennett. Bennett dealt with the crisis in prairie wheat sales by installing John A. MacFarland, an old friend and an expert in the grain business, as general manager of the pools' central selling agency. MacFarland's appointment merely postponed the crisis. The central agency collapsed in 1931, but MacFarland laboured on, with Ottawa's money, selling but more often buying wheat until, in 1935, he and Bennett agreed that a more permanent arrangement was required. A new Canadian Wheat Board was therefore established with the power to market the prairie wheat crop. In deference to the objections of Winnipeg grain traders, however, its full powers were not immediately used.

The wheat board was just one of many contrivances called forth to meet the emergency of the 1930s. Like many others, its origins predated the Depression, and the concepts associated with it lived on. Both the dominion government and several of the provinces tried to enhance the powers of co-operative marketing boards during the 1930s. The Bennett government introduced a Natural Products Marketing Act in 1934, hoping to establish a nation-wide network through which individual farmers could be compelled to market their goods. The NPMA, as it was sometimes called, came to grief on the shoals of the British North America Act in 1937. British Columbia's government had anticipated the result and enacted its own marketing act, which also compelled producers to market their goods co-operatively so long as a majority in each group – apple growers, chicken raisers, or whatever – agreed to do so. Ottawa co-operated, eventually, by exempting the provincial marketing boards from the operations of the national anti-combines law.

By 1939 there were boards to cover apples, pork, grapes, tomatoes, cheese, peaches, asparagus, pears, plums, and cherries, but not prairie wheat, where, thanks to Bennett's compromise, private marketing coexisted with voluntary pooling through the Canadian Wheat Board. It would take another war to terminate private trading in wheat on the Winnipeg Grain Exchange.

This account of agriculture during the 1930s has skirted the most commonly discussed aspects of the Depression on the farms, or on farming communities. But those were spectacular, and they lived in memories for decades afterwards. Drought, heat, dust, and grasshoppers were the experience of much of the Canadian west during the 1930s. Driving across Saskatchewan in the summer of 1936, a reporter for the *Winnipeg Free Press,* James Gray, recorded passing through 'village after village without a sign of life, past empty farm after empty farm.' Along the roadside the fence was sometimes 'completely covered, indicating drifted soil at least three feet deep.' Dust storms had carried off the topsoil; as far east as Winnipeg a westerly wind meant airborne grit, and sometimes darkness at midday. Drivers passing through found their cars covered not just with dust but with grasshoppers. In Weyburn, Gray wrote, 'we made a deal with the son of a garageman to clean the grasshoppers off our car for a dollar. It took him almost two hours and a gallon of coal-oil.'[3]

In some places, money virtually disappeared as a medium of exchange. It happened on the prairies, of course, but also elsewhere. An Ontario doctor reported in 1934 that previously prosperous farmers in his rural township could no longer pay for medical care. In the winter of 1933-4 he had received 'over twenty chickens, several ducks, geese, a turkey, potatoes and wood on account,' and at that he counted himself lucky. 'Many country doctors,' he observed, 'have trouble collecting sufficient to purchase the bare necessities of life.'

THE CITIES IN DEPRESSION

The stark images of the prairie dustbowl are complemented by equally depressing images of urban souplines. These long lines of Canadians, with downcast faces, waiting for a bowl of soup reveal much of the desperation of the 1930s. There was a stigma to accepting handouts – hence the eyes averted from the photographer – but for many Canadians there was little choice. By the 1930s, there were too few garden plots in Canada's cities to support a large unemployed population. In this respect, at least, rural Canadians had an advantage over urban Canadians.

Private charity through traditional agencies such as churches and service clubs was grossly insufficient, and the state was not yet ready to take on the burden. In Canada, relief for the unemployed and the destitute was still largely a municipal responsibility in the 1930s. The municipalities had, in the past, received provincial government assistance in times of serious need, and, occasionally, the federal government had given funds to meet emergencies. The structure, however, quickly collapsed under the weight of Depres-

3   James Gray, *The Winter Years* (Toronto 1966), 175-9

sion unemployment. The cities had relief offices which 'doled' out whatever 'relief' was available, but the conditions were stringent and the amount of relief was generally small.

In most cases, those who went on relief in the cities had to prove that the alternative was starvation. Then the normal form of relief was food vouchers which could be redeemed at local merchants. This permitted only the purchase of necessities, and, in most cities, necessities were very narrowly defined. Rarely was there enough left over for clothing, and all kinds of items including curtains, bedsheets, and rags were fashioned into children's and adults' clothing. Most Canadians seemed to accept that the destitute deserved no more than the basics, even though it had become impossible to believe that the unemployed had chosen their own fate. In Ontario, Mitch Hepburn's 'reformist' Liberal government threatened to cut off all aid to cities which gave relief beyond the maximum which the province had established.

In limiting their responsibilities, municipalities were especially tough in the case of single, able-bodied males. Most, in fact, were denied all relief. This naturally created fears that this army of young, unemployed males would cause trouble as they swarmed about Canada's city centres. The federal government, fearing the impact of this group on civic peace, organized relief camps under the aegis of the Department of National Defence. By 1934 those camps, which were usually placed away from the cities, were hotbeds of protest. Relief camp workers organized in Vancouver, and in 1935 began an 'On to Ottawa' trek to carry their protests about pay and conditions to the federal government. By early summer the trek had reached Regina, 2000 strong. The government decided to halt them there, and on 1 July 1935 the RCMP tried to arrest the leaders. A riot broke out, and many men and police were injured. The trek did end, but the Bennett government lost much credibility.

The Depression deeply affected working urban women as well as men. There was a predominance of women in the fifteen to thirty-four age group in the cities, and these women sought the same kinds of employment which they had found readily in the 1920s.[4] The working mother or wife was usually the first target of layoffs, and this procedure seems to have had general approval, even among some trade unionists. Single women – and other women – often maintained their jobs through the acceptance of lower pay. Undoubtedly, some of the financial and other gains which were made in the 1920s were lost. Women's wages remained much lower than men's wages in most occupational categories, ranging in 1931 from as low as 44 per cent in

4   See Veronica Strong-Boag, 'The Girl of the New Day: Canadian Working Women in the 1920s,' *Labour/Le Travailleur* 4 (1979): 131-64.

manufacturing to 71 per cent in clerical. The gap was not to be closed before 1939.

Trade unions seemed unable to protect their members in the early 1930s, and membership dropped as unemployment rose. More radical trade unionists moved to fill the void which was created. The Communist-dominated Workers' Unity League gained support in some industrial centres and was most important in organizing the 'On to Ottawa' trek. Of more lasting importance, however, was the Congress of Industrial Organizations, an American labour organization which promoted organization by industry rather than craft. In 1937 workers at the General Motors plant in Oshawa walked out in a strike inspired by CIO leadership and ideals. The Ontario government under Mitch Hepburn denounced the CIO as Communist-led and tried to crush the strike. It did manage formally to shut out the CIO from Oshawa, but there was a peaceful settlement, and the new industrial unionism had established strong roots in Canada. Those roots, however, extended across the boundary.

Canadian cities, then, reacted differently from the countryside to the Depression. This was in large part the product of the changes in social and economic organization which had occurred since 1900. In an urban society, the effect of economic depression were felt all the more keenly since most individuals now depended on wage labour. The self-sufficiency of the rural areas, itself too easily exaggerated, was lacking among the urban proletariat. Deprived of wages, there was little alternative to relief, and desperation was all too common. The old ways and traditional nostrums were no longer available, and it was small wonder that social and political protest took unusual forms.

CONCLUSION

It was commonly believed in the 1930s, and to some extent since, that the 'Big Interests,' whether in trade or in finance, had somehow exclusively 'caused' the Depression or exacerbated the pain it caused. In the United States, this feeling reinforced that country's existing anti-trust traditions in the later 1930s and resulted in a spasm of prosecutions. In Canada, where anti-trust laws were a milder and paler version of the ferocious American originals, the result was the Royal Commission on Price Spreads and Mass Buying, which grew out of a parliamentary committee on the same subject. The 1935 report urged a stronger Combines Investigation Act (the Canadian equivalent of anti-trust), and the regulation of trade practices that might drive the competition out of business. Where monopoly was inevitable, government should regulate prices and profits. Primary producers should group together to sell their products – sellers' monopolies, with the force of law behind them. Workers should join trade unions; and employers, trade associations. Almost none of this fell within the powers of the dominion government, a fact which did not bother the commission. It did bother other people, including the government, and helped to ensure the burial of the commission's populist report.

In examining those neglected documents, Canada's decennial censuses of 1931 and 1941, a curious fact becomes apparent. If we measure modern conveniences, such as automobiles, radios, or mechanical refrigerators, Canadians were better off in 1941, or even 1939, than they had been ten years before. In terms of radios, for example, Canada manufactured twice as many in 1937 as in 1929, even if production had fallen temporarily between 1931 and 1934. As for automobiles, there were 250,000 more on the roads in 1939 than there had been ten years before. There were more roads – some roadbuilding was a Depression phenomenon – and more drivers consuming more gasoline.

For some Canadians, therefore, the Depression decade meant a continuation of the modernization of the 1920s. In spite of the slump, white-collar jobs proliferated, especially in wholesale and retail trade and in the professions. Rural doctors might get their fees in chickens; urban doctors still got money. So did members of the civil service, who were paid less, it is true, but in dollars that were worth more. Professors and most teachers also had a steady income. Even at the University of Manitoba, where the bursar absconded with the endowment, the government kept the doors open. British Columbia, arguably better off, came closer to closing its provincial university, but other avenues were found for economy.

The careful historian must notice such things. The 1930s were a decade of depression, but also a decade of invention and modernization. A quarter of the population might be out of work, but three-quarters of the population could still subsist by its own efforts. 'Things were out of control,' some argued; 'nobody was in charge.' There was dissatisfaction and, even more, there was uneasiness. But there was not, and would not be, revolt. Creaking and groaning, the system held together.

16

Politics and Policy in the Great Depression

The 1930s were a decade of political change almost everywhere. In Britain, France, Germany, the United States – almost everywhere elections were held – the decade ended with a different leader from which it had begun. The Americans started out with Herbert Hoover, and finished with Franklin Delano Roosevelt. The Germans, who began the 1930s with a socialist government, finished with a national socialist one – and Adolf Hitler. Canada started 1930 with Mackenzie King, and ended 1939 with Mackenzie King. In between, no fundamental reforms disturbed the functioning of Canada's constitution. The country finished the decade with the same constitution it had started out with. The same political parties dominated politics, just as they had since 1867. There were, it is true, some changes, but only in Alberta had the electors refused to vote in either a Liberal or a Conservative government in the course of the decade. Manitoba had a 'Progressive' government, but it was drawing steadily closer to the Liberals.

Yet if much was the same, much had also changed. The forms of politics may have been the same, and even the vessels, if we include the good ship Mackenzie King. Canadians were concerned with very different things in the 1920s from what they were in the 1930s, and even members of the two 'old parties' saw politics, and political possibilities, in a different light in 1939 from that which had illuminated their perceptions of 1929. The possibility that capitalism had entered a state of crisis, and that the crisis might be permanent, had occurred even to the most obtuse, although their proffered solutions were kaleidoscopic. But, and it is an important but, the party system contained the crisis, just as it had contained the racial and social unrest of 1917 and 1918.

At first, nobody expected the Depression to take the form it did. The year 1930 seemed like a downturn, but it was a gentle downturn, sliding by degrees towards the abyss. Unemployment was up, and with it relief. Reports from the farms out west were bad. The dominion government responded parsimoniously. The finance minister reported a surplus. Prime Minister King rebuffed demands that Ottawa pass money on to the provinces for relief. They would only abuse the privilege, he told an astonished House of Commons, and use it as a siphon to get at the dominion's hard-earned money for their 'alleged unemployment purposes.' For such purposes, the prime minister concluded, 'I would not give them a five-cent piece.' It was not one of King's better days and he did his best in the months that followed to divert attention from his uncharitable remark to issues that really mattered: the tariff, for example. The tariff went up and down, to signal the start of an election campaign.

Parliament was dissolved, and an election called for 28 July. It was an election King expected to win. The Conservatives had chosen as their leader a Calgary corporation lawyer, Richard Bedford Bennett, whose talents had led him west from his native New Brunswick at about the same time another legal fledgling, Max Aitken, had displaced himself further east to become Lord Beaverbrook. From an early age, Bennett's ample girth had made him a cartoonist's delight. To match his spats, striped trousers, and morning coat, Bennett added a pince-nez, perched (at least in cartoons) on top of his jowls. All this must have comforted the Liberals. Unfortunately for them, Bennett was also active, intelligent, and eloquent. Some did not care for his rotund phrases as he projected them at his audience, but observers in Parliament and on the campaign trail considered him the best speaker of his generation.

The campaign of 1930 was Canada's first radio election. Both King and Bennett addressed coast-to-coast audiences over a national hook-up. It was not the national radio network proposed by a royal commission the year before, but it was sufficient to impress the politicians with the possibilities of combining technology with government money. To Canadians at the time, however, it seems to have made election campaigns last longer.

Long or short, the campaign went against the Liberals. Bennett at the outset told a Winnipeg audience that he would 'use tariffs to blast a way into the markets that have been closed to you.' King's protests were swept aside, and there were five provincial Conservative governments to help with the sweeping. They knew what he meant by his 'five-cent' speech and they believed that Bennett could not possibly be worse. Tariff rates, terms of trade, and fears of foreign competition swung crucial votes, especially in rural Quebec, to the Conservatives. And when the smoke cleared on election day, Bennett had his majority: 137 seats in the House of Commons out of 245, compared to 91 for the Liberals and 12 for the rump Progressives. (See Appendix 1.) 'The truth is I feel I do not much care, the load is very heavy,

'*My Government*'   R.B. Bennett and his cabinet, 1931
Arch Dale, *Winnipeg Free Press*

& I wd gladly do literary work for a while,' Mackenzie King told his diary.

And so it was Bennett, not King, who bore the political brunt of the Depression. The new prime minister had no thought of avoiding it. He knew his abilities and he was confident they would prove equal to the challenge. He raised tariffs. He journeyed abroad to meet with the great. He ruled his cabinet with a rod of iron. King's diary recorded the sequel, as minister after minister trailed off to tell him how little they liked the man who had elevated them to office, and how they longed for his contrition, if not his defeat. Bennett's parliamentary majority preserved him from that, in the short term. But it would not be long before his provincial outworks started to crumble.

One of the lasting consequences of the Depression was its effect on the political balance within Canada, as between Liberals and Conservatives. It would assist in the creation of new parties, the socialist Co-operative Com-monwealth Federation, or CCF, and the Alberta-based Social Credit party, and it would bury, once and for all, the remnants of the old Progressive par-ty. What is of most interest, however, is the manner in which the Depression altered the relations between the dominion or national government and the governments of Canada's provinces. The 1920s had been a decade of provin-cial rights, provincial projects, and provincial spending. The dominion had to fight, and sometimes fight hard, against demands by some provinces that it retrench by limiting its taxing practices to what they had been before 1916, abandoning the lucrative field of income tax to the provinces. The dominion could and did argue that it needed the money to pay off the debts left over from the First World War, a valid enough position but hardly a forceful one. The election of 1930 showed how difficult it was to budge Mackenzie King from his defence of the national treasury, and it showed how little either he or Bennett anticipated the demands that would be made upon it. What was worse, in the short term, was that the provinces had not anticipated the De-pression either.

During the 1920s the provinces had attached themselves to the British North America Act. As a consequence, they found themselves burdened during the 1930s with welfare and relief costs. They needed help from Otta-wa, and help was forthcoming. The Bennett government's attitude could hardly be described as gracious, and its help was at best unwilling. But be-cause it was the biggest and most solvent Canadian government it automati-cally improved its position vis-à-vis its provincial counterparts. The centrifugal forces of the 1920s were replaced by centripetal ones. Centrali-zation became the panacea for the disease of provincial insufficiency. This development, the most lasting legacy of the decade, has sometimes gone un-recognized, hidden by the artful politics and personal fireworks exploded by provincial politicians.

We cannot describe the situation in each province, but we can consider three examples: Manitoba, one of the worst-hit provinces, British Columbia, in between, and Ontario, one of the better off. In Manitoba the Depression hit early and hard. Unemployment was a serious problem as early as the winter of 1929-30. John Bracken's farmer government responded by helping out municipalities with winter works and with the cost of direct relief. There was, nonetheless, a heavy burden on individual municipalities, and it was obvious by the summer of 1930 that Manitoba's cities and towns would soon be at the end of their credit and tax resources. When the Bennett govern-ment passed its Unemployment Relief Act to provide dominion assistance to provinces and municipalities, Bracken found its conditions hard to bear. Ot-tawa would contribute to relief funds provided that municipalities funded fully 50 per cent of the total. The heaviest cost would go to the level of government least able to sustain it.

Compromises were made, but from Manitoba's point of view they could never go far enough. By January 1931 Bracken was asking Ottawa to pick up 80 per cent of the cost of direct relief, and pointing out that relief efforts should not be confined to the urban unemployed. Another federal relief act passed in August 1931 went only part way to meet Bracken's demands, but by then those demands had escalated. Manitoba could no longer afford to pay its share of old-age pensions. Would Ottawa assume the whole cost? Bennett responded grudgingly. He gave a little, and he added a constitutional lecture, noting that 'any effort on the part of the Dominion to undertake the direction of purely provincial or municipal undertakings would be in derogation of the constitutional rights of the provinces.'[1]

By the fall of 1931 Manitoba was cutting civil servants' wages (along with those of provincial ministers) and reducing any and all discretionary expenditures. On the axiom that union makes for strength, Bracken also invited Manitoba's opposition parties into his government; after prolonged negotiations, only the Liberals joined in 1932. The province needed money to meet its maturing obligations, and, reluctantly, Bennett agreed to cover it. Default by a province was not to be allowed, whatever the constitutional niceties of provincial rights.

The next few years simply repeated the pattern. The Manitoba government wore a path to its bankers' doors. The bankers would lecture the Manitobans on the need for a balanced budget, and in addition would extend some slight assistance to enable the province to limp onwards. When major obligations fell due, Manitoba turned to the dominion government, precipitating another round of lectures from Bennett. Rather than face default, however, with all that that entailed for the credit of Canada as a whole, Bennett would help out in paying off provincial bonds. He would emphatically not help Manitoba by further relief payments; instead, he earnestly implored the province to put its own financial house in order. But how would Manitoba do so? Taxes had risen and it was a real question how much more the hard-pressed provincial taxpayer would or could bear. Bracken nevertheless did what he could, with the result that the budget was indeed balanced by 1935 – always excluding relief. Appeased, Bennett could be relied on to pay the province's maturing obligations; but he would not give way on relief.

Instead, Ottawa's relief contribution was actually reduced in 1934, and although Mackenzie King's Liberals raised it again when they took office in 1935, it was never enough. Manitobans continued to show a measure of con-

1 Quoted in J. Kendle, *John Bracken: A Political Biography* (Toronto 1979), 114

fidence in their embattled government, returning it (under Liberal-Progressive colours) in 1932 and again in 1936, though in the latter year Bracken could barely scrape through with a minority administration sustained by the votes of the fledgling Social Credit party.[2]

Bracken's administration was in no position to exercise much initiative, but by combining and converting his party he was at least able to stay in power. His was the only government to do so between 1930 and 1940. British Columbia, by contrast, changed its government, and in this respect it was a much more typical province. Canada's westernmost province began the Depression with the Conservative government of S.F. Tolmie, elected in 1928. Like Manitoba, however, British Columbia had a large and volatile metropolis; and like Winnipeg, Vancouver very early had a large and vociferous group of unemployed. Taxes and the provincial debt rose, and the province's bank overdraft for unemployment relief alone reached $2.4 million by the spring of 1932.

To all this, the province's businessmen had a ready answer. Government expenditure, they proclaimed in 1932, could be reduced to a third of its existing level. The legislature and the cabinet were far too big and should be halved in size. The University of British Columbia should be taken off the provincial budget and left to fend for itself, surviving if it could. Other reductions suggested included the paring down of free public education, and, of course, no increase in social welfare.

A desperate Tolmie, like Bracken, sought salvation through coalition. Unlike Bracken, he had no takers. Having postponed an election until the last possible moment, November 1933, Tolmie was annihilated at the polls. The Conservatives ceased to exist as a major party. The Liberals won, with a large majority, but facing them across the floor of the legislature was a new opposition, the CCF, founded in Regina only that year. The new premier was Duff Pattullo, a transplanted Grit from southwestern Ontario.

British Columbia, Pattullo learned, depended on two things: its bankers, for overdrafts, and Ottawa, for salvation from default. As John Bracken could have told him, Bennett prized 'responsible finance' and that meant, as far as possible, a balanced budget. Instead, Pattullo proposed to spend more. He raised the level of relief payments, regulated hours of work, and fixed minimum wages, while the province's mining industry and fish processing plants got grants to help them out. Pattullo then asked Ottawa for money.

Sorely provoked, Bennett demanded that Victoria cut its cloth to suit. If it wanted Ottawa's money, then it would get it on Bennett's terms. Bennett's lectures provoked defiance from Pattullo. British Columbia would not have

2   The above is based on Kendle, *Bracken,* chapters 8 and 9.

its budget made in Ottawa. It would, instead, have 'equality of treatment,' which meant that Ottawa should absorb the province's money-losing Pacific Great Eastern Railway and pay out more subsidies. Pattullo got a little more money, but it would never be enough.

Flamboyant as Pattullo may have seemed to the cautious members of the Bennett government, he paled by comparison with some of the other political fauna that British Columbia produced. Gerry McGeer, the Liberal mayor of Vancouver, had his own unique solution to the province's financial problems. Let the four western provinces set up their own monetary system and get the presses rolling.

McGeer's schemes at least had the advantage that they were close enough to Social Credit to pass as almost the genuine article. When in 1935 a wave of economic and political rage swept over neighbouring Alberta, McGeer was exported across the Rockies to see whether he could persuade Albertans to vote the Liberal ticket under the delusion that some kind of monetary convulsion would follow. But as a provincial cabinet minister ruefully observed, 'If the Apostle Paul had been loose in Alberta for six months, he couldn't have stopped Social Credit.' Another British Columbian, Henry Angus of the University of British Columbia, got no further when he suggested that the 'effects of Social Credit were as obvious as those of arsenic.'[3] Obvious or not, the people of Alberta were determined to try the potion distilled by the Reverend William ('Bible Bill') Aberhart, and they elected Social Credit overwhelmingly in August 1935.

Meanwhile, more old governments were being exchanged for new. In Ontario the Conservative government of George Henry had had little more joy of R.B. Bennett than its Liberal and Liberal-Progressive counterparts in the west. But then, it must be admitted, politics were a reciprocal process. Bennett and Henry each had his problems, and each tried to solve them by thrusting them on the other. Provincial revenues went down by $3 million between 1930 and 1931 (representing 5 per cent of total revenues), and by $3 million more between 1931 and 1932. By the winter of 1932-3 the provincial government estimated that 10 per cent of Ontario's population was on relief. This caused Henry to suggest to Bennett that the dominion transfer personal income taxes to the provinces. Absolutely not, Bennett replied – not unreasonably under the circumstances. How could Ottawa surrender any of its revenues when it was bailing out half the country and casting a nervous eye over the other half?

Bennett could, and did, go further. When the western provincial premiers suggested that the dominion assume the entire burden of relief and establish

3   John Irving, *The Social Credit Movement in Alberta* (Toronto 1959), 317 and 329

its own system of unemployment insurance, Bennett told a dominion-provincial conference in January 1934 that the provinces were by nature wasteful and extravagant. Let them shape up, or let them disappear. As for Ontario and Quebec, they 'should not be receiving any assistance from the Dominion in connection with direct relief. They were rich and powerful enough to look after themselves.'[4] As the spring wore on, pleas from frantic provincial Tories did produce some action from their federal cousins, but by then it was too late. In June 1934 the provincial Liberals under Mitchell Hepburn routed the Conservatives at the polls. Ontario's voice in dominion-provincial relations would now sound a somewhat different note.

Mitchell Hepburn, 'Mitch' to friends and foes alike, was definitely a new variety of leader. 'Come on in,' he would say, welcoming visitors to his hotel suite in downtown Toronto, 'it's nice to see you.' The visitor confronted 'a smiling young man,' with 'a round cheerful face and a chin that was small but purposeful. He wore a well-tailored double-breasted suit and had the appearance and manner of a popular young-man-about-town. From the room behind him came the sounds of radio dance music and ice clinking in glasses and girls' voices.'[5] When he was new to office, Hepburn reverently kept a large colour photograph of Mackenzie King on display in his hotel home; later, presumably, it would be relegated to the dustbin along with Mackenzie King.

But that is to anticipate. Between 1930 and 1935 Mackenzie King had no more faithful admirer than Mitchell F. Hepburn, whose ample fund of irritation was concentrated on the bloated figure of Prime Minister R.B. Bennett. Hepburn was not alone in this. Most Canadians seemed to feel cheated by Bennett and his promises, and when the prime minister attempted to recapture their regard by promising reform, they reacted sceptically. On learning that the prime minister proposed to introduce an unemployment insurance bill, his erstwhile minister of trade and commerce, H.H. Stevens, wryly commented that he had been 'amused ... greatly' to see Bennett 'trotting out to the front in great shape.' Bennett was moved, among other things, by concern lest Stevens replace him, for his ex-minister had earned a considerable reputation through the Price Spreads Commission and hoped to put it to good use by deposing the ailing prime minister. But Bennett, spurred on by his closest advisers, his brother-in-law W.D. Herridge and his secretary Rod Finlayson, exploded a mine under Stevens and, incidentally, the rest of the Conservative party, in January 1935.

4   Christopher Armstrong, *The Politics of Federalism: Ontario's Relations with the Federal Government, 1867-1942* (Toronto 1981), 152
5   A. Jenkinson, *Where Seldom a Gun is Heard* (London 1939), 214

The prime minister, it was announced, would speak to the nation over the radio, via a special network of over thirty stations. Bennett was not a practised radio speaker, and the result, according to knowledgeable observers, was hasty and fumbled. But fumbled or not, Bennett's message was plain: the economic system must be brought under control in order to create employment and end relief. The dole must go, the prime minister said, for it 'was a condemnation, final and complete, of our economic system. If we cannot abolish the dole, we should abolish the system.' Reaction was mixed, especially inside Bennett's cabinet. Some thought it great stuff, while others reached for their resignations. The financial community in Montreal and Toronto was greatly disturbed. The prime minister did his best, such as it was. Coming out of cabinet one day he jovially slapped the venerable Sir George Perley, a veteran of the Borden era, on the back: 'How are you, comrade?'

Bennett's radio addresses – there were five of them – proposed a Canadian version of the 'New Deal' immortalized by American President Franklin Delano Roosevelt. Bennett next introduced legislation into Parliament. It was duly passed; and just as certainly it was, most of it, ruled *ultra vires* by the courts. Mackenzie King, who had forecast just such an outcome, could take satisfaction in his predictive powers. The Canadian constitution stood four-square against Bennett's attempt to create 'a dictatorship,' and the hallowed divisions of powers between the dominion and the provinces would baulk any such rash plans.

King was right, and thereafter events moved just as he wished. Bennett failed to carry large segments of his own party. H.H. Stevens, failing to displace the prime minister, founded his own Reconstruction party. It would elect only one member in the election to come, Stevens himself, but it would take 8.7 per cent of the vote, much of it, presumably, away from the Conservatives. Even an additional 8.7 per cent would not have helped Bennett. On 14 October, election day, the Conservatives won 29.6 per cent of the vote, compared to the Liberals' 44.8 per cent, and only forty seats compared to King's 173. The newly founded CCF received just 0.1 per cent more votes than the Reconstruction party, but because its support was more concentrated, it received seven seats. (The Social Credit party, based in Alberta, got seventeen seats, though with only 4 per cent of the national total.)

It would, therefore, be Mackenzie King who would finish out the Depression. Politically, the weather was fair. Seven provinces had straight Liberal governments; the eighth, Manitoba, was almost Liberal in its complexion, and only Alberta, under Social Credit, was anti-Liberal. Foremost among King's loyal supporters was Mitchell Hepburn. He had campaigned hard for King and against Bennett in the 1935 election. When King won, Hepburn might have been pardoned for believing that the millennium was at hand, with King cast in the role of saviour. It took Hepburn hardly any time at all to exchange King's halo for a devil mask, and in what followed the element of personal animosity cannot be ignored.

Hepburn's vision was not entirely fixed on Ottawa. He bowed towards the universal totem of 'economy' by auctioning off the previous government's limousines. He tilted at imaginary enemies by repudiating power contracts between Ontario Hydro and Quebec's private power companies. More constructively, Mitch enforced pasteurization on his province's reluctant farmers. It would be pleasant to report a related decline in tuberculosis, but our health statistics are not up to it. As reporting disease became more common and health practices more thorough, the number of cases appearing in statistics also rose. Nevertheless, pasteurization was a positive achievement for a government that had few.

What was missing in substance showed up as sound and fury as Hepburn tackled Ottawa. The dominion government was niggardly, and Hepburn discovered that King would not give Ontario as much as it wanted, when it wanted. King showed a disposition to place conditions on the use of federal funds, just as Bennett had. King would not let Ontario cover its electric power shenanigans by engaging in sham exports of energy. The two governments clashed over the proposed St Lawrence Seaway, and Mitch did his best to obstruct progress in discussions with the Americans. Despite his objections, a treaty was signed between Canada and the United States on the subject in 1941, only to languish in Congress for the following decade.

On the subject of power exports, and the Seaway too, Hepburn found he had an ally to the east. This time the ally was not a Liberal, but a Tory: Maurice Duplessis, the Union Nationale premier of Quebec. Duplessis, leader of the provincial Conservatives, had fashioned a political alliance with a group of dissident Liberals, the Action Libérale Nationale. Together the two groups commanded enough support in the Quebec assembly to obstruct the government of Louis-Alexandre Taschereau, which was shivering through a season of exceptional unpopularity. Duplessis succeeded in bringing the ALN under his direction, setting aside its titular leader Paul Gouin. 'I do not think any of us realized at the time what an energetic and forceful personality Duplessis was, and how easily he would establish his supremacy over Gouin and most of his followers,' Chubby Power, King's minister of pensions, wrote. But he did, and not only over the ALN. Taschereau's own followers were intimidated by Duplessis and, more particularly, by his hints of unpleasant revelations about their personal conduct while in office. Using the province's Public Accounts Committee as a forum, Duplessis conducted his own inquisition into the scandals, real or imagined, of Taschereau's disintegrating government. Finally, at the beginning of June 1936, Taschereau resigned. The legislature was dissolved and elections called for August. 'Avec un régime aussi dissolu,' Duplessis quipped, 'la dissolution s'imposait.'

The Liberals were defeated, and Duplessis took office. He presided over a grab-bag of Liberals, nationalists, and Conservatives, some of whom were, in the premier's own words, 'fanatiques et extremistes.' Duplessis had no time for the latter category. Strong on rhetoric and on symbolic acts, the Duplessis government had not the slightest intention of rocking the boat by practical change. The greatest difference between the departed Taschereau and the renovated Duplessis was that the new government took a more liberal attitude towards public expenditures.

The advent of the Duplessis government shook the foundations of the federal Liberal party. Mackenzie King's entire political strategy was founded on conciliation between English and French Canadians. Now his provincial allies in Quebec were scattered and in their place was a government that stressed the national unity of French Canadians and that coped with English Quebeckers mainly by omission. It is understandable that King and his Quebec lieutenant Ernest Lapointe should have an attack of nerves whenever they gazed across the Ottawa River at the strange and unpredictable province of Quebec.

In the dominion-provincial conflicts of 1935-41, however, Quebec played a secondary role. It would be Hepburn, Pattullo, and Aberhart who would repeatedly confront Mackenzie King. And it was towards Aberhart that King's eye first travelled.[6]

THE CRISIS OF FEDERALISM

Social Credit, if it was about anything, was about banking and finance. Banking is an indisputable aspect of federal jurisdiction in Canada, and any attempt to implement social credit was bound to run athwart the provisions of the British North America Act. At first, the Aberhart government proceeded cautiously. It had to deal with ordinary administration and it had to cope with Alberta's debt. That debt was great – almost certainly beyond the ability of the province to handle, unaided. The only thing more certain was that the price for aid from Ottawa would be politically unpalatable.

It seemed obvious that the whole of Canada had a vital interest in the credit worthiness of each of the country's nine provinces. A default on interest payments owing on a bond issue would undermine investor confidence in the reliability of Canadian finance and make the raising of future loans ei-

6 On Duplessis in this period see Conrad Black, *Duplessis* (Toronto 1977).

Premier Aberhart sings the praises of Social Credit to an unappreciative audience, 1936
Arch Dale, *Winnipeg Free Press*

ther more expensive or, in the worst case, virtually impossible. No province
of Canada had ever yet defaulted on its securities; but by 1935 only the
dominion government stood between most of Canada's provinces and financial ruin.

Under the circumstances, the dominion bailed away with guarantees and
emergency payments as successive provincial loans fell due. It did not take
long for the thought to occur that this was no way to run a country, for each
bailout rammed home the lesson that the dominion government was acting
as the bank of last resort for the provinces. Whatever a province had borrowed, Ottawa must ultimately pay, or so it seemed.

Australia, with a similar federal system, had solved the problem of federated debt by establishing a central loan council, whose sanction was necessary before an individual state could borrow funds. Surely something of the
kind was indicated for Canada if the provinces expected the dominion government, in the last resort, to foot the bill. The King government therefore

placed before the provinces, in December 1935, a proposal for a loan council. It was, in fact, a proposal for nine loan councils, one for each province, with the dominion minister of finance or his representative sitting on each, in tandem with his provincial counterpart. The effect would be to give the dominion a say in how a province raised its money; in return, provincial debt would be backed by the credit of all of Canada, and its interest charges would fall proportionately to reflect the higher credit rating of the Ottawa government.

Finance minister C.A. Dunning secured the apparent agreement of all the provinces to his proposal, which seemed to promise both regularity and security. But in March 1936 it became clear that Alberta's provincial treasurer and Premier Aberhart disagreed where the loan council was concerned. When the real meaning of the loan council – that Ottawa would have some control over his province's future borrowing – became clear to Aberhart, he backed out of the agreement. The dominion government, for its part, refused to advance any further funds to Alberta to meet the province's maturing obligations. Accordingly, on 1 April 1936 Alberta became the first Canadian province to default on its obligations. Thereafter, Alberta unilaterally reduced interest payments on outstanding debt, and efforts by bondholders to reach an accommodation with the Aberhart government proved fruitless.

The Aberhart government's actions were swiftly placed before the courts, which duly ruled against the Social Credit government. Interest was a federal, not a provincial, matter. Further legislative and legal skirmishes followed in 1937 and 1938. Aggrieved creditors finally petitioned the dominion government to exercise its powers of disallowance over Alberta's actions. Action was postponed pending the June 1938 election in Saskatchewan, where it was feared that decisive action by Ottawa might have the effect of nurturing Social Credit sentiments among the electorate. The Liberal party won that election, and within days of the Liberal victory justice minister Lapointe rose in the House of Commons to characterize certain Alberta acts as 'unjust in that they confiscate the property of one group of persons for another group.' Indeed, the acts were also discriminatory and confiscatory, as well as 'injurious to the public interest of Canada.' Two acts were therefore disallowed, although Lapointe prudently left the rest to the certain judgment of the courts. The battle did not end at this point. Alberta persisted, and further disallowance was the result, the last round coming in 1941-2.[7]

Debt, credit, and interest were not the only fields of struggle between Edmonton and Ottawa under Aberhart and King. Aberhart tried to issue his own paper currency – a form of the Social Credit 'social dividend.' And he

7 See J.R. Mallory, *Social Credit and the Federal Power in Canada* (Toronto 1954), especially chapters 6 and 7.

attempted to muzzle his domestic enemies inside Alberta as well. An Accurate News and Information Act, passed in 1937, obliged Alberta newspapers to publish government press releases issued to correct 'misinformation' appearing in their columns; worse, reporters were required to reveal sources for their stories, a power which presumably would be resorted to when those stories proved difficult for the government.

It is not surprising that relations between the dominion government and the government of Alberta descended to new lows. To punish the lieutenant-governor, an Ottawa appointee, for reserving certain acts (a kind of suspensory veto), the legislature did away with his expense allowance and cut off funds for his official residence. The lieutenant-governor retaliated during the visit of King George VI and Queen Elizabeth in 1939 by refusing to invite the premier of the province to his reception for Their Majesties. A bemused Mackenzie King, spotting Aberhart pacing up and down outside, escorted the premier in as his personal guest.

As for the general problem of dominion-provincial financial entanglements, the King government approached the question in two ways. First, it hared off in pursuit of waste; next, it proposed an extended meditation on dominion-provincial relations.

To bring the legacy of Bennett's supposedly wasteful policies under control, King and his minister of labour, Norman Rogers, appointed a National Employment Commission under the chairmanship of Arthur Purvis, the president of Canadian Industries Limited [CIL]. Purvis was a forward-looking man, who held more liberal views than the majority of his business contemporaries. But he was also a practical man, the sort who are often thought to possess magical powers which can exorcise the spectre of waste. This was premised on the deep-rooted conviction that relief in Canada meant waste and extravagance. If a solution could be found, the provinces would soon be spending less federal money on relief, a provincial responsibility. Meanwhile, the King government was obliged to stagger on with handouts to the improvident provinces. The amount of aid was reduced in 1936 in the hope of bringing the dominion's deficit under control. But unemployment remained high, and drought in the west produced special misery there.

The continuing crisis in the finances of the Prairie provinces encouraged officials in Ottawa to search for a longer-term solution. It had the same effect on John Bracken of Manitoba, who in December 1936 begged for a royal commission to investigate the tangled question of revenues and responsibilities under the Canadian constitution. After a Bank of Canada investigation of Manitoba's finances, it was learned that Manitoba might soon follow Alberta's lead and unilaterally reduce its interest payments on its bonds. Rather than face such a prospect, and abandon its position that aid for relief purposes must be temporary and minimal, the King government agreed, first, to provide emergency aid, and, second, to appoint a royal commission to examine dominion-provincial relations and finances.

To head the Royal Commission on Dominion-Provincial Relations the government appointed the distinguished chief justice of Ontario, Newton Rowell, J.W. Dafoe, editor of the *Winnipeg Free Press*, and Joseph Sirois, a Quebec City notary. Finally, for regional balance, the government selected Henry Angus, Aberhart's erstwhile opponent on the Alberta hustings, as British Columbia's representative, and Robert MacKay, a Dalhousie university professor. Alex Skelton, O.D. Skelton's son and an economist with the Bank of Canada, became the commission's secretary. When Rowell became ill part way through the commission's proceedings, Sirois took over as chairman, and from that accident the commission is universally known as the Rowell-Sirois Commission. It was one of the most important royal commissions in Canadian history.

The commission did not report until May 1940. What it had to say was nevertheless worth the saying. It recognized that there ought to be some kind of national Canadian standard of government services or, as the commission put it, 'normal Canadian services with no more than normal Canadian taxation.' This was the exact opposite of Hepburn's and Ontario's contention. Where a province could not provide these services for itself, the dominion government should assist it with National Adjustment Grants. These grants would be made from federal revenues. Those revenues were to be expanded by giving the dominion exclusive power to tax not only estates but also incomes, both personal and corporate.

The dominion government was also to assume the provinces' debts and, because of Quebec's different structure of debt, some municipal obligations in that province as well. The dominion was to finance the whole cost of unemployment insurance and old-age pensions – an unfortunate idea just at the beginning of the most expensive war in Canadian history.

Mackenzie King would have been content to let circumstances bury the Rowell-Sirois report, but his subordinates would not let him forget it. The federal government's position was strengthened by the concentration of power in Ottawa's hands during the war emergency. The King government was smashingly re-elected in March 1940, in a campaign explicitly designed to endorse King's leadership over Hepburn's. Maurice Duplessis had been put in the political wastebin by his own electorate in October 1939 when he challenged Ottawa's right to involve Quebec in Canada's war against Hitler. Nothing in the war had changed the basic facts that had called forth the commission, King was told. Now Canada had a war to finance, but how could it do so if its credit rating was dropping owing to the unconsidered and desperate actions of its provinces? Reluctantly, King hauled out the Rowell-Sirois report and, in September 1940, it was studied by a cabinet committee chaired by finance minister J.L. Ilsley. The committee recommended action, and Ilsley set out on a tour of the provinces. He got the reaction he could have expected. Some provincial governments favoured action along Rowell-Sirois lines. Others did not, objecting vehemently to any diminution in their powers.

The dominion government proceeded to call a dominion-provincial conference in Ottawa in January 1941. Mackenzie King, at least, had no high expectations of the conference, but he recognized that it was necessary to dispel doubt and clear up his own government's position. The dominion needed money to run the war, and it would soon have to raise more taxes whether the provinces made room for it or not. A statement of Ottawa's position would be helpful, and the conference would concentrate attention on what Ilsley had to say. As King wrote in his diary, 'It will lay the ground for such action as may shortly become imperative, and it should help to advance the necessary reforms by at least a step.'[8]

At the conference, most of the premiers were approving. Some may have found comfort in the fact that three provinces were certain to refuse to concede anything at all; but others, particularly Saskatchewan and Manitoba, were deeply dismayed. One observer at the conference described one of its sessions as 'the god damnedest exhibition and circus you can imagine.' Mitch Hepburn was in full flight. The Rowell-Sirois report, he claimed, was the spawn of 'three professors and a Winnipeg newspaper man, none of whom had any governmental administrative experience.' The report, indeed the whole conference, was just an excuse for an attack on Ontario, the most deeply patriotic of all provinces. Ontario's patriotism was affronted by an attempt to fiddle with the constitution while London literally burned under the attacks of the *Luftwaffe*. Aberhart and Pattullo chimed in.

Most of the publicity was reaped by Hepburn, and almost all of it was unfavourable. His oafish performance further undermined his position politically, while his calls to patriotism and appeals for war-winning action in fact played into the hands of King and his cabinet. Finance minister Ilsley delivered, as King wished, his analysis of the financial state of the nation. He told the premiers that, failing adoption of the Rowell-Sirois proposals, Ottawa would have to raise its own taxes, and that its action would certainly reduce provincial revenues. Despite Ilsley's warning that Rowell-Sirois and the war effort were in fact linked and not poles apart as Hepburn claimed, the dissenting premiers continued to obstruct discussion. King therefore adjourned

8   Quoted in Armstrong, *Politics of Federalism,* 223-6

the conference. He had, after all, achieved what he thought he was likely to get. The dominion government's position was fully ventilated. Its spokesmen had been moderate and persuasive. And Hepburn had received all the publicity that King could possibly have desired. When, shortly afterwards, Hepburn proudly reported a surplus in his provincial budget, he delivered himself even further into King's hands.

The other two dissenters, Aberhart and Pattullo, faced contrasting fates. Aberhart had only to account to his Social Credit faithful. He was not opposed to some arrangement with Ottawa that would bring revenues to Alberta while conceding taxes to Ottawa. When Ilsley and his officials came calling later in 1941, Alberta came to an agreement without too much trouble. Duff Pattullo, whose position on this issue was not far from Aberhart's, also was prepared to be reasonable, but in his case it was too little, too late. He had alienated a large part of his province's business community, and he found himself receiving brickbats from the press. It was rumoured that John Hart, Pattullo's finance minister, did not agree with his leader. At the end of the year, after an inconclusive provincial election, Pattullo was out, and John Hart was British Columbia's new premier, at the head of a coalition Liberal-Conservative government.

The new system which Ilsley proposed was called the War-time Tax Agreements, or, more succinctly, tax rental. In the event, somewhat modified, it lasted until 1962. The federal government collected income and corporation taxes, and in return offered the provinces what they had earned from those sources in 1940. Alternatively, the dominion government would hand over to a province an amount equivalent to its payment on its debt, less succession duties. Revenue from gasoline taxes and from liquor taxes was also guaranteed; this was important, because both sources were affected by wartime rationing. The War-time Tax Agreements gave each province a regular and predictable source of revenue in place of a system whose yields in wartime might prove erratic and unpredictable.

In several respects the 1930s had proved to be a centralizing decade. First of all, the fiscal fabric of Confederation had buckled under the strain of the Depression. Forced to underwrite the provinces' relief outlays and their debt service, and plagued by a serious deficit of its own, the dominion government could not stand on constitutional niceties: obliged to provide extra-constitutional subsidies, Ottawa had to worry about the constitution itself. The provinces might not like the results – proposals for loan councils; royal commissions; schemes for moving debts, taxes, and social service outlays from provincial to federal responsibility. But they could not prevent the schemes and proposals from emerging. Second, to the fiscal stresses was added an intellectual one: insofar as Canadians wanted more and better social services in the long run, the constitution seemed to pose an insuperable barrier – it gave the relevant responsibilities to the junior governments which, in turn, seemed unable to shoulder them. Constitutional reform thus became both a progressive and a nationalist cause, and its influence was probably strongest among those who were as yet too young, and too subordinate, to have the running of things. But men like Lester Pearson, Alex Skelton, Brooke Claxton, Jack Pickersgill, and Frank Scott could not be denied forever. When their turn came, the country would start out with a modern agenda worked up from their experience in the 1930s. The first step was taken in 1940 when, by means of a constitutional amendment which the provinces did not contest, the dominion took power to provide unemployment insurance. Finally, insofar as the intellectuals had begun to dream of 'planning,' or to hanker after the modern techniques of economic management which derived from the work of Keynes, it was obvious that Ottawa, not the provincial capitals, would have to house the experts and wield the powers. Hence the symbolic importance of such new and very centralized institutions as the Bank of Canada, the CBC, and Trans-Canada Air Lines.

In the face of these new realities, provincial government responses were many and varied. Generally speaking, the more bankrupt a province had become, the more willing was its government to shed powers and functions to Ottawa. Those who wanted change included Nova Scotia's Angus L. MacDonald, who argued for a redistribution of responsibilities and money that would give his people a chance at an equal standard of services on a national basis. John Bracken, the most persistent and responsible of provincial leaders, was also the most ardently centralizing. McNair of New Brunswick, Campbell of Prince Edward Island, and Patterson of Saskatchewan were less prominent, though equally postulant. Alberta was a special case: bankrupt it might be, but its Social Credit leadership believed itself to possess a message of monetary salvation which forced it to do battle with the Money Powers of Ottawa and Toronto. Tradition also played a part, as with Pattullo, who took his stand on British Columbia's traditional claim to 'equal treatment' (meaning more money and special treatment) within Confederation. Duplessis's approach to Rowell-Sirois probably falls into this category, although it is sometimes difficult to identify the rationale whereby Quebec's fun-loving ex-premier arrived at his conclusions. Hepburn, as we have seen, was in a class by himself. His arguments, like those of Pattullo, should not be treated as serious exercises in the arithmetic of fiscal federalism: even if Ottawa had turned over all the shared tax fields to the provinces, the richest of the provinces would have still been in trouble at anything like the rate-structures of 1938-9. And Ottawa, which was also in fiscal difficulties throughout the decade, certainly could not afford to abandon the income tax. But in arguing about the sharing, and in demanding a larger piece of the action, the provincial premiers were foreshadowing the future: such squabbles would, in the 1960s and thereafter, be the common coin of federal-provincial disputation.

17

The Making of Modern Times: Culture and Communications, 1919-39

Between 1976 and 1981 a group of American sociologists returned to study change and continuity in Muncie, Indiana, where Robert and Helen Lynd had carried out their pioneering sociological work in 1924 and 1925. The Lynds' *Middletown* was pre-eminently a study of change, for life in this small midwestern industrialized city exhibited either change or stress arising from failure to change at almost every point. A former resident returning to Middletown in 1925 after an absence of thirty years would not have recognized very much in the town, either its physical appearance or the way in which its residents approached life. However, the modern sociologists concluded that a Middletown Rip Van Winkle awakening from a fifty-year sleep in 1975 would not have had much trouble finding his way around town. There were certainly differences but, fundamentally, most of life in Middletown – its industrialism, its family values, and its materialism – would have remained clearly identifiable. The 1920s are, recognizably, part of our own times as the prewar times are not.[1] This is as true of Muncie as of St Catharines or Seattle or Vancouver.

Not only sociologists have pointed to the post-First World War era as distinctively modern; literary critics also have stressed how realism, experimentalism, and what has come to be termed 'modernism' became central in cultural history after the war both in Europe and North America. This is not meant to suggest that the triumph of 'modernism' and realism in literature came as quickly as the German collapse in the autumn of 1918. Indeed, during the interwar years in Canada most fiction which was published was of the romantic and escapist character that was familiar to prewar Canadians,

1 Theodore Caplow, Howard Bahr, Bruce Chadwick, Reuben Hill, and Margaret Holmes Williamson, *Middletown Families: Fifty Years of Change and Continuity* (Minnesota 1982), and Robert S. Lynd and Helen Merrell Lynd, *Middletown: A Study in American Culture* (New York 1929)

but today that work is forgotten. What is recalled is, for example, the work of Frederick Philip Grove, whose realism tested the limits of Canadian censors, and the *Canadian Forum, Canadian Mercury,* and *McGill Fortnightly Review,* where young Canadians like F.R. Scott, A.J.M. Smith, and Frank Underhill abandoned traditional metre and beliefs. In such journals they implicitly echoed F. Scott Fitzgerald's 1920 declaration that a new generation was taking command.

Of course, most Canadians did not grow up in this way: they maintained their faith and there were still wars to fight. Furthermore, motion pictures quickly replaced the romantic novel with a new escapist staple for the working and middle classes. In the Hollywood movies of the late 1920s and 1930s, romance and happy moral endings were inevitable. Nevertheless, most Canadians lived differently from their parents, not least because most Canadians after 1920 grew up in the city, not in the country. During the 1920s Canada, for the first time, became an urban nation, and gradually urban values established their pre-eminence.

The defeat of prohibition in the 1920s represented one aspect of the growth of urban values, for it had been rural Canada where prohibitionist sentiment had been strongest. Similarly, the union of the Methodist, Congregational, and Presbyterian churches which took place in 1925 was an indication that old religious differences were losing their force. The new United Church maintained many of the Social Gospel traditions of its founding churches, but lost its evangelicalism and confidence in belief. A.E. Smith and J.S. Woodsworth moved down from their pulpits into the public arena, Woodsworth as a socialist, Smith as a Communist. Their choice reflected the shift to secular values which marked the society as a whole. The psychology book or lecture replaced the minister's study as the source of consolation and understanding for many who were troubled and bereaved. The movie or Saturday night hockey competed with – and often contradicted – the sermon on Sunday morning. In the Canadian city of the 1920s and 1930s, new forces shaped moral and social values.

Many whose voices were influential in wartime and prewar Canada were baffled by these new forces. Archibald MacMechan, a prominent university professor and critic, expressed his anger with the new age in a 1920 article in the *Canadian Historical Review* entitled 'Canada as a Vassal State.' To MacMechan, Canada's values and its institutions, founded upon the traditions of British government and culture, were crumbling as American money and influence swept across the country. He, like many of his generation raised on imperialist lore and steeped in distrust of American ways, could not understand Canadian receptivity to American technology and entertainment. More fundamentally, however, his complaint was against the new age with its mass culture, more hectic pace, and aggressive democratic and egalitarian tone. He plaintively expressed his feelings in a question: 'How can a generation fed on movies and bred on motors understand Wordsworth?'[2]

In fact, contemporary educational theory was notably unsympathetic to the literary and classical education which MacMechan favoured. Educators did worry much more about motors than about Wordsworth. In 1925 British Columbia appointed a commission to examine the existing public education system in the province and to recommend future directions. The commissioners, Dr G.M. Weir, head of the Department of Education at the University of British Columbia, and Dr J.H. Putnam, senior inspector of schools in the Ottawa area, urged a less rigid educational system, one which reflected innovations such as the junior high school which had already appeared in the United States. Optional subjects, 'civics,' health education, and intelligence testing were also commended. The 'practical' needs of society were emphasized as was the importance of rearing young British Columbians to become democratic citizens. Recitation and 'reading, writing and arithmetic' had a much less important place in the curriculum of the new progressive school. Although progressivism met resistance in many parts of Canada, notably in rural areas where the one-room schoolhouse was saved by both traditional attitudes and the Depression, it profoundly influenced Canadian education between the wars.

During the 1920s teaching became a profession which demanded higher standards, and teacher education became an important part of higher education in Canada. The 'normal' schools and the educational schools in English Canada developed common aims in their curricula which reflected the progressive approach. Most of the instructors in teachers' colleges had themselves obtained their highest degree from the educational schools of the United States. These teachers – and the schools which produced them – became the strongest advocates of an extended education for Canadian youth, one which envisaged schools providing far more than the fundamentals of literacy. The 1920s and 1930s in Canada thus saw relatively little growth at the elementary level but considerable expansion of the high schools. The raising of school leaving age in several provinces made at least a couple of years of high school a normal adolescent experience.

The high school's expansion was, nevertheless, greatly retarded by the Depression. The university remained a distant dream for most Canadians, although its influence was great upon those who attended, and that influence was increasing. Still, the university's position in society in the interwar years

2   Quoted in S.E.D. Shortt, *The Search for an Ideal* (Toronto 1976), 47. An excellent survey of cultural affairs is found in John Thompson and Allan Seager, *Canada 1921-1939: Decades of Discord* (Toronto 1985).

must not be confused with its position today, when its role in research is significant.

EDUCATION AND THE NEW AGE OF SCIENCE

The federal government had not yet accepted that spending on universities served national needs. Although the federal government financed the National Research Council, which since 1916 had funded university research in the sciences, it gave no money for ordinary university purposes. Nor was the council lavishly funded – $464,382 in 1929-30. And the provinces were not much more generous. In 1929 total provincial subventions to universities were only $6 million. Furthermore, the funds were unequally distributed. In New Brunswick and the four western provinces there were five provincial universities which were grant-aided, and in British Columbia a tiny junior college also received some government money. In Ontario the provincial government concentrated its grants on the University of Toronto, which was overwhelmingly the best-financed public university in the country, although by 1925 the province was also giving small annual sums to Queen's and the University of Western Ontario. In Quebec and Nova Scotia, although the provincial authorities subsidized a few special-purpose institutions such as *L'Ecole des hautes études commerciales,* by and large the provincial authorities left university financing to fee-payers, donors, and churches. And in Prince Edward Island the government financed no more than a combination senior high school and junior college.

To an observer from the 1980s, it would seem that Canada's universities took little part in the growth of the 1920s and 1930s. Thanks to the National Research Council, admittedly, they were developing research capacities in science and engineering. By 1929-30 the council was providing fifty student awards and financing 111 university research projects. By that time, also, the council was already beginning to develop its own research laboratories in such fields as chemistry, physics, biology, and aeronautics. Alberta had a provincial research council which worked in close collaboration with its university, but it was small, ill-financed, and not very significant. In 1928 the Ontario provincial government set up a Research Foundation on the edge of the Toronto campus. The foundation raised an endowment of over $2 million, half of which came from the province. By 1930 it employed sixteen researchers, organized in departments of textiles, metallurgy, chemistry, veterinary science, and biochemistry. Although the Ontario Research Foundation was ready and willing to undertake contract work for ministries and industry, it is hard to believe that its labours contributed anything significant to the nation's prosperity.

It was by producing graduates, not new ideas, that Canadian universities made their chief contribution to economic growth and social betterment. As population and real income drifted upward, so did university enrolments. In 1920 Canadian universities and colleges enrolled 22,000 undergraduates and 383 graduate students. By 1929 there were 28,000 undergraduates and 1010 post-graduates. Women were few – in 1929, only 6400 undergraduates and a mere 269 graduate students. University education was still a training for the few. In 1931 it appears that only 3 per cent of the group aged between 18 and 22 was enrolled. But the tendency was upward, and the production of new graduates was relentless – 2889 bachelor's degrees and 237 earned higher degrees in 1920; and in 1939, 5467 bachelor's degrees and 746 higher degrees. Teaching staffs were small – in all Canada there were well under 3000 professors by the end of the 1920s. The universities themselves were small too – indeed, to observers in the 1980s, almost ludicrously so. In all New Brunswick, which contained at least five institutions of university rank, there were 730 undergraduate students and five graduate students during 1929. In British Columbia, with a single provincial university and a small junior college, total university enrolment was barely 2000. Course-offerings, naturally, were limited. But new programs, especially in commerce and engineering, were developed at many institutions during the 1920s. And the results could be quite impressive. By 1929, for example, Toronto's Department of Political Economy could boast that every graduate from its Bachelor of Commerce program had found work in Canada.

In elementary and secondary schools the same tendencies were at work. In public schools enrolments were rising – from 1.2 million in 1920 to 1.7 million in 1929 (average daily attendances). Within each province, furthermore, enrolments in the final grades were increasing rapidly. School teaching was a big industry. Yet the 'education industry' cannot possibly have absorbed many of the new graduates who flowed from Canada's universities during the 1920s. From 1920 through 1929 universities produced 41,582 new BAs. But the number of university graduates in the nation's schools seems to have risen by only 1480. Even allowing for some omissions, we have to conclude that most university graduates were finding their life work in industry, finance, and business.

BROADCASTING IN THE BRAVE NEW WORLD

Although the advance of education was not exactly speedy, neither was it glacial, and we must suppose that the development of secondary and higher education made some contribution to general enlightenment. The same cannot be said with certainty of radio broadcasting, whose development was one of the economic success stories during the 1920s.

The production of radios rose from 48,000 in 1925 to 150,000 in 1929. All these radios required something by way of a signal which they could receive. At that time the airwaves were less crowded than they were later to become; Canadians could readily 'Stay up all night to get / Pittsburgh on the crystal set,' as a popular song later observed. Nevertheless, there was room for Canadian-based broadcasting stations, and private enterprise was not slow to provide them.

In Montreal the Canadian Marconi Company began experimental broadcasting in 1919, and regular broadcasts commenced in December 1920, first as station XWA and then as CFCF. The Montreal station is considered by many the world's first station. By the fiscal year 1922-3 at least thirty-four private broadcasting stations were operating, and another twenty-eight had been licensed.[3]

The dominion Department of Marine and Fisheries issued the licences, both to broadcasters and to households, as it tried to prevent the various stations' signals from interfering with one another, but it took no interest in the content of broadcasting. Nor did it worry about ownership. Several stations, including CFCF, were run by companies that produced or distributed radio equipment, including batteries. Others belonged to newspapers, and still others were subsidiaries of various sorts of retail businesses, whose activities they promoted. Some were owned by the Canadian National Railways, and by 1929 one or two prairie stations belonged to provincial governments. A few were foreign-owned. In 1923 there were 9954 receiving licences in the dominion; by 1929, there were 297,398, and in that year there were eighty-five active broadcasting stations.

Each city was allotted one wave-length, or at most two; stations shared these wave-lengths, each operating for part of a day or a week. Canadian stations, moreover, were low-powered in comparison with American stations. Rural areas, therefore, could receive Canadian signals with difficulty or not at all. And even in the big cities, most Canadians seem to have tuned into American stations, especially in the evening.

The Canadian National Railways pioneered national broadcasting. In 1923 it began to develop a chain of stations, the first in the dominion. It put some receiving sets in railway parlor cars and hotels. It opened stations first in Ottawa, and then in Moncton, Montreal, Toronto, Winnipeg, other prairie cities, and Vancouver. In July 1927 the CNR's radio department arranged for the first nation-wide broadcasts. Tens of thousands of Canadians gath-

---

3   Much of this account derives from Frank Peers, *The Politics of Canadian Broadcasting* (Toronto 1969), and Bill McNeill and Morris Wolfe, *The Birth of Radio in Canada: Signing On* (Toronto 1982).

ered around their radios for the first North American coast-to-coast trans-mission. Some had primitive crystal sets, probably bought by mail, to which a headphone was attached. Others gathered near the loudspeaker, surround-ed by wires and batteries, to share the great national moment. In the most elegant homes the radios were housed in a mahogany or walnut cabinet, the wires and batteries carefully obscured. The marvellous new instrument occu-pied the most prominent location in the parlour, as was appropriate for an object which cost as much as a Model-T. More modest homes on the Saskat-chewan prairie or Toronto's Cabbagetown had boxes made of wires, usually positioned in the kitchen. Nevertheless, interest was equal if the cost was not.

The 1927 broadcast astounded Canadians and seemed to prove the proph-ets of radio correct: radio was the harbinger of a new and better age. In this spirit, and with appropriate hyperbole, the poet Wilson MacDonald com-memorated the triumph of the airwaves of Dominion Day, 1927:

A silence there, expectant meaning,
And then a voice clear-pitched and tense;
A million hearers, forward-leaning,
Were in the thrall of eloquence.

A pause, a hush a wonder growing;
A prophet's vision understood;
In that strange spell of his bestowing
They dreamed, with him, of Brotherhood.

MacDonald's effort was soon forgotten, but during the inter-war years the excitement of radio endured.

As Canadians of all classes went out and bought their 'Rogers Battery-less' or their 'Gold Medal Radio' (made in Uxbridge) in the late 1920s, the government began to face a demand for more Canadian programming. It also worried about the ease with which Canadian radio listeners tuned in to 'Jack Benny' and 'Amos 'n Andy,' two of the many popular American shows which, along with the weather, became the staple of corner grocery conver-sation in the 1930s. Canadians did have their own 'Hockey Night in Canada' which made hockey and Foster Hewitt famous. Hewitt did his first Toronto hockey game in 1925, but the national popularity of hockey on radio devel-oped most rapidly after 1931 when General Motors took over sponsorship. Starting with a small network, the GM transmission expanded to thirty-four stations and fifty-one broadcasts within three years. Telephone surveys sug-gested that almost three million Canadians listened to a Saturday night game. In Montreal, where three stations broadcast the Montreal Maroons in English and three stations broadcast the Canadiens in French, a telephone survey discovered that hockey outdrew 'Fu Manchu' and other programs by a three-to-one ratio. Hockey, listeners said, was a more gripping drama than any fictional drama. The sport's popularity exploded, with some declaring that they found games more interesting on the radio than at the Forum or Maple Leaf Gardens.

Hockey, however, was an exception – a Canadian program which led the ratings. In most time slots and for most radio stations, American programs captured the largest audience, except, of course, with French Canadians. Among francophones, who probably took to radio more eagerly than anglophones in the 1930s, programs often copied well-known American models. The popular comic team 'Nazaire and Barnabé' were advertised by the bilingual Montreal CBS affiliate CKAC as the 'Amos 'n Andy' of French Canada. In the absence of the language barrier, however, Canadians took their American programs in their original form, and this worried the Canadian government.

There was apparent chaos on the airwaves by the late 1920s, too many stations broadcasting too many programs which seemed to some to threaten patriotic, moral, educational, or other values. The CNR network's efforts were worthy but obviously insufficient. The second nation-wide broadcast following the July 1927 initiative occurred in December 1928, and regular nation-wide networking came only in 1929 – and then for three hours per week. The quality of programming was high. In 1929 the CNR began to carry the Toronto Symphony Orchestra on a national network. It carried comic opera, chamber music, school broadcasts, and by 1931 was dramatizing Canadian history. By renting time on privately owned stations it pioneered a pattern of public-private co-operation which the Canadian Broadcasting Corporation would later develop more fully. But its outlays were small – in 1923, $10,000; in 1929, $441,000, out of a total CNR expenditure of $215 million.

No one seemed to worry very much about the CNR experiments. Nor are we sure whether these broadcasts, many of high quality, were actually attractive to listeners. Much more controversial, and probably more influential, were the broadcasts of religious stations. By 1928 there were several such stations, of which some belonged to the Jehovah's Witnesses. The Witnesses' stations were not universally popular; minister of marine Pierre Cardin received many complaints regarding their programming, which was said to abuse other religious groups. Cardin revoked the Witnesses' licences, but in the ensuing controversy he announced that it was desirable to depoliticize not only the awarding of licences but also broadcast policy, and perhaps to follow the British model, by which a government-owned company would regulate broadcasting on behalf of the public.

In good Canadian fashion, Cardin proceeded to establish a royal commission under the chairmanship of Sir John Aird, the president of the Canadian Bank of Commerce. The commission began to work in autumn 1928, first travelling to Europe and the United States, then receiving briefs and arranging for open meetings and hearings. After consultation with the provinces, the commission reported on 11 September 1929 – less than two months before the stock market crash.

In its nine-page report the commission recommended that the dominion should nationalize all the existing private stations, close the redundant ones, and build seven high-power stations which could provide two programs, day and night, throughout the settled areas of the country. Programming, however, should be controlled not by the dominion but by the several provinces; national networking, however, was to occur from time to time. Money would come from the already-established listener licence fees, a dominion subsidy, and 'indirect advertising, that is, sponsored programmes without a direct sales message.'[4] Programs could be purchased from other countries, but there should be an effort to develop genuinely Canadian programming.

The defeat of the King government transferred the responsibility for dealing with the Aird report to the Conservative government of R.B. Bennett. Spurred on by the Canadian Radio League, a lobbying group formed in 1930 to advocate quality public broadcasting, and assisted by an important legal decision that broadcasting was a federal responsibility, the government set up the Canadian Radio Broadcasting Commission. Canada's radio broadcasting would henceforth be a blend of public and private programming and stations.

The Canadian Radio Broadcasting Commission set up shop in 1932 under the veteran Toronto Tory journalist Hector Charlesworth. The CRBC struggled valiantly with a meagre budget and a program schedule limited by its inability to carry 'commercial' programming outside Toronto. It swiftly became the focus for complaints from across the country, and its limited success stimulated the Mackenzie King government to reorganize and rename it in 1936 as the Canadian Broadcasting Corporation. Prime Minister King chose a Canadian who had worked for the BBC, Gladstone Murray, to be its chief (the responsible minister, C.D. Howe, had wanted a Canadian from one of the American commercial networks).

4   Peers, *Politics of Canadian Broadcasting,* 46

The CBC's task was scarcely enviable. By the late 1930s Canadians, at least in English Canada, knew what they liked. What they liked – baseball broadcasts, comedy programs, and even news shows – most often came across the border from the United States. During the day, Canadians mostly preferred soap operas – domestic dramas sponsored by soap companies aiming at the housewife market: 'Ma Perkins,' or 'Life Can Be Beautiful.' But in the daytime there was at least some Canadian competition: 'The Happy Gang,' with Bert Pearl, appeared every weekday after the one o'clock news (or, since it was carried live, at 10 in the morning in Vancouver) and, to judge by the ratings, it was largely successful. The Canadian programs, however, only rarely received better ratings in the evening hours, except on the French stations. In the late 1930s radio serials in French became highly popular in Quebec. The first of these, Alfred Rousseau's 'L'Auberge des chercheurs d'or,' began its three-year run in 1935 on CKAC and inspired several successful imitations.

In English and French, the CBC and private stations did their best for Canadian culture: historical dramas with home-made sound effects (a sieve of beans could produce a sound remarkably like rain) depicted Canadian heroes and heroines fighting off all manner of enemies, natural and unnatural. For many Canadians even in the more populated parts of the country it was their first chance to hear serious plays by authors both foreign and home-grown. And, as the decade wore on, radio brought newsworthy events into the home: the abdication speech of King Edward VIII in December 1936, or a mine disaster at Moose River, Nova Scotia, in 1936, the first live action broadcast; then, in 1938, there came the first live overseas radio reports, chronicling Nazi Germany's march to dominance in Europe, country by country, night after night.

While Canadians were depressed by news broadcasts, they were thrilled by the regular transmission of professional sports. The Americans had started it, but the Canadians were quick to learn. The private broadcasters generally used more live talent than they were later to find profitable. These 'stars' were not allowed to join US networks; the tape recorder had not yet been invented and there were problems of quality and copyright surrounding the narrow range of prerecorded material that was available; live local talent might have a local reputation that would pull audiences to stations that used it. Thus, while CBC Toronto hired actors, announcers, and musicians, CBC Montreal was doing the same, CKWX Vancouver procured Uncle Billy Hassell (whose name lent itself to memorable parody) to tell children's stories, and CJOR Vancouver had live singers mouthing kiddy-jingles, commercials masquerading as general-interest programming:

Look both ways before you cross,
And wait for cars that you see;
Then you'll be a true member of
Crone Safety Club with me.

It is to be hoped that Crone Moving and Storage reaped the reward of its pluck. In any event, the actors and singers were glad of the work.

Radio was not without its impact on Canada's high cultural life as well. The Toronto Symphony Orchestra, which after an earlier incarnation had been refounded in 1923, started broadcasting for an hour each week during the 1929-30 season under its permanent conductor Luigi von Kunits. Other orchestras soon followed: the Vancouver Symphony after 1933, the Quebec Symphony, the Concerts symphoniques de Montréal under Wilfrid Pelletier, in 1934, and the London Civic Symphony in 1937. Other forms of music were less frequent: opera consisted largely of Gilbert and Sullivan, or it depended on the efforts of the touring San Carlo Opera Company, out of New York. There were some home-grown specimens, it is true. In 1929 a Montreal company performed *l'Intendant Bigot,* a dramatization of the life and times of an eighteenth-century French colonial administrator; throughout the decade the Canadian National Exhibition in Toronto featured musical spectacles on subjects as diverse as 'Montezuma' or 'British history,' with casts ranging up to 1500 performers. It was a reminder that Canadian musicians had to work hard for their upkeep by pleasing the occasionally unsophisticated tastes of their audience. Von Kunits's successor as conductor of the Toronto Symphony, Sir Ernest MacMillan, found that rapport with his audiences involved squeezing his portly frame into a Santa Claus suit for the annual Christmas extravaganza, or into a little-boy costume for his annual audition to be a member of the orchestra's string section.

PICTURES, MOVING AND OTHERWISE

Canada did not exploit its early experience in making movies, although many Canadians such as Marie Dressler and Mary Pickford benefited personally from the movie craze which swept North America in the interwar years. The rococo palaces with their antique statuary and well-upholstered seats became a regular refuge from the cares of the day for millions of Canadians in the late 1920s and the 1930s. There were 950 motion picture houses in 1936, 102 in Toronto and 62 in Montreal. In smaller towns, old 'town halls' sufficed. Wherever Canadians went to the movies, they saw mostly American movies. Canada's hopes for a Hollywood of the North collapsed in 1928 when *Carry on Sergeant,* a $500,000 silent extravaganza, flopped completely. Henceforth Hollywood's stars – Harlow, Gable, Cagney, and the rest – would be Canada's stars as well. Canadians continued to take offence when their beliefs were attacked. In 1933, for example, the suggestion in a newsreel that Bermuda be handed over to the United States to pay off Britain's war debts led to such a ruckus in a Halifax theatre that the newsreel had to be halted.

Yet Hollywood after the 'talkies' arrived in 1928 lacked a direct political message. Its implicit message that individual effort led to success, and that hope was better than despair was as acceptable in Winnipeg as Peoria. Movies reflected popular culture more than they made it. Church groups and patriotic groups condemned the American movie for its materialist bias, fascination with sex and gangsters, and decidedly secular attitudes. The federal government tried in the early 1930s to break the control which distributors such as Famous Players had and to insist that Canadians have access to British movies. The effort was largely unsuccessful. A survey of schoolchildren in the 1930s identified the reasons as Hollywood's technical skill, stars, and representation of the conditions of everyday life.[5] It was much more than 'escapism' that led Canadians to the movies in the 1930s. Movies, like radio and the automobile, promised a richer and exciting future, one which made the pains of the Depression much more bearable. The foundations for a popular culture that was international and technologically derived were firmly laid in the 1930s. This popular culture celebrated the new, the different, and, above all, itself.

For Canada, film success came in the documentary which its National Film Board under John Grierson would raise to a new level of excellence during the war years. As with so much else Canadian, the state preserved a piece of the action for Canada when popular taste opted for the American way.

Other forms of pictures also preoccupied cultural enthusiasts. Art in its various forms went as far back as the origins of human settlement in Canada; to the home-grown variety, European immigrants added artefacts reminiscent of their cultural inheritance. Since 1880 Canadian and imported paintings had been housed in a diminutive National Gallery in Ottawa; an Art Museum of Toronto – the ancestor of the Art Gallery of Ontario – was founded in 1900, and other Canadian cities acquired art, and built buildings to house it, as occasion demanded.

The best-known Canadian artistic movement of the period was the Group of Seven, seven artists of varying ages and styles based in Toronto who sought to express through their art the uniquely Canadian landscape.

5   H.F. Angus, ed., *Canada and Her Great Neighbor* (New York and Toronto 1938), 370-1

Though some of their art looked remarkably Scandinavian, it nevertheless imprinted itself on the public consciousness as something characteristically Canadian. From its first exhibition in 1920 to its disbandment in 1933, the Group excited controversy and dominated the Canadian art scene. Although the work of the Group attracted much attention and its explicit nationalism matched the contemporary mood, their art did not bring them economic riches. By the 1930s the Group and its characteristic post-impressionist landscape art was too dominant in the Canadian art world. Galleries and collections in the Depression years clung to the safety of the Group and did not champion the young and experimental artists.

Important artists in this period who stood outside all groups included British Columbia artist Emily Carr, whose work reflected west-coast Indian motifs, David Milne, a highly individual and imaginative artist, and the Quebec artist Alfred Pellan, who returned to Canada from Paris in 1940. On a more popular level the caricaturist Robert LaPalme's cartoons and designs bridged the gap between contemporary artistic styles and popular acceptance. Sculptors were often as well known as painters in the interwar years. The postwar demand for war monuments gave regular work for realist sculptors in the 1920s. R. Tait Mackenzie received many commissions in Britain and the United States as well as in Canada. The influence of art nouveau and art deco can be seen in the work of several sculptors such as Alfred Laliberté and Elizabeth Wyn Wood. Nevertheless, the European movements, cubism and modernism, did not reach Canada until the 1950s.

Artists still needed patrons, whether institutional or personal. Vincent Massey, a Toronto millionaire, was perhaps the best known of the breed. He accumulated art and, in the process, subsidized its creators. Some of the art found its way to his foundation, Hart House (a kind of student union) at the University of Toronto. Hart House also had a theatre, in which important amateur dramatic productions were staged; Massey acted in some himself. To accommodate and recognize amateur theatrical production, Massey and the governor general, Lord Bessborough, organized a Dominion Drama Festival in 1933. A regular movement of amateur productions (the Little Theatre Movement) surfaced; some of its component theatres, such as the Ottawa Little Theatre or the Halifax Theatre Arts Guild, are still in existence. The effect was to offer greater variety of dramatic fare to Canadians than professional theatre could risk, or afford.

Canadian publishers also acted as patrons. English Canadians imported most of their books, usually through branches of British publishing houses located in Toronto. These publishers – Oxford University Press, Longmans, Dent, or Macmillan – enjoyed considerable local autonomy in an age when their owners took the view that the development of Canadian writing contributed, in no small way, to the reinforcement of British empire patriotism. Serious Canadian books did not make money except by accident, and government subsidy was unheard of, but there were ways and means for the deserving author to find first a publisher and then an audience. The publishers in turn looked for their reward in the happy hunting-ground of textbook sales to provincial departments of education, or through fortunate imports. When Macmillan of Canada published the American bestseller *Gone with the Wind* in 1936 it meant a bonus of two weeks' salary for all staff, ceremoniously distributed in small envelopes. There were native Canadian bestsellers too: Mazo de la Roche, whose *Jalna* won a $10,000 award from the *Atlantic Monthly*, or Grey Owl, a romantic Englishman who lived in the Ontario bush, posing as an Indian in a state of communion with nature.

Three presses, Ryerson, Macmillan, and McClelland and Stewart, promoted Canadian authors. Macmillan, a British-owned firm, probably published more Canadian fiction than any other house. Morley Callaghan and Mazo de la Roche were two of their best best-known authors of the interwar years. The influence of nationalist impulses upon Quebec publishing remained strong. Many of the major works of the period, including Léo-Paul Desrosier's *Les Engagés du Grand Portage* and the classic rustic novel, Philippe Panneton's *Trente Arpents*, were published in Paris.

O CANADA?

Canada did not usually strike outsiders as a particularly literary, or even a particularly cultured, place. A young Englishwoman crossing the dominion in 1930 commented that 'the Canadians I have met so far are utterly impossible people to talk to seriously. Their talk is all on the surface, of a type which we English people would consider *fearfully* bad form – everlasting[ly] praising themselves, their family, their town, their nation.' As for the life of the mind, she grumbled that 'So far I have come across no "educated" people in Canada. Those with whom I have spoken are interested in facts – mining, unemployment, the dollar, etc. – but ideas, thought and reading simply don't come into their lives.'[6] The wilderness was impressive (it was also the foundation of Canada's tourist trade) but its human inhabitants were, apparently, less so.

Some of the human inhabitants might have been tempted to agree with the criticism. Canada's frugally managed university system placed a premium on devotion and diversity as far as its staff were concerned: devotion could help augment a salary that the Depression reduced, and diversity

6   Katharine Götsch-Trevelyan, *Unharboured Heaths* (Toronto 1934), 55, 81

could compensate for a shortage of colleagues to teach the basic courses that students demanded. Imagination was required too in an age when university libraries were cutting back on expensive books and magazines and when in any case faculty were frequently too busy to read them. Not every university was equally afflicted. In some, research could be pursued, as in Toronto's Banting Institute where Sir Fred Banting, the nation's medical hero, still presided. Scholars in economics and history found an outlet for their talents in the Carnegie series on Canadian-American relations, or in work for the Royal Commission on Dominion-Provincial Relations, which spawned a shelf-full of special studies on Canada's history, economy, and society. Some academics, such as the University of Toronto's Harold Innis, shrank from involvement with government projects, or worried about the possibility of conflicting demands from federal and provincial governments, demands that might endanger the precarious political position of the several provincial universities. But others, such as McGill's Eugene Forsey and Frank Scott, Toronto's Frank Underhill, British Columbia's Henry Angus, or the Université de Montréal's Lionel Groulx, had no such qualms.

It could indeed be argued that Canada's universities, relatively impoverished and understaffed as they were, were nevertheless serving as a hothouse for new ideas, some imported but some domestically derived. To the universities in the 1920s and 1930s, came the currents of social thought common in other English-language jurisdictions: thoughts on pensions, health insurance, and family allowances. From them came publicity for advanced social thought and praise for foreign experiments in planning and social engineering. The League for Social Reconstruction was largely university-based, and its members played a prominent role in the foundation of the new Co-operative Commonwealth Federation party in 1932 and 1933. Interestingly, however, the CCF did not predominate among university faculty or even among those faculty who took an active reforming interest in politics: for them it would be the Liberal party, not the CCF, that was the appropriate, possibly the inevitable, instrument of political change. The future did not lie with McGill's socialist duo of Forsey and Scott, but with Norman Rogers of Queen's (minister of labour in Mackenzie King's 1935 government) and Brooke Claxton of McGill (another future Liberal minister).

What the professors wanted was not, even in 1939, very practical politics. The lines of federal-provincial jurisdiction continued to block any attempt at national solutions to the Depression and its attendant evils. The King government's preoccupation with foreign affairs in the last years of the decade were another impediment. For the generation that grew up in the 1930s the Depression was not merely a catastrophe but an incentive, a time of despair but also of hope. Its observations and its conclusions would determine Canada's national agenda for the forty years that followed.

18

The Dominion and the Dictators

At the beginning of the 1930s Canadians were hard put to discern any signs of trouble on the international scene. Everywhere, or almost everywhere, civilian, peace-minded governments were going about their normal business, and this did not include preparations for war or aggression. War was an expensive, unpleasant affair, and memories of the last war were too fresh to contemplate a new conflict. In Geneva the League of Nations was entering its second decade. In Europe the legacies of the Great War were gradually being dismantled, as the British and French prepared to withdraw their army of occupation from western Germany. Germany itself had achieved international respectability and joined the League, yet another stage in its reintegration into conventional and predictable international society.

And so, when R.B. Bennett took office as Canada's eleventh prime minister in August 1930, he had no reason to expect that foreign policy would cause him any great disturbance. Neither did the undersecretary for external affairs, O.D. Skelton, who laid before the new prime minister a list of 'pending questions' in Canadian foreign policy. These turned out mostly to concern trade, a natural enough preoccupation after an election that had turned on the state of the economy. The most urgent foreign issue, therefore, and the one requiring the most immediate attention, was a trade agreement with tiny and distant New Zealand.

In looking at Canadian foreign policy during the 1930s it is well to keep this emphasis in mind. For Canadians, the Great Depression was the overwhelming fact of the decade. Lines of unemployed, idle factories, crushing welfare costs, the collapse of the wheat trade, and prairie drought were the everyday reality that confronted the thinking citizen, and even more the government. Some aspects of foreign policy became extremely important, but these were economic: questions of trade, tariffs, and markets rather than arms and alliances. Coping with the Depression was enough; and if it were not, there was the lingering debt left over from the Great War of 1914-18. No Canadian government could contemplate lightly a policy which might require it to spend money on arms, soldiers, or ships – or on 'pump priming' for economic recovery.

Bennett's government was no exception. In fiscal 1930-1 it spent $23,732,000 on its army, navy, and air force. By 1932-3 this figure was down to $14,145,000, out of a total national revenue of $311 million. This money purchased the services of just under 3800 soldiers and 524 horses, a few trucks, a small number of ships and airplanes, and an obsolete tank or two left over from the Great War. Any Canadian government under the circumstances would have done the same, and would pursue a foreign policy that was circumspect in the extreme.

Fortunately, the government did not have to worry. Great Britain and the United States, Canada's most important neighbours and trading partners, were friendly. They had a depression too, and neither was inclined to follow a foreign policy that could get them into trouble or cost money. Germany, the great rival before 1918, was crippled until 1933 by unemployment and civil disturbance. France, Europe's strongest military power, faced east, towards the Rhine. And Russia, rebaptized the Soviet Union, had turned her attention inwards so as to pursue a program of industrial development and agricultural transformation.

To contemplate this outside world, Canada employed a small Department of External Affairs, founded, as we have seen, under Laurier. The department had grown during the 1920s. Under O.D. Skelton it reached out into academia for famished and discontented academics (even then government salaries were better than those the universities could pay). Two history lecturers from the University of Toronto, Lester Pearson and Hume Wrong, joined; so did a British Columbian (via Oxford and the United States), Norman Robertson. The army supplied Georges Vanier, and business and politics furnished men rich enough to undertake the not very arduous but comparatively expensive task of representing Canada abroad. Thus, Canada had Vincent Massey (and his wife Alice) as minister to the United States and then high commissioner to Great Britain, 1935-46. There was Sir Herbert Marler, like Massey a rich man and a former member of the Mackenzie King cabinet, as minister to Tokyo and then to Washington. There was W.D. Herridge, Bennett's brother-in-law, who was sent as minister to Washington between 1930 and 1935; much to everyone's surprise, Herridge was a smashing success in the American capital, where he became the confidant of first the Hoover and then the Roosevelt administrations. But Herridge's variety of initiative and competence was held to be unusual, and Dr Skelton preferred to receive substantial reports from less senior appointees, part of whose function was also to ride herd on their politically grateful superiors.

A glance through the dispatches that Canada's overseas missions sent home does not reveal a broad or deep grasp of the realities of the international system. As long as the news that the Washington, London, or Geneva mission retailed was good, this superficiality did not matter very much. But when it was bad, or contentious, there might be a problem. That problem was partly solved, but only partly, by a unique service provided to its dominions by the British government. Through the medium of the Dominions Office, a special department that concerned itself with relations between the mother country and Australia, Ireland, Canada, New Zealand, South Africa, Southern Rhodesia, and Newfoundland, dominion governments received regular printed anthologies of British diplomatic reportage and analysis. Compared to what they could generate themselves, it was impressive. But it had its flaws.

For one thing, it was not complete; and for another, it was seldom up-to-date. 'It is the same old story,' Pearson wrote to Hume Wrong in 1938. The British were having important discussions with the Irish, 'but they had given us no indication of the scope of the meetings, or even suggested that we might be interested in them .... After it is all over, they will send a telegram to Ottawa ...'[1]

Ottawa seldom noticed. Bennett has been described, accurately, as an unconcerned autocrat. Unkindly, some have suggested that his most intimate friend was himself. Certainly he had little use for his cabinet and, initially, for the Department of External Affairs. Bennett's first expedition to London, as prime minister in 1930, produced the comment that 'he consulted no one but Bill Herridge. The Ministers with him did not know from one day to the next what he was doing'; one of them picked up the paper one morning to discover that Bennett had just appointed the premier of Ontario, Howard Ferguson, to be his high commissioner to London. Bennett was not unmindful of the fact that Ferguson would now be 3000 miles away; as he would later discover, that was not far enough.[2]

Foreign policy was not widely discussed in Canada, and it was hard to learn much about foreign affairs. A couple of newspapers, most notably the *Winnipeg Free Press* of J.W. Dafoe, took note of overseas developments, and readers of 'serious' low-circulation periodicals like the *Canadian Forum* received their regular ration of foreign news and comment. British magazines like *The Economist* and American weeklies like *Time* and the *New Yorker*

1 Public Archives of Canada [PAC], Pearson Papers, volume 3, Pearson to Wrong, 17 Jan. 1938
2 PAC, Brooke Claxton Papers, volume 223, Claxton to J.W. Dafoe, 5 Jan. 1931. Claxton's source seems to have been Sir G. Perley.

furnished useful background. These magazines were read inside government as well as out. One future external affairs undersecretary, for example, was reported by the US embassy as depending 'upon strange media for his principal information regarding Britain and the United States. He is a cover to cover reader of the London *Economist* ... Except for the information he gets from the *Economist*,' the report continued, '[he] depends on the *New Yorker* which he also reads from cover to cover.'

There were, of course, other sources for Canadian information about the outside world. Some French-Canadian newspapers paid attention to foreign news and, as the 1930s drew on, more consideration was given in Quebec to the awful possibility of war. But newspapers were partisan, either on the side of the Liberal party, which enjoyed power in Quebec City down to 1936, or on behalf of its nationalist-conservative-reformist opponents – what the Liberal journalists scornfully dubbed 'la bonne presse.' It followed that newspapers would stress what best suited their party of political affection, and would report accordingly.

It is true that politicians in Quebec, as elsewhere, did attempt to sound public opinion, though without benefit of public opinion polls (these had not yet arrived in Canada). Election campaigns gave political leaders an opportunity to discover whether their educated guesses were right or wrong. In the 1930 federal election, for example, the Liberal high command discovered, in the words of C.G. Power, 'that references to conscription bored the audiences.' Astounded Liberal orators and organizers were instructed to talk about the tariff instead. Long afterward Power, the Liberals' main Quebec organizer, reflected on the 'incapacity and ignorance of the speakers' on this important question.[3]

What perturbed Liberals more than losing the 1930 election was the accumulating evidence of a decline in their electoral appeal as a provincial party. At first glance this may seem remote from considerations of foreign policy, but in fact the disintegration of the provincial Liberal party removed one of the bulwarks on which the federal leadership relied to get its message across to the Quebec electorate and, equally important, to keep untoward agitation from getting out of control. As we shall see, Liberal and Conservative leaders thought it necessary to address foreign policy issues in the 1935 federal election, but for the most part, as Power later recorded, 'conscription remained a dead issue' in that campaign.[4]

The sweeping federal Liberal victory in October 1935, a victory which included winning all but five of Quebec's sixty-five seats, encouraged the

3   C.G. Power, *A Party Politician: The Memories of Chubby Power,* ed. Norman Ward (Toronto 1966), 116
4   Ibid., 120

provincial Liberals to go to the polls. The Liberals barely retained a majority in the legislature. After a precipitate collapse in party morale, a second election had to be called in the summer of 1936. And that election was won by Maurice Duplessis's Union Nationale. It was the 'nationale' part of the 'union' that gave cause for concern. By emphasizing the particular qualities of the French-Canadian nation, the new government gave expression to feelings of separateness (not, we hasten to add, separatism). It reminded French Canadians that they could well have a different agenda in foreign policy questions from their English-speaking compatriots. This agenda was well to the political right, and heavily influenced by the views of some of the more radically nationalist members of the clergy, less prepared to see their values set aside by the English-Canadian majority in the dominion.

Ernest Lapointe, the senior Quebec Liberal in King's caucus, reacted with extreme caution, but a caution that was very forcefully expressed in his dealings with King. An opportunity now existed for real divisions to occur between the federal government and its provincial counterpart, and no appeals to party solidarity could mute Duplessis's nationalist appeal. Lapointe was determined to give no hostages to what he considered to be a very probable ill-fortune. And so, on questions of immigration (no admission of Jewish refugees), defence (no increase in the armed forces designed for overseas service), and foreign policy generally (no commitments to the automatic support of British policy), French-Canadian opinion, as interpreted by and expressed through Lapointe, acted as a brake on the King government. It was, perhaps, only the most obvious brake, for there was also considerable inertia on these issues in English Canada.

If the possibility of the movement of mass opinion concerned politicians, less concern was expressed about the elite variety. Since 1919, indeed since 1914, Canadian opinion-makers had concerned themselves to some extent with the educated discussion of foreign affairs. First through the YMCA and then through conferences sponsored by the Canadian Institute of International Affairs, discussions and orations were staged for the purpose of better informing Canadians of the realities of foreign affairs.

Three or four main currents are discernible in these discussions. There were, first, what were called 'imperialists,' which meant those who believed that Canadians should offer aid and sustenance to the British empire. Imperialists were fewer than they once had been, but their influence and their sentiments could easily be spied in the English-Canadian daily press and to some extent in the utterances of Conservative politicians. Dr Skelton, who regarded imperialists with somewhat less affection than he did the bubonic plague, hoped and prayed for their demise. Skelton in fact believed that the problem would solve itself in this way, because imperialists as a group, he thought, were older men, likely to be scythed by the Grim Reaper so that 'youth' might have its day. Regrettably for Dr Skelton there were many parts of the dominion, most obviously Ontario and British Columbia, where the young were frequently as attached as their parents to the 'old country' that they had never seen.

In looking at the Canadian Institute of International Affairs, grey is the predominant colour. The same may be said of the Canadian League of Nations Society, where elder statesmen like Sir Robert Borden and Newton Rowell lent their influence and prestige to the cause of 'collective security' – all for one and one for all in the international arena. Collective security assumed that peace was indivisible, and that aggression anywhere was the concern of all. Luckily the small wars and petty aggressions of the period between 1922 and 1931 did not call for much more than moral suasion and local action, in other words for the expenditure of nothing more than words and morality. The CIIA, as it was known, did not have an automatic path to the ear of the government, and still less to Dr Skelton's. At best decorative, at worst it could complicate the government's life as it wrestled with what it thought to be the more immediate problem of French-Canadian opinion. (French Canadians were very sparse in the CIIA, though somewhat more in evidence in the League of Nations Society.)

After imperialism and collective security came isolationism and pacifism. Isolationism, which we shall examine further below, often sprang from disillusionment with the conduct and consequences of the Great War. Some, including articulate army veterans like Frank Underhill, were early converts to the cause. Others, like Loring Christie, the former adviser to Borden and Meighen, took a little longer to give up on Europe and the British empire. In Christie's case, a fixed hostility to Europe and the League of Nations was in place by 1922 or 1923; the empire joined them in his demonology in 1925-6. This became significant when Christie rejoined the Department of External Affairs in 1935.

There were, finally, some pacifists who cleaved to the straightforward conviction that war is hell. The Great War furnished recruits to this viewpoint; those too young to have fought need only read the powerful war memoirs that retailed the experiences of soldiers or airmen – but not usually sailors – caught in the maelstrom of war on the Western Front. The cinema added its bit as well through movies like *All Quiet on the Western Front,* which promoted the not unreasonable argument that trench soldiers on both sides of the front had more in common with one another than with their superiors. As deduced from the 1914-18 war, pacifism had a considerable appeal. Would that war ever have begun, one Canadian author asked in the summer of 1936, if the soldiers on even one side had simply laid down their arms and refused to fight? He then added, 'I do not believe that any citizen army ... would follow their leaders against an unarmed foe. Not even the Nazis at their maddest.' Considering what the Nazis had already done to the 'unarmed foes' in their midst, this argument surely represented a triumph of optimism or ignorance. 'Pacifists only ask to be left at peace,' a Toronto commentator, Marvin Gelber, wrote in reply, 'but this the Fascists will never grant.'[5]

But what would they grant? That was not much discussed, possibly because it could be considered a matter of high politics, too remote for the academic minds of the *Canadian Forum*'s editorial board. As for high policy, that was located somewhere else, though where no one could tell for sure.

Even when abroad, Canadian diplomats were seldom concerned with questions of high policy. Writing from Washington in 1936, just before Sir Herbert Marler arrived as head of mission, Hume Wrong described his life as one of 'dreary routine,' with his principal task to 'fight the battles of the Bronfman frères,' Canada's premier distillers. 'Marler,' Wrong predicted, 'will be a trial here, and will be dazed, I expect, by the volume of business compared with Tokyo. I suppose I shall spend months explaining it all to him. About 95 per cent of it I can do while thinking of something else & the rest is just dull – like international double taxation and similar monstrosities.' Moved to Geneva, Wrong was no happier, writing in 1938 that 'Mr King' – by then back as prime minister – 'at heart regards all the offices abroad as irrelevant nuisances ... Our weekly bag recently contained two copies of the "Guide to Official Precedence in Ottawa" and nothing else.'

There were exceptions to this dismal rule. Serving in London (1935-41), Lester Pearson maintained a wide circle of friendships. Vincent Massey, his superior, sat in on Dominion Office briefings of the high commissioners. But so as to avoid committing Canada to any rash course of action, Ottawa insisted Massey could listen but not speak. Herridge enjoyed great success in Washington. Even in these cases, however, relations with the department at home, and with Skelton, were not always smooth.

Skelton's first task when Bennett became prime minister was to remain in office. Bennett, as leader of the opposition, had made angry sounds about the expansion of External Affairs into areas previously reserved for the British. But once in office, as frequently happens, Bennett found his perspective changing. Skelton was useful. He knew where things were. Indeed, on issues like dominion-provincial relations or the background of the Statute of West-

5 G.M.A. Grube, 'Pacifism: The Only Solution,' *Canadian Forum* 16 (June 1936): 9-10; Marvin Gelber, 'As It Is in Heaven,' ibid. (Sept. 1936): 16-18

minster, he knew more than anyone else in Ottawa. As befitted a good political scientist in an age of civil service reform, he understood the principles of non-partisanship as applied to the servants of the people. If Bennett would direct, then Skelton would serve. And serve he did, for the duration of the Bennett regime, and afterwards.

Skelton's perspective on his work also deserves some comment. According to the American minister to Ottawa, writing on the occasion of Skelton's death in 1941, the undersecretary was 'an exponent of the North American point of view ... a great patriot and staunch friend of the United States.' Those with any understanding of Ottawa and its ways also knew that Skelton took a jaundiced view of things British, and that he was forever on the alert for imperial plots to inveigle Canada into dangerous foreign adventures. Some of Skelton's distaste for imperial co-operation was ideologically or historically founded, but some of it derived from his interpretation of recent Canadian history.

War, Skelton believed, brought in its train the squandering of 'tens of thousands of lives of ... young men, bringing [Canada] to the verge of bankruptcy, risking internal splits and disturbances.' The Great War had demonstrated what would happen, the only difference in the 1930s being that the instruments of warfare were more awful and more deadly. If Skelton trembled as he contemplated war, he trembled because of the lessons that recent history had taught. 'We are the safest country in the world,' the department line ran, 'as long as we mind our own business.'

Skelton was, therefore, disposed to drag his feet on co-operation with Great Britain. The British connection brought little security and much peril to Canada. The United States, in contrast, was rather more favourably regarded, if only because it was altogether likely to protect Canada from foreign danger. As for the League of Nations, it was primarily an instrument for the European great powers. The Soviet Union and the United States were not even members, and without their participation the League could hardly be called universal. In a crunch, it might not even be effective.

The crunch came sooner than anyone predicted. One of the legacies of the prewar age of imperialism was the sovereign presence of foreign great powers in China. Britain, France, and the United States all kept garrisons there; but the largest body of foreign troops was Japanese, concentrated in that part of northeastern China which is generally called Manchuria. In September 1931 there was an incident between the Japanese army in Manchuria and the troops of the local Chinese warlord. Before the incident was over, the Japanese had occupied the whole of Manchuria, amputating it from China proper and proclaiming it to be an independent state known as Manchukuo.

Both China and Japan were members of the League of Nations, and to the League China took its grievance. The League, as was its duty, studied the issue through most of 1932. A report, known from its principal author as the Lytton report, was presented at a special League session in December of that year. Once the report was received, the League's alternatives narrowed. In cases of aggression, as the Japanese occupation of Manchuria surely was, the League was to impose sanctions on the aggressor. Woodrow Wilson, the League's founder, had sought to give to the field of international law and conduct the same certainty and predictability to be found in a domestic or municipal legal code. If there were aggression, therefore, there would have to be sanctions.

Representing Canada at the League of Nations special session was C.H. Cahan, a Montreal Conservative who occupied the position of secretary of state in the Bennett cabinet. (The secretary of state then dealt with patents and similar matters.) Cahan duly received his instructions from Ottawa, as well as a draft speech to deliver to the League assembly. These instructions had been drafted both in light of Ottawa's own perception of events in the Far East and in consultation with the American government, which took a grave view of what Japan was actually doing. Cahan was to acknowledge what could not be denied, that right lay with the Chinese, and to urge that the dispute be solved peacefully through the establishment of an autonomous but still Chinese regime in the disputed territory.

Cahan did not much like what he was told to read. After conferring with the British foreign secretary, Sir John Simon, who was in Geneva, and showing him what he proposed to say, Cahan got up and delivered his own highly personal gloss on his instructions. Although Cahan did in fact include what he had been told to say at the end of his speech, the bulk of his oration was reasonably construed as pro-Japanese. The Japanese were delighted, and the Chinese were cast down. Dr Skelton was dumbfounded, receiving with what grace he could manage the congratulations of the Japanese minister in Ottawa, on the general principle that Canada must remain friends with someone. Cahan was nonchalant, taking the attitude that if Bennett didn't like it, he could fire him. Bennett did not fire him.

The Cahan incident was not a harbinger of smooth relations with the League. Eventually, the Manchurian question turned out as badly as anyone could have expected. The Japanese stayed in Manchuria and withdrew from the League. The League wrung its hands and declined to do anything much. The United States loudly protested, but also refused to do anything concrete to punish the Japanese. And while the League and its remaining supporters dithered, the Japanese gobbled up another couple of Chinese provinces for good measure. Japan's government could no longer control its army, a fact demonstrated for all to see when in 1932 the army, or a part of it, undertook to murder Japan's government and largely succeeded.

And while these events were unfolding, the international system received another blow. In January 1933 Adolf Hitler, the leader of an extreme nationalist party, became chancellor of Germany. Within a few months his Nazis had abolished all other parties, suspended constitutional guarantees, and imprisoned opponents great and small. In a noisy and noticeable way the persecution of the Jews, Hitler's particular bugbear, began in earnest.

Hitler's rise to power did not go entirely unobserved in Canada. As early as 1930, when Hitler first won a large bloc of seats in the German Reichstag, the *Canadian Forum* noted the appearance of 'a new and terrifying danger.' Of course, Germany was not entirely to blame for this development, some people reasoned. The Treaty of Versailles was unequal and unjust. The democracies were playing into the hands of extremists like Hitler by exacting reparations and by failing to agree on economic co-operation, which might combat the spreading economic depression. Other commentators, then and in the years to come, stressed that Germany could and should be accommodated by timely concessions. Even after Hitler came to power, it was argued, it was not too late. Those on the political left referred to what they thought to be a self-evident fact: that wars are caused by economic competition. Remove or lessen the competition, and war would vanish. This reasoning appealed to others besides Marxian socialists.[6]

These arguments could be found in any of the former belligerent powers, at least on the allied side. There was, however, a peculiar Canadian twist to some of the reasoning which was advanced to keep Canada out of Europe and out of war. One commentator, Frank Underhill of the University of Toronto, summed up attempts to mobilize an alliance against Hitler as simply 'retired burglars versus would-be burglars.' As for the argument that Canada's interest was the same as the British empire's and that Canada's true interest was bound up in strengthening Britain's, Underhill was unimpressed. 'But, of course, if we try to stay out of Europe, we shall drift into the orbit of the United States. And here is the final, unanswerable clear moral issue. Any sacrifice of men and money in Europe would obviously be justified to keep us free from American influence. So let us prepare for the crusade. We have yet time to do it in a style befitting our national dignity. For they say that Germany will not be ready to fight till 1937 or 1938 at the earliest.'[7]

Underhill, writing in 1936, was right about one thing. Germany would not be ready to fight until 1938. A breathing space was afforded the allies between 1933 and 1938, when Nazi demands first spilled over Germany's

---

6   R. de Brisay, 'The Trend of Events,' *Canadian Forum* 11 (Nov. 1930), 43-5
7   F. Underhill, 'That Clear Moral Issue,' ibid., 16 (April 1936), 5-6

frontiers. What did the allies do with it?

France, not surprisingly, took the rise of Hitler most seriously. 'France views German Nazis as Gangsters,' readers of Toronto's *Financial Post* read in July 1933. Hitler's government, the *Post*'s special correspondent learned, was in the opinion of the French foreign office composed of 'men of the basest character' who would 'stop at nothing' to get their way.[8] German rearmament would give the Nazis their opportunity, and in stages between 1933 and 1936 they announced what they had already managed to accomplish. There would be conscription and an air force, both prohibited by the Treaty of Versailles. The demilitarized zone in the Rhineland, protecting France's eastern flank, vanished early in 1936, when German troops marched in unopposed.

Against this danger, French and occasionally British statesmen attempted to form a common front. To be effective, such a front should include as many continental European powers as possible. A key candidate was Italy, a wartime ally. Italy, although ruled by a fascist despot, Benito Mussolini, was not unwilling, but Italian co-operation had a price. The price was the absorption into the Italian empire of the independent empire of Ethiopia in eastern Africa. Mussolini came to believe that Britain and France had promised to permit this expansion, and as far as the French were concerned he may have been right. The British probably wished that the whole issue would simply go away; it is always uncomfortable for democratic statesmen to argue the public case for choosing the lesser evil over the greater, and in the event the British found the argument sticking in their throats.

Mussolini's timetable of conquest coincided with the autumn 1935 session of the League of Nations. As with Japan and China, Italy and Ethiopia were both members of the League; unlike Japan, Italy's actions were easily predictable as men and machines were shipped south through the Suez Canal to be ready for the end of the rainy season in east Africa. As the summer of 1935 drew to its close, war seemed very close at hand.

It was at about this point that Ethiopia first impinged on Canada. In the spring of 1935 the prime ministers of the self-governing empire gathered in London for George V's Silver Jubilee. To their dominion colleagues, British ministers presented a very gloomy picture. Germany was rearming, and Britain was having to take steps to re-equip and strengthen its own military forces. There was 'grave danger' of 'serious developments' in Ethiopia, and such developments would arouse not merely the British government (an unlikely prospect) but the British public (which was altogether likely). The connection between events in Europe and Africa was all too clear, as Bennett im-

8 *Financial Post*, 22 July 1933, 1

mediately pointed out.

Bennett, however, was in no position to do anything much to help. Personally well-informed – he wrote as early as 1933 that Hitler was generally believed to pose a menace to world peace – the prime minister had no high expectations of Canada's influence at the League or in Europe generally. 'Our military prowess in the next war is regarded as of little concern,' he told a clerical correspondent. As for Canada's unaided, if moral, voice, he asked, 'What can one man do who represents only ten and one half million people?' Bennett may even have exaggerated Canada's influence – except in one quarter.

As part of the British empire, Canada was among those countries Britain looked to for help if war should in fact break out. The British could be confident of a sympathetic hearing from Bennett himself. But Bennett might not always be around. What of Canada as a whole? To investigate what the empire thought, Sir Maurice Hankey, secretary to the UK cabinet, undertook a round-the-world study vacation in 1934. Australia and New Zealand, he discovered, were sound and still boasted a 'fervid Imperialism' that in Britain was by then passé, at least in the sophisticated circles of Whitehall. The warmth of Hankey's reception in Canberra and Wellington was matched by the chill he found at Ottawa, or, more properly, in certain circles there. The Canadian Institute of International Affairs, for example, was not unusual in having defeatists among its members. The League of Nations Society was no better: it had what he termed 'extremists of all kinds – "highbrows," isolationists, French Canadians, Irish disloyalists, with a sprinkling of sound people who for one reason or another – sometimes because they know too much – take no leading part.' Bennett was properly contemptuous of such people, Hankey was happy to say, but a more moderate and perhaps more representative point of view was expressed by Arthur Meighen, government leader in the Senate, and General A.G.L. McNaughton, chief of the general staff. They told Hankey that 'if our cause was just, if every effort to maintain peace had been exhausted, and it was clear to the world that war had been forced upon us, then Canada would come along.'

This description may tell us more about Hankey than about Canada, but it has an importance nevertheless. Hankey's perception that Canada was doubtful, that its help might not be infallibly available, was reported home to the cabinet. Although there was a tendency to lump together all the overseas members of the empire as 'the dominions,' it was understood that some dominions – Canada, South Africa, and Ireland – were more reluctant than others to commit themselves to deeds as well as words in the defence of the status quo or, as the phrase of the day had it, to 'collective security.'

That being the case, it must have come as a considerable surprise when, in October 1935, Canada's delegation to the League of Nations voted to condemn Italy as an aggressor against Ethiopia (the invasion had begun on schedule, at the beginning of the month). There was further astonishment when Canadians in Geneva spoke vigorously against Italy and for sanctions to discourage the aggressor. And when Canada's permanent delegate to the League, Walter Riddell, proposed that Italy's oil supplies be cut off on 2 November 1935, it was reported around the world.

Inevitably it was reported in Canada, where the news was received with a shudder. An election was just past. Bennett was out, Mackenzie King was in, and the new government was barely a week old. Foreign policy had played a part in the election campaign, and the voters, especially in Quebec, had been allowed to gain the impression that the new Liberal government would keep Canada out of war. The Italo-Ethiopian war was divisive for another reason. Italy was a Latin, Catholic state. Mussolini had a certain appeal in Quebec and, while in ordinary times his appeal had no political significance, it just might be important if Canada set itself against Italy and the confrontation developed into war.

So at least reasoned some of the French-Canadian members of the King cabinet. French Canadians and English Canadians thought differently on foreign policy. King hardly needed to be reminded of this fact. The memory of the 1917 election and of the conscription riots that followed was fresh in his mind, and fresh in the election rhetoric of a generation of Liberal orators in Quebec who reminded voters that a vote for the Conservatives was a vote for conscription and war. A vote for the Liberals, however, was a vote for peace.

Nor were all English Canadians advocates of support for the League. 'Sanctions,' wrote Loring Christie, who was back in External Affairs, were 'Swiss for war.' Skelton, who feared the British and trusted in distance, agreed. Sanctions should be avoided at all costs, and if they could not be excluded altogether then at least Canada ought not to step out in front. King, who privately believed that Italy's course was unconscionable, also agreed. Ernest Lapointe added his voice to the chorus. The Canadian government adopted such sanctions as the league had already agreed on, and hoped there would be no more.

It came as something of a shock, therefore, when Riddell's 'Canadian proposal' made the headlines. The proposal was unauthorized by Dr Skelton, Mackenzie King, or anyone else. Riddell, the man on the spot, had been caught up in what was sometimes called 'the spirit of Geneva,' and the spirit had wafted him away to the very heights of policy. Whose policy? Riddell's own, to be sure, but also one that was agreeable to the British and French

Mr King at the podium, 1938   Courtesy Robert LaPalme

delegates to Geneva.

King waited to see whether the 'Canadian proposal' would be buried and forgotten. When it was not, he authorized Lapointe to bury it himself. On 1 December Lapointe, who was acting prime minister while King and Skelton vacationed in the south, announced that Riddell had spoken on his own initiative at Geneva and not on behalf of the government of Canada. Riddell was

Ernest Lapointe   Courtesy Robert LaPalme

informed that the decision to publicize the difference of opinion between himself and Ottawa was taken 'reluctantly ... under pressure of incessant press comment on [the] danger of war attributed to [the] "Canadian proposal."' This was true enough. Nor was there any great disagreement in Ottawa, as a correspondent afterward wrote, 'on the question of sanctions.'

Skelton and Christie acted together on the issue, and with the support of the prime minister. It was not, as some have claimed since, a French-Canadian cabal assisted by Christie.[9]

Riddell's career never recovered, although he remained in the diplomatic service for another ten years. The fate of his proposal illustrates the difficulty in long-distance policy-making, and the danger of allowing a diplomat to take on the colouration of his assignment. Ignorant of the political problems his action would cause at home, or uncaring about these repercussions, Riddell acted as he thought best. King and Lapointe in turn acted as they knew best.

The only casualty was Ethiopia. In the spring of 1936 Italy completed its conquest of that hapless country. The League of Nations, which had supported Ethiopia and opposed aggression, was rendered ridiculous. Italy withdrew from the League and signed an alliance with Germany. In Europe, Britain and France faced one more enemy while the erstwhile supporters of collective security bickered among themselves over who should be blamed for what had transpired. German rearmament continued; British and French rearmament had barely begun.

Spain's civil war, which broke out in July 1936, produced a curious diversion in Canadian policy. Canada had no diplomatic representation in Madrid, and no direct involvement in events there. The Liberal cabinet were duly and devoutly grateful for this fact, in that the Spanish war was almost perfectly calculated to divide English from French Canadian. The Catholic church in Quebec had no doubts as to where the right of the matter lay. Devout Catholics suffered persecution from the infidel Spanish republic, the legitimate government. Defenders of Spain's Catholic values and traditional order, Franco's Falangist rebels, rose in revolt to stop the spread of godlessness and worse. Propagandists for these rebels strove, with considerable success, to identify the cause of the republic with that of Karl Marx. So, for precisely opposite reasons, did the Canadian Communist party, which, with other Communist parties elsewhere in the world, regarded the Spanish civil war as a heaven-sent opportunity to enlist young recruits in a good cause. They hoped that the recruits would remember who their friends were after the war was over, and perhaps even join them.

In dribs and drabs young men drifted out of Canada, eventually to arrive in Spain to enlist in the Mackenzie-Papineau battalion of the International Brigades fighting for the republic. Their departure, and subsequently the fact of their existence, caused some embarrassment for the Mackenzie King government which saw them as symbolic not of youthful and misguided

9 Queen's University Archives, Grant Dexter Papers, volume 5, Chester Bloom to Dexter, 16 Jan. 1948

idealism but of the fundamental divisions that lurked between Canada's English and French communities. Fortunately for the government's purposes, not too many went, and the cause of Spain tended to sink in importance as other, graver events superseded it in the public consciousness. The government also failed to notice that in a minor way espionage was beginning in Ottawa, where a left-leaning young lady in the British high commission was furnishing copies of secret documents to Soviet agents. Whether the Soviet Union derived any advantage from her activity is, of course, another question.

The brouhaha over Spain did not deflect the government from other considerations. No matter what stand one took on the Spanish issue, it could not be doubted that the world was closer to war in 1936 than it had been the year before, or the year before that. Hume Wrong, looking at events in Ottawa from the perspective of Washington, told his friend Pearson that there was 'a serious conflict of opinion within the cabinet, which reflects a conflict of opinion within the country. All the sectional lines of division in Canada are at present simultaneously very apparent, and the task of governing the country is even more unhappy than usual ... The external crisis is opening all the old sores.' Wrong was writing in March 1936, just after Hitler's militarization of the Rhineland, an event which faced the King cabinet with the first specifically German-oriented international crisis of its term.

· In the end Canada did little about the Rhineland. In the summer of 1936 Mackenzie King toured Europe, where, to adapt very slightly a famous remark by J.W. Dafoe, he ushered the League of Nations into the outer darkness with assurances of the most distinguished consideration. For King, the great event of 1936 did not involve considerations of aggression or domestic political difficulties. The abdication of Edward VIII in December brought a flood of delectable gossip creeping across the border in the Sunday supplements of US newspapers, and then a first-class constitutional crisis: Edward wished to marry a divorcee! Propriety was satisfied by Edward's abdication and the accession of his brother, George VI. George would be crowned in May 1937, and King, his senior ministers, and other luminaries of Canadian society would be there in Westminster Abbey.

Since virtually everyone who counted in the empire's political firmament would wish to attend the coronation, it was an obvious time to convene an imperial conference. Although questions of trade and money would surface, the conference agenda was weighty with questions of armaments and alliances, questions that could no longer be decently avoided. As for armaments, Canada faced its own day of reckoning in February 1937 when the estimates of the Department of National Defence reached the House of Commons. The defence minister, Ian Mackenzie, told the House the government wanted to spend $36 million on defence in fiscal 1937-8; that figure represented a large increase over the figure for 1935-6.

It was true that the meagre defence budgets of the mid-1930s did not allow the armed forces to do much more than buy postage stamps. There were no bombs for airplanes to drop. There were no anti-aircraft guns. The field artillery could bang away at an enemy for precisely ninety minutes, after which, ammunition exhausted, its members would have to creep away as best they could. These figures were so obvious and so compelling that they brought the cabinet to the point of doing something; but they did not go so far with individual members of the House of Commons. The Conservatives accepted the estimates without a twitch, but then they had been recently in government. The real opposition came from the semi-socialist CCF, which was tinged with pacifism and good intentions, and from within the Liberal party. The estimates passed, of course, but with warnings ringing in ministers' ears, just as Mackenzie King began his spring travels.

He went first to Washington, where he and President Franklin D. Roosevelt spent an evening concocting a plan for a conference designed to secure universal peace. The conference would be held in the Canary Islands, and its object would be to bring international supply and demand more nearly into balance. If this could be done, and if the theory that political disputes grew out of real or perceived economic grievances proved true, then world peace must follow. The British ambassador in Washington labelled this modest plan 'western vapourings.' When the plan reached London, in summary form, at the end of March 1937, the permanent undersecretary at the Foreign Office commented pungently that 'Mackenzie King seems to lose rather than gain in intelligence as he gets older. This is drivel, and dangerous drivel. I hope he will be sternly discouraged from "thinking" along these lines.'[10]

When King set off for the imperial conference – a judicious leak to the *Financial Post* told the world about the message of peace he was bearing – he may have seriously intended to secure the consent of the other nations of the empire to his and Roosevelt's plan. On all matters of detail it consisted of theory and good wishes rather than concrete proposals. But as in all imperial conferences, King had something else in mind. It was essential to avoid making commitments that would automatically commit Canada to act with Britain in case of a still hypothetical aggression by Germany or any other power. It was precisely such a commitment that the British wished to have.

The British failed in their object. Wearisome sessions produced no Canadian guarantees of troops or, almost equally important, supplies. In the

10 Public Record Office, Kew, FO 371/20670/A2082, Sir R. Lindsay to Sir R. Vansittart, 8 March 1937, and comment by Vansittart, 31 March 1937

intervals between negatives, King hymned the virtues of economic appease-
ment and Anglo-American co-operation. To the British, anxious for dominion help to compensate for their own economic and military weakness, these
platitudes had an unwelcome ring of self-righteous indifference. Rather than
permit the conference to break up in disagreement, British ministers, headed
now by Prime Minister Neville Chamberlain, subscribed to King's carefully
nuanced platitudes. Sir Maurice Hankey, who watched the conference un-
fold, found little with which to console himself in its results: 'all our efforts
at the conference failed to obtain from Canada any really satisfactory assurance that we should be able to count with certainty on obtaining supplies
from her in time of war.'

But was the conference really as unsatisfactory as the British believed?
King constantly told them that he knew what was best, and refused to be
instructed on the state or potentialities of Canadian opinion. In this he was
almost certainly right, since British estimates of King and Canadian public
opinion in this period were poorly informed and reasoned. From the point of
view of Canadian opinion, recently displayed over the defence estimates, to
omit a commitment to the British was better than to refuse a commitment,
as a large section of Canadian opinion would actually have preferred. Nor
were British concessions to King's caution misplaced. King left the conference confident that he had made his mark, that the British government took
the necessity of American friendship more seriously, and that Chamberlain
agreed with him that an effort should be made to appease Germany on economic matters. Better still, he left with the impression that Chamberlain
wanted war no more than he himself did, which was certainly the case, and
that if war nevertheless resulted it must be from some other cause, for which
neither Chamberlain nor Britain could fairly be blamed.

King left London for Berlin, where he interviewed the Führer himself, as
well as Hitler's henchmen, air minister Goering and foreign minister von
Neurath. King's memorandum of the discussion survives, and a great deal of
fun has been made of its naïve tone and patronizing conclusion that Hitler
was little more than a simple peasant. This misreading of Hitler's character
is doubtless deplorable, but it is irrelevant to later Canadian policy. That
policy was clearly stated in King's discussions in Berlin, and ironically it was
far more clearly stated to the Germans than it ever was to the imperial conference. King did, however, tell the dominions secretary, Malcolm MacDonald, what he had in mind. He proposed to tell the Nazi leader 'that if
Germany should ever turn her mind from constructive to destructive efforts
against the United Kingdom all the Dominions would come to her aid and
that there would be great numbers of Canadians anxious to swim the Atlantic!' In Berlin, King was as good as his word. And by the time he returned to

Canada the prime minister had laid down the policy that Canada would in fact follow, if occasion offered.

The occasion almost occurred the very next year. In March 1938 Germany annexed Austria, its smaller southern neighbour. Soon afterwards agitation began about the fancied wrongs suffered by the German minority in neighbouring Czechoslovakia, a French ally. After a summer of tension, during which the British government dithered over what to do and how to do it, Hitler's demands for the cession of Czech territory became more immediate and more compelling. He was, as we now know, prepared to invade Czechoslovakia, so perceptions of the danger of war were real enough. The danger frightened the British government, which believed that in such a war it would be at a heavy disadvantage. But it could hardly avoid involvement if Hitler attacked the Czechs, thereby bringing in the French, and possibly the Russians as well. Chamberlain therefore went to see Hitler not once but twice, only to find the German dictator's attitude more unbending and unreasonable than before. By the middle of September war seemed likely, and Britain began to mobilize.

It is sometimes thought – indeed some thought it at the time – that in such a war Canada would have remained aloof. The evidence contradicts this interpretation. Some elements in the Canadian government, especially Skelton and Christie, were opposed to war. It is possible that Ernest Lapointe was also opposed, although this is unclear. King, however, knew right from the beginning what should be done. His diary for 31 August 1938 reads: 'I made it clear to both Mackenzie and Power [respectively minister of national defence and postmaster general] that I would stand for Canada doing all she possibly could to destroy those Powers which are basing their action on *might* and not on *right,* and that I would not consider being neutral in this situation for a moment. They both agreed that this would be the Cabinet's view.' On 13 September, as the crisis worsened, King told another minister that Canada had 'a self-evident national duty' under the circumstances. Although Skelton and Christie twisted and turned, they could not escape their master's will. By 27 September King had decided that Canada faced 'one of the great moral issues of the world.' The only thing that is remarkable about these developments, which were no particular secret among the well-informed in Ottawa, is that the British seem not to have known or understood what was intended.

Providentially, relief came at the last moment. Chamberlain flew to Munich on 29 September, and an agreement partitioning Czechoslovakia was reached among the British, French, Germans, and Italians. The Czechs were not invited. With their country partitioned, the rump of Czechoslovakia slipped under German control, to be finally dismembered by Germany in mid-March 1939.

What followed is well known. Chamberlain awakened belatedly to the impossibility of reaching a lasting or honourable agreement with Hitler. Although war was still not a sure thing, it was obvious by the spring of 1939 that it was much more likely than not. In anticipation, King and Lapointe pledged that in any conflict, Quebec would do its part; at the same time, they promised there would be no repetition of conscription. Robert Manion, an ex-Liberal and the new Conservative leader, agreed.

In May, attention was distracted, as far as Canadians were concerned, with a tour by George VI and his consort Queen Elizabeth. The two were rapturously received, even in Quebec City, and Mackenzie King took the occasion to bask in the royal favour and the prominence it afforded to a politician on tour. He was by then thinking of an election, and, so one story holds, asked Chamberlain towards the middle of August what he thought of Canada going to the polls in the fall.

Chamberlain, the story continues, advised postponement. There was likely to be a spot of trouble to the east, in Poland, and it might be well to keep the Canadian Parliament in readiness for the occasion. And so in August 1939 King prepared for the worst. Now there was no hesitation, just as there had been none in September 1938. Speeches in Parliament by both King and Lapointe in March had shown which way the wind was blowing, for in his speech Lapointe had explicitly accepted the possibility of war and committed himself and his party colleagues to Canadian involvement. Canada would, as far as its cabinet was concerned, go united into the crisis.

Or almost united. The Canadian Communist party, strong against fascism during the late 1930s, had a change of heart as soon as its international homeland, the Soviet Union, signed a non-aggression pact with Hitler on 23 August 1939. (It was a non-aggression pact only as far as Russia and Germany were concerned, since the chief end of the pact, a partition of eastern Europe, could hardly be attained without Soviet and Nazi aggression.) Some French Canadians, including a couple of members of Parliament, and some residual English-Canadian isolationists and pacifists, including Skelton, still opposed war. But Skelton's resistance under the circumstances had no significance. He would not resign on the issue and seems not even to have contemplated the possibility.

Hitler invaded Poland on 1 September 1939. On 3 September Britain and France declared war on Germany. On 6 September South Africa did likewise, Australia and New Zealand having accepted the British declaration as their own. Ireland remained neutral. In Canada, Parliament was summoned, in fulfilment of King's pledge that 'Parliament will decide.' There was no doubt what Parliament would decide. With only a few MPs declaring themselves against, a resolution declaring war on Germany was quickly approved. On 10 September Canada found itself at war for the second time in a generation.

19

The Politics of War, 1939-45

A sensible Canadian, looking at the country's future in September 1939, might have been forgiven a considerable measure of apprehension. Canada had not come well through the 1930s. The decade had been characterized by federal-provincial feuding and it seemed to make little difference whether a Conservative or a Liberal prime minister was in power in Ottawa. Unemployment continued high, though not as high as in the early thirties. Certainly, no one could say that the federal government had evolved a clear or consistent strategy for dealing with the phenomenon. After two decades of pretending that Canada had no foreign policy, the government had launched itself and its supporters into a war that the Liberal party's French-Canadian wing had vociferously opposed. It remained to be seen whether the party could stand the strain.

Canada's political system at the end of the 1930s was a curious mixture of dependence and antagonism. Obviously antagonistic were the four parties – Liberal, Conservative, Social Credit, and CCF – represented in the federal House of Commons. Yet among the three parties with hopes of appealing to a national constituency there was a tacit agreement as to what could, and what could not, be mentioned. Liberals, Conservatives, and CCF were all in agreement over the necessity for war. They agreed, too, that in prosecuting the war there should be no conscription, the most divisive issue during the previous conflict. They disagreed, however, over the depth of commitment the war required, and the most effective means of winning it.

Politics was not exclusively federal. All national parties had their federal and provincial wings. Although a provincial leader like Duff Pattullo or Mitch Hepburn might publicly disagree with Mackenzie King and place British Columbia or Ontario into formal opposition to the national government's plans or desires, it did not follow that British Columbia or Ontario Liberals felt the same as their excitable chieftains. 'After all,' as Paul Martin, a Liberal MP from Windsor, remarked, 'our political organizations were composed mostly of the same people.'[1] The strength of one part was the strength of the other, and even the public antagonism between Hepburn, in particular, and Mackenzie King failed to result in any deep or long-lasting fissure between the provincial and the federal wings of the Liberal party. It was also true that the weakness of one part could feed the weakness of the other, a maxim of politics that Mackenzie King never forgot; as we shall see, other wartime politicians were not so retentive.

King did not begin the war with any long-term political strategy save one: he wished to avoid repeating the mistakes of the First World War. The same could not be said of Canada's principal opposition party, the Conservatives. Their leader was a Catholic ex-Liberal, 'Fighting Bob' Manion, who had come over to the Tories in Sir Robert Borden's day. Manion's hold on the affections of his party was tenuous at best. Party members, especially in Toronto, let it be known that their leader was a temporary figurehead; while Manion orated in the House of Commons or around the country, telling Canadians that conscription was dead and that the war could and should be won without it, his ostensible followers laid plans for a better day in which he would not figure.

The CCF had problems of its own. Its leader, J.S. Woodsworth, opposed Canada's entry into the war as a matter of conscience. Plainly, he could no longer lead the party when most of its members supported the war, and in his stead Canada's socialists chose a scholarly ex-schoolteacher from Saskatchewan, M.J. Coldwell. It did not matter very much. The CCF was so far, in terms of popular support, from the seat of power that it could not hope to influence the results of any election called in the measurable future. And Mackenzie King was determined that such an election would soon be called.

King had left a hostage to fortune. In adjourning the emergency session of Parliament in September, he had let it be understood that Parliament would meet again before any new election. The promise stood in the way of King's instinctive political timetable. He had wanted an election in the fall, but war had intervened. In the ordinary course of events an election would have to be held by October 1940, and the Liberals' political options narrowed with every passing month. It might have been possible to extend the life of Parliament as Borden and Laurier had done in the First World War and as the British were to do in the current war, but King disapproved of the idea. It had not worked well twenty years earlier. King, who turned sixty-five in December 1939, was well aware of the dangers of political senility encouraged by electoral idleness.

---

1   Paul Martin, *A Very Public Life:* I: *Far from Home* (Ottawa 1983), 237

War posed a special dilemma to a political party. It was important to be non-partisan, in the interest of the greater national purpose of winning the war. It was obvious that petty political scandals of the kind that had trailed after Sir Sam Hughes in the First World War would do the government no good. The whiff of favouritism that clung to the reputation of Ian Mackenzie after the luckless minister of defence tried to ensure the manufacture of Bren light machine guns in Canada before the war was sufficient to cause the appointment of a non-partisan War Supply Board to look after war purchases; it was also sufficient to turn Mackenzie out of National Defence into the minor and, King hoped, low-profile appointment of Pensions and National Health. This was, on balance, a political advantage, or so King believed, and more than compensated for the loss of patronage for the faithful.

The first months of war brought little in the way of war contracts. An expeditionary force was raised and sent to Britain for training under General McNaughton. A couple of by-elections were held. Parliament got ready to resume in January. The opposition fulminated that too little was being done, and that little badly. It was, on the federal level, a tranquil political scene.

It was anything but tranquil in Canada's two central provinces. Mitch Hepburn and Maurice Duplessis had made much of their rivalry with Ottawa before the war; now, with war declared, they had little in common except a reckless hatred of Mackenzie King. Both premiers wanted King out; neither cared very much how.

Duplessis had a pressing reason. His province was virtually out of funds. Ottawa now controlled Canada's credit, and access to foreign money markets was dispensed by the Bank of Canada. A shortage of money was not an especially good issue with which to go before the electorate, and Duplessis did not choose to use it. Instead, in a bizarre series of announcements, Duplessis dissolved the Quebec assembly and scheduled elections for 25 October. The issue? 'I say,' Duplessis told a class reunion in Trois-Rivières, 'that never, absolutely never, as long as I am Prime Minister and the electors renew their confidence in me, will I permit the assimilation of the Province of Quebec. Cooperation always; assimilation never!'

What did he mean? It appeared to be a challenge flung in the face of Ottawa and, in particular, of Ernest Lapointe, King's Quebec lieutenant. The Liberals in Ottawa took note. King called the Quebec election 'a diabolical act' – but only in his diary. His Quebec colleagues, Lapointe, Cardin and Power, told King that they wanted to go public. Duplessis had challenged them, and if they failed to pick up the challenge their ability to lead and guide Quebec would be undermined if not entirely destroyed. They must respond, and they did. Lapointe, Cardin, and Power announced that they would resign from the cabinet if Duplessis won.

At first, Chubby Power later wrote, the Liberals were unaware of 'the inherent weaknesses in Duplessis' position.' There was dissent within his Union Nationale. The nationalists were – some of them – distant and disillusioned. Duplessis did nothing to improve matters when, on 4 October, he delivered a resounding campaign speech, again in Trois-Rivières. As the premier's biographer later explained, that night 'his diction was clear, his voice thunderous, but he was, literally, roaring drunk.' Whether it was Duplessis's chosen mixture of gin and champagne speaking or the authentic voice of the Union Nationale, the message delivered outside Quebec and to English Montreal was plain. 'A vote for the Liberals,' Duplessis was quoted as saying, 'is a vote for participation, conscription and assimilation.'[2] The Liberal response was easy. Duplessis might well be right, King's ministers proclaimed, but only if the electorate repudiated its effective representatives in the federal cabinet. Electing Duplessis would not be a bulwark against conscription; it would destroy the existing bulwark, embodied in Lapointe's pledge that there would be no conscription.

The Liberals had no difficulty in putting their message across. For one thing, they had a great deal of money, some of it raised from outside the province. For another, the English-language community of Montreal recoiled from the extremist rhetoric of the Union Nationale. J.W. McConnell of the Montreal *Star* switched his paper's allegiance; he did more, travelling to Ottawa to pledge his support to Mackenzie King in person.[3]

When the smoke cleared on 25 October, Duplessis was back in opposition; his party took 39.2 per cent of the vote and fourteen seats, while the Liberals secured 54.2 per cent and seventy seats. The Liberal leader, Adélard Godbout, took office as premier. The election results were rather less lop-sided than they appeared. The Liberal victory was largely an urban phenomenon, with much of their vote concentrated in Quebec's two largest cities. The Liberals also enjoyed, for the first time, the overwhelming support of the province's English-speaking minority. In the countryside, which held the bulk of the seats, the margin was much narrower, a problem which only redistribution could cure. Godbout, to his later sorrow, never came to grips with this problem.

Duplessis's debacle removed the first of Mackenzie King's provincial adversaries. Mitch Hepburn now rushed to fill his fallen partner's shoes. Hepburn was brooding over Ottawa's failure to match his personal standards of hyperactive patriotism while cultivating an increasingly close attachment to the person and policies of George Drew, the leader of the provincial Conser-

---

2 Conrad Black, *Duplessis* (Toronto 1977), especially 208-9
3 On finance see R. Whitaker, *The Government Party: Organizing and Financing the Liberal Party of Canada, 1930-58* (Toronto 1977), 287-8.

vatives. As usual with Hepburn, his private feelings did not take long to become public property. Mackenzie King, hearing what Hepburn had to say, concluded, accurately, that Hepburn and Drew had decided 'to make matters as difficult for us as possible.' They would not succeed because, in his opinion, Toronto's point of view did not even carry to the rest of Ontario, far less to the rest of Canada. But on 18 January 1940 the Ontario legislature passed a resolution denouncing the federal Liberals' conduct of the war; it passed over the votes of a minority of provincial Liberals who preferred Mackenzie King to their own increasingly erratic leader.

The news reached Ottawa with a week to go before the promised resumption of Parliament. After consulting a few senior ministers, King decided that Hepburn's resolution offered him an opportunity he could hardly decline. When Parliament met it would be dissolved and an election called for 26 March. And so it was. The opposition, caught off guard, could only splutter objections. Then King held a caucus. 'I said,' he told his diary, 'I would expect every man to be one hundred percent loyal to myself and the ministry. There could be no other than Mackenzie King Liberals as candidates, who would be recognized as such.' Those who were not were invited to leave the room, and the party.

The campaign that followed was a rout for the official opposition, which renamed itself the National Government party for the occasion. On 26 March the Liberals took over 50 per cent of the vote and 184 out of 245 seats in the House of Commons. Fighting Bob Manion, among others, had lost his seat and, as it turned out, his leadership of the Conservative party as well: a coup dethroned him as soon as the Conservative caucus had a chance to meet. King found his erstwhile rival a job; he later recorded his satisfaction at Manion's subsequent 'confession ... that he should never have left the Liberal Party; of how badly he had been treated by the Conservatives and how decent I had been to him at all times.'[4]

For the next two years the national Conservatives enjoyed, if that is the word, a temporary leadership remarkable for its ineffectiveness in the House of Commons: R.B. Hanson and his lieutenant, Gordon Graydon. They were parliamentary leaders only – no party convention was held until 1942. Indeed, the national leader of the Conservative party would not again sit in the House of Commons until 1945, a circumstance which must go some way to explain the dominance of the federal Liberals in national politics during the war.

The momentum created by the general election of 1940 was sufficient to carry the King government through the disasters sustained by allied arms in

4   Public Archives of Canada [PAC], King Papers, King Diary 3 July 1943

France and the Low Countries in the spring of 1940; past an anachronistic agitation for National Government in the same year; and past supply shortages and disruptions in the winter of 1940-1. Although the political climate worsened somewhat during 1941, a number of precedents had by then been established that were to assist the government in managing Canada's political climate for the next four years of war. A most important precedent was the manner in which war supply was dealt with in Parliament. The government presented an omnibus War Supply motion, under which fell all the war-derived expenditures. Details which might give aid and comfort to the enemy were omitted and the scope of the expenditures, which reached into the billions, was so vast that it was difficult if not impossible to seize any single part for detailed scrutiny. The opposition, handicapped by lack of staff and information, in any case chose to 'play the game' and refrained on patriotic grounds from questioning national secrets. Nor did the subsequent establishment of a Commons committee on war expenditures change matters; it met in camera and issued toothless reports.

The Conservatives were constrained by another important consideration. The Department of Munitions and Supply, which handled most war contracts, was stocked with business executives on war duty, and many of those executives were ordinarily Conservative partisans, serving to deflect or defuse partisan attacks on a war effort of which they were a prominent part.

The government's policies were in any case surprisingly popular, and for the first time in Canadian history the government could rely on something other than guesswork or instinct to tell it so. The Gallup Poll came to Canada in 1941 and started publishing its research in Canadian newspapers that fall. What it had to tell Canadians about themselves was reassuring. For example, late in 1941 76 per cent of Canadians approved wage and price controls and 66 per cent approved Mackenzie King's performance; 90 per cent approved the government's regimentation of industry during the war; and 78 per cent favoured a ban on strikes in war industries.

When it came to transforming this support into possible votes, the news was equally encouraging for the government party. The Liberals had the support of 44 per cent of the entire electorate at the beginning of 1942 while the Conservatives lagged with 24 per cent. It was true that the Conservatives were ahead of the undecided, who counted 20 per cent, and far ahead of the CCF, sustained by a mere 8 per cent of Canadians. As might be expected, the Liberal lead was founded on massive support (59 per cent) in Quebec, but in every region the party was ahead. Only in British Columbia were things even close: there the Liberals were supported by 28 per cent, the Conservatives by 23 per cent, and the CCF by 21 per cent. The CCF was also strong on the prairies, where 17 per cent would plump for socialism; but it was very weak in Ontario, Quebec, and the Maritimes.

The government, though not King, studied the polls anxiously. The government ran polls of its own to sound out Canadians' feelings on such issues as aid to Britain (Conservatives were more likely to favour it than Liberals) or on conscription. On these subjects, feelings were emphatic and divided. French Canadians did not want conscription, and they did not much want aid to Britain of the kind the government was preparing to dispense. English Canadians, however, did want such things, and they went further, boosting aid to Russia, Canada's ally since June 1941, and predicting a harmonious postwar world in which the Russians would help the various countries of Europe to get governments of their own choice. French Canadians, when asked, had no such hope. It did not take extraordinary perspicacity to conclude that French and English Canadians differed fundamentally in their perceptions of the world and more particularly of the role that Canada should play in it. It was the old foreign policy and defence debate carried forward into the war and it was still as dangerous as it had ever been.

Events at the end of 1941 brought these differences to the surface. The most important occurrence was the Japanese attack on the American naval base at Pearl Harbor and the United States' entry into the war. Canadians were naturally encouraged by the fact of direct American participation, but they were also imbued with a sense of heightened crisis. It was a crisis that the Conservatives could respond to.

The Liberals faced a dilemma. They had boxed themselves in by pledging to combat conscription in both the Quebec election of October 1939 and the federal election of March 1940. Lapointe and his colleagues from Quebec had promised to resign from any cabinet that brought in compulsory military service abroad (conscription for home defence, instituted in June 1940, was all right as far as they were concerned, and it was supported by opinion inside Quebec). It is difficult to know how Lapointe would have responded to the reappearance of conscription on the national political agenda, for on 26 November 1941 he died. The gap created by his demise was difficult to fill, but after some hesitation King decided to go outside Parliament and outside politics. He selected a distinguished Quebec City corporation lawyer, Louis St Laurent, the former counsel for the Rowell-Sirois Commission, to be minister of justice.

By-elections were called in four constituencies for the beginning of February 1942. In one, Welland, the electors were asked to ratify King's choice of an old craft unionist, Humphrey Mitchell, for the post of minister of labour, and although Hepburn, true to form, tried to block Mitchell, he failed. In the second, Quebec East, Louis St Laurent was running for the House of Commons on a platform that, significantly, did not include a promise to resign from the cabinet if conscription were implemented. This caused the entire Quebec East organization to walk out in protest, but with help from Chubby Power, St Laurent prevailed anyway. The most important by-election, from King's point of view, was in York South, a safe Tory seat in the suburbs of Toronto. There Arthur Meighen decided to run in anticipation of a return to the Conservative leadership from which he had been removed fifteen years before. If Meighen were elected he would bring back into the House of Commons more than a whiff of Union government; and that in turn could hardly be dissociated from the issue of conscription for overseas service. King dreaded Meighen's reappearance in Parliament more than anything else; but fortunately for the Liberal leader's peace of mind, events were in train which would halt Meighen's career and blow him out of national politics altogether.

It went without saying that the albatross of Ontario politics, Mitch Hepburn, supported Meighen vociferously. The federal Liberals took a dim view of this collaboration, so dim that they determined to take advantage of an old Canadian electoral courtesy – namely, that the leader of a political party not be opposed in a by-election. The CCF, latecomers to the election game, were not bound by this hoary convention and therefore had no difficulty in nominating Joe Noseworthy, a schoolteacher, to run against Meighen. The national Liberal organization then donated funds to the Noseworthy campaign, while Norman Lambert, the national organizer, urged any and all of the local Liberals to vote for Noseworthy, the lesser evil, against Meighen, the greater. To judge from the results, Lambert, rather than Hepburn, was successful. Meighen frankly appealed for conscription. The CCF demanded conscription of wealth as well as manpower, and the CCF prevailed. Mackenzie King was overjoyed.

To handle the conscription question, King resorted to an unusual but not unprecedented device. Since the people had ratified the Liberals' pledge of no conscription for overseas service in March 1940, let the people decide whether to hold them to it in the changed circumstances of the spring of 1942. The government, citing the necessity of freeing its hands from a too rigid promise, asked the electorate simply to approve releasing it from its commitment. The Conservatives could hardly oppose the government on the issue; they were, after all, asking for the same thing themselves. The real contest was not between the two old parties with their opposing traditions and convictions, but within the province of Quebec. There, the request for a 'yes' vote in the plebiscite was interpreted as an avowal, as Chubby Power saw it, 'that the government would bring on conscription at no distant date.' So English-Canadian conscriptionists believed; otherwise, why have the plebiscite? French-Canadian anti-conscriptionists believed this too, and they shaped a 'non' campaign accordingly.

In the event, the 'yes' forces won, nationally, 2,945,514 to 1,643,006. The armed forces in Canada voted 84 per cent yes, and those overseas 72 per cent yes, a phenomenon which C.P. Stacey interprets, doubtless correctly, as more an anti-government vote than a show of no confidence in conscription. In Quebec, however, the 'Nons' had it. A subsequent Gallup Poll, showed that, if anything, opinions had hardened: 90 per cent of French Canadians opposed conscription, although 82 per cent proclaimed their willingness to bear arms if Canada itself were directly invaded.

Mackenzie King actually had no intention of imposing conscription under existing circumstances, but he was keen on removing the urgency from the issue. In this, it would seem, he largely succeeded, and it would be two years before conscription surfaced again as a serious issue outside Quebec. Inside Quebec it was a very different matter. There the Liberal party was divided on the issue. Some Liberals, like St Laurent, explained that they would do whatever was best for the country. Some, like Chubby Power, stressed the fact that there was no conscription for overseas service at present and therefore no immediate cause for alarm. Some, like P.J.A. Cardin, distanced themselves from Mackenzie King; Cardin resigned from the cabinet on the issue and held himself aloof from the Liberal party for the next two-and-a-half years. Still others left the Liberals altogether and formed a new opposition party, the Bloc Populaire, in conjunction with non-Duplessiste elements among French-Canadian nationalists.

During the first half of 1942 the conscription issue obscured an equally important political change. The first indication occurred in the fall of 1941 when the Liberal government of British Columbia went to the polls. The premier, Duff Pattullo, thought the election 'a cinch,' but it was not. The Liberals descended from thirty-one seats and a majority in the legislature to twenty-one, with no seats at all in Vancouver. The Conservatives rose to twelve seats, and the CCF to fourteen. When Pattullo resisted coalition with the Conservatives to keep the CCF out, his party abandoned him. At the beginning of December 1941 he lost the Liberal leadership and resigned as premier, making way for John Hart and a Liberal-Conservative coalition which would hold power for the next decade. British Columbia politics had just been redefined, and in such a way as to emphasize a right-left split, with no perceptible middle ground.[5]

In the British Columbia election the CCF attracted 33 per cent of the popular vote. At first this might have been explained as an aberration, but opinion polls during 1942 showed that it was not. The CCF began 1942 with the

5 On this and other British Columbia subjects, Margaret Ormsby's elegantly written *British Columbia: A History* (Toronto 1958) repays perusal.

support of 10 per cent of a national poll sample. By December CCF support was up to 25 per cent, one percentage point more than the Conservatives and within shooting distance of the Liberals' 36 per cent. That result was to some extent skewed by the CCF's miniscule showing in Quebec; in the Maritimes the socialists attracted 14 per cent, in the prairies 36 per cent and in British Columbia an astonishing 40 per cent, far more than either of the old parties and almost as much as both of them put together.

That the polls were right would be demonstrated in Ontario. There the discredited Mitch Hepburn finally resigned as premier. His two short-term successors had to face the polls within a year, and when they did, on 4 August 1943, they were practically wiped out. The Liberal vote touched bottom at 31 per cent, down 20 per cent from the previous provincial election, and the party lost fifty seats. The CCF, just behind George Drew's resurgent Tories, would be the official opposition. Mackenzie King found what consolation he could in the defeat of Hepburn's closest associates, but he did not conceal from himself the dire possibility that Canadian politics were becoming realigned along a clear right-left axis, 'which,' he wrote, 'may be the beginning of the end of the power of the Liberal party federally.'

What had, in fact, happened? Investigation by the Gallup Poll confirmed what was statistically obvious: the CCF had got its support largely from ex-Liberals. The majority of the upper income bracket had supported the Conservatives; the middle class had split three ways, with the Liberals lagging even there behind the CCF; and at the lower end of the economic scale the CCF outdistanced both Liberals and Conservatives. Why had people voted CCF? 'Time for a change' was the reason most frequently cited, followed by the belief that 'they will help the working man' and 'platform.' 'Time for a change' could have meant everything and anything. It probably included disgust at Hepburn's antics, disapproval of the old party system, and a rejection of the Liberals' last-minute attempts to recapture credibility. A few weeks after the election, Mackenzie King noted that members of the cabinet had come to believe that the dominion government's liquor regulations had played a part in the Liberal defeat; taken a little more broadly, it meant that after four years of war and restrictions, the government's controls were finally wearying and annoying the electorate. There was also the suspicion, as voiced to one rural MP, 'that Quebec is running our Government.' It was a heavy burden, and one with which faithful Liberals were increasingly uncomfortable. What looked logical, necessary, and inevitable from Ottawa did not seem so in the provinces.

The crisis in the Liberal party's affairs was reached in the late summer of 1943. The war was by then going moderately well. Italy had surrendered and the German army was in retreat on all fronts. Canadians were turning

Mitch Hepburn
Courtesy Robert LaPalme

Premier Bracken of Manitoba accepts the Conservative leadership, 1942, as Lord
Bennett looks on
Arch Dale, *Winnipeg Free Press*

their thoughts to what would happen after the war and what they might expect from their government in the aftermath of victory. 'Reform,' variously
defined, was in the air. As of September 1943 Canadians were noticeably
more reform minded (71 per cent) than the British (57 per cent) or the
Americans (32 per cent); of Canadians, the CCF supporters were most likely
to want reform (85 per cent for it), and Liberals least (61 per cent). The
Conservatives occupied an uneasy middle ground.

The Conservatives at least had done something about reforming their
public image. A group of Conservatives, meeting at Port Hope, had adopted
positions considerably in advance of anything the party had supported to
date; they would afterwards be called the 'Port Hopefuls.' A formal party
convention, meeting in Winnipeg in December 1942, had added
'Progressive' to the party label, and taken on board as leader John Bracken,
the erstwhile Progressive premier of Manitoba. Bracken chose to reform his
party first, reserving until a general election his entry into the House of
Commons, and it was while Bracken was touring the country, burnishing the

Progressive Conservative party's new image, that the Liberals met in Ottawa to consider the low estate to which their party had fallen.[6]

How low, the polls showed. In September 1943 the Liberals and Conservatives were running neck and neck in popular favour, tied at 28 per cent each. The CCF had emerged as the party favoured by more Canadians than any other, at 29 per cent. Some prominent Liberals, like C.D. Howe, were becoming convinced that the government party had shot its bolt and should await the end of the war and dignified oblivion. Others were not so inclined to give up without a fight, and even Howe's melancholy proved to be a passing phase. Mackenzie King's secretary J.W. Pickersgill urged the path of reform on his leader. Brooke Claxton, the exceedingly active Montreal MP who was the prime minister's parliamentary assistant, agreed. Chubby Power's partisan juices were also stirred by the possibility of danger to the party. When the Liberals' advisory council met in September 1943, Claxton reported that 'the boys are drifting into town and things are boiling in many directions. A good many are beginning to see that the existence of the Liberal party may depend on what we do here.' The Gallup Poll results certainly helped things along.[7]

Norman Lambert and Brooke Claxton, interested participants at the national council, agreed on the deficiencies of King's political performance. The national leader, Lambert said, was trying to have it both ways. He blamed bad organization for the Liberal defeat in Ontario, but in the next breath proclaimed the government's entire devotion to winning the war while excluding party matters. 'Pounding away with "we must win the war first,"' Claxton wrote, 'just irritates and that is what the Prime Minister et al are doing.' The Liberals were simply not responding to concerns that were seeping into the public mind not only from CCF propaganda but from CBC broadcasts, church sermons, and public think tanks 'in the fields and in the manner that the CCF has made peculiarly its own.'

To redress the balance, Claxton and his supporters steered a series of forward-looking resolutions through the advisory council. The government would spend more to create full employment after the war. There would be more social security, including better old-age pensions. And, just possibly, there would be family allowances, a proposition whose public appeal had not yet been firmly established, outside Quebec.

It was a beginning. The King government took note, and soon afterwards the cabinet began to discuss just what it would do in the winter session of Parliament to provide for the postwar future. When Parliament met, the as-

6 On this assessment see J.L. Granatstein, *The Politics of Survival: The Conservative Party of Canada, 1939-1945* (Toronto 1967).
7 PAC, Claxton Papers, volume 32, Claxton to G.V. Ferguson, 24 Sept. 1943

sembled politicians learned that the government intended to do quite a bit: comprehensive assistance for veterans, to be embodied in a special veterans' department; revision of the national housing policy; reconstruction, with a department to match; even a special department of social welfare. The measures were passed into law by the early summer, and in October the new departments of Veterans' Affairs, National Health and Welfare, and Reconstruction were set on foot. Ian Mackenzie, a political warhorse from British Columbia who had recently championed the cause of social security and health insurance inside the cabinet, became minister of veterans' affairs. Brooke Claxton became minister of national health and welfare, a reward for work well done and in anticipation of more. C.D. Howe became minister of reconstruction in a role more powerful and influential than King had initially wished to contemplate. Politically, the government had done all it could; it remained to give administrative flesh to the legislative bones.

It was by then October 1944. The Liberal party had through the year enjoyed a slow rise in the public opinion polls, from the low of 28 per cent in September 1943 to 30 per cent in January 1944 to 35 per cent in June and 36 per cent in November. The Conservatives stayed approximately where they were, and the CCF started to decline. It bottomed out at 21 per cent in June 1944, and rose slightly to 23 per cent in November; but for the rest of the war it stayed safely behind the Conservatives and, needless to say, considerably behind the Liberals. No one could then tell that the CCF's peak had passed for good.

In June 1944 the Liberals suffered another electoral reverse. The Patterson government in Saskatchewan faced the electorate for the first time in six years and it was drubbed. Survivors returning to Ottawa told a dismal tale. As in Ontario, there was 'heated opposition to the various wartime controls and regulations,' the Saskatchewan minister of highways reported. 'There was a strong resentment against the Income Tax on the lower incomes and the freezing of wages.' The military vote had gone overwhelmingly to the CCF, and the Conservative vote had simply collapsed. 'Speaking generally,' King was told, 'the young people of the Conservative families were almost all CCF supporters.' What the result signified varied from correspondent to correspondent; what mattered was that King had already decided what it all meant. 'The essence of Liberalism,' he told a Liberal advocating a return to the purest Gladstonian individualism, 'is the securing of more in the way of equality of opportunity for all men. Social services properly conceived and administered should greatly further that end.'[8]

8   King Papers, volume 358, King to R.J. Deachman, 24 June 1944

Quebec was in wartime politics, as in so many other things, the province least like the others. The Godbout government had to face an election by the end of 1944. Its record was by no means discreditable. It had given the vote to women, the last Canadian province to do so. It had nationalized Montreal Light, Heat and Power and created Quebec Hydro, a publicly owned entity to serve the metropolis. Hydro's new president, the veteran Liberal Senator T.D. Bouchard, promptly announced rate reductions and pay raises. Then Bouchard went on to more important matters in a speech to the Senate on 21 June 1944.

Ordinarily, speeches in the Canadian Senate, however meritorious, have little resonance. Bouchard's was an exception. A fervent anti-clerical democrat, Bouchard applauded national unity and damned French-Canadian nationalists with equal enthusiasm. It had taken him years, after a clerical education, to learn that 'Canadians of English descent were not all cloven-footed and did not all bear horns.' How had he ever believed such nonsense? He had had a French and Catholic education at the hands of the church in Quebec. Other products of the Quebec system had not survived as well as he: they accounted for the 'hidden fascists' Bouchard perceived in the ranks of the Quebec Conservative party and the Bloc Populaire. He was promptly fired as president of Hydro-Quebec by the desperate Godbout, who was within months of an election, but the damage was, apparently, done. Conscription was not enough; the wartime regulations were not enough; Bouchard had revived a century's worth of antagonism between the Catholic church of Quebec and the Liberal party, and it hardly mattered under the circumstances what were the rights and wrongs of the matter.[9]

The Quebec election was held on 8 August 1944. The Godbout organization stumbled from the first. The splits that had occurred at the time of Taschereau had never completely healed. Godbout apparently did not see the necessity of healing them, and election post mortems condemned the blind optimism which held that 'Victory was in sight just the same.' If Godbout's organization was bad, Duplessis's organization was correspondingly good. The former premier was rejuvenated after a prolonged stay in the hospital, his problems with the bottle a thing of the past. He knew how to organize, and he did his best. 'He has a very good Organization,' Chubby Power conceded in July, 'and he has good candidates in the field.' It was important that he did, because there was a rival, ultra-nationalist party in the field, André Laurendeau's Bloc Populaire. The Bloc Populaire suffered from the same defects as its Action Libérale Nationale predecessor a decade earlier, and, 'with the exception of three or four men,' Power rated its candidates as

9 Black, *Duplessis,* 278-9

nobodies. The federal minister remained optimistic until the end, but he did point to the essential feature of the campaign: 'Godbout is being made the scapegoat for our sins' and there was little or nothing that could be done about it.

The scapegoat was duly sacrificed on 8 August. In terms of the popular vote, Duplessis received 36 per cent to Godbout's 37 per cent; the Liberal margin is attributable to the huge majorities Liberal candidates piled up in English-speaking Montreal, where the electors had not forgotten or forgiven Duplessis's anti-participationist stand in 1939. The Bloc Populaire got 15 per cent of the vote, almost all of it French Canadian, and Duplessis's biographer correctly concludes that French Canadians repudiated the Liberals by a margin of roughly three to two. Because of his predominance in the provincial backwoods, Duplessis got the majority of seats in the Quebec assembly. Nationalist government had returned to Quebec.[10]

It was too late for Duplessis's victory to make any significant difference to the Canadian war effort. August 1944 saw the allies break out from Normandy towards the Seine and Paris. By the end of the month, Canadian troops were approaching Belgium and Germany's collapse appeared imminent. Mackenzie King and his cabinet seriously considered calling an election for the fall, but instead they resigned themselves to recalling Parliament in November for one last pre-election session. With these decisions safely out of the way, the minister of national defence, Colonel Ralston, took off on an inspection tour of the Canadian army in Europe.

When he returned, on 18 October, Ralston went to see King, and the next day told the cabinet's war committee what he had found. Casualties had been heavy in the previous months, with the result that the infantry units of the Canadian army in Europe were operating under strength. Reinforcements were needed, and in Ralston's opinion they could only be found among the 'NRMA men' – conscripts who had not volunteered for overseas service. Subsequent reports confirmed this fact: there was no readily available manpower reserve, in Canada or in Britain, that could be drawn upon. The conclusion was inescapable: Canada would have to send conscripts overseas.

King would not agree. He prized national unity too highly. The issue was dragged before the full cabinet, but no agreement was possible. King feared that ministers favouring conscription would begin to plot against him unless he acted decisively, and, on 1 November, he took drastic action. Ralston had submitted his resignation two years earlier and, King told the cabinet, he 'had never withdrawn it.' (He had, of course, been persuaded not to act on

10 King Papers, volume 369, Power to King, 20 July 1944; Black, *Duplessis*, 290-1

it.) King now proposed to accept it. Ralston, stunned, shook hands all round and left the room. He was replaced by General A.G.L. McNaughton, who had been commander of Canada's troops in Europe between 1939 and 1943 and who, not coincidentally, hated Ralston, his former superior. McNaughton promised to find the necessary volunteers for overseas service, and the proconscription ministers in the cabinet decided to wait and see whether he could.

McNaughton had, effectively, three weeks. Out of 42,000 NRMA men, a grand total of 694 stepped forward. By 22 November it was obvious that McNaughton's faith in the volunteer system had not been justified. Parliament was to meet that day (it had been recalled on 13 November), and the pro-conscription ministers were determined to bring matters to a head. To make matters worse, McNaughton received word that his senior officers might well resign, and that one already had. When the cabinet met in the evening of 22 November it was widely believed that this meeting would be their last as a government; but at the last moment events took a different course.

To the amazement of most of his ministers, King and McNaughton reversed themselves. Conscripts would be sent after all. The conscriptionist ministers, who had proposed to resign in a bloc, had had their way, without having formally to confront their leader on the subject. Chubby Power, the sole survivor of the three Quebec stalwarts who had promised to resign should conscription ever be implemented, did resign, but St Laurent, Lapointe's successor, did not. He had made no such pledge, and in the interest of party and national unity he stayed.

The conscription crisis was the most serious political challenge for the wartime cabinet. No other issue of policy had the same emotional power and, in all probability, no other matter could have toppled the government. It is striking, in examining the conscription crisis, that the parliamentary opposition was almost irrelevant. What counted was trouble in the army, which led King to conclude that the military was preparing to defy the civil power, and the forcefully expressed views of some of the most powerful members of the cabinet. It was, in other words, a crisis internal to the government.

The Liberal party did not fall apart as a result of the conscription crisis. Many, though certainly not all, of King's French-Canadian followers conceded that their leader had done all he could to avoid conscription, and they could hardly expect to better their lot under anyone else. There were certainly rumours around Quebec in the months that followed that Cardin, Power, or both would succeed in derailing the Liberal party in the province. By then, however, the war was definitely on the wane and the collapse of

Nazi Germany in the spring of 1945 effectively removed conscription from the national political agenda.

The only casualty of the conscription crisis was General McNaughton. The general had somehow to get elected to Parliament, and the chosen means was to run him in an Ontario by-election. The campaign straddled Christmas, but for McNaughton it was anything but a season of peace and charity. A fire and brimstone evangelist came out from Toronto to establish McNaughton firmly in the voters' minds as a minion of the Pope and the devil (not necessarily in that order), and the result would seem to indicate that he was preaching to the converted.

The minister was beaten. He would be beaten again in the forthcoming general election. He finally retired from politics to return to the more comfortable field of administration and diplomacy, in which capacity he yielded the country another twenty years of service.

With conscription past, King was working to win four more years of office. More accurately, his assistant J.W. Pickersgill was working to that end, along with Brooke Claxton and Bob Kidd of the advertising firm of Cockfield, Brown. The slogan for the campaign had nothing to do with the abstractions of victory and foreign policy. Instead, it stressed what the polls said Canadians were mostly concerned with: 'Liberal Policies Create Jobs.' Some members of the cabinet were not as enthusiastic as Claxton thought they should be, and questioned whether Claxton's shiny brochures were really a reflection of policy. But King approved. 'When I realized that Mr. King was in effect approving our work,' Claxton later wrote, 'I almost burst into tears.'[11]

The campaign did not formally begin until April. By then, Howe had brought down his White Paper on employment and income, and party propagandists had nailed the flag of 'full employment' (words carefully omitted from the White Paper) to the party mast. Mackenzie King was off in San Francisco demonstrating to the public that he was a world-class statesman, the very man to steer the country through the perils of the postwar era. Though not as well-financed as in 1940, the Liberals had enough money to make an appeal where it counted, and they were assisted by the popularity and prominence of several of their ministers, notably J.L. Ilsley, the best-known minister after King himself, and C.D. Howe.

The polls showed that the Liberals were gaining support after the election was called, from 36 per cent in April to 39 per cent at the beginning of June to 41 per cent on polling day. It was enough for a squeaker, and more than enough to overwhelm the Conservatives, who polled only 29 per cent of the

11 Claxton Papers, volume 224, draft memoirs

popular vote. Such a division was sufficient to put the Conservatives in opposition for a decade. But what was really significant was the fate of the CCF, which managed only a disappointing 15 per cent. The government party received 125 out of 245 seats, a working majority. The political revolution of 1945 had not occurred.

It had seemed so logical, so probable, that the Canadian electorate would opt for socialism at war's end. Their British cousins did it barely a month later; the polls had seemed to be pointing in the approved direction; planning was in the air – to those who had not been planners the war was thought to have shown the way. Why, then, had Canadians not chosen to follow the CCF slogan, 'Left Turn, Canada?'

The answer is rather complicated. In the first place, socialism and socialist appeals had almost no resonance in French Canada, which remained obdurately conservative in social attitudes and political views. The CCF therefore began with some 30 per cent of the electorate predisposed against it. In the second place, it would seem that the electorate was more concerned with stability than with a genuine restructuring of Canada's economic and social fabric. Canadians remembered the Depression of the 1930s, and feared its return, but they were also impressed by the security and stability achieved during the war. Therefore, the combination of depression and war may have been not a radicalizing experience but a stabilizing one as far as the voters were concerned. Given the choice between experimentation and a reliance on older symbols, they plumped for tradition, whether Bracken or King.

It is true that all parties competed to show how renovated they truly were. Each outdid the other in affirming a commitment to social security, full employment, and government management, if and when necessary. If the rhetoric was in most cases the same, it would seem that continuity had the edge; the success the incumbents had shown in managing the war effort qualified them to lead the country in peace, or so a plurality of Canadians thought. The Second World War had not strained the Canadian political system, as the First World War had done. There was no fatal inheritance to overcome, as conscription had been for Meighen and his unfortunate successors. The political history of the Second World War may have been a series of near misses, but in politics, a miss was as good as a mile. The Liberal party continued to dominate Canadian politics, and Mackenzie King would hold office until, figuratively, he dropped.

20

Fighting the War

The population of Canada when war broke out in Europe in 1939 was estimated to be 11,267,000; by 1945 it would be 12,072,000. Of these totals, some 1,100,000 persons, men and women, served in Canada's armed forces during the war. Not all served at the same time, of course; at its peak the Canadian army totalled 495,804, including 15,845 women. The Royal Canadian Navy, at its peak, held some 92,000; while the Royal Canadian Air Force expanded to a maximum, at the end of 1943, of 206,350 personnel.

It was a formidable effort, and one which the politicians who took Canada into the Second World War in September 1939 did not expect to see. Nor was there much on which to build. Between 1935 and 1939 force levels rose somewhat, and some new equipment was bought; but the military's political masters had to keep in mind that Canada was officially a country bound to do little or nothing in the event of war. Too much or too conspicuous expenditure would rouse suspicions in Quebec, allergic since 1917 to the prospect of war, or among the left. The government did what it thought it could get away with, but that was not very much.

Both politicians and military planners tacitly assumed that Canada would have time to react to war and the prospect of war. In the first instance, Canada would be defended by Great Britain and France, and, if an enemy ever landed on Canadian shores, by the United States too. President Roosevelt had pledged as much in a speech in Kingston, Ontario, in 1938. Politicians emphasized home defence as a means to get money out of a reluctant public, but in fact the military had not the slightest expectation of having to fight a war close to home. Europe was the inevitable battlefield in any war that the military could imagine, and as events proved, they were right.

Once war was declared, on 10 September 1939, events moved rapidly. Mobilization of Canada's reserves and the enlistment of volunteers produced over 60,000 soldiers by the end of September 1939. By then the government had decided to dispatch an expeditionary force overseas. At the beginning of October Major-General A.G.L. McNaughton was appointed to command the 1st Canadian Division. There was soon a 2nd, which, the government revealed in January 1940, would also be sent overseas. A 3rd Division was authorized in May 1940, and before summer the government started raising men for a 4th.

The first Canadian troops arrived in England in December 1939. Without equipment and requiring considerable training to bring them up to fighting form, they were too late to play much of a role in the 1940 campaigns, although as the Germans advanced into France in June 1940 part of the Canadian 1st Division was sent on a tour of Brittany by truck and rail in the futile hope of stopping the Germans. Long before Canada's soldiers met any of the enemy, the division was re-embarked for England with only minimal losses of men and equipment. The French surrendered without benefit of Canadian assistance.

Over the next three years Canada's army gradually accumulated in southern England. The first three divisions were infantry; the 4th was converted to armour, and a 5th Division was also armour. There were many other Canadian units overseas, but these were the principal ones. Together they justified the creation, first of a corps and then of an army, the First Canadian Army, under McNaughton, now promoted to full general. At its height, in March 1944, the Canadian army overseas totalled 242,000.

The air force and the navy underwent a similar expansion. For the air force, the great priority was the creation of a British Commonwealth Air Training Plan (always abbreviated as BCATP). This plan was agreed among the several Commonwealth governments in December 1939. Canada's remote skies, far from enemy activity, were ideal for training British flyers. A network of schools and airbases was opened across the dominion, with a heavy concentration on the prairies and in southern Ontario. Between 1940 and 1945, 131,553 aircrew graduated from BCATP schools. Of this total, 73,000 were destined for the RCAF, 42,000 for the British RAF, and just under 17,000 for the Australian and New Zealand air forces. The BCATP involved a heavy commitment of Canada's men and money, a commitment which grew heavier in 1940 when circumstances prevented Britain from supplying the equipment it had originally promised.

The Royal Canadian Air Force quickly began to send what it could to Britain, and over time Canadian airmen served in transport, coastal patrols, reconnaissance, fighters and bombers. Some forty-six squadrons of the RCAF served overseas, and a large element of the RAF's Bomber Command was Canadian. We shall deal below with some of the detailed history of this enterprise, and with some of the complications that ensued.

The Royal Canadian Navy also played an active role; its best-known assignment was the protection of the western side of the Atlantic, particularly the convoys sailing from New York or Halifax bound for Britain. Using destroyers and destroyer escorts (corvettes), the navy was to escort ships to a point in the mid-Atlantic where they would be picked up by an allied force. RCN ships also played a role in the defence of Britain itself and in various allied amphibious operations.

It was assumed from the beginning that Canada's armed forces would serve with their British counterparts. The uniforms, training, and traditions were much the same. The equipment was standard as between Canadian and British units. Many of the officers had served together during the First World War, or had trained together in the 1920s and 1930s, as the higher ranks of Canada's armed services had all received advanced training from the British. Thus, the history of Canada's soldiers, sailors, and airmen at war is also to some degree the story of the larger British formations of which they were part. It is on the whole a creditable story, but not without friction or inconsistencies. And it throws a revealing light on the ability of a junior partner in an alliance to control its own destiny, as well as the fates of the men and women it sends to fight.

It was plain from the beginning that, except under the most unusual circumstances, Canadian troops would fight in combination, where their contribution would most of the time be outweighed by the contributions of the British or, later, the Americans. Command would therefore go to one or the other (or both) of Canada's senior partners. Also, planning and staff work would tend to be reserved for British and American officers. Given the scarcity of professionally trained and experienced Canadian staff and line officers this was not surprising, especially at the beginning of the war when Canada boasted no serving officers who had commanded more than a brigade.

There was no problem with the command of strictly Canadian army units. It had been established during the First World War that Canadian units would be commanded by Canadian officers. Because Canada had too few specialist staff officers, Canadian staffs would be bolstered by British officers. As time passed, however, the suspicion grew that for the British the moment would never come when Canadian officers were regarded as the equals of themselves, at least as far as brains were concerned. This impression contended with another – that senior British officers were insufficiently educated in political developments over the previous fifty years and that they failed to proceed with due regard for dominion sensibilities. The British, for their part, regarded senior Canadian officers as far too prone to play politics, by which they often meant that Canadian officers were able to invoke the influence of their home government on behalf of themselves or their units.

With Canada's tacit consent, the grand military strategy of the war was left to the senior allies: the French and British, in 1939-40; the British by themselves in 1940-1; and the British and Americans, from 1941 to 1945. Prime Minister King resisted attempts to convene imperial conferences, and as a result he visited Great Britain only twice during the war, in 1941 and 1944. (There was a conference in the latter year.) The Canadian government's reticence is underlined by the fact that when Prime Minister Churchill and President Roosevelt conferred with their high military and political advisers in Quebec City in August 1943 and September 1944, all Mackenzie King asked was the privilege of acting as their host. The resultant photographs proved the old saw that a picture is worth a thousand words or, in this case, many thousand votes. Appearance triumphed over reality, for once the photographers were gone, King quietly retired from the scene to await dinner. The multitude of hovering photographers and reporters were treated to a lavish outpouring of alcohol, ration-free. Those lucky enough to be on the spot were also treated to the spectacle of Canada's minister of national defence for air, Major Power, removing his trousers before taking a run down a corridor at the Château Frontenac. Power was eventually collared by the lieutenant-governor of Quebec, who was instructed to get him out of the city and keep him out.[1]

If Canada either excluded itself from the highest level of conferences or was excluded by the conferees, how did the Canadian government keep track of what was going on? The answer seems to be, 'with great difficulty.' The British and American war efforts were co-ordinated by a series of bilateral bodies headquartered in Washington, under the authority of the Combined Chiefs of Staff (the American chiefs of staff meeting with very senior British officers representing the British chiefs of staff). As a result of decisions taken at the Combined Chiefs level, Canadian troops could be shipped hither and yon, invasions launched, armistices arranged, and strategy debated. Canada learned about the decisions of the Combined Chiefs or their subordinates through a discreet network of contacts in Washington under Lieutenant-General Maurice Pope. Pope did his job well, and when the Combined Chiefs moved to Quebec City for their conferences, Pope was brought up too, to lurk in corridors and waylay friendly allies who might possibly know something that the Canadian government would like to learn. Canada was informed after the fact, but usually before the manoeuvre decided upon had taken place, though not always. When the Allies landed in

1   Public Archives of Canada, King Papers, King Diary, 14 and 19 Aug. 1943

France on 6 June 1944 and Canadian troops went with them, Mackenzie King learned of the invasion from an RCMP constable on duty at his home, Laurier House. The constable had heard it on the radio.[2]

The consequences of some of these decisions could be severe as far as Canada was concerned. To test the German defences on the French Atlantic coast in 1942 the British proposed to stage a reconnaissance in force. The target chosen was the Norman city of Dieppe. The progenitor of the Dieppe raid appears to have been Lord Louis Mountbatten, cousin of the king and, in 1942, a glamorous young officer high in favour with Winston Churchill. Mountbatten was promoted rapidly to high rank and responsibility.

Dieppe was, in its origins, a political exercise, mounted to compensate for the absence of a second front, which the Americans as well as the Russians would have liked to see. It held promise, according to its originators, as a perfect combined operation, and it may be that if land, sea, and air forces could have been got to work together the results would have been worthwhile. Air and sea were the responsibility of the British and, in particular, Mountbatten; land was an overall British responsibility, and the responsibility was assigned to General Bernard Montgomery, the general commanding in southeast England.

Montgomery had Canada's overseas army under his command. He had not been getting on especially well with the Canadians, and some of them viewed Montgomery as hypercritical of their high-ranking officers. When Montgomery assigned the 2nd Canadian Division under General Roberts to the Dieppe raid, he may well have been trying to show a belated confidence, as well as to secure valuable experience for troops who had yet to see a shot fired in anger.

The assignment was an honour. But it was also, unfortunately, a mistake. The 2nd Division fought bravely, but it could not overcome strong German defences. The Canadians were repulsed from Dieppe on 19 August 1942. They left behind more than half their number, as dead or prisoners. In all, the 2nd Division suffered 3367 casualties, including almost 2000 prisoners of war, out of just under 5000 men landed.

Why had it happened? We have seen that the origin of the raid was political rather than strictly military. Dieppe was the wrong choice, because of high cliffs and strong German defences. A German analysis of the raid argued that the raid failed for four main reasons: lack of artillery support; an underestimation of the strength of the German defences; superior German weaponry; and the sinking by the Germans of almost all the landing craft intended to evacuate the troops. To this might be added the failure of the

2 The problems of high strategy are considered in C.P. Stacey, *Arms, Men and Governments* (Ottawa 1970).

combined operations strategy to provide what it had promised: adequate cover through air support or artillery, sufficient to keep the Germans in their bunkers and out of their artillery pits.

Dieppe by itself should not lead us to conclude that Canada's generals in Europe were unfit for their jobs or were promoted beyond their safe capacity. But it is indisputable that some Canadian officers were not held in high regard. The luckless General Roberts was one of them. (Montgomery hoped that he would be balanced by his senior staff officer, Colonel, later General, C.C. Mann.) General McNaughton was another. For whatever reason, both General Montgomery and General Sir Alan Brooke, the chief of the Imperial General Staff, regarded McNaughton as unfit for his duties. When Montgomery was posted to Egypt in August 1942 to take command of the British Eighth Army, Brooke took up the struggle with McNaughton. By the summer of 1943 Canadian politicians were being told that grave doubts existed about McNaughton's fitness to lead his army into battle. Finally, in the fall, defence minister Ralston was compelled to take the painful decision to relieve McNaughton on the strong and very explicit recommendation of Brooke and General Bernard Paget, commander of British home forces.

McNaughton was succeeded by Harry Crerar, a quieter soldier and, some thought, a better one. Crerar's placid exterior masked a sharp and opinionated view of the world. Asked after the war what he thought about Montgomery, Crerar told the story of how he had first asked a knowledgeable British friend about the then unknown general. 'Well, Harry,' his friend replied, 'all I can tell you about Monty is that he's an efficient little shit.'[3] Crerar led the Canadian army to the beaches of Normandy in June 1944 and commanded the First Canadian Army all the way from the beachhead to the northwest coast of Germany.

Crerar was not universally liked. From the start he did not enjoy Montgomery's complete confidence. (Montgomery was commanding the invasion of Normandy and, thereafter, the Canadian and British armies in northwest Europe.) Crerar, Montgomery wrote, was 'fighting his first battle and it is the first appearance in history of a Canadian Army H.Q. He is desperately anxious that it should succeed. He is so anxious that he worries himself all day!! I go and see him a lot and calm him down.' Less charitably, and less accurately, Montgomery blamed Crerar for the refusal of a senior British general under his command to accept his orders.[4] It may well have been that had Crerar been a British general he would not have got or kept his assignment; but he was Canadian, and there was little that Montgomery or anyone else could do to him. It seems that the Americans got the impression

3 Quoted in C.P. Stacey, *A Date with History* (Ottawa 1983), 235
4 N. Hamilton, *Monty, Master of the Battlefield* (London 1983), 780

that Crerar looked down on them; and they returned the favour, as they saw it. What the Americans objected to may have been nothing more than stiffness, the effect of a cold official personality. As a general, Crerar did not display notable imagination or flair for command; he could be optimistic and, on occasion, over-optimistic, but, on balance, he made no bad mistakes.

From his post in England, Crerar commanded three divisions, rather more than half of Canada's fighting soldiers. The remaining two were shipped out from England in 1943 to join in the Sicilian and Italian campaigns. The long inactivity of the Canadian field army in England was, it was believed, affecting morale both among the troops and at home. The idea of raising an army the bulk of which saw no combat for four-and-a-half years (the time that elapsed between their arrival in England and the invasion of France in June 1944) gave even Canada's manpower-conscious politicians pause. And so it was for reasons which were only tangentially military that Canadian troops were shipped to the Mediterranean sector to replace certain British units which were already there.

When they arrived they found, inevitably, Montgomery, whose Eighth Army they were to join. Montgomery regarded his new troops fondly, although he thought them at first rather fat and out of shape. He even liked their commander, General Guy Simonds. His Canadian soldiers performed creditably in battles in Sicily during July and August 1943. Then, in September, the Eighth Army crossed the Straits of Messina and invaded the Italian peninsula. The Canadians went with them. Now a corps of two divisions, the Canadian army in Italy fought through two winters, mostly on the eastern side of Italy, ending up in a battle for the Gothic Line, the German defensive position in northern Italy. In February 1945 the Canadians were withdrawn, and trans-shipped to join the remaining three Canadian divisions in northwest Europe.

On 6 June 1944, D-Day, allied forces landed in Normandy by air and sea. Of the five seaborne divisions, two were American, two British, and one Canadian. The Canadian force, the 3rd infantry Division, pushed inland towards the city of Caen, some ten miles inland. But the Canadians, and the British divisions on either side of them, were to be looking towards Caen for the next five weeks, as German resistance stiffened and crack German units were moved in to oppose them. Heavy and desperate fighting characterized the Canadian sector of the Normandy battlefield. There the Germans concentrated the bulk of their armour, containing the Canadian and British forces at the cost of being worn down themselves. Finally, at the end of July, the Americans broke through the western end of the German line. From there they moved into Brittany, to the west and south, and towards Orleans on the east. The Germans facing the British-Canadian armies were at risk.

Hampered by an ill-conceived counterattack ordered by Hitler, the German armies were slow to withdraw from their exposed position and risked being surrounded.

Encirclement depended on the British and Canadians closing a ring around the German army from the north, in order to meet the Americans coming up from the south. The battle that ensued is commonly known as the battle of the Falaise gap, from the town of Falaise in the middle of the battlefield. General Crerar had responsibility for the northern hinge and, to some degree, he was responsible for the prolonged character of the battle. Every day that the Allies failed to close the gap was crucial to the Germans, permitting the escape of more of their troops. As C.P. Stacey, Canada's official military historian, commented, 'A German force smaller than our own, taking advantage of strong ground and prepared positions, was able to slow our advance to the point where considerable German forces made their escape.' Although, as Stacey noted, the Americans had contributed their share to the allied failure, that 'should not blind us to our own shortcomings.' General Charles Foulkes, one of Crerar's senior commanders, later observed: 'When we went into battle at Falaise and Caen we found that when we bumped into battle-experienced German troops we were no match for them. We would not have been successful had it not been for our air and artillery support.'[5]

Normandy was nevertheless a tremendous victory, and Canadian troops played their part well, improving and improvising as they went along. The best German field army in Western Europe was destroyed. In the aftermath, the Germans had no choice but to evacuate France and Belgium. When the Canadians next ran into an organized German front it was north of the Belgian port of Antwerp, at the end of September 1944. The Allies needed Antwerp, a river port, to resupply their armies, which were then at the end of a supply line stretching all the way back to Normandy. But the Germans held both sides of the river Scheldt northwest of Antwerp, and they were dug in. Nature favoured the Germans. The lower reaches of the Scheldt were one huge bog, hampering advance by land but not flooded sufficiently to allow allied landing craft to sail over them. The Scheldt campaign, which lasted through October and November 1944, was therefore difficult and costly. But when it ended, ships could freely sail up the river to Antwerp, and the Allies could be resupplied in time to cope with a winter German offensive in eastern Belgium.

The cost, in Normandy and in the Scheldt, was considerable in Canadian lives and wounds. It was the heavy fighting that lasted from June until No-

5   C.P. Stacey, *The Victory Campaign* (Ottawa 1960), 276

vember, with little respite, that precipitated the reinforcement crisis of October 1944 and the subsequent painful decision by the King government to send conscript soldiers to join the army in Europe. Some 16,000 were sent, and they were needed.

The final battles of the war were fought, as far as the Canadian army was concerned, on the lower Rhine River, along the border between Germany and the Netherlands. Canadians fought their way up to the Rhine, crossed it, and spread out into the north German plain, reaching the North Sea on 15 April 1945 and cutting off the Germans in the Netherlands. On 4 May the German forces in the region surrendered to Field Marshal Montgomery (as he had become), and on 5 May a cease-fire took effect along the Canadian lines. On 7 May Canadian troops crossed the line to liberate the cities of Amsterdam, Utrecht, and The Hague; German troops were shipped out in the other direction, back to Germany.

The campaign in northwest Europe had lasted eleven months. During that time there were 44,339 Canadian casualties, including just over 11,000 fatalities.

AIR AND NAVAL WARFARE

The army was incomparably the largest aspect of Canada's military effort, but it was hardly the only one. Nor was it, proportionately, the most risky. The army between 1939 and 1945 suffered 22,917 killed and 52,679 wounded; the RCAF, though considerably smaller, lost 17,100 dead in places as far away as Burma, Poland, and Iceland, as well in Western Europe. Some were also killed in Canada – 2300 in fact, their deaths a testimony to the hazards of flying and flight training.

The Royal Canadian Air Force had two principal theatres of activity. At home the air force was responsible for coastal defence in the Atlantic and reconnaissance in the Pacific, while the British Commonwealth Air Training Plan turned out pilots for the several Commonwealth air forces. The Western Air Command operated as far afield as the Aleutians off Alaska, and managed to down a Japanese fighter, the only aerial victory by a home-based RCAF aircraft during the war. In 1943, when the Japanese menace receded, some of the western squadrons shifted to Britain. The Eastern Air Command had graver duties, being responsible for anti-submarine patrols off the east coast.[6]

When graduates of the BCATP were sent abroad they could be posted to their own specific national formations, or they could be absorbed into the

6 On the RCAF at home see W.A.B. Douglas, *The Creation of a National Air Force: The Official History of the Royal Canadian Air Force*, volume 2 (Toronto 1986).

RAF. Military necessity and the efficiency of the service were the prime considerations here, but it was hoped that as time passed RCAF units would come into being to absorb Canadian flight crews. This ran counter to the RAF's inclinations, at least on the operational level. Each Canadian pilot was warmly welcomed and treated as an equal; but the idea that the RCAF should have a separate identity even on the level of the squadron was very reluctantly conceded. By the end of 1941, therefore, of 8595 Canadian BCATP graduates serving overseas, a scant 500 were actually serving in RCAF squadrons. The rest belonged to the RAF.

This news was not warmly received by senior Canadian officers. A prolonged dispute followed, in the course of which several RCAF officers made themselves distinctly unpopular with British air commanders. The politicians on both sides proved to be more supple, but the final solution to the problem was found not on principle – dominion autonomy or the like – but in money. Canada would pay to have RCAF squadrons. The RAF and the British Air Ministry were sensitive to the power and lucidity of this argument, and during 1943 Canadian squadrons were created at a rapid rate.

There would eventually be forty-eight RCAF squadrons. The largest number were in British Bomber Command, flying Wellingtons, Halifaxes, and Lancasters to destinations on the Continent. For most of the time the target was Germany. These massive bombing raids were designed to disrupt German life and morale, but their effect has been repeatedly called into question. Certainly they did not bring the Germans to their knees, although the devastation they caused added considerably to postwar difficulties in the reconstruction of Germany. Prior to the Normandy invasion in the spring of 1944 the bombing effort was switched to the interdiction of transport to and from the French Atlantic coast. Every bridge over the Seine was hit from Paris downwards to the sea, and railway yards were repeatedly struck. There can be no doubt that this had a great effect on German mobility and it doubtless contributed to the initial success of the allied landings.

Besides bombers there were fighters, mostly Hurricanes and Spitfires. Canadian pilots flew in fighters too, either as escorts to bombers going in over occupied Europe or on their own, shooting or bombing German air, road, or rail traffic in vulnerable areas. By the summer of 1944, when allied command of the air over Western Europe was virtually complete, the Germans preferred to hide during the day and march at night to avoid the unwelcome attentions of allied airmen. Fighter units also were grouped together for the tactical support of army units, and bombers occasionally let loose their tonnage of bombs to clear the way for an attacking force. Unfortunately, various factors sometimes interfered with the precision of such tactical bombing, and there were several occasions in 1944 when Canadian troops on the ground were bombed by their own side's aircraft, with resultant casualties.

The task assigned the Royal Canadian Navy was largely, but not exclusively, defensive. One of the greatest dangers to the allied cause was the threat of German submarine action. It had practically put the British out of the war during 1917, and it threatened to do so again after 1940. The submarine campaign increased in severity as the war went on. In November 1942, the worst month of the war, 807,754 tons of allied shipping went to the bottom of the ocean.

To meet the problem the Royal Navy, with the co-operation of the Royal Canadian Navy, organized convoys from North American waters. The northwest sector of the Atlantic became a Canadian responsibility, and through it Canadian destroyers or destroyer escorts shepherded numbers of ships bound for Britain. In Newfoundland, St John's became a principal anti-submarine base and a centre of RCN activity; by 1944 no fewer than 5000 naval personnel were based there. This strength, added to army and air force contingents sent to Newfoundland, gave Canada a large and visible presence in the island dominion; Canadian authorities were careful to keep their presence apparent given that many American troops also were stationed in Newfoundland.

By the summer of 1942 Canada had placed 13 destroyers, sixty-eight corvettes, twenty minesweepers, and sixty minor vessels into anti-submarine duty in what would come to be known as the Battle of the Atlantic. This was a major contribution, and it was reflected in the proportion of total convoy duty undertaken by Canadian ships – 48 per cent by the beginning of 1943. The expansion of the RCN and its readiness to tackle a large, difficult, and, in North Atlantic weather, unpleasant duty are no small accomplishments. But, as a recent historian has argued, the RCN's accomplishments in the anti-submarine campaign may well be less than its input.[7]

The Royal Navy was not backward in criticizing the RCN. Canadians were awkward, sloppy, and careless, some wartime critics (and some postwar ones too) asserted. The criticism was admittedly true, especially in the early years of the war, because the expansion of the RCN was managed by diluting the small permanent navy and spreading the few available professional sailors around the new ships. It is difficult to see any alternative, but the results in the short term are undeniable. Also, the RCN's expansion was not great enough; by the autumn of 1942 it was being asked to perform a very large number of tasks, and its resources were, as a consequence, stretched too thin. Finally, its equipment was run-down or obsolescent. That said, it is

7 See the path-breaking work by Marc Milner, *North Atlantic Run: The Royal Canadian Navy and the Battle for the Convoys* (Toronto 1985).

plain that the RCN handled a few of its tasks very badly and that some of the convoys it escorted met catastrophic fates. As a consequence, the RCN lost operational responsibility for the mid-Atlantic region early in 1943, while many of its ships were sent for crew-retraining in British waters.

In the first six months of 1943, when the Battle of the Atlantic rose to crisis, the RCN was not as much in evidence as it had once been. The RN now commanded in the middle of the ocean. Better equipment, and more of it, was assigned to the battle. Training was emphasized. Air patrols moved further out into the ocean from the British Isles. Temporarily, twenty RCN ships were transferred to British command; when they returned they were the better for the experience, and more able to play their proper role in the defence of the North Atlantic.

CONCLUSION

Canada's military effort in the Second World War was the largest of any secondary power. Canadians were not used to thinking of themselves in such terms. By 1945 the RCAF was the fourth-largest air force in the world; the navy had reached an impressive size; and the overseas army was the largest sent by any Commonwealth nation save the British. Underlying these military efforts, and making them possible, was a national economy that was increasingly mobilized, regulated, and centrally directed. Furthermore, Britain's own war effort depended on that regimented Canadian economy, and even the United States found Canada helpful – indeed, in some respects, essential. An army marches on its stomach. But if cool heads do not manage the commissariat, that stomach will go unfilled.

21

The War Economy, 1939-45

For Canada's governors, administrators, industrialists, and farmers, the Second World War posed unparalleled problems both of production and organization. To some extent lessons could be learned from what was done – and undone – in 1914-18. But the demands on the system in 1939-45 were to prove far greater, and the military system – the Grand Alliance, or the United Nations – was somewhat more complex and demanding. If 1914 found the dominion economy sliding into a slump, 1939 found that economy – now much larger and more fully developed – still unrecovered from a Great Depression that had already lasted for a decade. But there was an important difference. In 1914 the number of competent and experienced dominion officials might plausibly have been counted on the fingers of a three-toed sloth; in 1939 the careful observer might have to use both of his own hands – and perhaps his feet as well. Further, thanks to theoretical work that had been done both in Britain and in the United States during the preceding quarter-century, the mechanics of economies in general, and of war economies in particular, were much better understood in 1939 than in 1914. Fortunately, some Canadians had followed and assimilated this theoretical work, without contributing to it. And some of these Canadians already worked in the national capital, while others would drift to Ottawa or be summoned there, before many months had passed.

In terms of expertise and understanding of economic processes, the dominion was far better served in the Second World War than in the First. In 1939 the Department of Finance possessed a few officials, including its deputy minister, who understood the working of the economy. The nation possessed a central bank whose small but efficient staff was knowledgeable and experienced. In the universities, especially at Queen's and Toronto, there were academic economists who could be drawn into government service. The Department of External Affairs and the Department of Trade and Commerce contained men who were experienced in international negotiation, and who worked closely both with British officials and with American in the trade negotiations of the period 1935-8. In 1914 there had been no remotely comparable body of experience and skill either in the dominion civil service or outside it. Prime Minister King distrusted these experts. Reminding himself that he too was an economist who possessed a PhD, he often suspected that the officials ignored political realities. Nevertheless, the officials were able to get their way to a considerable extent, and although the first nine months or more were marked by disorder, confusion, and an inability to get much done, in due course the result was a well-orchestrated and managed war effort.

In some respects the Second World War was less of a demographic disaster than the First. Naturally it caused many deaths in action – some 40,000 Canadian servicemen and women. But the First World War had cost 62,000 Canadian lives at a time when the population of the dominion was considerably smaller. Also, in the Second World War, unlike the First, the birth rate rose perceptibly. The crude birth rate rose from 20.6 per thousand in 1938 to 24.3 in 1945, while the total number of live births increased from 237,000 to 301,000. The same pattern appears when we look at the fertility rates for each age group. These rates were not nearly as high as the ones which would appear during the later 1940s and the 1950s. Nevertheless, although no one noticed at the time, the stage was being set for the postwar baby boom.

The war brought overseas immigration almost to an end. From 1940 through 1944 only 21,800 immigrants arrived at Canada's ocean ports, and the large majority of these immigrants were women and children. British families evacuated their offspring to Canada; Canadian servicemen married, begat, and sent their new wives and children to the dominion. Besides the overseas migration, another 28,000 arrived in Canada by land, so that total immigration during these four years amounted to 49,500, of which 78 per cent were of British and Irish descent. Identifiably Jewish immigration, a mere 1900, was pathetically and disgracefully small, nor are matters much improved if we argue that some of the 1750 immigrants from Germany and Austria were probably Jewish.

Immigration could not help Canada find the men and women that would be needed for the forces and the civilian war effort. In due course the national stock of person-power would be mobilized – and much more thoroughly than in 1914-18. But the same could be said of the economy as a whole.

MOBILIZING THE ECONOMY

In organizing and regulating the wartime economy, Ottawa's politicians and officials had at their command a powerful engine, the War Measures Act. This inheritance from the First World War allowed the dominion government to govern by decree to a quite remarkable extent. Many of the important measures of wartime economic management – price control, foreign-exchange control, the reorganization of labour relations – were taken under the general authority of the War Measures Act. Orders-in-council would be issued, and that would be that. Ordinary legislation could be used as well – for instance, to conserve foreign currencies and to set up the Department of Munitions and Supply. (That department had sweeping powers under its own act.) Budgets, budget speeches, and new tax programs were introduced and debated in the same old parliamentary way; how the money was spent was not. The War Measures Act allowed the government to avoid parliamentary debate, and to act promptly and decisively. Prime Minister King must have been grateful for the former, and C.D. Howe, the minister of munitions and supply, for the latter.

During the First World War the Canadian government concerned itself largely with the financial burden which the war created – the very considerable outlays to which Ottawa became committed. During the Second World War many Ottawa officials, and some politicians, were more sophisticated: it was somewhat more clearly recognized that the 'cost of the war' was the national resources which would have to be committed to the war effort, and that the 'financial cost' simply reflected, and followed from, that cost in terms of real resources – manpower, the capacity of the nation's factories and farms, the exports which would be needed to pay for essential imports, and the goods which would be sent overseas to help Canada's allies.

In retrospect it is possible to see that the mobilization of the economy corresponded to the emerging problems that arose, one after another, in connection with these real resources. First, almost immediately after the outbreak of war, came control over foreign exchange, because it was certain that Canada would have a deficit with the United States. Imports would tend to rise, while there was no reason to expect a comparable stimulus to exports. But for the first nine months, the period which was then called the 'phony war' because so little was happening, there was plenty of slack in Canada's domestic economy, and plenty of room to meet the slowly increasing demands for military hardware and overseas supply. Indeed, as Britain, anxious to conserve foreign exchange, was reluctant to order munitions in Canada, preferring to confine her orders to foodstuffs, the Canadian authorities had to press for more British munitions orders so as to justify the expansion of military production within their own borders. In early summer 1940, with the fall of France, the phony war was obviously over, and Ottawa responded by introducing a large but still incomplete system for allocating key raw materials. It also imposed new restrictions on imports from the United States. But there was no need to ration civilian goods, or even to control most of their prices, because the domestic economy was still far below full employment. For the time being the government put its faith in macroeconomic fiscal policy to restrain consumer demand: it would tax away excess income to finance its war effort, leaving the population with a spendable income in proportion to the production of consumer goods and services. As the months passed, however, the pressure of war demand increased, and so did the weight and complexity of government controls over prices and production.

Depending on the ways in which the relative data are arranged, economic mobilization can be made to look rapid or slow. Unemployment, for instance, rose slightly in 1939 and fell only a little in the following year, when it remained over 9 per cent of the labour force. In 1941-2 the number and the percentage of unemployed fell dramatically, and in 1943-5 less than 2 per cent of the labour force was unemployed. Other indices also show a slow start in 1939. Federal government spending on goods and services, for instance, rose only $37 million between 1938 and 1939, in which year it was still only 3.4 per cent of GNP. But in 1940 there was a great leap forward: federal government outlays on goods and services rose to $694 million, or 10 per cent of GNP. In the next four years the increases were dramatic and cumulative, so that by 1944 the dominion was spending 37.6 per cent of GNP – a grand total of $4.4 billion, of which $3.2 billion was military pay and allowances. In 1945, as war ended first in Europe and then in Asia, government outlays fell to 26 per cent of GNP and military pay and allowances went down to $1.8 billion.

Even though full-scale industrial mobilization did not really begin until the Department of Munitions and Supply commenced operations in April 1940, by spring 1941 a great deal had been accomplished. Although Canada still produced no aero engines, the dominion was building four models of fighting aircraft, and six kinds of trainers. In the chemicals industry, which was expanding rapidly, there were sixteen plants, making a dozen varieties of war-related chemicals and eight of explosives. The department planned to make fourteen types of land and naval guns and ten types of gun mountings; already the nation's factories were mass-producing rifles and machine guns, as well as several types of light gun and massive quantities of anti-aircraft gun barrels, together with bombs, grenades, depth charges, anti-tank mines, and twenty-two types of ammunition. The production of military motor vehicles, including some new types, had reached 135,000. More than one hundred small naval vessels – corvettes and mine-sweepers – had been launched, as well as some 350 small auxiliary vessels, and there were plans to build merchant ships as well. Many kinds of optical, technical, personal, and camp equipment were in large-scale production.[1]

Canada had never seen anything like the Department of Munitions and Supply. In the First World War, Britain arranged its own Canadian procurements through the Imperial Munitions Board. In September 1939 it began in much the same way, by sending a supply mission to Ottawa. Canada's own military needs, meanwhile, were to be handled through a civilian board of businessmen – at first, the Defence Purchasing Board, and then the War Supply Board. But when, in April 1940, the dominion government began to take mobilization seriously, it proclaimed the Munitions and Supply Act which had been hurried through Parliament in September 1939, abolished the War Supply Board which had achieved little except confusion, and turned the newly created department over to C.D. Howe, who at once began to recruit business advisers and commodity controllers. 'The Munitions and Supply Act allowed the Minister "in his absolute discretion" to "mobilise, control, restrict, or regulate" whatever he thought necessary for war supply and production. Armed with Howe's orders, and equipped with their own extensive knowledge of the Canadian economy, the government's "dollar-a-year men" fanned across the country to mobilize, organize, control, restrict, and regulate essential supplies, and to provide for their transformation into necessary war equipment.'[2] In the summer of 1940 the department took over responsibility for procuring first British war needs, and then American. Now, in principle, there could be no confusion, duplication, or waste motion: the department would do whatever had to be done so that Canada could contribute her all to the war effort.

The system worked because Howe delegated real responsibility to the businessmen he had recruited. Not bothered by the paucity of official statistics, they knew their industries well and acted accordingly. They built new plants, arranged for additions to old plants, placed orders, negotiated the terms for contracts, and, increasingly, controlled scarce raw materials. Indeed, it was in this way that Canadians became aware of just how great the war effort was to be. To save foreign exchange, oil control was established in June 1940. More than 80 per cent of Canada's oil needs were then supplied through imports. The refineries were told to produce more fuel oil at the expense of gasoline production, and there were shortages in the summer of

1 A.F.W. Plumptre, *Mobilizing Canada's Resources for War* (Toronto 1941), 54-6
2 R. Bothwell, 'Who's Paying for Anything these Days? War Production in Canada, 1939-45,' in N.F. Dreisziger, *Mobilization for Total War* (Waterloo 1981), 62

1941, followed by rationing in April 1942. The power controller banned electric space heaters, imposed daylight saving time against the wishes of the dominion's farmers, and planned the expansion of hydroelectric generating stations. Steel mills grew, and so did almost everything else. From 1939 to 1944 Ottawa built ninety-eight new war plants, which it ran for itself, and spent $166 million on additions to private plants, whose owners ran them on behalf of the crown. Furthermore, the department took over several hundred million dollars' worth of plant which the United Kingdom had built in Canada during the early years of the war.

At first the new department was more than a little disorganized: no one really knew just how much money was being spent, or what commitments, both domestic and foreign, had been made. The Department of Finance was naturally anxious that Howe control his spending, especially of American dollars; the minister, however, wanted to give priority to the war effort more or less regardless of the cost. The result, in the winter of 1940-1, was interdepartmental strife, resolved by the Hyde Park Agreement of April 1941, which eliminated most of the worries about American dollar spending, and by an improvement in the flow of information, which allowed Howe to keep track of what was really happening not only in his department but in the economy at large.

Before 1939 Canada's industries were already concentrated in Ontario and Quebec; although there were important industrial plants in other parts of the country, central Canada accounted for most of the national capacity in many industries, and for all the output in industries such as vehicles. Wartime mobilization did little to change that pattern. The new plants were largely 'add-ons' to existing plants, or to existing arrangements for transportation and processing. Thus, for instance, when Polymer built its government-owned plant for synthetic rubber, the plant was at Sarnia because that town's oil refineries produced plenty of the materials on which Polymer would depend. Strangely enough, it was easier to move labour than to relocate centres of industrial activity. Indeed, Ottawa helped with the movement by building suburban townsites for the new industrial workers. Howe and his department would exploit productive possibilities wherever they could be found, but their main criteria had to be efficiency and speed, not 'regional balance.'

Nevertheless, Canada being what it was and is, regional politicians and capitalists wanted whatever crumbs might fall from the table. Their desires were especially pressing in 1939-40, when the national economy was still painfully underemployed, and turnover and profits were low. War, as the Liberal campaign managers told the voters of Saskatoon in a by-election in 1939, meant production and jobs: 'Will Saskatoon get its share?' Perhaps, by casting their votes for the Liberal candidate.

In the event, because the emergency was great, in 1940 all ordinary restraints were removed, financial as well as political. Indeed, in order to concentrate on the war effort, Howe secured the cabinet's consent to ignore all ordinary political factors. This meant that Howe was free to hire or contract with anyone he chose, regardless of political affiliation. It also meant that he could ignore the ordinary regional pressures. However, Howe did not ignore the chances of scattering orders, or of distributing purchases to the more remote parts of the dominion, if he and his controllers thought that a job could be done well, efficiently, and on time. Provincial authorities were invited to make their potential contributions known, and when, for instance, Manitoba complained that it was being left out, Howe sent one of his officers, who conferred with a member of the provincial cabinet; orders quickly followed.

Not every provincial initiative was well received. In June 1940 the British Columbia government attempted to inject itself directly into war production by urging Ottawa to appoint its own minister of lands and forests as the national timber controller. Howe firmly rejected the notion, arguing that such a local political figure would detract from, rather than strengthen, the national war effort in timber. In any case, no government department could tolerate the presence of two active politicians. Instead, Howe announced the appointment of H.R. MacMillan, a former dominion and British Columbia civil servant who had risen to prominence in the province's lumber industry. Further, MacMillan would rule his forest realm from Ottawa. There were, after all, trees galore in central Canada and in New Brunswick.

Regional demands did not abate, of course. In June 1941, for instance, it was reported that many Alberta organizations were asking for more war orders. While it was true that unemployment had virtually ended in Alberta, the local officials gave the credit to the temporary boom in airport building; many of the province's skilled unemployed had left, drawn to other provinces by the lures of lucrative employment in Howe's war industries, so that even the Edmonton railway shops were having trouble in finding enough workers. If the workers had left, how could new contracts be fulfilled? Such questions, smacking as they do of excessive rationality, did not trouble the regional suppliants.

Yet by late 1941 the prairies were benefiting from the second stage of Howe's war production program, the 'bits and pieces' stage which emphasized subcontracts so as to secure the full utilization of existing facilities. In Winnipeg, war orders for aircraft parts, gun components, and other steel parts had enriched local factories and markedly eased local unemployment. In Regina the local General Motors assembly plant, encouraged by government restrictions on the civilian goods it could still produce, was switching over to the production of naval guns. More orders, it was hinted, would come only if there was enough electricity for a bigger productive effort.

Winnipeg, with large resources of accessible water power, appears to have been immune to problems involving electricity. Defence Industries Ltd, a subsidiary of Canadian Industries Limited, employed almost 4000 at the end of 1941 in producing a smokeless explosive. But although CIL was the largest, it was by no means the only important Winnipeg contractor. The British Commonwealth Air Training Plan spun off repair and overhaul functions to such companies as Trans-Canada Air Lines, Canadian Airways, and Mid-West Aircraft, while the CNR, the Vulcan Iron Works, and Manitoba Bridge and Iron rejoiced in gun and shell contracts. By mid-1942 wartime industrial employment in Winnipeg had passed 60,000, and it remained at that level for the duration.

Vancouver was the other important industrial centre in western Canada. In Canada's war economy the city was especially important as a focus for lumber production, aircraft manufacturing, and shipbuilding. In aggregate terms, Vancouver did very well: its gross industrial production rose from $101 million in 1939 to $289 million in 1944, by which time war-related industrial employment had gone up to 89,000 persons.

For Vancouverites, the most dramatic manifestation of the city's war contribution was the Boeing aircraft factories which rose from almost nothing on the mudflats of Sea Island. But the centrepiece of British Columbia's war industry was shipbuilding. At the height of production, in 1943, shipbuilding even became the province's most important industry. Although initial growth was hampered both by official reluctance and by a shortage of skilled labour and machine tools, by autumn 1940 production was in full swing. Yet, as was the case further east, full utilization of British Columbia's industrial potential awaited the eventual tour of one of Howe's production team. 'Most of the orders placed here,' one local businessman sourly commented, 'have had to be fought for.'

Part of the problem in the shipbuilding momentum derived from confusion within Howe's shipbuilding apparatus. H.R. MacMillan, having attempted a coup against his minister, was sent to Montreal to take charge of cargo shipbuilding, which was then divorced from ship repairs and naval shipbuilding. By October 1941 MacMillan was securing results. Although Howe's officials estimated that the cost of sending steel out to British Columbia would be considerable, they regarded the facilities on the west coast as essential, therefore more than justifying any extra cost.

MacMillan recognized that a shipyard 'is actually an assembly plant in which [subcontractors'] components are put together.' Using British prototypes, British specifications, and a considerable number of British executives and foremen, MacMillan made steady progress, despite the absence in Canada of huge ship assembly lines like those of the Kaiser company south of the border. Early in 1942 the yards were producing a ship every eight days; by 1943, they were readying one every two days. As shipping was diverted for Pacific war needs, or suffered from submarine action, MacMillan's cargo tubs proved to be invaluable.

As for timber, in 1940 MacMillan, while still timber controller, acted to ensure the 'co-ordinated productive capacity of the B.C. saw-mills over a period of months.' British Columbia's timber would be especially important, given the wartime construction that would have to occur both in Canada and in United States, and given Britain's isolation from her normal timber supplies in Scandinavia. Most of the staff of the timber control came directly from the trade associations and lumbering companies, who paid their salaries throughout the war. In terms of production, the results were officially described as spectacular. But the course of timber control was not entirely smooth. Labour shortages were a serious problem from 1942 on, and Howe's hybrid officials were not happy at the prospect of labour unions infesting the spruce forests. Further, there were some inherent dangers in the regulation of an industry by its own managers, and in timber control some of these nightmares became realities. The controllers had dealt with timber shortages not by allocation but by all-out cutting. As a result, there appeared to have been a good deal of waste, and the shortage of labour was exacerbated. Nor were lumber shortages altogether avoided, as the summer of 1942 and the winter of 1943 showed all too clearly. The timber controller was quickly demoted, and then, several months later, eased out altogether.

Labour shortages were not unique to the lumber industry. As the economy moved towards full employment, labour problems tended to increase and spread. The civilian economy and the armed forces were expanding in parallel, and without sufficient co-ordination. During 1942, for instance, problems arose in connection with coal, which was then of prime importance for industrial processes, railways, and home heating. 'Serious labour shortages' first appeared in the western coal fields in the summer of 1942, precisely when the American war economy was absorbing more of the potential production from the Pennsylvania fields from which Ontario and Quebec normally drew most of the coal they used. In October 1942 Ottawa's Coal Administration submitted the first of fifty-five reports on the manpower shortage in the coal fields. An angry Howe protested to the cabinet that coal was 'the basis for transportation and industry as well as the chief source of heat for domestic purposes.' But production was running 350,000 tons a month behind the 'ascertained capacity of the mines,' with a shortfall of three million tons expected in 1943. 'It is obvious,' Howe concluded, 'that we are headed for disaster.' In March 1943 coal was officially 'controlled' and brought under Howe's department; in May, King announced that coal miners could not leave mining before the winter of 1944, and that no one should continue to employ in a non-mining job anyone who had mined coal since 1935; in autumn 1943 the Department of Labour and National Selective Service began to send miner-soldiers back to the mines, while an Emergency Coal Production Board strip-mined lignite in Alberta and Saskatchewan.

Petroleum fuels presented Ottawa with a different sort of problem. When war broke out, Canada produced slightly more coal than she imported; although imports rose much more than domestic production during the war, even in 1944-5 Canada's own mines were supplying 40 per cent of her coal needs. But in 1939 Canada's oil wells produced only 18 per cent of the nation's needs, and although domestic production was raised by 25 per cent during the war, imports had to rise more rapidly still, so that by 1945 Canada was importing 87 per cent of the crude petroleum she used. Some of the oil came from Venezuela, where Imperial Oil had large interests, and some from Trinidad and Peru, but most came from the United States, which still produced far more oil than she used. The crude arrived in various ways – by ship to the east coast and British Columbia, by pipeline and lake steamer to Ontario and Quebec refineries, even by expensive tank cars. The war would disrupt tanker services, especially on the Atlantic; it would increase domestic demand for fuel oil and aviation gasoline.

Although some oil was produced in New Brunswick and southwestern Ontario, Canada's major domestic source was the Turner Valley field in Alberta. Along with all other aspects of oil and gas production and consumption, Turner Valley found itself operating under the jurisdiction of Canada's crusty oil controller George Cottrelle. As Cottrelle wrestled with the thorny task of reducing civilian supply across the country, his officials in Alberta turned their attention to maximizing Turner Valley's output. After a visit to Calgary by Cottrelle in the fall of 1940, western refiners increased their storage capacity so as to smoothe the flow of crude between well and refinery. As Cottrelle explained, the imports of foreign crude which had previously topped up the refineries' needs might soon be unavailable. Nevertheless, prairie consumption exceeded production by over two-and-a-half million barrels in a given year; the difference had to come from the United States and, in the form of processed products, from refineries in eastern Canada.

Further regulations and innovations followed. Thanks to the war emergency, the controllers could ignore the ordinary provincial power over natural resources, these powers having been transferred to the dominion for the duration. Nevertheless, the Alberta Public Utility Commission was consulted regarding the new regulations which were prepared to govern the financing of oil wells. In succeeding years there were tax concessions and higher depletion allowances, and in 1943 the field price of crude oil was raised 15 cents a barrel; in 1942 the average price of Canadian domestic crude was just $1.55, so this increase was not insignificant, but it did not prevent production from falling in 1943, 1944, and again in 1945. To encourage production in other ways, a crown company, Wartime Oils Ltd, was incorporated in April 1943, with broad powers to prospect for oil properties and to drill wells. Wartime Oils had as its first preference the financing of private wells; under its subsidy scheme some ten wells were drilled and brought into production during its first year of business. The effect on the national fuel balance, however, was not great. More significant, perhaps, was the discarding of provincial output control. Under prewar provincial conservation regulations, the daily 'allowable' production at Turner Valley had been about 20,000 barrels per day; in 1942 Munitions and Supply ordered an increase to 28,000 barrels per day.

Under wartime conditions, extensive prospecting would not have been feasible, nor could the country have found the equipment for a massive program of well-drilling. But one visionary development was undertaken – the Canol pipeline, exploiting the field at Norman Wells in the far Northwest Territories which had first produced in 1920. Canol was meant to provide aircraft fuel for the Northwest Staging Route, by which planes flew through Canada on their way to Alaska. Like Wartime Oils, Canol made little difference to the national energy picture.

Petroleum had other uses besides fuel. Almost all military explosives used in the Second World War were made by a mixture of nitric and sulphuric acids. The best-known source of nitrate is Chile saltpetre, but the substance can also be manufactured from ammonia, which in turn can be made from natural gas. When, in March 1940, it was decided to use ammonia in explosives-making, nothing was more natural than to look for a site in Alberta. In June 1940 Ottawa decided to build the plant in Calgary. Two companies, Consolidated Mining and Smelting (Cominco) and CIL became joint owners of the newly founded Alberta Nitrogen Company Ltd. Two hundred acres in the Bow River valley south of Calgary were purchased, close enough to take advantage of the city's abundant housing and surplus labour.

What resulted was the 'first plant of its type in the world,' the largest of the four ammonia plants in Canada. So successful was the plant that by 1943 it was producing far in excess of its rated capacity. By late 1943 some of the output could be diverted to producing nitrogen fertilizer, using a unique formula which had been developed at Calgary. In the long run the Calgary ammonia works developed a thriving export business, selling fertilizer to the Americans.

Alberta nitrogen met two of Howe's most important criteria: it was economical and its output was needed. As Howe explained to his director general of chemicals in 1941, in reference to a second Calgary project, 'If the product is not needed, the plant should not be built.' There was no question of using wartime investments to shape or transform the later direction of a regional economy. But by early 1942 it was obvious to all that Calgary should have the second plant, an alkylate installation to produce high-octane aviation fuel for the prairie training fields. The reciprocating piston engines of World War Two burned very high quality gasoline, not the kerosene which would fuel the jets of a later era. And they were thirsty. The Calgary project in fact proved to be the only alkylate project completed remotely on time, and without substantial cost-overruns.

Calgarians continued, as before, to worry about the state of agriculture and to preoccupy themselves with the long-term prospects of the oil industry. Wartime prosperity, with its accompanying influx from the farms into the city, still appeared to be a temporary phenomenon. In October 1945 a group of local businessmen grunted, 'If young men persist in their desire to live in the city where there are modern conveniences,' then unemployment was certain. As for oil, the American consul reported the next month that 'firms show evidence of drifting out of this Province where they have spent millions in the past few years and have opened up no new important crude fields as yet.' The great days that would follow the Leduc discovery were in the future; in 1945 they were not foreseen.

And what of Saskatoon? Did it get its share? Sad to say, Saskatoonians did not think so. As the province complained in 1944, 'The province owes comparatively little to the advent of new industries, the erection of new plants or the extension of existing ones, for war production. Neither increase in capital investment, nor of population, have contributed to the general improvement. Indeed,' it gloomily added, 'Saskatchewan has lost population as a result of recruiting and of the migration of workers to war industries in other provinces of Canada.' Postwar reconstruction, not the stimulus of the war, would have to provide the base for an industrial future. And as yet no one had envisaged the oil, potash, or pulp mills.

In fact, between 1939 and 1944 all of Canada's provinces showed an increase in industrial employment. The Maritimes gained 56,000 jobs, central Canada 494,000, the prairies 56,000, and British Columbia, 72,000. But when interprovincial migration is considered a somewhat different story has to be told. Allowing for natural increases in population between the 1941 census and the summer of 1944, we find net movements to only three provinces – Nova Scotia gained 8000 new residents, Ontario, 58,000, and British Columbia, 90,000, while the Prairie provinces and the smaller Maritime provinces were not retaining their natural increase.

Those western cities which had labour, industrial space, and experience – Vancouver and Winnipeg – boomed. So did Calgary, endowed as it was with critical industrial raw material. Those cities which lacked these advantages, such as Regina and Saskatoon, contributed their labour to other areas of the country where geography and historical circumstances had created the basis on which wartime needs could be satisfied. This is not to say that the other western cities and towns did not prosper. The revival of prairie agriculture meant more trade. So did the presence of so many Commonwealth Air Training stations. But it is important to underline that the contribution of the four western provinces to Canada's industrial war effort was conceived and run as part of a national program, and in response to requirements that were by no means all within Canadian control. At a time of full employment and shortage, it was obvious that any facility not hopelessly disadvantaged would be put to work in the common cause. Although some regional cavilling was heard, the experiment in national direction and central control did not provoke serious criticism, particularly from the western provincial governments who were delighted to find a firm financial footing. After ten years of drought and depression, Canada's national government had accomplished something that worked.

MONEY AND THE WAR

The Second World War, like the First, produced an export boom for Canada. But it also produced an import boom – the inevitable result of the rapidly expanding domestic economy and of the exports themselves. The dominion's industries were called to supply Britain with a wider range of manufactures than in 1914; many of these factory products incorporated American components, as did the consumer goods which were churned out for Canada's own households. To pay for American goods, Canada needed American dollars. Exporting massively to Britain, she could not expect the British to pay American dollars: London properly wanted to keep her dollar holdings to pay for her own purchases from the United States. The 'North Atlantic Triangle,' by which Canada ran an export surplus with Britain, an import surplus with the United States, and covered all or part of her deficit with the latter through drawings on the former, would not work in wartime.

Fortunately, in 1939 Ottawa had a few officials who understood the problem and knew that only a careful control over external transactions, such as that which Germany had operated since 1931, would prove effective. Canada's own holdings of gold and foreign currencies were not large: in 1939 the Bank of Canada had only $290 million in such assets – an amount which would not go far. Imports from the United States, therefore, would have to be controlled so as to match export earnings in the form of US dollars. Nor could the dominion allow an outward movement of capital funds, especially to the United States. Thus on 16 September 1939, under the authority of the War Measures Act, Ottawa imposed exchange control and set up the Foreign Exchange Control Board to administer the new system.

Domestic finance, by contrast, was far less of a problem. Naturally the government, and especially the prime minister, worried about the cost of the war. There were efforts to calculate the dominion's fiscal capacity, and thanks to the system of 'tax rentals,' which we describe in Chapter 16, tax rates became uniform throughout the dominion. Having the First World War in mind, the officials intended that taxation should be used to pump out purchasing power, thus, on the best Keynesian model, reducing or perhaps preventing inflation. No one could be sure the system would work, and certainly there had to be provision for government borrowing. In this respect the situation was much brighter than in 1914, when the dominion had recourse first to the printing press and then to New York and London before it involved itself in the domestic financial system. Since 1914 a good deal had been learned. The experience of successful domestic borrowing, both in the First World War and thereafter, had not been forgotten. The domestic bond business had developed apace, and the financial system was a great deal more sophisticated. The departments of Finance and External Affairs now had small but expert staffs who understood economic and financial matters. The gold standard was long gone and almost forgotten. Most important of all, the dominion now had its very own central bank – the Bank of Canada. Its Governor, Graham Towers, could be trusted to give good advice; its services, as lender and manipulator of the financial system, could be trusted to provide whatever funds the dominion government might require. This time, there would be no need to finance the dominion by borrowing in London or New York.

In the course of the war, the dominion had to tax much more heavily. In 1938 personal income tax collections had been only $47 million, or 1.1 per cent of households' personal income; in 1944 they were $771 million, or 8.6 per cent. Corporation taxes rose from $77 million in 1938 to $636 million – nearly half of corporate profits – in 1943, and in 1944 they were almost as high. Indirect tax revenues rose also, as rates were pushed ever upward. So far as households were concerned, it was 1941 which marked a dramatic break with the past, as personal income tax rates rose dramatically.

In the Second World War, unlike the First, the dominion tried to cover a high proportion of outlays from taxation. But the new taxes could not and did not cover all the new spending. Deficits occurred, and in 1942-5 they were very large indeed. In 1939 the federal deficit, on the 'national accounts basis,' was $2 million; in 1944 and 1945 it was $1.9 billion. In the course of the war, from the end of 1938 to the end of 1945, the dominion raised $15.7 billion from the sale of securities, and its net debt, after allowing for some refunding of old loans, rose from $3.6 billion to $17.9 billion.

Little of the new debt consisted of extra currency. Since the establishment of the Bank of Canada in 1935, the dominion had given up the power to issue new paper currency of its own. But the Bank could buy dominion bonds and issue its own notes. During the war the Bank bought $1.7 billion of dominion bonds and issued $0.8 billion of extra currency, 'monetizing' barely 6 per cent of the new dominion debt. The bank's purchases of bonds, and its issue of currency, provided the extra reserves on which the chartered banks could expand. But the banks did not buy many new government bonds: their holdings appear to have risen by just over $2 billion, while the life insurance companies may have bought another $1.6 billion. And in the Second World War, unlike the First, the dominion did not borrow abroad. The Canadian public therefore seems to have bought about $9 billion – something like 63 per cent of the total new dominion debt, which amounted to $14.3 billion.

The war saw a series of Victory Bond campaigns, all orchestrated with energy and skill. The government borrowed much more cheaply than in the First World War – usually at 3 per cent or less as opposed to 5 per cent or more in 1914-18. The public, urged to save for victory or postwar security, was able to buy large numbers of bonds because it was very prosperous indeed. There were payroll deduction plans, by which people could buy bonds on the instalment plan. There were 'War Savings Stamps and Certificates,' in denominations as low as $0.25, through which school children could contribute their mites. There were even experiments with compulsory savings, by which taxpayers contributed a surcharge in the form of a loan, repayable after the end of the war.

To supply itself with money for spending within Canada, the dominion government could tax, borrow, or, in the last resort, sell its bonds to the Bank of Canada. With respect to its need for American dollars, none of these expedients would suffice. Admittedly, in principle Canada could have borrowed in the American market. But the Ottawa authorities did not want to do so, and it was far from clear, especially in 1939-40, just how the market would have received a new Canadian loan. Hence the importance of exchange control.

Although the powers of the Foreign Exchange Control Board applied symmetrically to all foreign monies, in fact it applied them only to transactions in American dollars. British pounds were not 'scarce'; indeed, Ottawa had far more sterling than it knew what to do with, because in 1939-41 it was taking some sterling in payment for its exports to Britain. All exports to non-sterling countries had to be paid for in American dollars, or in currencies which were freely convertible into American dollars. In turn, anyone who received any such currencies had to sell them to the board, through chartered banks or other authorized agents of the board. The exchange rate, which had been floating since 1929, was pegged at 90 American cents to the Canadian dollar, plus or minus a small margin which was meant to cover the board's operating cost. Imports had to be paid for in Canadian or American dollars, but the board would supply these only under permit. Any transactions in securities and other property required a licence from the board. There were no restrictions on payment of rent, interest, dividends, or old debts – those incurred before 16 September 1939. Other capital payments to non-residents in dollar countries were, in general, not permitted.

At first, import licences were freely issued. The board made little real effort to limit current spending in the United States; its main concern was to prevent a flight of capital from the Dominion of the North to the Great Neutral to the south. When Hitler overran Western Europe in the early summer of 1940, however, the controls were tightened considerably. Tourist travel to the United States was ended, and dollar imports were restricted, first by the War Exchange Tax of 24 June, and then by the quotas and prohibitions of December. Nevertheless, in 1940 Canada ran a very large deficit with the United States. The situation was saved only because the United Kingdom agreed to supply Canada with $248 million in gold and American dollars. In 1941, however, Britain could not help in this way, and Canada's purchases from the United States, fuelled by the return to full employment and by war demands, increased by 19 per cent while export earnings rose by much less. As in 1940, the dominion had to draw on its holdings of gold and American dollars. What saved the day was a small and unexpected capital inflow from the United States.

Help, however, was on the way. In April 1941, in the Hyde Park Agreement, the United States committed itself to make substantial purchases of defence-related materials in Canada; it also agreed to supply goods under Lend-Lease which Canada would instal in the things she was making for Britain, without requiring that Canada herself should accept Lend-Lease commodities. The point was important to Canada for at least two reasons. First, American policy was to require the recipients of Lend-Lease to divest themselves of all, or substantially all, their American assets; Canada was not anxious to do that. Second, it was believed that the main cause for Canada's dollar problem was her production for Britain.[3] Indeed, the provisions about 'Lend-Lease components' for Britain never worked well, although in time they played a significant role. The other parts of the Hyde Park arrangements were much more helpful. But even they did not wholly solve the problem.

Meanwhile, Britain and the sterling area were buying more from Canada, while selling less. How was this immense gap filled? In 1940-1, 32 per cent was derived from selling assets in Canada; 17 per cent came from Britain's transfer of gold and American dollars; the rest was financed by the Canadian government.

After 1941 Britain's purchases went on up, while her exports to Canada fell to insignificant amounts. In 1943, and even more in 1944 and 1945, Britain earned large amounts of Canadian dollars through the overseas outlay of the Canadian government, which now found itself supporting a large expeditionary force. The British paid the cost of the Canadian army in Europe, and billed the Canadian government. Nevertheless, a great gap still yawned. It amounted to more than half of Canada's sales to the sterling zone. In 1942, though not in later years, Britain sold off more assets in the dominion. In the same year the dominion gave Britain a billion dollars and lent another $700 million, eliminating the prior build-up of Canadian government holdings of sterling and preventing any new ones from accumulating. Britain was believed to hold a remaining $700 million in Canadian securities; it was agreed that if any of these were sold or transferred to another country, the dollars thus acquired were to be applied against the $700 million loan, which would bear no interest until after the war.

On 29 April 1941 the minister of finance announced that Canada would not allow a shortage of Canadian dollars to impede Britain's procurements in Canada. One observer notes[4] that this formal assurance could not have been given, and was not given, until after the Hyde Park Agreement had made Ottawa less uneasy about the American-dollar implications of a massive and continuing program of Canadian-British aid. In May 1943, after a variety of further shifts had kept Britain afloat for the first months of that year, Ottawa announced its own 'Mutual Aid' plan, which paralleled the American Lend-Lease scheme. Canadian government departments would buy the Mutual Aid goods; Canada's new Mutual Aid Board would administer the program; physical aid, not financial aid, would pass from Canada to Britain and the United Nations at large. During 1943-5, 85 per cent of Canada's mutual

---

3 See F.A. Knox, 'Canada's Balance of International Payments, 1940-1945,' *Canadian Journal of Economics and Political Science* 13 (Aug. 1947): especially 349.

4 Ibid., 354

aid went to the United Kingdom and almost all the rest to other sterling area countries. In addition, Britain again began to supply small sums of gold and American dollars, while the Canadian government continued to provide small amounts in special payments. Thus the yawning chasm was filled.

If Mutual Aid disentangled our financial relations with wartime Britain, the Hyde Park Agreement helped to perform the same task in our relations with the United States. From 1941 through 1945 the United States government spent $1187 million in Canada because of the agreement. That was 12.8 per cent of our American-dollar earnings in those years – but it was 791 per cent of our cumulative current-account surplus of $150 million on our transactions with the United States. In fact, because Canadian businesses and junior governments borrowed $1149 million in the United States during 1941-5, and because Americans continued to buy Canadian securities, the dominion's war effort could have survived without Hyde Park. But the result would have been a painfully hand-to-mouth existence, with tiny exchange reserves and great and continuing unease about the balance of payments. In the event, Hyde Park allowed Canada to continue servicing old dollar debt and to build up the national holdings of gold and American dollars.

This cold account of the wartime arithmetic cannot convey any sense of the excursions, alarms, misunderstandings, and passions which accompanied the day-to-day and month-to-month management of international war finance.[5] As usual, there were mixtures of motives on all sides, and misunderstandings were rampant. The Canadian government, and especially Prime Minister King, worried ceaselessly about the budgetary cost of its aid program. The Americans believed that by buying things from Canada they were providing something analogous to aid, and they watched the dominion's foreign exchange reserves with hawk-like attention. The British, however, knew that they were suppliants, but consistently managed to convey the opposite impression to an annoyed King. Meanwhile, on the Canadian side, while there was an eagerness to help the common war effort, there was also the desire as well to help the government's electoral prospects by 'winning markets' for Canadian producers, both agricultural and industrial. Thus, the Ottawa authorities were agitated, at various times, about insufficient British ordering, low British prices for bulk purchase, and the risk that more generous American aid policies would divert British purchases from Canada to the United States. Ottawa also felt obliged, from time to time, to press Britain for the release of gold and American dollars. Nor was Ottawa under-

5 What follows relies heavily on Hector Mackenzie, 'Mutual Assistance: The Finance of British Requirements in Canada during the Second World War,' D.Phil. thesis, Oxford University, 1981.

standing when, after the fall of France in 1940, the British wished to borrow the gold which France had deposited in Canada for safekeeping. 'A Sacred Trust,' King said; the gold would be kept for the French and returned to them after liberation, not diverted to wartime uses. As for Britain's own assets in Canada, Ottawa was not inclined to ignore them in assessing Britain's ability to pay for Canadian goods. The Canadian government did not force the British to divest themselves as completely as the American government did. But divestiture there certainly was, and the British were obliged to defend their portfolio of Canadian stocks and bonds by arguing that, of course, after the war the interest and dividends would be spent on Canadian goods.

THE INTERLOCKING OF SUPPLY AND PLANNING

Canadian-American co-operation in defence production began with an American agreement in August 1940 to channel purchases through Canada's Department of Munitions and Supply. Then came the Hyde Park Declaration. In July 1941 collaborative Joint Economic Committees were set up in the two countries. These bodies worked on policy with respect to export control, shipping, Canadian expansion of production of feed grains and oil seeds, and the seasonal movement of farm machinery and labour across the border – no easy matter in peace time. They also recommended that there should be a Joint War Production Committee. This body coexisted with the Materials Co-ordinating Committee (United States-Canada), which already existed, and which set up ten subcommittees covering 'all the important fields of war production' – tanks, motor vehicles, ammunition, small arms, artillery, chemicals and explosives, signal equipment, aircraft, and shipbuilding. The result was a successful avoidance of duplication. For instance, because the United States could meet Canada's needs for aero engines, the dominion abandoned any plan it might have had to build such engines. But Canada built air frames for American dive-bombers. It also supplied shells, fuse parts, components, and complete rounds of ammunition, helped start the American corvette program, and supplied chemicals and explosives. Each country maintained its own war production program, but the two programs were extensively co-ordinated.

Ten days after the Hyde Park Declaration, the dominion Department of Munitions and Supply joined with the American War Production Board to set up the Materials Coordinating Committee. This was a small body – two men from each country – which allocated and stockpiled metals, natural rubber, and the ingredients for synthetic rubber production on both sides of the border. As Sydney Pierce and Wynne Plumptre , two wartime officials, explain, 'Its operations were considered effective and it was thought advisable not to disturb them.'[6]

Besides the formal apparatus for co-operation, there was a large network of informal co-ordination between officials in the two countries. As both countries extended their domestic systems for allocation of materials and intermediate products, which in turn became increasingly scarce as war efforts accellerated, there was increasing need for such co-ordination. For some considerable time, both before and after December 1941, the United States authorities insisted on licensing every export transaction, no matter how small. The procedure could cause weeks or months of delay, and these stoppages were especially trying for Canada, whose industries still depended in so many instances on materials and components from the United States. Eventually, however, the Canadian officials persuaded the Americans to require no licences on shipments to Canada. When the American government began to apply a system of priorities to various defence programs, Canadian needs were soon accorded equal treatment, so that if American aircraft manufacture, for instance, had 'first priority' claim on allocations of materials, Canadian aircraft manufacturers were also 'first priority' claimants. To rate Canadian programs without undue delay, the US War Production Board set up an Ottawa office. Similarly, when the Americans moved from the 'priority' system to the direct allocation of materials and components, Canadian requirements were treated as if they were American, not foreign, requirements. The same occurred insofar as the scheduling of orders was concerned. On the American side, military and other buyers were allowed to place orders in Canada without any special formalities. And to grease the wheels of the whole complicated mechanism, there were Canadian representatives attached directly to the armed forces and to the more important American economic agencies – the War Production Board, Office of Defense Transportation, Petroleum Coordinator, Office of Price Administration, and even the Department of Agriculture. If Canada depended on American supplies of many materials, fuels, fibres, and components, the United States depended on Canada for important amounts of aluminum, copper, lead, zinc, asbestos, and nickel, among other goods.[7]

With respect to civilian supplies, also, there was a great deal of co-operation. The Combined Food Board allocated many products which both countries imported. Canadians took part in civilian 'requirements committees' which blossomed on the American side of the border during 1942. Both countries came to restrict civilian allocations by roughly the same propor-

6   S.D. Pierce and A.F.W. Plumptre, 'Canada's Relations with War-Time Agencies in Washington,' *Canadian Journal of Economics and Political Science* 11 (Aug. 1945): 406
7   For the resultant official euphoria see ibid., 411.

tions, on the principle that misery should be shared equally. Nor did the Americans fuss about the measures which Canada had been obliged to take for the sake of saving American dollars – the War Exchange Tax of 10 per cent, imposed in July 1940 on imports from dollar areas, and the War Exchange Conservation Act of December 1940, which restricted or prohibited many 'non-essential' articles from American-dollar countries, such as the United States and Cuba. After Pearl Harbor both countries quickly moved to ration many consumer goods, but the ration lists and allocations were by no means always the same – a fruitful source of irritation and carping comment, but hardly a threat to wartime co-operation.

Each country controlled prices in its own way, and at its own chosen times. The result, for a considerable period, was that Canadian ceiling prices were below American. The devaluation of the Canadian dollar, which occurred at the outbreak of war, had the same effect. Canada had to control exports, so as to 'prevent Canadian supplies from disappearing across the border.' As Pierce and Plumptre say, 'In the early days of price divergence this sometimes used to happen literally overnight.'[8] The export controls were specially necessary for natural products; many Canadian manufactures remained uncompetitive, and were in any event regulated and allocated through the joint systems described above. As for export controls, they were never sufficiently tight to prevent waves of hungry Americans from driving across the border, and filling the car trunk with unrationed Canadian foodstuffs. Canadian housewives fulminated; Canadian officials counted the earnings in American dollars, and reminded themselves that, in any event, thanks to American gasoline rationing, the forays could not really be much of a problem.

To some extent the war had the effect of diverting Canadian demand from British sources to American. British industry could not maintain its shipments to Canada, especially after 1940; Canadian manufacturers found their only feasible suppliers in the United States, and also found that the interlocking supply bureaucracies could and did provide the American-sourced inputs they needed. Conversely, Americans found that for some products the Canadian manufacturer actually could offer competitive prices.

There was, of course, nothing immutable about these wartime rearrangements. With peace, Hyde Park would lapse, and British firms would be able to re-enter the Canadian market place. For the time being the war helped to integrate the Canadian economy more closely with the American. But unless new and different developments were to occur during the postwar period, that integration would prove to have been transitory.

FARMERS AND THE WAR

Remembering how well they had done in the early years of the First World War, the wheat farmers of the Prairie provinces increased their acreage in the spring of 1940. However, the Second World War was different from the First: before the crop had been harvested, German troops had overrun all the continental European countries which had once bought Canada's wheat. The very good crop of 1940 therefore was somewhat of an embarrassment, and in the spring of 1941 the dominion government began to plan for a reduction in wheat acreage. The hope was to reduce the sown acreage by 35 per cent. Acreage fell still further in 1942 and 1943, at which time it was 42 per cent of what it had been in 1940. Coarse grains, meanwhile, were sown in ever larger amounts, so that by 1943 the total output of prairie coarse grains was far larger than the output of wheat, even though wheat still accounted for 57 per cent of prairie farm cash income. Ottawa encouraged this shift partly by providing subsidies for the transfer of land, and partly by fixing minimum prices for oats, barley, and flax in March 1942. By 1943, acreage reduction was costing the dominion $31 million per year.

The coarse grains were needed to feed livestock, which in turn the dominion wanted to provision both Canada and the United Kingdom. Beef and butter, for which minimum prices were fixed, went mostly to the domestic market, but export contracts helped to clear that market. The prices of cheese, hogs, and eggs were supported through contract prices which were negotiated between Ottawa and the British Ministry of Food. The dominion subsidized butterfat producers and provided subsidies for the interregional movement of grain, so as to stimulate production while controlling domestic consumer prices.[9]

So far as prairie farmers were concerned, the effects were dramatic. The wheat monoculture economy of the Prairie provinces diversified rapidly into a much more complicated and adventurous system.[10] Furthermore, prairie farmers became a great deal more prosperous. Their total cash income including government payments rose from $345 million in 1939 to $726 million in 1943; in 1944, with a dramatic revival of wheat production and continued development on the livestock front, prairie farm incomes rose farther still – to a figure which was 72 per cent more than the figure for 1928, and 205 per cent of the 1939 figure.

What did the prairie farmers do with their money? Few consumer durable goods were available, especially after 1941. But tractors and combines

9 Andrew Stewart, 'Stabilization of the Income of the Primary Producer,' *Canadian Journal of Economics and Political Science* 11 (Aug. 1945): 359ff
10 V.F. Fowke, 'Economic Effects of the War on the Prairie Economy,' ibid., 378

were still being manufactured, and Fowke reports that from 1939 through 1944 the prairie farmers seem to have bought 10,029 tractors and 3,605 combines – rather more than they bought in 1926-30. Although they did not bid up the price of rural land as they had done during the First World War, they bought farm land and urban houses, paying a substantial proportion in cash. Finally, to a remarkable extent prairie farmers paid off their debts and arrears of taxes. The Dominion Mortgage and Investments Association estimated that by December 1944 they had reduced their debt by 50 per cent.[11] In 1937 Saskatchewan rural municipalities collected 8.5 per cent of the taxes that were due to them; in 1944 the collection rate was 47 per cent.

In spite of the wartime controls on wheat production and marketing, the war did splendid things for the prairie farm economy, putting it in a good position to seize the opportunities of the postwar world. Debt had been reduced, new equipment obtained, and experience gained with respect to agricultural diversification. Nor had land values been inflated. In agriculture, as in industry, the economy of the Second World War was much better managed than it had been during the First.

Coarse grains are used chiefly for distilling, brewing, and livestock feed. From 1939 to 1945 Canada doubled its production of beer and increased its sales of proof spirits by 80 per cent. During the latter part of the war spirits were rationed, but beer was not, and it is obvious that many people spent some of their extra real income in the beer parlour or the provincial liquor store. Even teetotallers often bought their entitlements of spirits: liquor was a valued gift, and it could be bartered. The chairman of the Wartime Prices and Trade Board, Donald Gordon, was believed to collect liquor rations like baseball cards. As a bottle-a-day man he could do no less. Although the number of milk cows stayed more or less unchanged while the number of horses went down, other livestock became much more numerous. And the payoff came in extra meat production. For instance, from 1939 to 1945 the nation's output of beef rose 86 per cent.

Where did all this production go? Much of the output was exported. Foreign markets, chiefly in the United Kingdom, took 35 per cent of the extra beef, 59 per cent of the extra pork, and 56 per cent of the extra cheese. In addition, there were more dairy products. Egg exports soared, from about a million dozen in 1939 to 114 million in 1945. Even wool exports rose. Nevertheless, there was plenty left over to improve Canadians' diet. Butter, wheat flour, and egg consumption per capita did not increase, but each Canadian gobbled up ever-rising quantities of pork, chicken meat, milk, cheese, and potatoes. Beef consumption per capita rose from 53.2 pounds per year in

11 Ibid., 380-1

1939 to 67 pounds in 1945. Per capita ice cream consumption almost doubled. Thus, while some Canadians found solace in the beer parlour, others, it appears, found surcease in the ice cream parlour.

For prairie farmers themselves, another kind of solace was found in the abolition of private trading in grain through the compulsory 'pooling' for which many farm groups had been pressing since the end of the First World War. But while pressures to close the Winnipeg Grain Exchange had been building for some time, the decision to close was taken suddenly and unexpectedly. Long afterward, the chairman of the Canadian Wheat Board still remembered sticking his head out of his Ottawa hotel door to see the cabinet, led by King, striding down the hall towards him. The moment had come. On 27 September 1943 Ottawa suspended trading on the Winnipeg Grain Exchange, fixed the initial payments to farmers for 1943-4 and 1944-5 at $1.25 per bushel, transferred all commercial wheat inventories to the Wheat Board, and arranged that the board should be the sole marketer of western wheat. Only inventories on farms were outside its control.

Why was this done? At the time, speculation centred on four possibilities. First of all, because the transport system was congested, there were large farm stocks but inadequate supplies for current sale, producing a sharp discount on wheat futures and denying producers any advantage from the high spot price. Second, it appeared likely that wheat prices would rise in the near future, because supplies and demands were increasingly out of balance. Third, because of low prices and relatively low delivery quotas, western farmers had not been doing well out of the war economy. Thus, in 1942, Saskatchewan farmers' cash income was only 66 per cent of what it had been in 1926, while Quebec's farmers received 178 per cent as much as in that year. Finally, because the open market price was higher than what the Wheat Board was offering by way of initial advance, for some months previous the board had not been pulling in much wheat – a trying situation for the government, which had to regulate the flow of wheat to markets at home and abroad. If all the crops and inventories could be brought under a single control, allocation would be much easier to manage.[12]

Like the modification of Canada's labour code discussed in Chapter 22, compulsory wheat-pooling came by accident, the unplanned result of wartime conditions. Like the labour relations system which was created in 1944, the Wheat Board system of 1943 would have a long history. Forty years later it is still alive and well, and there are no signs of its disappearance. Nor has it evolved significantly. Here is one place where the would-be planners of the Left got their way: a piece of wartime Ottawa interventionism was

12 L.A. Skeoch, 'Changes in Canadian Wheat Policy,' *Canadian Journal of Economics and Political Science* 9 (Nov. 1943): 565-9

indeed carried bodily into the postwar era. Fortunately, the Wheat Board had no organic connection with the rest of Ottawa's wartime interventionism – the system of exchange controls, price controls, priorities, rationing, and allocation, which officials and politicians agreed should be dismantled as quickly and as completely as possible.

CONCLUSION

By 1945 Canada's government and Ottawa's officials could look back with considerable pride on five years of economic achievement. When war broke out, none of them had much by way of a plan for economic mobilization, for the management of the domestic economy under war conditions, or for the re-design of Canada's trading and financial systems. In the event, partly because American officials and Canadian business people proved co-operative and partly because at last Ottawa contained some expertise, Canada was able to innovate creatively. The nation moved from unemployment to full or even overfull employment; it mobilized the workforce more extensively than ever before; avoided serious inflation; placed no strain on living standards; and distributed burdens and benefits in a fashion that was widely perceived to be fair. This was a record of which everyone, not simply cabinet members and mandarins, could properly be proud.

But at bottom it was the wartime political system which had to manage the wartime economy; co-operativeness and technical expertise could take the country only so far. And bottom water is proverbially said to be muddy water. So it was to prove in wartime Canada.

22

The Second World War at Home

By 1945 most Canadian families had sent one or more members into the armed forces, and a high proportion of these citizen soldiers, sailors, airmen, and women had served outside Canada. Defence installations, furthermore, were widely spread across the country, not only for Canada's own forces but for the British Commonwealth Air Training Plan. The military life, therefore, was brought very close to most Canadians – probably closer than in the First World War. In addition, and far more successfully than in that earlier war, Ottawa was managing the flow of goods, services, and information, while regulating the work lives of Canadians in new and adventurous ways.

THE CONSTRAINED CONSUMER

Dramatic though Canada's military effort certainly was, consumers did not suffer. Real consumption rose throughout the war, as did real consumption per head, which went from $731 in 1938 to $992 in 1945. Household income rose more rapidly still, and in the absence of most consumer durable goods, especially after December 1941, households had no real choice but to save. The tax burden was rising, but it was really onerous for comparatively few families, and in 1945 it was offset wholly or in part by the new family allowances – the 'baby bonuses' which were meant partly to sustain consumer spending in the expected postwar slump. So far as households were concerned, things got better in 1939-42; thereafter the pressure on the economy was too great to leave much room for higher consumption, although consumption per head did rise a little more in 1943-4.

In the Second World War the dominion government was far more willing to control consumption than it had been in the First. In 1939-41 the economy was still too underemployed for much control to be necessary, although some imports became scarce because earnings of American dollars were being used for war needs. Indeed, when food and gasoline rationing came in 1942, it was introduced partly to save foreign currency and partly to spread the supplies of tropical goods which had to come from afar. With Japan's entry into the war in December 1941, and with the increasing risks from submarines on the Atlantic sea lanes, the nation could not maintain peace-time importation of such goods as rubber, sugar, cocoa, tea, or coffee. Other products, such as butter, were rationed to enable the dominion to send enough to Britain. And many goods, such as bananas, simply vanished from the market, the victim of foreign-exchange control and shortage of shipping. Until the beginning of 1942 most consumer durables, such as cars and radi-os, continued to be produced and sold in large quantities. But early in 1942 no more were produced for civilian use. Similarly, house construction was buoyant through 1941 and then fell sharply, as the authorities rationed the necessary raw materials and concentrated new building in the places where the armed forces and the munitions workers wanted to live. The result, out-side most large Canadian cities, was a series of 'federal villages,' instantly recognizable because the houses were built in a few standard designs which recurred without variation from coast to coast. Even so, there was not enough 'wartime housing' to meet the demand. In the cities, families doubled up. Around the burgeoning military camps, people paid high rents for very little space. As for textiles, clothing, and footwear, such things were not rationed, but they were often very hard to find. Meanwhile, at the na-tion's dinner tables, Paraguayan yerba maté was substituted for India tea, and honey replaced the rationed sugar; even margarine, long illegal because of the dairy lobby, was a real possibility. Everywhere people were growing 'victory gardens,' where peas, beans and turnips competed with weeds and ignorance.

Eventually, along with wage controls and retail price controls came con-sumer rationing. Like price controls, rationing had been almost unnecessary during the first two years of the war, although by mid-1940 Ottawa was in-troducing maximum output ceilings for some consumer durable goods, such as cars. In October 1941, also, Ottawa began to control the terms of con-sumer credit, and during 1941 there was a spreading system of priorities which produced shortages of some consumer goods, such as gasoline and coal. Actual rationing, however, began in the winter of 1941-2, and spread quite rapidly – tires and tubes, sugar, gasoline, tea and coffee, butter, meat, preserved fruits and sugar substitutes, and evaporated milk. Meanwhile, sys-tems of allocation by permit were introduced for electric stoves, residential lighting fixtures, new farm machinery, tires and tubes, typewriters and of-fice machinery, standard railway watches, protective rubber garments, small arms ammunition, automobiles, and trucks. Thereafter, right through most of 1944, there was a general tendency for rationing to become more stringent. Meanwhile, the controllers of the economy worked to save resources by simplifying and standardizing such things as clothing, textiles, and many consumer goods which were allocated to the various regions, and to each individual retailer, on the basis of 1941 sales. More and more goods, furthermore, simply vanished from the shelves, 'controlled' out of production or shut out by the controllers of imports. As for alcoholic beverages, in December 1942 Ottawa imposed production and distribution restrictions, while the various provincial liquor control authorities devised their own rationing plans – and began that evil expedient of watering the spirits, a stratagem they have never since abandoned.

For many Canadian households, automobile controls symbolized the 'war effort.' All over the dominion the love affair with the private motor car raged unabated, undeterred by the poor state of many Canadian roads, or by the fact that in many Canadian localities the arrangements for eating, drinking, and sleeping which faced the motor traveller were dismal at best and sordid at worst. Unfortunately, cars impinged on the war effort in all sorts of ways. They ran on rubber tires; they burned gasoline, more than 80 per cent of which was produced from imported crude oil; they could be driven across the border into the United States (indeed, given the state of Canada's roads, that was often the natural way in which to drive them). But crude oil and foreign travel used American dollars, which were scarce from the beginning of the war and which had to be husbanded throughout. As for the vehicles themselves, car building needed imports, employed scarce engineering capacity, and swallowed enormous quantities of steel, energy, non-ferrous metals, and textiles. Civilian car production was first restricted, then ended; gasoline was first made scarce, then rationed; tires were rationed with special severity. Canadians compromised, grumbled, and worried. Would the tire controllers allocate a retread replacement for that bald back tire? Could the gas ration stretch to cover that absolutely necessary family duty call on grandma? Would the old Terraplane keep trundling along?

Public transport became very crowded indeed. Intercity train and air travel came under regulation quite early in the war, as the movement of servicemen and freight imposed heavy demands on the system. Local transport was unrationed, but it was congested, slow, rickety, and irritating. Streetcar systems were still widespread and a few electric interurban railways moseyed along, forgotten by their owners and by the citizenry until the outbreak of war. For example, from Vancouver an interurban electric line snaked seventy miles eastward to Chilliwack, passing close by one of the larger bases for the Commonwealth Air Training Plan. For trainees with day-leave passes, the interurban was a lifesaver: it would take them to Vancouver, where they would discover drizzle, one 'supper club,' beer parlours, and a general air of Presbyterian gloom. For the poor souls at Trenton, Camp Borden, Summerside, or Gimli, there was no such easy escape. As for civilians, public transport made life and work possible but not pleasant. On the streetcar systems the rolling stock largely dated from before the First World War. Toronto was the only city which had bought any large amount of rolling stock since 1929. Theorists of public transport sometimes ask themselves why Canadians were so quick to scrap their streetcar systems in the 1950s. To those who remember Canadian streetcars in the Second World War, the answer is obvious. No move could be so readily equated with modernization.

Congestion, shortages, and rationing were painful, and it was annoying that some goods were not for sale at all. Foreign tourism was impossible, because the authorities would not supply American money for the purpose. American periodicals were sometimes hard to get, for the same reason. Instead, the Canadian homegrown comic book enjoyed a brief flowering because there was little or no allocation of American dollars for the importation of *Superman, Batman,* or *Captain Marvel.* For those Canadians who paid income tax, the new and much heavier wartime imposts were painful. Since many of these people found their pretax incomes frozen at prewar levels, their real incomes certainly did go down. Liquor rationing, too, dampened many a wartime celebration.

People did not feel better off. However, the well-informed knew that in Britain, and even in the United States, things were a great deal worse. The United States carried food rationing much further than Canada did. In Britain almost everything except bread and potatoes was rationed, and the burden of taxation was a great deal heavier than in Canada, so in general real consumption fell substantially. Canadians responded by sending parcels to their British relatives, ignoring complaints in the British press that British Columbia canned salmon was 'really dolphin.' From time to time the British would reciprocate in odd ways. Hearing that toilet paper had become scarce in Vancouver, one Scottish family sent British Wartime Biffy Paper – hard, glossy, and unyielding – to its Canadian kin as a Yuletide gift. Such thoughts were appreciated, even if the objects themselves were not.

MOBILIZING LABOUR

All-embracing though the Department of Munitions and Supply appeared to be, it did not control the allocation of labour, perhaps the most important element in the war effort. Under the National Resources Mobilization Act of June 1940 there was authority to conscript men not only for the armed forces but for other work as well. Military call-ups began in September 1940 under the management of a new civilian Department of National War Services, which was set up in July 1940. At first, the conscripts were to serve only for a month, but in February 1941 the period of service was extended to four months, and in June 1941 Ottawa decided to retain conscripts in the domestic Reserve army for the duration of the war. Volunteers, meanwhile, were welcomed into the active forces, that component of the army whose members could serve overseas.

Thus the armed forces grew from 7000 men in 1938 to 779,000 men and women in 1944. The civilian labour force shrank, as men and women joined the armed forces, while the number of unemployed shrank too, as jobs and the forces absorbed them. Even so, and even allowing for the growth in the population, the unemployed were too few to provide all the bodies which the forces and the factories wanted. Where were the extra bodies to be found? In statistical terms, from a higher 'participation rate' – that is, a more intensive involvement of adults in the workforce. In human terms, from women.

Most of these new 'participants' seem to have been women. School terms were not shortened to release teenagers for war work, and there is little reason to suppose that many adolescents abbreviated their schooling for this purpose. As for women workers, to some extent the war merely redistributed them from low-paying work in trade and domestic service into better-paying factory work. Undoubtedly, however, a higher proportion of adult women sought work and found it. Of course, many of the industries whose outputs grew so rapidly, such as foods, beverages, textiles, and clothing, had always depended on female labour to a considerable extent. Drawing more women into such work did nothing to change the traditional roles, or stereotypes, about 'women's work.' Nor did the considerable expansion of government clerical and secretarial work, a process which went so far that in Ottawa the authorities had to erect a sort of civilian barrack, or secular convent, for their burgeoning female staff. As for the metal-working trades and the other heavy industries, no one seems to believe that in Canada these were yielded over to women. Nevertheless, we know little about this topic, and it may be that careful research will disclose more penetration than we acknowledge.[1] In manufacturing, by 1944 34 per cent of supervisory and office workers and 28 per cent of production workers were women. Canada produced no popular song to match the Americans' 'Rosie the Riveter,' but American Rosie certainly had sisters north of the 49th parallel.

1 From 1941 to 1944 the number of male workers fell by 215,000, while the number of female workers went up by 413,000, so that by 1944, women made up 31.5 per cent of civilian employment.

For the first part of the war the government left the mobilization and direction of civil labour to market forces. Wage rates, too, were unregulated. In 1939-41 civilian employment was growing slowly, and it was the growth of the armed forces which accounted for most of the fall in unemployment. Moreover, the population was growing, as was the civilian labour force, with no help from any rise in the participation rate. Hours of work, however, became somewhat longer, partly through overtime and partly through the spread of shift work. Government provided a variety of short trade courses, and in 1940 it set up a Wartime Bureau of Technical Personnel, originally to find chemists and engineers but later to locate machinists and other technicians. Finally, in 1940 came the national compulsory unemployment insurance scheme, which began to operate in July 1941. There had been a dominion-provincial employment service since 1917, but no one had to register and few vacancies had ever been filled through the service. In any event, for a decade there had been few vacancies to fill. But with compulsory unemployment insurance things were bound to be different: the unemployed could receive benefit only if they also registered for work with the new National Employment Service.

In 1941 things quickly began to change. On the average, only 4.6 per cent of the civilian labour force was unemployed, and in the later months of the year the percentage must have been smaller than this low figure. The armed forces were growing fast, and the reservists were now to be kept on duty until the end of the war. The nation's war effort was growing greater, and would become even bigger in the years ahead. Now there was real risk of wage-push inflation. Accordingly, the government promulgated wage guidelines, first for defence contractors and then for the civilian economy as well. At last, on 24 October 1941, by PO 8253, wages and salaries were frozen; employees would receive cost-of-living bonuses, but no other increases until after the war.

Since prices were also frozen, these measures ought to have had the effect of freezing real wage rates. Perhaps they did, but, as we have seen, real consumption rose, and this must have happened because people were working longer hours, there were now two breadwinners in many households instead of one, and many people moved from low-pay to higher-pay work. Controls did not prevent all movements in retail prices. Between mid-1941 and mid-1945 the cost-of-living index rose by 7.76 per cent. This was, however, a gentle increase, especially compared with that of the First World War when consumer prices rose 48 per cent in four years.

Furthermore, after 1941 the government found it necessary to control the movement of workers among industries, and even among firms. By 1943 'postponement orders' could be used to keep draftable men in essential industries, seasonal occupations, and agriculture. For each locality there were elaborate labour priorities. The offices of the National Employment Service were, with insignificant exceptions, the only routes through which workers were allowed to look for jobs, or employers to look for labour. Nobody could quit work without giving seven days notice to the Employment Service, which also issued the permits without which no employee or employer could seek, offer, or accept employment. Those unemployed for more than a fortnight could be assigned to any job that the service considered suitable. There were special provisions covering the direction of labour into coalmining, east-coast longshore work, woodcutting, fishing, fishprocessing, and farm labour. No farm workers could leave agriculture, except for seasonal work, without a permit. After 20 September 1943 government permission was needed before any workers in an essential industry could quit or be discharged. There was even considerable compulsory reassignment of labour from low to high priority work. Thus the civilian labour force was mobilized at least as fully as the military.

Not all Canadian workers laboured diligently and without self-seeking in the interest of allied victory. There were labour disputes, and union membership rose a good deal – from 382,000 in 1939 to 724,000 in 1944. Furthermore,.there were plenty of strikes – 1463 from 1939 through 1944. Indeed, in 1943 there were more strikes than in any other year from 1901 to 1960. But most of the strikes were short. Even in 1943, strikes cost less than one-third as many lost days as in 1919. On the whole, therefore, the process of war production was not much disturbed through labour militancy.

The government, nevertheless, worried about the labour situation. Indeed, a government headed by Mackenzie King could hardly be expected not to worry about it. In the first two years of the war there was concern because some unions were led or organized by Communists. With Hitler's invasion of the Soviet Union in June 1941, this worry receded: Canadian Communists could be trusted to forward the war effort now that the Socialist Motherland was in danger too. But what could or should Ottawa do about unions, strikes, agitations, and so on?

By 1939 the provinces had captured from the dominion the pre-eminent responsibility for labour matters. In peacetime, Ottawa could legislate only with respect to workers in federally regulated industries such as the railways, except where provinces specifically delegated their powers to the dominion. But with the outbreak of war everything changed; with the proclamation of the War Measures Act, 'Canada's second constitution,' as Frank Scott was to call it, came out of the closet. The inherited legislative framework was King's own Industrial Disputes Investigation Act of 1907 – the IDIA – which provided for conciliation but gave no special protection to unions. Furthermore, conciliation was voluntary, except in certain public utilities and mines. In agreeing to a conciliation board, an employer gave a sort of de facto recognition to a union, but there was no arrangement for the selection of bargaining agents, nor was there any requirement by which employers could be required to recognize unions or bargain with them.

Voluntarism, in the misty mind of the prime minister, was all. But the end of voluntarism was at hand. In 1940 the dominion extended the IDIA provisions for compulsory conciliation to cover all war industries. In June 1940 Ottawa issued a statement of principles – another voluntary statement – asserting that employees should be free to form unions and to bargain collectively; any collective agreement, furthermore, should contain grievance machinery. In December 1940 questions of wage-bargaining were taken away from the unions through the imposition of wage-controls on war industries. As we note elsewhere, the step was taken mostly to produce a better cost-control in these industries, so that the government could more rationally negotiate terms with employers. With the extension of wage control throughout the economy in the autumn of 1941 the scope of labour disputes was further diminished. Or so one might have supposed. But as Woods explains,[2] in the early years of the war there were many disputes about 'individual rights related to freedom of association,' and about ensuring 'that negotiations would take place.' In 1940 and 1941 both the two national labour federations, the Trades and Labor Congress (or TLC) and the Canadian Congress of Labour (or CCL), were agitated about these issues, and pressed the government to impose new obligations on employers. The Canadian Manufacturers' Association, however, saw no need for change. In 1941 the TLC proposed that there should be special commissioners who would have power to investigate cases in which employees appeared to have been penalized for union membership. In June 1941 the government accepted this recommendation, providing for the appointment of industrial disputes inquiry commissioners who could make preliminary studies of any industrial dispute. The new procedure was more speedy than the IDIA procedure because the minister of labour could act on his own initiative; he did not have to wait for a strike vote. It also had the effect of securing employees the right to unionize.[3] In September 1941 the government provided for compulsory supervised strike votes in war industries, where striking was now contingent on a majority vote. In 1943, during a wave of wartime strike activity, both British Columbia and Ontario made provision for the compulsory recognition of unions, with which employers were then obliged to bargain. Although such ar-

2   H.D. Woods and Sylvia Ostry, *Labour Policy and Labour Economics in Canada* (Toronto 1962), 65
3   Ibid., 68

rangements had existed in the United States since the mid-1930s, they were new in Canada.

In 1944 the dominion took the final steps. In all war industries, in all industries normally subject to dominion jurisdiction, and in any province which might make the new dominion regulations applicable to other industries, there were to be standard arrangements for identifying and certifying bargaining agents, for requiring employers to bargain with such agents, for compulsory arbitration of grievances, and for compulsory conciliation.

Strikes about union recognition thus became unnecessary, and other aspects of the arrangements made jurisdictional strikes among competing unions impossible. Furthermore, strikes could occur only when no collective agreement was in force, and only after a conciliation board had reported to the minister. The 'right to strike,' in other words, was severely curtailed, but many of the issues which had been provoking strikes – disputes among unions, efforts to bring employers to the bargaining table, arguments about the meaning and applicability of existing collective agreements – had been regulated out of existence.

The order was certainly meant to produce industrial peace. But it cannot properly be seen as anti-union – or, for that matter, as anti-management. What would it mean in the long run, after the end of the war? It would then lapse, because the War Measures Act would no longer be in force. However, in the event that it formed the basis for postwar dominion and provincial legislation, it provided something of a common framework – not a national labour code, but certainly a distinctively Canadian system of labour relations.

EXHORTATIONS, DEPORTATIONS, INVESTIGATIONS

Besides rearranging consumption and labour relations, the dominion manipulated public opinion as best it could. Obviously, the government wished to give itself favourable publicity and to avoid circulating information detrimental to its own or its allies' best interests. At the same time, however, it had to make its deeds believable, and to do so it had to moderate the controls it exercised over the national flow of words.

There were a number of government agencies to hand. There was a National Film Board, established in 1939, and commanded for the duration by a distinguished British film-making emigré, John Grierson. Grierson had made a name for himself through the dramatization of everyday events, and it was to be expected that his cinematic efforts would be directed at making events intelligible to the average citizen, whether on the farm, in the factory, or at school. At the same time, Grierson hoped to redefine the categories of events considered newsworthy or cinematically appropriate. Under Grierson,

Canada's official cinematic output was both grittier and less vainglorious than a previous generation would have considered desirable; but it may by that token have had more impact. Two NFB series, 'Canada Carries On' and 'World in Action,' were regularly displayed in 600 commercial theatres in English and in sixty in French for the edification of the people; but in addition there were rural, industrial, and trade union circuits and discussion groups which, the NFB claimed, generated monthly audiences of over half a million. All this was in the direction of 'mass education,' a concept which, it was hoped, would have a profound impact on the way Canadians thought about themselves, their country, and the world. Unfortunately, as with most artistic theories, we have no means of assessing its true impact on the hearts and minds of the people. The only certain thing is that it produced few if any discernible political consequences.

While the NFB assaulted the eye, the CBC bombarded the ear. The national radio network took seriously its educational task, but since it was also a major purveyor of immediate news it had to splice earnestness with attraction. And so there was 'Fighting Navy,' a weekly soap opera about the Naval Reserve on the North Atlantic ('Roll along, wavy Navy, Roll along'). There was the nightly news, with Lorne Green, who retailed tales of allied triumphs and disasters with appropriate sonority and authority. But while the tone in which the news was delivered was important, the content was equally so.

Allied propaganda during the First World War was an important controlling factor. The vivid retailing of imaginary excesses by the beastly Hun proved an effective means of stimulating patriotism, but it had its side effects, both during the war and after. During the war it made rational communication difficult and encouraged more and more excessive language and threats directed at the enemy, threats that came home to roost when peace was negotiated. After the war, when the truth about German atrocities (some real but mostly imaginary) came to be known, the public recoiled. The allies' propaganda, in order to be believed, had to avoid the wilder flights of fancy that had characterized the First World War. Ironically, the Germans in the Second World War managed most of the atrocities they had been accused of during the First, but the full horror of the Nazi regime's activities was not known until near the end of the conflict. Using the Wartime Information Board set up in September 1942, the government did its best to inspire its friends and make fun of its foes; and it must be said that Adolf Hitler co-operated in this enterprise.

The other side of purveying information was the withholding of it. There was censorship throughout the war. Many activities were held to be secret: troop movements, convoy sailings, and secret weapons projects. But to a reader in the 1980s the Canadian press throughout the war appears to have been surprisingly unfettered. It would have been possible to put together a chart of Canadian war production using only published sources. The names and products of Canadian factories were known to any attentive reader of the *Financial Post,* and the Department of Munitions and Supply made sure that its activities were well publicized. Within limits, Canadian newspapers were free to criticize the government. The most obvious limit on freedom of speech and of the press during the war was the suppression of overt fascist propaganda and, during the period when the Soviet Union was maintaining a friendly neutrality towards Nazi Germany, of Communist propaganda as well.

The government regulated not only words, written or spoken, but those who uttered them as well. Fascist sympathizers, German, Italian, or native Canadian, were placed under surveillance or actually locked up. The War Measures Act permitted internment without trial, and many Canadians of greater or lesser eminence found themselves placed in northern Ontario or New Brunswick for the duration of the war. The most famous detainee was Camillien Houde, the mayor of Montreal, who spent four years behind barbed wire for denouncing registration for national service in the summer of 1940.

With the Japanese attack on Pearl Harbor in December 1941, Canadians of Japanese descent faced a special problem. They were an unpopular, highly visible minority concentrated in coastal British Columbia. There had always been strong anti-oriental feeling in British Columbia, where people of Asian ancestry were discriminated against in a variety of ways. The outbreak of the Pacific war gave British Columbia racists their opportunity, and there began an agitation to remove the Japanese entirely from an area where the Japanese army and navy were expected to land at any time.

The government, or most of it, understood that there was no immediate military danger, and officials in Ottawa were extremely sceptical of claims that Canada's Japanese minority posed a threat to national security. Both the police and the army were reasonably assured of the contrary, but it proved impossible to quell the hysterical demands uttered by prominent BC politicians for the expulsion of the 'disloyal' Japanese minority. The King government delayed, but finally buckled under. If the Japanese were not removed they might become the victims of vigilante action from their neighbours and so, in February 1942, removed they were, to camps in the interior run by the government. Most property had to be abandoned. Placed in official custody, it was sold at derisory prices and at considerable economic loss to the luckless deportees.

Perhaps in an era when whole nations were bundled off to extermination camps, the wrong done to the Japanese might not have seemed very great. Nobody lost life or limb as a result, and the resettled Japanese, or most of them, eventually re-entered Canadian society where they played a large and distinguished role after the war. But what the Japanese suffered was the major injustice committed in Canada during the war, and it has been plausibly argued that it should be judged by native Canadian standards and not those of Soviet Russia, Nazi Germany, or Imperial Japan. It is not very unusual that people on the Pacific succumbed to panic, or that, panicking, they reacted in an unpleasant way. The government may have felt that it faced a choice of evils, the deportation of a minority group or the possibility of mob action and civil disorder. It is assuredly inexcusable that Japanese-Canadians were persecuted in this fashion, but if Ottawa felt obliged to conduct the persecution, it might at least have prevented the giveaway of their assets. As for the internment itself, it is at best understandable, which does not make it less morally wrong.

Because many German prisoners of war and 'enemy aliens' were brought to Canada from Great Britain for safekeeping, the Japanese camps were not the only ones in the dominion. It was easier to feed the prisoners in northern Ontario than in Britain; if they escaped they would do far less damage; and anyway, where would they escape to? One or two Germans actually did escape from custody and found sanctuary in the neutral United States prior to December 1941, and an imaginative movie, *The 49th Parallel,* showed what could happen when a band of desperate Nazis got loose in peaceful Canada.

The army looked after the camps, and the RCMP looked after other aspects of national security. Its tasks ranged from trivialities to keeping espionage agents at bay; and from the silly, such as watching 'subversive' Jehovah's Witnesses, to shadowing currency speculators and controlling the other unpleasant fauna that a regulated economy throws up. It cannot be said that the government's security standards during the war were particularly strict. Indeed, the historian may wonder just how the standards might have been defined. Nazis and Fascists were presumably natural enemies. But there were few such in Canada. As for Communists and other left-wing sympathizers, Canada was never at war with the Soviet Union, which, indeed, was our ally after June 1941. Hence it should cause no surprise that many individuals with pronounced left-wing views were hired as scientists, propagandists, and diplomats. As is well known, a few of these people were later proved to have acted disloyally, but it was Moscow, not Berlin or Tokyo, to which they transmitted state secrets.

Security clearances, spy-watching, the dispersal of the Japanese, the channelling and manipulation of public opinion through government-owned media – all these were wartime eructations that few Canadians expected to linger after the outbreak of peace. The CBC and NFB would continue the task of nation-building with which they were charged by statute. But their tone would be less strident than it became in the 1970s and 1980s simply because the 'national unity question' was still considered to be manageable through negotiation and compromise rather than through confrontation and collision. Though national unity was on people's minds, it was something that could safely be left to Mackenzie King. Long before the end of the war, politicians and officials began to think instead about postwar reconstruction, but in doing so they had far more mundane matters in mind.

23

Planning for Reconstruction

In the middle of February 1944 Mackenzie King, suffering from insomnia, prowled into his library looking for something to read. Secreted among the worthy Victorian biographies that he favoured there nestled a work of recent history, George Dangerfield's *Strange Death of Liberal England,* published some eight years before. Dangerfield's subject was the eclipse and near-demise of the great British Liberal party, so confident, dominant, and secure in the decade before the Great War. King took the book to bed with him and read a chapter before he nodded off. Dangerfield's book, he told his diary the next day, 'interests me as much as any I have ever read in my life.' So concerned was King that he preached to the cabinet on the subject: 'I wished they would all read it. They would see wherein the Liberal Party had lost out through concerning itself only with constitutional and other matters, but forgetting altogether the great social programmes, working classes and the like, which lay at the basis of all else. I said there was a great danger of Liberal Government in Canada sharing a similar fate if we did not keep in closer touch with the people.'[1]

Fortunately, the Liberal government had tools to hand which had been unavailable to their British counterparts a generation earlier. As we have seen, they had a much more sophisticated understanding of how the economy worked. They had seen the social disruption that had followed the earlier war. They had public opinion polls – secret ones as well as public – to tell them that ordinary Canadians, apprehensive about the future, wanted government to secure their future employment and social security.

Consciously and unconsciously, the government had already taken certain steps along these lines. The enactment of unemployment insurance in 1940 was a belated reaction to the 1930s. Certain veterans' benefits had already

1 Public Archives of Canada [PAC], W.L.M. King Papers, King Diary, 17 Feb. 1944

appeared as needed during the war, and shortly there would be more. In the obscure Department of Pensions and Natural Health, officials dusted off old schemes for universal health care while lay committees of experts concocted more. Ian Mackenzie, since 1939 relegated to the safety of that department, wanted to re-establish his political reputation by becoming the father of a Canadian welfare state, and to that end he periodically erupted into cabinet with bright ideas for the glowing postwar future. The Department of Finance, whose duty it was to worry about costs, generally opposed Mackenzie's schemes or diverted them into politically innocuous channels. Health insurance, for example, which Mackenzie was strenuously promoting in 1943 and 1944, was sent both to a House of Commons committee on social security, where the public was treated to the spectacle of Christian Science healers, chiropractors, and ordinary doctors competing for a slice of the health money pie, and to a committee of government experts who were instructed to find a way to make Mackenzie's proposals accord more closely with economic reality.

The best known, if not the most effective, of the wartime proposals for social security was the so-called Marsh Report, the product of Leonard Marsh, a social scientist working for a blue-ribbon lay committee on reconstruction, known from its chairman as the James Committee. Marsh evolved a sweeping scheme for social security in its many aspects, and his proposal certainly focused debate on the area. But any appraisal of the Marsh Report should also take into account the very real hostility it aroused among the professional civil servants, particularly in the Finance Department, and the embarrassment that Mackenzie King believed it had caused his government. The Marsh Report, and its author, were discreetly buried in the bureaucracy. The significance of the report, therefore, is primarily intellectual and symbolic; its impact on the development of policy was slight.

There was a natural tendency during the war to lump all the ideas for Canada's postwar future under the general heading 'reconstruction.' Reconstruction is an omnibus word meaning, as the politicians gratefully realized, many things to many people. It could imply a program of job security and full employment, directed by a wise and all-seeing government in Ottawa. This meaning was the most commonly found, although its broadest expression came from the political left. CCF politicians argued from the experience of the war that it was entirely feasible to provide a full employment economy through 'planning.' Planning was another all-purpose word, generally uttered, in the jaundiced opinion of C.D. Howe, the government's principal industrial minister, by those who had no idea what planning was really all about. He and his advisers were in any case sceptical of a planning millennium in which wage control, for example, did not play as large a part as price control. Both kinds of control had been necessary to keep inflation within bounds between 1941 and the end of the war, and to achieve full employment planning the same control mechanisms would have to be maintained afterwards. But Howe and his advisers were also doubtful that Canadians would really wish to keep such a stringent regime in being. It is also doubtful whether the dominion possessed the necessary constitutional authority in peacetime.

Was Canadian public opinion compatible with Howe's scepticism? King, typically, hesitated before he attempted an answer. For the 1944 parliamentary session, which most people expected would be the last before the next election, King and his ministers prepared a quadruple legislative package. There would be, first of all, family allowances, an idea which came most immediately out of the National War Labour Board as an expedient for bolstering low incomes without having to throw wage control overboard. Then there would be three new departments, expressing the government's administrative priorities for the postwar period: Veterans' Affairs, an obvious creation; National Health and Welfare, which absorbed the former Department of Pensions and National Health; and Reconstruction.

Although these items were promised in January 1944 and passed before summer, it took some time to implement them. Family allowances, for example, were not to be distributed until after the next election to avoid the appearance of bribing the electorate with its own money. The new departments waited until October, at which time King appointed the relevant ministers. Health and Welfare went to a new cabinet appointee, King's parliamentary assistant Brooke Claxton, a relatively young and extremely vigorous Montrealer. Veterans Affairs passed to the warhorse Ian Mackenzie, a reward for loyalty and partisanship if not sobriety. And Reconstruction went to C.D. Howe.

It had taken King a long time to reconcile himself to Howe as minister for reconstruction. Howe had rough edges, King knew. He was perceived, accurately, as close to business. He posed difficult conditions for taking the job, demanding that his new department have real responsibilities as well as a budget all its own. As minister of reconstruction Howe would pursue independent policies rather than act as co-ordinator of the actions and expenditures of other ministers, which had been King's original intention.

The policies Howe proposed to pursue were well known to his fellow ministers. When reconstruction was debated in cabinet in March 1944, the prime minister sourly noted in his diary that 'Howe seemed to think the only purpose of a Reconstruction Bill was a reconversion of industry. Taking for granted all this would be done under his department.'[2]

What did the 'reconversion of industry' mean? To Howe and his lieutenants, it meant that they would continue to do what they were already doing. That is, they would offer assistance and incentives to industry to reorient itself from military production to civilian demand. Even this task was a complicated one, involving as it did the cancellation of contracts, the determination of fair compensation, and the provision of incentives for re-equipping the relevant industrial plant. The technique had been perfected during the war, when the changing military situation had demanded first one item of equipment and then another. When victory began to seem both more likely and more imminent in the fall of 1943, the Munitions and Supply Department began to make provision for the disposal of some of the equipment it had accumulated. Categories of equipment or plant destined for disposal were established. In December Howe made it known that he would set up a war assets disposal corporation, and leaked his choice for its president. In February 1944, long before cabinet had determined what form the Reconstruction Bill was to take, Howe's department issued a manual for ending war contracts to its clients.

Nor were the minister's views on the general state of the economy any secret. Addressing the Maritime Chambers of Commerce in November 1943, Howe predicted that there was no reason to fear unemployment when peace returned. 'Work for All,' proclaimed headlines over reports of Howe's speech. 'Let's not Fool Ourselves,' the Montreal *Gazette* editorialized in reply. The *Gazette*'s fears were more 'fiction' than fact, Howe told a press conference in December. For those like the *Gazette* who thought that a sudden end to the war would bring disruption as it had in 1918, Howe had reassurance. There was still the war against Japan, he told the Montreal Reform Club in late November. It would go on longer than the German war, and it would ease the transition from war production to peace.

How did reconversion actually work? The answer appears to be as follows. First, it was voluntary. A businessman who wanted to convert from wartime production to peacetime consumerism could expect help and advice of all kinds, but the timing and direction were left to his choice. Second, the government allowed necessary capital outlays to be deducted from taxable income at a much higher rate than normal. Thus, taxes in 1944, 1945, and 1946 – to use one example – would be much lower than if the business were not converting. But the blow would fall in 1947, when the deductions were all used up. This system was called '*double* (or accelerated) depreciation.'

2   Quoted in R. Bothwell and W. Kilbourn, *C.D. Howe: A Biography* (Toronto 1979), 184

The new policy began to work on schedule. By the end of April 1945, just two weeks before the end of Hitler's war, Howe reported that 274 applications for $54 million work of double depreciation had been received and approved, and of that total about 38 per cent were in Ontario, Quebec, and British Columbia, the three main centres of industry. About 70 per cent of the total was for new machinery, especially in iron and steel. Buildings costing just over $2 million had been sold for rather more than half their cost; machinery originally costing $2.37 million had gone for $942,000. Complete establishments (buildings and machinery together) went for rather less, but 'in general,' Howe reported, 'it was sought to get a return of 60% of cost.' Judging by early results, that return was never reached. Nevertheless, the 40 per cent and 50 per cent rates of return characteristic of the disposal of assets in 1945 contradict subsequent charges of a 'fire sale' of the people's property.[3]

As sales of capital goods took off, Howe turned his department's attention to the dismantling of controls. Controls had been intended to secure needed supply for munitions plants. Their imposition indicated that a condition of scarcity existed; the disappearance of such scarcity was the criterion for the removal of controls. Wartime controls continued beyond the period covered in this book, but by the end of 1945 most of them were gone. With them went the bureaucracy that had administered them, and with the bureaucracy went some of the dreams of a 'planned' postwar economy.

The staged return to 'free enterprise' took place relatively smoothly. There was little effective political protest because Howe's predictions of labour scarcity proved to be more accurate than the widely expected labour surplus. There was some unemployment in regional pockets, it is true, carefully monitored by the government through a secret labour survey. It was not sufficiently widespread to cause serious disquiet among the electorate, and for the most part local incentives sufficed.

The question must be raised whether Howe's reconstruction policy was the result of a 'hidden agenda' conceived by Canada's industrial elite to turn the clock back to pre-socialist time. Such a question, though beloved of certain historians and other social scientists, is to some extent unanswerable since it presupposes data which seem never to have existed. Howe himself knew that business would prefer to continue in a condition where its markets were guaranteed, and where normal risk factors were as far as possible banished by the overflowing public purse. As early as October 1944 he informed the Canadian copper industry that they should be 'placed in the same position that we found them prior to the war, that is, in private busi-

3 PAC, Privy Council Papers, Cabinet Reconstruction Committee minutes, April-July 1945

ness enterprise.' No consideration seemed to Howe compelling enough to alter his view. There would be no unemployment if copper production shut down. 'Canada has a very serious shortage of labour of that type,' he knew from wartime experience, 'and the same condition will continue for a long time. There is no purpose whatever in encouraging copper mining which is not needed.'[4] For a country of Canada's size and limited resources no other position was possible than to recommend, and enforce, the most efficient distribution of labour and capital as determined, ultimately, by supply and demand. Howe took it for granted that neither labour nor capital would like this situation.

The refusal to intervene within broad limits applied to Canada's internal situation. External affairs were another matter entirely.[5] Canada was represented at an international monetary conference at Bretton Woods, New Hampshire, in the summer of 1944. Its object was to discover and establish a means of regulating the currencies of the world, whose fluctuating values were thought to have bedevilled world trade during the 1930s. Because of the high calibre of the Canadian delegation, Canada was able to make a strong and positive contribution to the discussions, which resulted in the International Monetary Fund and the International Bank for Reconstruction and Development, later known as the World Bank.

Canadian officials and ministers also kept an anxious and gloomy lookout for anything that might mean a limitation on Canada's postwar export opportunities. It was known that Britain's postwar economic condition would be parlous, and towards the end of the war the Canadian government initiated discussions with the British with the object of limiting any disruption to trade that might occur once the cushion of interallied war credits was removed. What most Canadian officials – and even the ministers most directly concerned – preferred to see was a liberalized international economic system with as few barriers to trade as could be negotiated. But no one was foolhardy enough to believe that this millennium would arrive in the foreseeable future. In the meantime, Canadian diplomats husbanded their resources, counted up what was owing to the country, and awaited events with a brave smile fixed on their faces.

What the diplomats and politicians wanted was what Canadians had always wanted – the largest possible vent for the products of the nation. The wartime experience had in this respect been enormously exciting. Both Britain and the United States had absorbed Canada's goods on an unprecedent-

4 PAC, Howe Papers, volume 69, Howe to G. Bateman, 4 Oct. 1944
5 For a broader description of the measures taken at the end of the war to stabilize world trade and finance see Robert Bothwell, Ian Drummond, and John English, *Canada since 1945* (Toronto 1981), Part Two.

ed scale. But there was no reason to suppose that either country would continue to do so after the end of the war. It was recognized in Ottawa that Britain would be painfully short of dollars, both Canadian and American. Tariff negotiations with the United States promised a great deal – but what could the American negotiators deliver, in the face of a parochial and obstructionist Congress? American protectionism was certainly not dead; the prudent Canadian hoped for much, but expected little. And unless there were successful new trade arrangements with the United States, the Americans could be expected to resurrect the normal barriers of tariffs and quotas which routinely kept Canadian goods from freely entering the American home market. The Hyde Park arrangements were not permanent; they would expire with the end of the war, or very soon thereafter. Nor could Canada count on converting her sterling earnings into American dollars, thus covering her excess imports from the United States; Britain would be short of American dollars too. It was recognized that Canada would have to try to buy more from Britain, so as to help Britain buy more from Canada. Furthermore, it was hoped that Britain would eventually be able to let Canada convert more of the dominion's overseas earnings into American dollars. Canada therefore had a special interest in any arrangements which would help Britain achieve this result. Tariff reductions were thought to be in Canada's interest, because if the Americans and the other countries could be persuaded to cut their tariffs, Canada's peacetime exports were bound to be helped. Admittedly, Canada would have to lower her own tariffs as well, but with clever tariff bargaining the dominion might 'gain' more from the tariff cuts of others than she would 'lose' through her own tariff reductions.[6] Remembering, perhaps, the trilateral trade talks of 1937-8,[7] Canadian officials might well have been confident in their ability to manage such tariff bargaining.

In thinking about postwar reconstruction, Ottawa's officials and politicians were not committed either to free trade or to continental integration with the United States. Prewar markets in continental Europe and the overseas Commonwealth countries were to be recaptured if possible. The British market was to be preserved and developed. After all, these overseas markets wanted certain Canadian goods, such as wheat, for which the American outlet would always be small or non-existent. There was no question of diverting goods from overseas to the United States. At the same time, the American market was a large and a rich one. Britain was only one-quarter as populous

6 Economic theory shows that tariff cuts generally help the cutter as well as the 'cuttee.' Politicians, however, rarely see things that way.
7 See J.L. Granatstein, *A Man of Influence: Norman A. Robertson and Canadian Statecraft 1929-68* (Toronto 1981), 56-79.

as the United States, and most of the Commonwealth countries were too small or too poor to buy very much from Canada, even in the best of times. Lord Beaverbrook, the expatriate Canadian who owned the *London Daily Express*, might long for 'empire free trade,' or at least an economic integration of the Commonwealth. Certainly there were theorists in London who hoped for a Commonwealth economic bloc which could 'look the Americans in the eye.' There were no such theorists in Ottawa, but neither were there people who wanted to abandon overseas markets or to rely on American largesse. For Ottawa, it was 'Both – And,' not 'Either – Or.'

Nobody expected postwar prosperity without a thriving export trade. Wartime events had underlined a fact of life: Canada would prosper when its trade prospered. However, besides reinforcing this old lesson, wartime experience had provided a new one. The taxing and spending of the federal government could be used to smooth the movement of the economy, reducing inflationary pressure when events were overheating, and raising the levels of income and unemployment when times were not so bright. Of course, the system would work best when other countries, especially Britain and the United States, were doing the same thing. But there was reason to hope that the same Keynesian lessons had been learned in Washington and London as in Ottawa.

It might seem that all would be plain sailing. In good times, Ottawa would run surpluses and pay off debt; in bad times, it would run deficits and incur debt for the sake of 'high and stable employment.' There were, however, two main problems.

One problem was the parliamentary process. Oppositions were all too likely to criticize surpluses, debts, and sudden changes of tax and spending policy. Journalists, too, might be expected to carp and complain, whenever the government got its sums wrong – or even when it got them right. Indeed, one group would moan when the government successfully practised Keynesianism, and another group would moan if it did not.

The second problem was Canada's federal system. The Rowell-Sirois Commission had skilfully diagnosed the resultant illness; it remained to discover whether anybody would swallow an appropriate medicine. In peacetime, the Canadian provinces spent as much as Ottawa, or more. What was to prevent them from running bigger deficits when the correct medicine was surpluses? Or bigger surpluses when Ottawa was trying to produce bigger deficits for the sake of the unemployed? Also, in peacetime the provinces and not the dominion controlled most of the more manageable kinds of spending program – most capital works, almost all welfare schemes – the sorts of thing which would have to be rationally managed for the sake of high employment and price stability in the postwar world. Family allowances, introduced in 1944 under the dominion's general constitutional power to spend as and when it liked, would provide some underpinning for consumer spending. But this would probably not be enough, nor could the allowances be made larger or smaller according to the need for overall economic balance. The government issued a White Paper on Employment and Income – a policy pronouncement without legislative effect – committing itself to 'high and stable employment.' The drafter was an economist and temporary civil servant, W.A. Mackintosh, who had wanted the White Paper to say 'full employment.' Howe responded that full employment was impossible, and that to promise it was political madness. The cabinet sided with Howe. But without some new dominion-provincial understandings, even 'high and stable employment' would be more than Ottawa could deliver. There would have to be a dominion-provincial conference on reconstruction.

This conference, the first since 1941, met on 6 August 1945, only eight days before Japan's surrender.[8] The provinces rejected Ottawa's proposals for a fiscal recasting of Confederation. The immediate result was bitter disappointment in Ottawa; in the long term, the rejection condemned Canada to its postwar fate – an indefinite federal-provincial squabbling over shared tax fields, joint spending programs, social welfare, medicare, and the counter-cyclical management of the economy. The recession of 1981-3, Canada's first since the 1930s, may have made Canadians wonder whether the price of 'provincial rights' may not have proved to be rather high.

In 1945 Canada could look back on a half century of rapid population growth, where immigration had been of immense importance but where natural increase had also been significant. Canadians had continued to drift out of the country, but immigration had more than offset that outflow. Urbanization, immigration, and prairie settlement had gone hand in hand. Though less densely populated than it would be in the 1980s, Canada by 1945 was peopled in a way that the citizens forty years on would not find surprising. Winnipeg was a genuinely multicultural, diverse society, even if the cultures existed side by side rather than mixed together. Both in Toronto and Montreal there were small Italian communities, and rather larger communities of Jews. But Toronto was still what the poet Earle Birney had called it: 'Anglo-Saxon Town.' Vancouver was even more so. Indeed, because of the wartime expulsion of its Japanese residents, it was more Anglo-Saxon than ever. In Montreal the 'two solitudes' warily regarded one another. Most Canadians now lived in cities, and in the larger cities the way of life would not be unfamiliar, even though that way of life was often cautious, stodgy, limiting, and dull. By 1945 no one could doubt that Canada would be an

8 For a full account of the conference see Bothwell, Drummond, and English, *Canada since 1945*, 91-6.

urbanized country, like the societies of the United States and Western Europe. The prairie farmlands were as populated as they were ever likely to be, and few people now believed that the frontier of agricultural settlement could be pushed much farther north or northwest. Whether natural increase or immigration were to raise the nation's population, in the future the cities would grow and the rural population would not. Because of the westward march of Soviet totalitarianism, once postwar refugees had been absorbed there would not be many immigrants from Eastern Europe. Sifton's peasants in sheepskin coats would not be seen again. Instead, there would be new peasants, from new lands. But they would settle in cities – above all in Montreal, Toronto, and Vancouver, which by 1945 had seen little of them.

Whatever was happening to Canadian population was unsatisfactory to someone. The objectors kept complaining, before 1945 and since. In the early 1900s Sifton and the rest of the government wanted to settle the prairies, but the bulk of immigrants drifted to the cities. By 1914, and again in the 1920s, intellectuals and politicians wanted more 'assimilable' immigrants, and they wanted to place these migrants on the land. Nor were they always anxious to see much immigration. Yet immigration remained large, and, as before, most of those migrants went to the cities. Francophones worried about the immigration of Anglophones, or those who would become Anglophones. That immigration nonetheless continued. Both Francophones and Anglophones worried about the emigration of the native-born. So far as Francophones were concerned, the prosperity and urbanization of 1900-29 stemmed the drain. So far as Anglophones were concerned, neither prosperity nor urbanization had the effect which might be expected: Canada was growing, but many Anglophones still thought they would do better in the United States. Only in the 1930s, when depression and government policy shut off both immigration and emigration, did things go according to plan. Or did they? There were few immigrants and few emigrants, but all too few babies. Unnoticed by politicians, publicists, and intellectuals, a great demographic transition had begun: without a revival of immigration, the birth rate, or both, Canada would remain an assembly of comparatively small and scattered city nodes. And that was an outcome which nobody wanted.

In the event, things went remarkably well after 1945 – not only demographically, but in most other respects. However, that is another story – and one which we have told elsewhere.

Appendix 1

	Maritimes	Quebec	Ontario	West	Overall	Popular Vote (%)
General Election of 1900						
Liberal	27	57	37	12	133	51.2
Conservative	12	8	55	5	80	47.4
Other	0	0	0	0	0	1.3
General Election of 1904						
Liberal	26	53	38	21	138	52.0
Conservative	9	11	48	7	75	46.4
Other	0	1	0	0	1	1.5
General Election of 1908						
Liberal	26	54	37	18	135	50.4
Conservative	9	11	48	17	85	46.9
Other	0	0	1	0	1	2.7
General Election of 1911						
Liberal	19	38	13	17	87	47.7
Conservative	16	27	73	18	134	50.9
Other	0	0	0	0	0	1.4
General Election of 1917						
Unionist	21	3	74	55	153	57.0
Opposition	10	62	8	2	82	39.9
Other	0	0	0	0	0	3.1
General Election of 1921						
Liberal	25	65	21	5	116	40.7
Conservative	5	0	37	8	50	30.3
Progressive	1	0	24	39	64	22.9
Other	0	0	0	5	0	6.1

	Maritimes	Quebec	Ontario	West	Overall	Popular Vote (%)
		General Election of 1925				
Liberals	6	59	11	23	99	39.9
Conservatives	23	4	68	21	116	46.5
Progressives	0	0	2	22	24	8.9
Other	0	2	1	3	6	4.7
		General Election of 1926				
Liberals	9	60	26	23	128	46.1
Conservatives	20	4	53	14	91	45.3
Progressives	0	0	2	18	20	5.3
Other	0	1	1	4	6	3.4
		General Election of 1930				
Liberals	6	40	22	23	91	45.2
Conservatives	23	24	59	31	137	48.8
Progressives	0	0	1	11	12	2.8
Other	0	1	0	4	5	3.2
		General Election of 1935				
Liberals	25	55	56	37	173	44.8
Conservatives	1	5	25	9	40	29.6
C.C.F.	0	0	0	7	7	8.8
Others	0	5	1	18	24	16.7
		General Election of 1940				
Liberals	19	61	57	44	181	51.5
Conservatives	6	1	25	8	40	30.7
C.C.F.	1	0	0	7	8	8.5
Others	0	3	0	13	16	9.3
		General Election of 1945				
Liberals	19	53	34	19	125	40.9
Progr-Conserv.	6	2	48	11	67	27.4
C.C.F.	1	0	0	27	28	15.6
Others	0	10	0	15	25	16.2

Source: J. Murray Beck,
Pendulum of Power Canada's Federal Elections
Scarborough 1968. 174-5, 188-9, 202-3, 220-1, 238-9, 256-7

Bibliography

There is an abundance of literature, historical and primary, on the period 1900-45. In the forest of material there are some convenient pathways and reliable signposts. Since we cannot hope to list the material tree by tree or book by book, we intend to concentrate on those books and references which will be most useful for the general reader. To update and expand the bibliography on a particular topic, one should consult J.L. Granatstein and Paul Stevens, *A Guide to Canadian Historical Literature* (Toronto 1982), and the bibliographies which regularly appear in the *Revue d'histoire de l'Amérique française* and the *Canadian Historical Review,* the latter of which was published throughout our period, although known down to 1920 as *Review of Historical Publications Relating to Canada.* From 1935 onwards the *Canadian Journal of Economics and Political Science* also provided not only specialized bibliographies but also commentaries on the trend of events.

The most obvious, and usually the most available, reference is the *Canada Year Book.* As the title suggests, the *Year Book* was an annual, containing a combination of statistical material and general essays on various aspects of Canadian affairs. Other statistics are to be found in the decennial *Censuses* and in the two editions of *Historical Statistics of Canada* (1965 and 1982). Note that the two editions contain different sets of data, so that one must be ready to use both. An important unofficial annual publication was *The Canadian Annual Review* (the title varies slightly), published in Toronto under various auspices from 1901 until its demise in 1937. *Canada and its Provinces* (23 volumes, Toronto 1913-17), an encyclopedic treatment of history and society, is an invaluable source for the pre-World War One period. *The Canadian Encyclopedia* (three volumes, Edmonton 1985) contains a wealth of information – historical, biographical, and economic.

For the period between the wars the *Report* and the subsidiary studies of the Royal Commission on Dominion-Provincial Relations (Ottawa 1940 and thereafter) are extremely valuable, both for historical commentary and as a kind of snapshot of the way Canada was governed, on the local, provincial, and national levels. There is a documentary series produced by the Department of External Affairs, *Documents on Canadian External Relations* (volumes 1-9 and 12, Ottawa 1968-80), known to the trade as the DCER. The analogous publication of the American State Department, *Foreign Relations of the United States* (several volumes, Washington: Government Printing Office, annual) is also useful for Canadian and Canadian-related topics.

Another contemporary series that retains much utility is the vast project on 'The Relations between Canada and the United States,' sponsored by the Carnegie Endowment for World Peace and published between 1936 and 1945 by Ryerson Press in Canada and by Yale University Press in the United States. It contains volumes on such subjects as immigration, public opinion, and foreign investment, as well as more orthodox treatments of Canadian-American relations.

Over the past twenty-five years McClelland and Stewart have produced three volumes in a 'Centenary Series' which treat the period 1900-1945: R.C. Brown and Ramsay Cook, *Canada 1896-1921: A Nation Transformed* (Toronto 1974), John Thompson and Allan Seager, *Canada 1922-1939* (Toronto 1985), and Donald Creighton, *Canada 1939-1957: The Forked Road* (Toronto 1976). The first two merit close reading, providing as they do a wealth of useful and intelligent comment. There is plenty of comment in Creighton's work, but in our opinion and in that of most critics it lacks balance and background. Morris Zaslow's *The Opening of the Canadian North 1870-1914,* another centenary volume, treats only part of our period.

During our period Canada fought in three wars, and in peacetime much effort was spent avoiding war and involvement in war. There is, not surprisingly, a rich literature on Canada's external relations and upon its participation in the British Empire, the Boer War, and the First and Second World Wars. John Kendle, *The Colonial and Imperial Conferences* (London 1967), deals with the administrative side of imperialism; Carl Berger's *The Sense of Power* (Toronto 1970), treats what might be called its spiritual side. Desmond Morton, *Ministers and Generals: Politics and the Canadian Militia* (Toronto 1970) examines the complex development of Canada's military. Max Beloff's *Imperial Sunset* (London 1969) is a sensitive and sensible examination of the decline of the British Empire, 1897-1921. Intended as the first volume of many, it is now a striking monument to what might have been. Philip Wigley, *Canada and the Transition to Commonwealth: British-Canadian Relations, 1917-1926* (Cambridge 1977), is a first-class treatment of a crucial period. The military side of World War One has filled shelves of books; the standard official account is G.W.L. Nicholson, *The Canadian*

Expeditionary Force, 1914-1919 (Ottawa 1962). More readable is John Swettenham, *To Seize the Victory* (Toronto 1965).

There has also been a considerable outpouring on the interwar period. James Eayrs, *In Defence of Canada* (two volumes, Toronto 1964 and 1965), covers the years from 1919 to 1940. It is lively, opinionated, but incomplete and now dated in its research. A compilation of articles and original documents is Robert Bothwell and Norman Hillmer, eds., *The In-Between Times* (Toronto 1975). J.L. Granatstein's *A Man of Influence* (Ottawa 1981) describes the career of a Canadian diplomat, Norman Robertson; another diplomat, Hugh Keenleyside, has done the job for himself in his exhausting but interesting *Hammer the Golden Day* (Toronto 1981). The first volume of L.B. Pearson's memoirs, *Mike,* treats our period. It is fascinating although oblique. Charles Ritchie's diary-memoir, *The Siren Years* (Toronto 1974), presents a charming and penetrating view of Canada's external relations as seen by a junior diplomat. The military are represented by General Maurice Pope's undeservedly neglected autobiography, *Soldiers and Politicians* (Toronto 1962). Robert Holland's *Britain and the Commonwealth Alliance* (London 1982) is incomplete in its documentation and frequently inaccurate in its depiction of Canadian events. On Canadian attitudes abroad at this time see R.A. MacKay and E.B. Rogers, *Canada Looks Abroad* (Toronto 1938).

The basic account of the direction of Canada's war effort between 1939 and 1945 is C.P. Stacey, *Arms, Men, and Governments* (Ottawa 1970). Thorough and reliable, it is a starting point for all research on the period. Events during the war were covered by a series of admirable official histories; a recent resurgence of interest in World War Two has supplemented but not supplanted these so far as the army is concerned. The navy, however, is now seen in a different light: Marc Milner, *North Atlantic Run* (Toronto 1985), has expanded our knowledge of the stresses that war and convoy duty placed upon Canada's sailors. J.L. Granatstein, *Canada's War* (Toronto 1974), is readable and thorough. Robert Bothwell, *Eldorado* (Toronto 1984), deals with some of Canada's wartime atomic diplomacy. The same topic may also be viewed from the British side in Margaret Gowing's thorough and excellent study, *Britain and Atomic Energy* (London 1964); not all of her conclusions were accepted by Canadian participants in the atomic energy program. There is also a rare view of wartime Canada as seen by an American diplomat in N.H. Hooker, ed., *The Moffatt Papers* (Cambridge, Mass. 1956).

Canadian politicians are plentifully represented in the literature of biography. Sir Wilfrid Laurier's first biographer, O.D. Skelton, remains his best. Skelton's *Life and Letters of Sir Wilfrid Laurier* (Toronto 1921) stimulated the Winnipeg editor, J.W. Dafoe, to write an extended review; his *Laurier* (Toronto 1922) offers a useful contemporary commentary on Sir Wilfrid. Richard Clippingdale has written a fine popular biography: *Laurier: His Life and World* (Scarborough 1979). David Hall, *Clifford Sifton* (two volumes, Vancouver 1981, 1985), largely supersedes Dafoe's 1931 biography of his employer. H.B. Neatby, *Laurier and a Liberal Quebec* (Toronto 1973) is a convincing account of the way in which the Liberal party established its pre-eminence in that province under Laurier. Sir Robert Borden, unlike Laurier, wrote his own *Memoirs* in two volumes (Toronto 1938). They have been superseded by an excellent scholarly biography, R. Craig Brown's *Robert Laird Borden: a Biography* (two volumes, Toronto 1975, 1980). Borden's successor, Arthur Meighen, has been memorialized in a three-volume work by Roger Graham, *Arthur Meighen* (Toronto 1960-5).

William Lyon Mackenzie King can be studied either through his own words or through the prism of scholarly analyses. His invaluable diaries are available on microfiche at most large libraries. His former assistant, J.W. Pickersgill, with the assistance of D.F. Forster, edited a selection from his war-time diaries, and these were published as *The Mackenzie King Record* (four volumes, Toronto 1961-70). Work on an official biography was begun by R. MacGregor Dawson, who died with the project still incomplete, and was carried to completion by H.B. Neatby, whose *William Lyon Mackenzie King* (Toronto 1958, 1976) repays close study. C.P. Stacey, *Mackenzie King and the Atlantic Triangle* (Toronto 1976), is a perceptive survey of King's basic policies in foreign affairs. The same author's *A Very Double Life* (Toronto 1976) caused a storm of controversy when it appeared because of its unflattering conclusions about King's private life; while not all historians accept Stacey's conclusions, the book is nonetheless well written and interesting. Equally controversial is Joy Esberey, *Knight of the Holy Spirit* (Toronto 1980). There is no standard study of R.B. Bennett.

Among King's ministers, C.G. Power left behind an edited memoir, *A Party Politician* (Toronto 1966), which accurately reflects its author's charming but sometimes disorganized intelligence. *C.D. Howe: a Biography* (Toronto 1979), by Robert Bothwell and William Kilbourn, deals with King's powerful wartime supply minister. Paul Martin, King's secretary of state, has written two volumes of memoirs, *A Very Public Life* (Ottawa 1983, 1985), which give the reader a fascinating account of life in Ontario in the 1920s and 1930s, as seen from the point of view of a promising lawyer and professional politician. Vincent Massey was only briefly a politician, but his deep involvement in politics, diplomacy, and culture is traced by Claude Bissell in *The Young Vincent Massey* and *The Imperial Canadian* (Toronto 1981, 1986).

Party politics on the national level are represented by Reg Whitaker's excellent study of the national Liberals, *The Government Party* (Toronto 1977), and J.L. Granatstein's *The Politics of Survival: The Conservative Party of Canada 1939-1945* (Toronto 1967). An earlier period is covered in John English, *The Decline of Politics* (Toronto 1977). The CCF is treated in Walter Young's schematic and frequently unconvincing *The Anatomy of a Party* (Toronto 1969); more useful are David Lewis' autobiography *The Good Fight: Political Memoirs 1909-1958* (Toronto 1981), Desmond Morton's *Social Democracy in Canada* (Toronto 1977), and Ivan Avakumovic's *Socialism in Canada* (Toronto 1978). This is not an exhaustive list of works treating the CCF, which, despite its small size, has continued to fascinate historians and other intellectuals. Social Credit has been little studied as a national phenomenon; its significance is conveyed in J.R. Mallory's superb *Social Credit and the Federal Power in Canada* (Toronto 1954) and J.A. Irving, *The Social Credit Movement in Alberta* (Toronto 1959); C.B. Macpherson's *Democracy in Alberta* (Toronto 1953) is less useful for historians. William Rodney's *Soldiers of the International* (Toronto 1968) is a useful survey of communism's early period; for later developments see Ivan Avakumovic, *The Communist Party of Canada* (Toronto 1975).

Although there has recently been much greater interest in provincial politics than heretofore, the coverage in the literature is still uneven. Ernest Forbes' *The Maritime Rights Movement 1919-1927* (Montreal 1979) traces the history of a decade of Maritime discontent with what was perceived to be central Canadian domination. But the individual Maritime provinces have not been fully explored. There are several biographies of Nova Scotia's politicians, but none that should be mentioned here. New Brunswick has produced a lively but somewhat trivial book, *Front Benches and Back Rooms,* by Arthur T. Doyle (Toronto 1976), and Prince Edward Island has Wayne MacKinnon, *The Life of the Party* (Summerside 1973), on the Island's Liberals. Frank MacKinnon, *The Government of Prince Edward Island* (Toronto 1951), has much valuable information.

Information on Quebec is much more plentiful. There is an extraordinary series, Robert Rumilly's *Histoire de la Province de Québec* (Montreal 1940-69), in forty-one volumes; it is a variable but inescapable source of unattributed information. P.-A. Linteau, René Durocher, and J.-C. Robert have collaborated on two invaluable volumes, *L'Histoire du Québec contemporain 1867-1929* (Montreal 1979), which cover Quebec politically, economically, and socially. Susan Mann Trofimenkoff, *A Dream of Nation* (Toronto 1982), is less useful and less thorough in its coverage. Trofimenkoff's *L'Action nationale* (Toronto 1975) surveys a Quebec nationalist movement of the 1920s, whose leader, Lionel Groulx, has left his own *Mémoires* (four volumes, Montreal 1970-4). Georges-Emile Lapalme, later Liberal leader in Quebec, has written a charming and informative volume of *Memoires, Le bruit des choses reveillées* (Montreal 1969), which deals with his early political experiences.

There are numerous treatments of the Quebec Conservative party and its successor, the Union Nationale. Marc LaTerreur, *Les tribulations des conservateurs au Québec* (Quebec 1973), deals primarily with the federal branch of the party. Réal Bélanger has written very useful biographies of Conservative-Nationalists: *Paul-Emile Lamarche* (Quebec 1984) and *L'impossible défi: Albert Sévigny et les conservateurs fédéraux (1902-1918)* (Quebec 1983). Herbert Quinn, *The Union Nationale,* in several editions, deals with the ramifications of the party in an academic and rather remote fashion. To be preferred is Conrad Black's well-researched *Duplessis* (Toronto 1977). On the Liberal side there is Bernard Vigod, *Taschereau* (Montreal 1984), and Richard Jones, *Vers une hégémonie libérale* (Quebec 1980). Not to be omitted are T.-D. Bouchard's lively *Mémoires* (Montreal 1960). Denis Monière, *Ideologies in Quebec* (Toronto 1981), tells us more about the author's Marxist categories than about the ideas and events it purports to describe. Nonetheless, it received a Governor General's Award.

Ontario is similarly rich in the literature of political history. Robert Bothwell, *A Short History of Ontario* (Edmonton 1986), gives an overview of the province's history. Joseph Schull, *Ontario since 1867* (Toronto 1978), is better on events prior to 1900 than after; a lively supplement is Hector Charlesworth, *Candid Chronicles* and *More Candid Chronicles* (Toronto 1925, 1928). Charles Humphries, *Sir James Pliny Whitney* (Toronto 1985), adds considerably to our knowledge of Ontario before 1914. Peter Oliver, *Howard Ferguson, Ontario Tory* (Toronto 1977), presents a favourable view of the premier and his party in the 1920s. H.V. Nelles, *The Politics of Development* (Toronto 1974), is an invaluable description of public policy and its assumptions; Christopher Armstrong, *The Politics of Federalism* (Toronto 1981), outlines Ontario's relations with the federal government down to 1941.

West of Ontario the historical literature, like the population density, becomes thinner. Manitoba is covered in W.L. Morton's classic *Manitoba: A History* (second edition, Toronto 1977), but this book is less satisfying on events after 1920 than on the earlier period. D.J. Bercuson, *Confrontation at Winnipeg* (Montreal 1974), gives a strongly reasoned account of Winnipeg's labour history leading to the 1919 General Strike. G. Friesen, *The Canadian Prairies: A History* (Toronto 1984), is best on the early period. The standard history of Saskatchewan is John Archer, *Saskatchewan: A History* (Saskatoon 1980). Also valuable is David Smith, *Prairie Liberalism: The Liberal*

Party in Saskatchewan, 1905-1971 (Toronto 1975). Apart from the 1950s' works on Social Credit which were noted above, Alberta history has been little examined. British Columbia possesses a solid and well-written standard treatment in Margaret Ormsby's *British Columbia: A History* (Toronto 1958, 1971). There is also Martin Robin's *The Company Province* (two volumes, Toronto 1972, 1973), but it has been criticized for narrow focus and for occasional sloppiness.

The literature on the economic history of the period 1900-45 is dominated by questions of economic policy. The three general textbooks – W.T. Easterbrook and H.G.J. Aitken, *Canadian Economic History* (Toronto 1956), Richard Pomfret, *The Economic Development of Canada* (Toronto 1981), and W.L. Marr and D.G. Paterson, *Canada: an Economic History* (Toronto 1980) – are therefore unable to provide a complete coverage of actual economic events. Marr and Paterson include a valuable select bibliography, which should be used in conjunction with their notes. There is no other general bibliography beyond the lists in the *Canadian Historical Review*, which can be used to up-date Marr and Paterson.

Statistical material became a great deal more plentiful after the foundation of the Dominion Bureau of Statistics in 1918. A very high proportion of the Bureau's work was embedded in the *Canada Year Books*. The Bureau's entire output is listed and indexed in Statistics Canada, *Historical Catalogue of Statistics Canada Publications 1918-1980* (Ottawa 1982), which, in spite of its title, also lists pre-1918 materials. It was only during World War Two that the Bureau began to prepare national output, income, and expenditure accounts; annual estimates for each year since 1926, much revised since the wartime estimates, are in Statistics Canada, *National Income and Expenditure Accounts* (Ottawa 1976). In that the estimates for the period 1926-45 are revised from time to time, it is important not to depend on earlier publications for information about GNP and its components. For the years before 1926 there are private estimates, most notably those of O.J. Firestone, in *Canada's Economic Development 1867-1953* (Cambridge 1958). A team of economists at Queen's University has been elaborating new estimates for the period 1867-1926, but these are not yet published.

The financial adventures of the various governments are reported in appalling detail in the annual volumes of each government's *Public Accounts,* but these are obscure and specialized materials which the beginner should shun. Government tax and revenue policies are treated with magisterial thoroughness by J. Harvey Perry, *Taxes, Tariffs, and Subsidies* (two volumes, Toronto 1955), which does not attempt to provide a full treatment of expenditures, surpluses, and deficits.

Details of imports, exports, the balance of payments, and the balance of international indebtedness can all be found in various Bureau of Statistics publications. Specialized works on Canada's tariff policies are Douglas Annett, *British Preference in Canadian Commercial Policy* (Toronto 1948), O.J. McDiarmid, *Commercial Policy in the Canadian Economy* (Cambridge, Mass. 1946), and John Young, *Canadian Commercial Policy* (Ottawa 1957). J.H. Dales' important and influential work, *The Protective Tariff in Canada's Development* (Toronto 1966), may perplex non-economists.

The best general guide to monetary policies is still R.C. McIvor, *Canadian Monetary, Banking, and Fiscal Development* (Toronto 1958); see also Irving Brecher, *Monetary and Fiscal Thought and Policy in Canada 1919-1939* (Toronto 1957). For more detail on the evolution of financial institutions see E.P. Neufeld, *Bank of Canada Operations and Policy* (Toronto 1962) and *The Financial System of Canada* (Toronto 1972). There are numerous official histories of the banks and the other financial institutions. See in particular Merrill Denison, *Canada's First Bank* (Toronto 1966). But these works are uneven in coverage and uncertain in quality. Canada's trading and monetary policies of the 1930s have been treated by Ian Drummond in *Imperial Economic Policy 1917-1939* (London 1974) and *The Floating Pound and the Sterling Area* (Cambridge 1981); both books place Canada in a Commonwealth context. Two recent works attempt to cover the Bank of Canada and the Department of Finance: Douglas Fullerton, *Graham Towers and His Times* (Toronto 1986), and Robert Bryce, *Maturing in Hard Times* (Montreal 1986); Fullerton's is, however, a very limited treatment. The political and economic background of social policy is treated in James Struthers, *No Fault of Their Own* (Toronto 1983).

The periods of boom and slump, war and peace, have not all been studied in the same degree of detail. On the slump of the 1930s the standard work is A.E. Safarian, *The Canadian Economy in the Great Depression* (Toronto 1959; reissued Toronto 1970). World War One, World War Two, and the boom of the 1920s still await their economic historians, although some papers by H.A. Innis *(Essays in Canadian Economic History,* Toronto 1956) can usefully be consulted. The Wheat Boom of 1900-13 has given rise to a large literature. Many scholarly papers, as listed in the Marr and Paterson bibliography, have treated the process of prairie settlement. V.W. Fowke, in *The National Policy and the Wheat Economy* (Toronto 1957), has interpreted western adventures in a national context. C.A. Wilson, *A Century of Canadian Grain* (Saskatoon 1978), treats the marketing of prairie wheat, superseding such earlier treatments as that of MacGibbon. Comparatively little, however, has been written about urban and industrial development during the period 1900-30. On hydroelectricity in Quebec, see J.H. Dales, *Hydroelectricity and Economic Development* (Cambridge, Mass. 1957);

Nelles' *Politics of Development,* which was noted above, exemplifies the political and policy orientation that is not always informative with respect to actual economic developments. Electric development in British Columbia has been traced by Patricia Roy in several papers, most notably 'Direct Management from Abroad: the Case of the British Columbia Electric Railway,' *Business History Review,* 47:2 (1973). Merrill Denison, *The People's Power* (Toronto 1960), is a popular history of Ontario Hydro. On urban development, the *Urban History Review* is a source both of articles and of bibliographies. With encouragement from Ottawa, a series of illustrated urban histories is now appearing; see, for example, John C. Weaver, *Hamilton: An Illustrated History* (Toronto 1982), J.M.S. Careless, *Toronto to 1918* (Toronto 1983), James Lemon, *Toronto since 1918* (Toronto 1985), Alan Artibise, *Winnipeg: an Illustrated History* (Toronto 1977), and Patricia Roy, *Vancouver: An Illustrated History* (Toronto 1980). On Montreal, Paul-André Linteau's *Maisonneuve* (Montreal 1982) is essential.

Few Canadian manufacturing industries have been studied in any detail, but with respect to the iron and steel industry something can be gleaned from William Kilbourn, *The Elements Combined* (Toronto 1957); Merrill Denison's *Harvest Triumphant* (Toronto 1948), E.P. Neufeld's *A Global Corporation* (Toronto 1976), and W. Phillips' *The Agricultural Implement Industry in Canada* (Toronto 1956) all treat the farm equipment firms. Similarly, it is hard to find recent scholarly work on most components of the mining industries, although O.W. Main, *The Canadian Nickel Industry* (Toronto 1955), remains an excellent treatment. Foreign direct investment, which was important not only in mining but also in manufacturing, received its first scholarly examination in H.F. Marshall, F.A. Southard, and K.W. Taylor, *Canadian-American Industry* (New Haven 1936; reissued Toronto 1976), a work which is still of great value. The American perspective on external direct investment can be traced in the various works on Mira Wilkins.

In the past twenty years a great deal of work has been done on the history of labour. Much of this is embedded in the pages of specialized journals, such as *Labour/Le Travailleur* and *Histoire sociale/Social History,* but some has appeared in book form: see in particular Bryan Palmer, *A Culture in Conflict* (Montreal 1979). A different strand of labour history is represented by David Bercuson's *Confrontation at Winnipeg* (Montreal 1974) and R. Babcock, *Gompers in Canada* (Toronto 1974). In parallel with the work of the labour historians there has been a renewed interest in living standards. Two representative books are those of Michael Piva, *The Condition of the Working Class in Toronto 1900-1921* (Ottawa 1979), and Terry Copp, *The Anatomy of Poverty* (Toronto 1974). These treat the condition of the workers in Toronto and in Montreal. The former, it should be noted, has received some serious criticism for faulty research.

There has also been a new interest in the economic histories of the several Maritime provinces. Many contributions have appeared in the specialized regional journal, *Acadiensis,* whose reviews are a further guide to the regional literature.

Railways continue to attract scholarly interest. H.A. Innis' early work, *A History of the Canadian Pacific Railway* (London 1923; reissued Toronto 1971), is obscure and almost impossible to fathom. Fortunately it has been superseded for the general reader by W.K. Lamb, *History of the Canadian Pacific Railway* (New York 1977). Other railway histories are T.D. Regehr, *The Canadian Northern Railway* (Toronto 1976), A.W. Currie, *The Grand Trunk Railway of Canada* (Toronto 1957), G.R. Stevens, *Canadian National Railways* (two volumes, Toronto 1962), and J.F. Due, *The Interurban Electric Railway in Canada* (Toronto 1966). Other forms of transport, like many other Canadian industries, still await their historians.

Although the period 1900-45 is often depicted as increasingly materialistic in spirit, the intellectual and religious history of the period has attracted some of our finest historians. As we have mentioned above, the classic study of the ideas of Canadian imperialists is Carl Berger's *The Sense of Power* (Toronto 1970). Berger's *The Writing of Canadian History* (second edition, Toronto 1986) has a broader focus than its title implies. On Quebec see Serge Gagnon, *Le Québec et ses historiens de 1840 à 1920.* Intellectual life in the university is covered well in S.E.D. Shortt, *The Search for an Ideal* (Toronto 1976), and Brian McKillop, *A Disciplined Intelligence* (Montreal 1979). Ramsay Cook's award-winning *The Regenerators* (Toronto 1985) traces the career of diverse Canadians who responded in different ways to the waning of the age of faith. The ideas of the women's movement are discussed in Carol Bacchi, *Liberation Deferred* (Toronto 1983). Trends in Quebec at the same time are traced in Fernand Dumont et al., *Idéologies au Canada français, 1900-1929* (Quebec 1974). Thompson and Seager, *Canada 1921-1939,* noted above, has outstanding sections on culture, popular and otherwise.

Index

Aberdeen, Lord 113
Aberhart, William 265, 269-72, 275
Accurate News and Information Act
  (1937) 272
Action Libérale Nationale 268, 331
Adams, Thomas 103
Agriculture 2-6, 18, 56, 62-4, 70, 80-1,
  83, 169-70, 172-7, 195, 211, 213-19,
  221, 223-5, 246, 248-9, 252-5, 259,
  273, 276, 351, 360, 366-7, 370-3, 381,
  395, 398; and demography 2, 4, 18,
  56, 62, 170, 172, 211, 213-15, 246,
  295, 360-1, 398; exports 62, 68, 70,
  80, 169-70, 172, 174-7, 216, 218-19,
  221, 223, 224, 253, 361, 370;
  wheat 3, 6, 56, 62-5, 68, 80, 170,
  172-3, 175-7, 215-16, 221, 224, 248-9,
  252-4, 295, 370-2, 395
Air Force (Canadian). See Defence, air
  force
Aircraft 174-5, 346, 352, 356, 367-8
Aird, John 287
Aitken, Max (Lord Beaverbrook) 59,
  69-70, 74, 260, 396
Alaska Boundary 112, 117
Alberta 3, 38-9, 43, 60, 65, 158, 205,
  207-8, 218, 226, 230, 241, 259, 262,
  265, 267, 270-2, 275, 282, 355, 358
Alberta Nitrogen Company Ltd 359-60
Alberta Public Utility Commission 359

Alcock, John 199
Alderson, E.A.H. 142-3
Alger, Horatio 18
Algoma Steel 74
All Quiet on the Western Front
  (movie) 300
Allan, George 131
Allen, Richard 89
American Association for the
  Advancement of Science 201
American Federation of Labor (AFL).
  See Labour unions
American Labour Union 96
Amery, Leo 224
Ames, H.B. 15
Ames, Herbert 101
Amiens 149
'Amos 'n Andy' 285
Angell, Norman 155
Angus, Henry 265, 273, 293
Anti-Semitism 247, 299, 350
Army (Canadian). See Defence, army
Art Gallery of Ontario 290
Arts 187-8, 192-3, 196-7, 280-1, 286,
  290, 383-4; movies 192, 197, 280-1,
  289-90, 300, 383-4, 386
Asquith, H.H. 48, 145
Asselin, Olivar 100
Atholstan, Lord. See Graham, Hugh
Atkinson, Joseph 10

Atlantic Monthly 292
'L'Auberge des Chercheurs d'or'
    (radio) 288
Austria, annexation of 314
Automobile 2, 7, 9, 23, 66, 72, 74, 80-1,
    171-3, 195, 199-201, 208, 214-17,
    219, 224, 226, 241, 251-2, 258, 281,
    285, 290, 354, 375-7
Autonomy Bills 38, 44

Babcock, Robert 95
Balance of payments 180
Baldwin, Stanley 237
Balfour, Arthur 238
Balfour Report 238
Bank of British North America 79
Bank of Canada 73, 250, 273, 276, 319,
    349, 362-3
Bank of Commerce 77, 177-9, 287
Bank of Montreal 184
Bank of Nova Scotia 77
Banks. *See* Financial institutions
Banting, Frederick 293
Bastedo, Alf 154
Battle of the Atlantic 347-8
B.C. Electric Company 67
Beautiful Joe 191
Beaverbrook, Lord. *See* Aitken, Max
Beck, J. Murray 43
Bell Telephone Company of Canada 8,
    75-6
Bennett, Richard Bedford 243-4, 250,
    254, 256, 260-8, 272, 287, 295-7,
    301-3, 305-7
Bercuson, David 162
Berger, Carl 103
Bernhardt, Sarah 192
Berthiaume, Trefflé 10
Bessborough, Lord 291
Beynon, Frances 192
Birmingham, Robert 51
Birney, Earle 397
Black Friday (25 October 1929) 222,
    246
Blair, A.G. 38

Bliss, J.M. 174
Bloc Populaire 225, 331-2
Board of Commerce 176
Board of Grain Suppliers 175
Board of Trade 102
Boeing 356
Boer War 42, 45, 53, 108-12, 115, 120
Borden, Frederick 116
Borden, Robert Laird 38-9, 43-9, 53-4,
    93, 118-29, 131-4, 137, 140, 143,
    145-6, 152, 158, 163, 179, 202, 229,
    231, 235, 239, 300, 318
Bouchard, T.D. 331
Boundary Waters Treaty (1909) 114
Bourassa, Henri 38-9, 42, 45, 47-8, 50,
    54, 100, 123-4, 126, 131
Bourinot, John 187
Bracken, John 208, 262-4, 273, 276,
    328, 335
Bradbury, Bettina 18
Bren sub-machine gun 319
British and Canadian Theatre
    Organization Society 192
British Columbia 7, 10, 15, 27-8, 44-5,
    55, 57, 60-2, 64-6, 73, 75, 95-8, 125,
    158, 172, 175, 181, 203, 217-18, 226,
    254, 258, 262, 264-5, 277, 281-3, 300,
    317, 322, 325-6, 330, 355-8, 360-1,
    378, 382, 385-6, 393
British Columbia Electric Railway
    Company 79
British Columbia Federation of Labour.
    See Labour
British Commonwealth Air Training
    Plan (BCATP) 337, 345-6, 356, 361,
    375, 377
British Commonwealth of Nations 209,
    217, 229-30, 238, 313, 395-6
British Ministry of Food 370
British North America Act 25-35, 74,
    239-41, 243, 254, 262-3
Broadfoot, Barry 246
Brooke, Alan 342
Brown, Arthur 199
Brown, George 50

Brown, R. Craig 137
Brownlee, John 207-8
Bruce, S.M. 237
Bruchési, Archbishop 192
Bryce, James 102, 114
Buckley, Kenneth 219
Budget 34, 241, 262-4, 270, 272, 276, 296, 312, 351; federal 34, 241, 262, 276, 296, 312; provincial 34, 241, 263-4, 270, 272, 276
Burns, E.L.M. 148, 152
Burns, Tommy 196
Byng, Julian Lord 147, 206-7

CFCF (radio) 284
CJOR (radio) 288
CKAC (radio) 286, 288
CKWX (radio) 288
Caen 343
Cagney, James 290
Cahan, C.H. 303
Caisses Populaires. See Financial institutions
Calder, James 129
Caldwell, H.J. 318
Calgary Eyeopener 86
Callaghan, Morley 292
Campbell, Thane 277
'Canada Carries On' (NFB series) 384
Canada Cement Company 74
Canada Food Board 176
Canada Foundries 74
Canada Temperance Act 157
Canadian Aeroplanes Ltd. 175
Canadian Airways 356
Canadian and Catholic Conference of Labour. See Labour
Canadian Bankers Association 182
Canadian Broadcasting Corporation (CBC) 276, 286-8, 384, 387
Canadian Congress of Labour (CCL). See Labour
Canadian Council of Agriculture 134
Canadian Expeditionary Force. See Defence, army

Canadian Federation of Labour. See Labour unions
Canadian Forum 280, 297, 301, 304
Canadian General Electric 74, 79
Canadian Historical Review 280
Canadian Industries Limited (CIL) 272, 356, 359
Canadian Institute of International Affairs (CIIA) 299-300, 306
Canadian League of Nations Society 300, 306
Canadian Manufacturers' Association 94, 382
Canadian Marconi Company 284
Canadian Mercury 280
Canadian National Exhibition 289
Canadian National Railways 178, 241, 284, 286, 356
Canadian Northern Railway 64, 66, 76, 79, 177-9
Canadian Pacific Railway (CPR) 3, 7, 55, 64, 66, 76, 86, 96
Canadian Radio Broadcasting Commission 287
Canadian Radio League 287
Canadian Socialist League 95
Canadian Westinghouse 74, 79
Canadian Wheat Board 177, 215, 254, 372-3
Cape Breton Island 55, 62, 68-9
Capitalism 18-22, 69, 87, 187, 259
Cardin, J.A. 286, 319, 325, 333
Carnegie, Andrew 189
Carr, Emily 291
Carson, Sara Libby 101
Carstairs, J.S. 51
Cartwright, Richard 38
Carvell, Frank 129
Censorship 190, 196, 272, 280, 322, 384-5
Census (1901) 1, 3-4, 10, 188-9, 193, 195, 215; (1911) 146, 158, 189, 215; (1921) 136, 158, 189, 212, 215; (1931) 212-13, 215, 258; (1941) 258, 360-1

Chamberlain, Joseph 115-17, 223
Chamberlain, Neville 313-15
Chanak Crisis 205, 235, 237
Chapais, Thomas 192
Charlesworth, Hector 287
Chinese Immigration Act (1923) 213
Chown, S.D. 132
Christie, Loring 229-36, 300, 309-10, 314
Churchill, Winston 48, 199, 235, 340-1
Citizens Committee of One Thousand 166
Clark, C.S. 16-18
Clark, Michael 230
Clark, S.D. 3
Clarke, E.F. 51
Claxton, Brooke 276, 293, 329-30, 334, 391
Coal. See Natural resources
Cockfield, Brown (advertising) 334
Cody, H.J. 131
Combine Investigation Act 257
Combined Food Board 368
Commission of Conservation 103
Committee of Imperial Defence 48
Commonwealth. See British Commonwealth of Nations
Communications 8, 10, 23, 34, 75-6, 187-9, 195, 197, 222, 248, 260, 267, 272, 276, 279, 283-94, 297-8, 322, 329, 341, 384-7; books 190-1, 195-7, 279-80, 291; broadcasting 8, 197, 251, 260, 267, 276, 283-90, 329, 341, 384, 387, 396; newspapers 10, 16, 23, 187-9, 195, 222, 248, 272, 284, 297-8, 322, 385, 396; telegraph 8, 23, 189; telephone 8, 9, 75-6
Communism 89, 163-4, 246, 257, 280, 315, 381, 385-6
Communist Party of Canada 315
Concerts Symphoniques de Montréal 289
Conference on the Operation of Dominion Legislation (CODL). See Imperial Conference, 1929

Congress of Industrial Organization (CIO). See Labour
Connaught, Prince Arthur of 113
Connor, Ralph. See Gordon, Charles
Conscription 123, 126-8, 131-2, 134, 146-7, 159, 163-4, 202, 298, 315, 318, 320, 323-5, 331-5, 378-9
Conservative party 39-53, 91, 97, 120-1, 125, 137, 202-7, 225, 234, 241, 243, 254, 259-61, 264-9, 307, 317, 321-3, 325-6, 328-31, 334; federal 39-40, 42-50, 53, 125, 202-3, 205-6, 243; provincial 39-40, 44-5, 51-2, 91, 125, 135, 158, 204-5, 241, 260, 264-6, 268-9, 326, 331
Consolidated Mining and Smelting (COMINCO) 359
Constitution 25, 30, 206-7, 229, 235, 239-40, 242-3, 259, 263, 267, 273, 275-6, 390, 397. See also British North America Act
Construction 63, 67, 223, 250-1, 351-5, 375
Cook, Ramsay 137
Coolidge, Calvin 200
Co-operative Commonwealth Federation (CCF) 262, 264, 267, 293, 312, 317-18, 322-6, 328-30, 335, 390; provincial 324-6, 330
Cotes, Mrs Everard. See Duncan, Sara Jeanette
Cottrelle, George 358
Craig, Grace Morris 153-4
Credit unions. See Financial institutions
Crerar, Harry 342-4
Crerar, Thomas A. 129, 134-6, 202-4
Crime rates 156
Crone Moving and Storage 289
Crowe, Eyre 237
Crown lands 28, 64, 70, 73, 241
Crowsnest Pass Rates 76
Culture 32, 40, 44, 101, 153, 187-9, 191-7, 200-1, 279-94
Currie, Arthur 143, 148-9, 178-9
Curtis, Lionel 118

Curzon, Lord 233, 237
Czechoslovakia, partition of 314-15

D-Day (6 June 1944) 340-3
Dafoe, John W. 128, 273, 297, 311
Dalhousie University 194, 273
Dangerfield, George 389
Darwin, Charles 201
Dawson, R. MacGregor 230
Deficit 34, 169, 179-80, 223, 273, 276,
  296, 363-4
Defence 34, 45-8, 50, 111-12, 116,
  139-52, 311-12, 296, 299, 332-3,
  336-48, 375, 379-80, 386; air
  force 296, 312, 336-7, 345-8, 375;
  army 116, 140-2, 144-5, 147-52, 179,
  296, 312, 336-7, 339, 341-4, 348, 375,
  379, 386; Canadian Corps 147-9,
  151; Canadian Expeditionary Force
  (World War I) 122, 126, 142, 144-5,
  147-51, 319, 322, 337, 365; Great
  Britain and 111-12, 169; navy 45-8,
  50, 296, 336-8, 347-8, 375;
  Newfoundland Regiment 144;
  policy 116; 13th Royal
  Highlanders 146; 16th Canadian
  Scottish 146; 46th Battalion (South
  Saskatchewan) 145-6; 58th Ontario
  Battalion 146
Defence Industries Limited 356
de la Roche, Mazo 292
de Lotbinière, Henri Joly 38
Demography 1-4, 11, 14, 17-18, 40,
  55-8, 60-2, 65, 189, 212-13, 215, 241,
  247-8, 280, 282, 312, 337, 350, 360,
  379-80, 397-8; census (1901) 1, 10,
  13, 17, 62, 65, 215, 247-8; (1911) 65,
  215, 247; (1921) 61-2, 65, 212, 215;
  (1931) 212-13, 215, 247;
  (1941) 247-8, 360-1
Dent (publisher) 291
Department of Agriculture (US) 368
Departments, federal: Department of
  External Affairs 113-15, 231, 236,
  295-7, 300-2, 309, 349, 362;

Department of Finance 183-4, 220,
  222-3, 250, 271, 349, 354, 362, 390;
  Department of Labour (Labour
  Department) 94, 181, 239, 272, 358,
  382; Department of Marine and
  Fisheries 284, 286; Department of
  Munitions and Supply 322, 351-4,
  359, 367, 378, 385, 392; Department
  of National Defence 242, 256, 311,
  319; Department of National Health
  and Welfare 330, 391; Department
  of National War Services 379;
  Department of Reconstruction 330,
  391; Department of Soldiers Civil
  Re-establishment 151; Department
  of the Secretary of State 115, 117,
  303; Department of Trade and
  Commerce 349-50; Department of
  Veterans Affairs 330-91; Dominion
  Bureau of Statistics 219;
  Intercolonial Railway 75, 178;
  National Selective Service 358;
  Pensions and National Health 319;
  Post Office 75, 190; Public Works
  Department 75
Depression (1913-15) 161, 167, 169,
  170; (1920-2) 171, 185, 218-19;
  (1930s) 216, 220-3, 246-59, 261, 273,
  281, 290-3, 295, 335, 349
Desrosiers, Leo-Paul 292
Dewey, John 195
Dieppe 341-2
Dollar 181-4, 220, 361, 364-5, 369, 395
Dominion Arsenal 174
Dominion Bureau of Statistics. See
  Departments, federal
Dominion Mortgage and Investments
  Association 371
Dominion Notes Act 73
Dominion Securities 74
Dominion Stores 211
Dominions Office (Great Britain) 297,
  301
Dressler, Marie 289
Drew, George 320-1, 326

Drury, E.C. 135-6
Duncan, Sara Jeanette 103, 191
Dunning, C.A. 204, 271
Dunsmuir, James 93
Duplessis, Maurice 268-9, 274, 277, 299, 319-21, 331-2

Eastern Air Command (RCAF) 345
Eaton's 5, 9, 74, 211
Ecole des Hautes Etudes Commerciales 282
Economist, The 297-8
Economy 55-84, 169-72, 187, 211-27, 241, 246-77, 349-73, 389; Great Boom (1900-13) 55-84, 104, 211, 220. *See also* Depression
Education 27, 32-3, 43-4, 91, 124, 126, 187, 189, 193-6, 226-7, 258, 264, 281-3, 292-3, 331, 349; bilingual schools issue 91, 124-6; provincial responsibility 27, 124, 126, 195, 227, 281; separate schools, and 91, 195; universities 33, 101, 193-4, 258, 264, 281-3, 292-3, 296, 349
Edward VIII 288, 311
Edwards, Bob 86
Einstein, Albert 199, 201
Elections (1891) 41; federal: (1896) 41; (1900) 41-2; (1904) 41, 43, 47, 49; (1908) 41, 44, 47, 49; (1911) 41, 43, 49, 54, 122-3, 134; (1917) 131-2, 208, 229; (1921) 136, 202-3, 208, 226, 235; (1926) 207-8, 227; (1930) 260-2, 298; (1935) 263, 267-8, 298-9; (1940) 274, 321, 323; (1945) 334-5; provincial: Alberta (1921) 136, 208; (1935) 265; BC (1928) 264; (1933) 264; (1941) 325; Manitoba (1922) 136; (1916) 158; (1932) 264; (1936) 264; Nova Scotia (1925) 205; Ontario (1919) 135; (1943) 326, 329; Quebec (1936) 269, 299; (1939) 274, 319-20, 323; (1944) 331-2; Saskatchewan

(1938) 271-2; (1944) 330
Eliot, Charles 201
Elizabeth, Queen Mother 272, 315
Emergency Coal Production Board 358
Emigration 55-6, 58, 212
Ethiopia (invasion of) 305, 307-10
Exchange controls. *See* Foreign Exchange Control Board
Excise revenues 28, 180, 223, 225
Exports. *See* Trade
External Affairs. *See* Departments, federal; Great Britain, foreign policy

Falaise Gap (Battle of) 344
Family allowances 293, 329, 375, 391, 396-7. *See also* Mothers' allowances
Famous Players (theatre chain) 290
Farmers movements 134-7, 167
Farthing, J.C. 132
Fascism 231, 247, 301, 305, 315, 331, 385-6. *See also* Nazis
Federal-provincial relations 25-32, 90, 239-46, 262, 265, 268-75, 277, 287, 293, 301, 317, 396-7; conferences: (1927) 241-3; (1934) 266; (1941) 274-5; (1945) 397
Ferguson, Howard 124, 205, 242-3, 297
Fielding, W.S. 38, 46, 204, 238
'Fighting Navy' (radio) 384
Finance Act (1914) 183-4, 220, 223
Financial institutions 19-20, 27-9, 33, 73-4, 77, 80, 174, 180, 182-4, 211, 214, 216, 218, 220-3, 240, 249-50, 253-4, 263-4, 270-1, 363; banks 19-20, 27, 73-4, 77, 174, 182-4, 211, 214, 216, 218, 220-3, 240, 249-50, 253-4, 263-4, 270-1, 363; caisses populaires 77; and capitalism 20; credit unions 77; insurance companies 29, 33, 74, 77, 180, 363; securities 74, 77, 218-19, 221-2, 270-1; trust and mortgage companies 28, 33, 74, 77-80, 180
Financial Post 305, 312, 385
Finlayson, Rod 266

First World War. *See* World War I

Fisher, Sydney 14

Fisheries. *See* Natural resources

Fitzgerald, F. Scott 199-200, 280

Flavelle, Joseph 45, 54, 89, 162, 174

Flett, John 94-5, 98

Ford of Canada 72, 74, 79, 219

Ford, Henry 23

Foreign Exchange Control 362-4, 375

Forestry. *See* Natural resources

Forke, Robert 204

Forsey, Eugene 293

Forum (Montreal) 286

Foster, George 45, 133, 164

Fowke, V.F. 370-1

Franchise 30. *See also* Womens' issues

Franco, Francisco 310

Fraser, W.A. 191

Fred Victor Mission 101

Freemasons. *See* Religion

French, John 144

French Canada 43-7, 50, 90, 100, 120, 122-6, 128, 131-2, 136, 155, 190, 194, 202-5, 212, 268-9, 286, 299-300, 306-7, 310, 315, 317, 323-5, 331-3, 335, 398

Freud, Sigmund 23, 193, 199-200

Froebel, Friedrich 195

'Fu Manchu' 286

Fussell, Paul 153

Gable, Clark 290

Galbraith, John Kenneth 59

General Motors 257, 285, 355-6

George V 230, 305

George VI 272, 311, 315

George, David Lloyd 127, 145, 231-6

Germany 110, 140-50, 175, 224, 231-2, 239, 259, 288, 295-6, 304-5, 310, 313-15, 326, 332, 334, 337, 341-8, 362, 370, 375, 384; air force 305; army 120, 140, 142-5, 147-9, 326, 332, 337, 341-5; navy 110, 144, 150, 175, 232, 345, 347-8, 375

Ghosts 193

Gilbert, Arthur 45

Ginger Group 204-5

Glengarry School Days 191

Godbout, Adélard 320, 331-2

Goering, Hermann 313

Gold 362, 365-6

Gold standard 181-4, 211, 220, 250, 362

Goldie and McCulloch 20

Gompers, Samuel 94-6, 98-9, 163

Gone with the Wind 292

Gordon, Charles 21, 55, 87, 91, 98, 105, 155, 161, 190-1, 196

Gordon, Donald 371

Gouin, Lomer 204

Gouin, Paul 268

Governor general 26, 113, 206-7

Graham, Hugh 10, 53

Grand Trunk Pacific 66-7, 76, 79, 177-9

Grand Trunk Railway 66, 76, 94, 177-9

Gray, Charles F. 166-7

Gray, James 89, 156, 255

Graydon, Gordon 321

Great Britain 26, 29, 35, 41, 46-8, 108, 110-13, 115-18, 139-50, 169, 179, 184, 191, 205, 223-5, 229-39, 243, 249, 259, 295-7, 302, 305-6, 312-14, 336-48, 350, 357, 361, 364-7, 370-1, 378, 394-6; army 139-40, 144-5, 147-9, 298, 305, 339-45; British Expeditionary Force (BEF) 139-40, 144-5, 147-9; Colonial Office 111-13, 233; foreign policy and Canada 41, 43, 46-8, 230-9, 243, 302, 312, 336; imperial affairs 115-16, 118, 229-30, 233-9, 301-2, 305-6, 312; legal relations with Canada 26-9, 35, 230-1, 233-5, 237-8, 243, 312, 367; Royal Air Force 338, 341-2, 346, 348; Royal Navy 110-11, 233-4, 341, 347; trade relations with Canada 4-6, 108, 169, 173-4, 184, 223-5, 249, 296, 350, 363-6, 371, 394-6

Green, Lorne 384

Grey, Lord 113-14

Grey Owl 292

Grierson, John 290, 383-4
Gross National Product (GNP) 219, 223, 246, 352
Groulx, Lionel 293
Group of Seven 290-1
Grove, Frederick Philip 280
Gwatkin, Willoughby 140

Haig, Field Marshal Douglas 144, 148
Halifax Theatre Arts Guild 291
Hamilton Herald 10
Hamilton Philharmonic Society 17
Hankey, Maurice 306, 313
Hanna, W.J. 176
Hanson, R.B. 321
'Happy Gang, The' (radio) 288
Harlow, Jean 290
Hart, John 275, 325
Hart House (U of T) 291
Hassell, 'Uncle Billy' 288
Hawley-Smoot tariff 225
Health insurance 75, 101, 185, 202, 226, 293, 330, 390, 397
Heaps, Abraham 206, 227
Hearst, William 158
Hemingway, Ernest 199
Henry, George 265
Henshaw, Julia N. 191
Henty, G.A. 119
Hepburn, Mitchell F. (Mitch) 256-7, 266-9, 273-5, 277, 317-20, 323-4, 326
Herridge, W.D. 266, 296, 297, 301
Hertzog, J.B.M. 238
Hewitt, Foster 285
Hewitt, John 51
Hitler, Adolf 274, 304-6, 311, 313-15, 344, 364, 381, 384, 393
Hocken, H.C. 44
'Hockey Night in Canada' 285-6
Home Bank 214, 221
Hoover, Herbert 259, 296
Hopkins, J. Castell 191
Houde, Camillien 385
House of Commons 26, 30, 206-8, 230, 241, 260, 272, 311-12, 317-18, 321,

324, 328
Housing 31, 63, 67, 85, 219, 250-1, 330, 375
Howard University 194, 201
Howe, C.D. 287, 329-30, 334, 351, 353-8, 360, 390-4, 397
Howland, O.A. 101
Hudson Bay Railway 204-5
Hudson's Bay Company 28, 64, 74
Hughes, Sam 42, 119, 122-4, 140-3, 152, 319
Hughes, W.M. 232
Hughson, J.E. 156
Hutton, Maurice 193
Hyde Park Agreement (1941) 354, 364-7, 369, 395
Hydro Québec 331

Ibsen, Henrik 193
Ilsley, J.L. 274-5, 334
Immigration 2, 40, 49, 55, 57, 58, 61, 63, 82, 205, 211-14, 241, 246, 290, 299, 350, 397-8
Immigration Act (1906) 56; (1910) 58, 166-7
Imperial Conference (1921) 232-5; (1923) 236-8; (1926) 238, 243; (1929) 243; (1930) 243; (1937) 311-13; (1944) 340
Imperial Munitions Board 162, 174-5, 353
Imperial Oil 358
Imperial War Cabinet 223, 232
Imperial War Conference 230
Imperialist, The 191
Imports. *See* Trade
Income Tax. *See* Taxation
Indians 31-2, 248
Industrial Canada 94
Industrial Disputes Investigation Act (1907) (IDI) 98, 381-2
International Joint Commission 112, 114; Alaska Boundary 112; Boundary Waters 114
Inflation 162, 176, 181, 183-4, 362, 373,

380, 391, 396
Innis, Harold 293
Insurance companies. *See* Financial
  institutions
Intercolonial Railway 7, 75, 178, 241
International Brigades (Spanish Civil
  War) 310
International Labour Organization. *See*
  Labour
International Monetary Conference
  (Bretton Woods) 394
International Monetary Fund 394
International Wheat Agreement
  (1933) 249
Inventions 4, 188
Investments 63, 66, 78-9, 169-70, 211,
  218-21, 250-1; American 78-9, 211,
  218, 221; British 78-9;
  domestic 169-70, 218-21, 250-1;
  value of 63, 78-9, 219-21, 250-1

'Jack Benny' 285
Jackson, Gilbert 222
Jalna 292
James, Henry 193
Jazz Age 199, 208
Jews 247-8, 299, 304, 350, 397
Joint Economic Committees (Canada-
  US) 367
Joint War Production Committee
  (Canada-US) 367
Judicial Committee of the Privy
  Council 26, 29, 124, 230
Jury, Alfred 51

Kealey, Gregory 51
Keefer, Thomas 6, 7
Kelly, Thomas 52
Kerr, Philip 117-18
Keynes, John Maynard 250, 276, 362,
  396
Kidd, Bob 334
Kindred of the Wild, The 191
King, William Lyon MacKenzie 16, 39,
  93, 94, 98, 100, 105, 117, 136-7,

200-7, 209, 222, 224, 227, 235-9,
  241-2, 259-63, 266-9, 271-5, 287, 296,
  299, 301, 307, 310-15, 317-26,
  329-30, 332-5, 339-41, 350-1, 358,
  366, 372, 381, 387, 389, 390-2
Kipling, Rudyard 119
Kitchener, H.H. 110, 140
Knights of Labour 95-6

Labour 75, 81-2, 87, 93-100, 129, 132-3,
  136-7, 161-7, 202, 211, 231, 256-8,
  350-1, 354, 356-8, 360-1, 367, 373,
  378-83; American Federation of
  Labor (AFL) 94-6, 163; British
  Columbia Federation of Labour 163;
  Canadian and Catholic
  Confederation of Labour 167;
  Canadian Congress of Labour
  (CCL) 382; Canadian Federation of
  Labour 100; Congress of Industrial
  Organization (CIO) 257;
  International Labour
  Organization 231, 239-40; Knights of
  Labour 95-6; Trades and Labour
  Congress (TLC) 95-6, 98, 100, 163-5,
  167, 382; United Brotherhood of
  Railway Employees 96; Western
  Federation of Miners 96; Western
  Labour Conference 165; Workers
  Unity League 257
Labour party 135
Laliberté, Alfred 291
Lambert, Norman 324, 329
Langford, Sam 196
LaPalme, Robert 291
Lapointe, Ernest 124, 201, 204, 209,
  242, 269, 272, 299, 310, 314-15,
  319-20, 323
La Presse 10, 53, 189
Laurendeau, André 331
Laurier, Wilfrid 13, 18, 35, 37-9, 42-3,
  45-7, 49, 51, 53-4, 56, 76, 90, 93,
  112-14, 120-1, 123-9, 131, 136, 192,
  200, 202-3, 236, 296, 318
Laut, Agnes C. 191

Law, Andrew Bonar 236
Law 25-6
Leacock, Stephen 54, 85-7, 99-100, 102-5, 159, 190
League for Social Reconstruction 293
League of Nations 209, 231-2, 238-9, 295, 300, 302-3, 305-7, 309-11
Le Devoir 48
Lemieux, Rodolphe 57
Lend-Lease 364
Lenin, V.I. 199
Les Engagés du Grand Portage 292
Liberal party 38-42, 44-5, 49, 91, 97, 113, 120-1, 123, 125, 137, 185, 200, 202-7, 225-6, 234-6, 239-41, 256, 259-61, 263-9, 272, 293, 298-9, 307, 312, 317-18, 320, 322-6, 328-30, 332, 334, 389; federal 38-9, 42, 44, 49, 185, 200, 202-3, 206, 226, 267, 269, 298, 318, 323, 326, 334; provincial 39, 53, 91, 123, 125, 135, 158, 203-5, 207, 241, 256, 263-6, 268-9, 272, 298-9, 318, 320, 322, 325-6, 330, 332
Liberalism 38, 42, 45, 54, 112
Libraries 189-90, 293
Lieutenant-governors 29, 272
'Life Can Be Beautiful' (radio) 288
Lippmann, Walter 200
Literacy 188-90, 192, 195-7, 281
Literature 187, 189-93, 279
Loblaws 211
London Civic Orchestra 289
London Daily Express 396
Longboat, Tom 196
Longmans (publisher) 291
Lord's Day Act 87, 92
Low, G.J. 12
Luftwaffe 275
Lynd, Helen 279
Lynd, Robert 279
Lytton Report (on Manchuria) 303

'Ma Perkins' (radio) 288
'MacAdam shovel' 140
MacDonald, Angus L. 276
MacDonald, John A. 29, 42, 108, 202
MacDonald, Malcolm 313
MacDonald, Ramsay 201
MacDonald, Wilson 285
MacFarland, John A. 254
Mackenzie, Ian 311, 314, 319, 330, 390-1
MacKenzie, R. Tait 291
MacKenzie, William 64, 77, 179
Mackenzie-Papineau Batallion (in Spain) 310
Mackintosh, W.A. 397
Maclean, A.K. 129
MacMechan, Archibald 280-1
MacMillan, Ernest 289
MacMillan, H.R. 355-7
Macmillan of Canada (publisher) 291-2
Macphail, Agnes 208
Macphail, Andrew 120, 193
Manchuria 302-4
Manion, Robert 315, 318, 321
Manitoba 3, 7, 28, 44, 52, 56, 91, 125, 132, 158, 203, 207-8, 226, 241, 259, 262-4, 267, 273-4, 328, 355
Manitoba Bridge and Iron 356
Manitoba Free Press 128, 193
Mann, C.C. 342
Mann, Donald 64, 77, 179
Manufacturing 2, 18-19, 61, 63, 68, 70, 72-80, 170-1, 174-6, 204, 211, 217, 225, 248, 251, 284, 295, 352-60, 366, 371, 379; and demography 2, 18, 61, 68, 217-18, 224
Maple Leaf Gardens 286
Marconi, Guglielmo 8, 23
Maritime Chamber of Commerce 392
Maritime provinces 7, 14, 21-2, 30, 52, 56, 60, 65, 68-9, 172, 203-4, 215, 241-2, 323, 326, 360
Maritime Rights 205, 242
Marler, Herbert 296, 301
Marr, William 79

Marsh, Leonard 390
Marsh Report (on social security) 390
Martin, Paul 317-18
Marx, Karl 104, 310
Marx Brothers 192
Massey, Alice 296
Massey, Vincent 238, 291, 296, 301
Massey, W.F. 232
Materials Coordinating Committee 367
McBride, Richard 45
McClelland and Stewart
    (publisher) 292
McClung, Nellie 90, 92-3, 154, 157-8,
    161, 208
McGill Fortnightly Review 280
McGill University 15, 153, 194, 199,
    293
McGreer, Gerry 265
McLaughlin, Sam 2
McNair, R. 276-7
McNaughton, A.G.L. 306, 319, 333-4,
    337, 341
Medicare. *See* Health insurance
Meighen, Arthur 135-7, 158, 166, 202,
    205-7, 227, 231-6, 300, 306, 324, 335
Merchant's Bank 184
Merchant's Bank of Halifax 77
Métis 31, 248
Mid-West Aircraft 356
Military Service Act 128, 147
Military Voters' Act 128, 158
Miller, J.O. 159
Milne, David 291
Milner, Lord 118, 223
Mining. *See* Natural resources
Minto, Lord 113
Mitchell, Humphrey 323
Mitchell, Walter 204
Molson's Bank 184
Money. *See* Dollar
Monk, Frederick 44-5, 47-8, 123
Mons 149-50
Montgomery, Bernard 341-2, 345
Montreal Canadiens 286
Montreal *Gazette* 392

Montreal Light, Heat and Power 331
Montreal Maroons 286
Montreal Reform Club 392
Montreal *Star* 10-12, 53, 189, 320
Moore, Tom 165
Moose Jaw *Evening Times* 139
Moral and Social Reform Council of
    Canada (1907) 87, 91
Morgan's 74
Morris, Basil 154
Morris, Ramsey 154
Morton, W.L. 134, 208
Mothers' allowances 208-9, 226-7
Mountbatten, Lord Louis 341
Movies 200, 208, 211. *See also* Arts
Mowat, Oliver 38
Mulock, William 94
Munitions and Supply Act 353
Murray, George 129
Murray, Gladstone 287
Mussolini, Benito 231, 305
'Mutual Aid' plan (financial) 365-6

National Adjustment Grants 273
National Council of Women 92-3
National Employment Commission 272
National Employment Service 380-1
National Film Board 290, 383-4, 387
National Gallery of Canada 290
National Government party 321
National Research Council 282
National Transcontinental Railway 66,
    68, 76, 177-8
National War Labour Board 391
Nationalists (Quebec) 45-8, 50, 122-4,
    127; Nationalist-Conservative
    Alliance 45, 48, 122-3
Natural Products Marketing Act
    (1934) 254
Natural resources 28-9, 34, 66, 68-70,
    72, 99, 170-1, 205, 211, 214, 217-19,
    225, 252, 264, 351-3, 355-6, 358-60,
    368, 369, 394; coal 357-8;
    fisheries 66, 68, 72, 264; forest
    products 66, 72, 170, 217-19, 225,

252-3, 255, 356-7; mining 66, 68, 72, 99, 170-1, 195, 211, 214, 217-19, 252-3, 264, 292, 357, 368, 393-4; oil 69, 171, 218, 353, 358, 360

Natural Resources Mobilization Act (1940) 378-9

Navy (Canadian). *See* Defence, navy

Naylor, Joe 163

'Nazaire et Barnabé' 286

Nazis 301, 304-5, 384, 386

Neatby, Blair 204-5, 222, 236

Nelles, H.V. 102

New Brunswick 26, 32, 76, 132, 158, 203, 241, 260, 282-3, 355, 358, 385

New York Central Railroad 178

New York Stock Exchange 246

New Yorker 297-8

Newfoundland 8, 27, 68, 199, 347

Newfoundland Regiment 144

Nighbor, Frank 196

Normandy invasion. *See* D-Day

Norris, T.C. 158

Northway, John 20

North-West Territories 3, 7, 28, 43, 56, 60

Noseworthy, Joe 324

Nova Scotia 10, 21, 26, 32, 68, 132, 158, 204-5, 217, 226, 241, 282, 361

O'Donoghue, D.J. 51

Office of Defence Transportation (US) 368

Office of Price Administration (US) 368

Oil. *See* Natural resources

Old-Age Pension Act (1927) 227

Old-age pensions 31, 75, 185, 202, 206, 208, 211, 226-7, 241, 263, 274, 329

'On to Ottawa' Trek 256-7

Ontario 3, 4, 7-10, 15, 21, 27-9, 32, 38-9, 42-3, 45-7, 50, 55, 60-1, 65-6, 69, 94-5, 102, 124-5, 132, 135, 158-9, 172-4, 188, 191, 202-5, 207, 214-18, 226, 242, 251, 256-7, 262, 265-8, 273, 275, 282, 300, 317, 321, 323, 326, 333, 354, 357-8, 360, 382, 385-6, 393;

agriculture 3, 4, 132, 135, 172, 214-17, 268; demography 3, 15, 60-1, 65, 69, 75, 102, 215; education and 124, 226, 282; French language rights 124; labour and 94-5, 251; provincial governments 38-9, 135, 256, 265, 268, 317, 321

Ontario Hydro 102, 226, 268

Ontario Research Foundation 282

Orange Sentinel 51

Orders-in-Council 351

Ottawa Little Theatre 291

Oxford University 194, 201, 296

Oxford University Press 291

Oxley, J. Macdonald 191

Pacific Great Eastern Railway 265

Pacifism 300-1, 312

Paget, Bernard 342

Palmer, Bryan 97

Panneton, Philippe 292

Paris Peace Conference 199, 207, 230, 232

Parker, Gilbert 190-2

Parliament 26, 239-40, 260, 315-16, 318, 322-3, 329-30, 332-3, 351, 396

Passchendaele 147-8

Paterson, Donald 79

Patronage 44, 51-3, 69, 75, 122, 131, 135, 140, 159

Patterson, G. 277, 330

Pattullo, Duff 264-5, 269, 275, 277, 317, 325

Pearl, Bert 288

Pearson, Lester B. 276, 296-7, 301, 311

Pellan, Alfred 291

Pelletier, Wilfrid 289

Pensions 30, 75, 223, 226-7, 241, 293; teachers and civil servants 75; veterans and war disabilities 150, 223, 226. *See also* Old-age pensions

Perley, George 143, 267

Perry, J. Harvey 241

Petroleum coordinator (US) 368

Pickersgill, Jack W. 276, 329, 334

Pickford, Mary 200, 289
Pierce, Sydney 367, 369
Plebiscite on conscription (1942) 324-5
Plumptre, Wynne 367, 369
Poland (invasion of) 315
Police Gazette 190
Polymer 354
Pope, Joseph 57, 114-15
Pope, Maurice 340
Population. *See* Demography
Power, C.G. 268, 298, 314, 319-20,
    324-5, 329, 331, 333, 340
Presbyterians. *See* Religion
Prices and wages 169, 171, 173, 175-7,
    181-3, 188, 214-17, 219, 221, 248-9,
    252, 257, 370-1, 375-6
Prince Edward Island 27-8, 34, 69, 75,
    132, 158, 181, 226, 241, 282
Progressive party 135-6, 202-8, 230,
    248, 259-60, 262
Prohibition 86, 89, 90-2, 100, 131,
    135-6, 150, 156-7, 159, 161, 168, 208,
    226, 241, 280; provinces and 90-2,
    135-6, 156-7, 226, 241
Protestants. *See* Religion
Province of Canada 26
Public Accounts Committee
    (Quebec) 268-9
Public opinion 298, 322-3, 325-6,
    329-30, 334, 383, 386-7, 389, 391;
    Gallup poll 322, 325-6, 329
Public works 223, 262, 396
Purvis, Arthur 272-3
Putnam, J.H. 281

Quebec 3-4, 7-8, 10, 15, 21, 25, 27, 30,
    32, 38-9, 42-3, 45-8, 50, 55-6, 60-1,
    65-6, 69, 76, 90-1, 95, 123, 131-2,
    158, 161, 165, 167-8, 172-3, 178, 195,
    203-4, 215-18, 226, 235, 242, 247-8,
    260, 266, 268-9, 273, 282, 288, 298-9,
    307, 310, 315, 319, 322, 323, 325-6,
    329, 331-3, 336, 354, 357-8, 372, 393;
    agriculture 3, 4, 172, 215-17;
    demography 3, 15, 60-1, 65, 69, 215,

247-8; labour and 90-1, 95;
    provincial governments 38-9, 268-9,
    319, 329, 332
Quebec Symphony Orchestra 289
Queen's Quarterly 11
Queen's University. 193, 236, 282, 293,
    349
Queen's University Alumni Conference
    (1900) 13

RCAF. *See* Defence, air force
Railways 3, 6-7, 27, 29, 33-4, 55, 61,
    63-4, 66, 68, 70, 74-6, 79-80, 83, 170,
    177-9, 181, 183, 205, 211, 217,
    219-20, 240, 242, 251, 264, 284, 286,
    357, 381
Ralston, J.L. 242, 332-3, 342
Rationing 176, 276, 352-3, 368-9, 371,
    375-8
Rauschenbusch, Walter 88
Reciprocity Agreement (with US) 46-7,
    49-50, 134, 224
Reconstruction (post-World War
    II) 387-98
Reconstruction Bill 391-2
Reconstruction party 267
Red Cross 158, 164
Regina *Leader* 139
Relief. *See* Welfare
Relief Corps 256
Religion 12-13, 21, 37, 41, 43-4, 46-7,
    87, 91-2, 101, 123-4, 136, 155-6, 161,
    167, 189, 191-2, 194-6, 200-2, 207,
    213, 232, 280, 286, 290, 310, 318,
    329, 331, 334, 378, 386;
    Anglican 13, 51, 90, 131-2, 191;
    Baptist 13; Christian Science 390;
    Congregational 280;
    Doukhobors 213; Freemasons 51;
    Hutterites 213; Jehovah's
    Witnesses 286, 386; Lutheran 13;
    Mennonites 213; Methodist 13, 21,
    87-91, 101, 124, 132, 280;
    Orangemen 51; Presbyterian 13, 21,
    90-1, 101, 202, 280, 378;

424   Index

Protestants 13, 21, 44, 87-8, 90, 92, 136, 155-6, 161, 168, 195; Roman Catholics 12-3, 37, 43-4, 46-7, 56, 90-1, 100, 123, 131-2, 161, 167-8, 192, 194-5, 232, 310, 318, 331; United Church 280
Rhodes, E.N. 205
Riddell, Walter 307, 310
Ridley College 159
Ritsohl, Albrecht 88
Riverside Church 201
Roberts, Charles G.D. 191
Robertson, Gideon 129, 163, 166
Robertson, John Ross 53
Robertson, Norman 296
Roblin, Rodmond 91
Rockefeller, John D., Jr. 201
Rogers, Norman 272, 293
Rogers, Robert 52
Roosevelt, Franklin Delano 259, 267, 296, 312, 336, 340
Ross, Charles 174. See also Ross Rifle
Ross Rifle 122, 141
Rostow, W.W. 62
Rousseau, Alfred 288
Rowell, Newton Wesley 91, 124, 128-9, 240, 273, 300
Rowell-Sirois Commission. See Royal commissions
Royal Bank of Canada 77, 184
Royal Canadian Mounted Police 166-7, 256, 341, 386
Royal Canadian Navy. See Defence, navy
Royal commissions 96, 162, 167, 178, 241, 257, 260, 266, 273-6; Dominion-Provincial Relations (Rowell-Sirois Commission) 273-5, 277, 293, 323, 396; on labour 96, 162, 167; on Maritime Claims (Duncan Commission) 205, 241; on national radio network (1929) 260, 287; on Price Spreads and Mass Buying 257, 266; Smith-Drayton-Acworth Commission 178

Royal Society of Canada 187
Russell, Bertrand 110
Russell, Robert 165
Rutherford, Ernest 199
Ryerson (publisher) 292

Safeway 211
San Carlo Opera Company 289
Santayana, George 37
Saskatchewan 3, 38-9, 43, 60, 65, 158, 188, 204, 241, 252-3, 255, 274, 285, 330, 358, 360, 371-2
Saunders, Margaret Marshall 191
Scheldt Campaign (for Antwerp) 344
Scott, F.R. 276, 293, 280, 381
Scott Act (1878) 90
Senate 26, 30, 227
Shaw, George Bernard 188, 193
Sheard, Verna 191
Shell Committee 122, 174
Shortt, Andrew 193
Siegfried, André 41, 47-8, 194
Sifton, Arthur 129
Sifton, Clifford 38, 44, 46-7, 52, 54, 56, 61, 97, 103, 159, 398
Simon, John 303
Simonds, Guy 343
Simpson, James 87, 89, 93
Simpson, R.M. 52
Simpson's 15, 74
Sirois, Joseph 273
Skelton, Alex 273, 276
Skelton, O.D. 5, 236, 239, 295-6, 299-300, 301-3, 309-10, 314-15
Smith, A.E. 89, 280
Smith, A.J.M. 280
Smith, David 51
Smith, Ralph 96
Smuts, J.C. 232
Social Credit party 262, 264-5, 267, 270-2, 275, 277, 317
Social Gospel 88-9, 98, 100, 102-3, 168, 280
Social Service Council of Canada 87, 91, 93

Social services 27, 32, 75, 87-92, 185,
    202, 206, 208, 211, 226-7, 255,
    329-30; provincial responsibility 27,
    32, 239-43, 255
Socialism 87-93, 97, 101, 203, 266, 280,
    318, 329-30, 335, 389-90, 397; labour
    and 93, 97, 203; religion and 87-8,
    280; social reform and 87-92, 101-5,
    125, 185, 202, 208, 266, 276, 280,
    326, 329-30, 335, 390-1, 397
Socialist Party of Canada 97
Somme offensive 144
Spanish Civil War 310-11
Spencer's 74
Sports 194, 196-7, 280, 285-8
St Laurent, Louis 323-5, 333
St Lawrence Seaway 268
Stacey, Charles P. 42, 237-8, 325, 344
Statute of Westminster 301
Stead, Robert 155
Steel Company of Canada 74
Stevens, H.H. 266-7
Strange Death of Liberal England 389
Strathcona, Lord (Donald Smith) 86
Strikes 94, 96, 98-9, 134-5, 161-2, 164,
    167, 322, 381-3; mining 99;
    railway 96; Winnipeg General
    Strike 134-5, 164-7
Superman (comics) 378
Supreme Court 26, 240

Taft, W.H. 114
Tariffs 28, 33-4, 68, 70-3, 80, 108, 112,
    134-5, 202-5, 219, 223-5, 252-3,
    260-1, 295, 298, 395; National
    Policy 68, 70, 108, 134; 'New
    National Policy' 134, 136
Tarte, Israel 38, 42
Taschereau, Louis-Alexandre 268-9,
    330
Taxation 28, 30, 34-5, 75, 157, 160,
    163, 180-1, 204, 223-6, 241-2, 252,
    262-5, 273-7, 330, 351-2, 359, 362-3,
    375, 377-8, 392-3, 396-7; on bank
    note circulation 180; of

corporations 30, 180-1, 226, 241-2,
    273, 275, 362; of gasoline 30, 226,
    241, 276; on insurance
    premiums 180; of liquor 30, 157,
    226, 241, 276, 326, 377-8; of personal
    income 30, 75, 160, 163, 180-1, 226,
    241-2, 252, 262-5, 273, 275, 330, 352,
    362; powers of 28, 30, 81, 226,
    241-2, 262-3, 265, 273-7, 397; sales
    tax (federal) 226, 241
    (provincial) 226; on trust and loan
    companies 180; war profits tax 180
Taylor 'Cyclone' 196
Temiskaming and Northern Ontario
    Railroad 66
Teskey, Adelaide M. 191
The 49th Parallel (movie) 386
Thompson, John 108
Thompson, Phillip 51
Time 297
Tolmie, S.F. 264
Toronto District Labour Council 98
Toronto *Globe* 42, 53, 117, 235
Toronto News 42, 54, 131
Toronto Star 10, 12, 199, 235
Toronto Symphony Orchestra 286, 289
Toronto *Telegram* 53
Towers, Graham 362
Trade 4, 6, 62-3, 70-3, 80-1, 99, 108,
    169, 172-4, 180, 217-21, 223-5,
    249-50, 252-3, 260, 268, 295-6, 311,
    350-2, 358, 360-1, 364-5, 368-9, 371,
    377, 394-6; exports 4, 6, 62-3, 70-2,
    80-1, 108, 172-4, 180, 217-21, 223-5,
    249-50, 252-3, 268, 295, 351, 360-1,
    364-5, 369, 371, 395-6; imports 63,
    72-3, 99, 108, 169, 180, 223-5, 351-2,
    358, 361, 364-5, 377, 395
Trades and Labour Congress (TLC). *See*
    Labour unions
Trans-Canada Airlines 356
Transfer payments to provinces 28, 30,
    34, 226, 242, 273
Transportation 4, 7, 9, 27, 31, 34, 64-5,
    73, 78, 113, 150, 169, 172, 177-9,

189, 218, 354, 357, 372, 377-8
Trente Arpents 292
Trust and mortgage companies. *See* Financial institutions
Tupper, Charles 39, 42
Turner, Richard 143

Underhill, Frank 280, 293, 300, 304
Unemployment 151, 161, 165, 167, 171, 175, 218-20, 246, 248-9, 252, 255-6, 259-60, 262-6, 273, 292, 295, 317, 329, 334, 352, 355-6, 360-5, 373, 379-81, 392-4
Unemployment insurance 75, 185, 226-7, 266, 274, 276, 380, 389
Unemployment Relief Act 262-3
Union of Canadian Municipalities 101
Union Government (1917) 128-35, 137, 156, 159-60, 163-4, 202-3, 230, 324
Union Nationale 268, 299, 320
United Brotherhood of Railway Employees. *See* Labour
United Empire Loyalist Association 51
United Farmers 135-6, 203, 205, 207, 208; of Alberta 136, 207-8; of Manitoba 136; of Ontario 135, 203, 205, 207
United States 3, 35, 41, 43, 46, 111-12, 114, 192, 194-5, 201, 217, 224-5, 231-4, 237-8, 249, 253, 257, 259, 268, 279-81, 284-5, 288-90, 296, 302-4, 323, 336, 339-40, 342-4, 347-8, 350, 357-8, 360-2, 364-9, 378, 382, 386, 394-6, 398; Canadians in 3, 201, 398; relations with 35, 41, 43, 46, 111-12, 114, 201, 217, 224-5, 231-4, 337-8, 253, 268, 280, 284-5, 288-90, 296, 302, 304, 336, 347-8, 350-1, 357-8, 360, 364-9
Université Laval 192, 194
Université de Montréal 293
University of Alberta 194
University of British Columbia 264-5, 281, 293
University of Cambridge 194, 201

University of Chicago 201
University of Manitoba 258
University of Toronto 153, 193-4, 201, 222, 282-3, 291, 293, 296, 304, 349
University of Western Ontario 194, 282
Utilities 75-6, 79, 100-2, 218, 226, 268, 331, 382

Vancouver Symphony Orchestra 289
Vanier, Georges 296
Veblen, Thorstein 86
Versailles, Treaty of 230-2, 239, 304-5
Verville, Alphonse 98
Veterans: World War I 150-2, 223, 226, 235-6; World War II 329, 389-90
Victory Bonds 363
'Victory Gardens' 376
Villeneuve, Cardinal 158
Vimy Ridge 127, 147, 154
Von Kunits, Luigi 289
Von Neurath, Baron 313
Vulcan Iron Works 356

Wage and price controls 322, 351-2, 370, 380, 382, 390-1, 393
Wages 162, 164-5, 252, 256-7, 263-4, 292, 296, 322, 330, 376, 378, 380. *See also* Prices and wages
Walters, James 163
War Exchange Conservation Act (1940) 369
War Exchange Tax (1940) 364, 369
War Measures Act 121, 351, 362, 381, 383, 385
War Production Board (US) 367-8
War Savings Stamps and Certificates 363
War Service Gratuity 151
War Supply Board 319, 322, 353
Wartime Bureau of Technical Personnel 380
Wartime Elections Act 129, 158, 203
Wartime housing 376
Wartime Information Board 384
Wartime Oils Limited 359

Wartime Prices and Trade Board 371
Weaver, John 102
Weber, Max 103, 193
Weir, G.M. 281
Welfare 226-7, 249, 253, 255-7, 259-60,
   262-7, 273, 276, 295, 396
Western Air Command (RCAF) 345
Westminster Abbey 311
Wheat. See Agriculture
White, Thomas 180-2, 184
White Paper on Employment and
   Income 334, 397
Whitney, James 45, 125
Wickett, S. Morley 102-3
Wilhelm II 109-10, 112, 120, 131
William Davies Company 173
Williams, J.S. 51
Willison, John 38, 42, 54
Willys-Overland of Canada 175
Wilson, Woodrow 303
Winnipeg Free Press 255, 273, 297
Winnipeg General Strike. See Strikes
Winnipeg Grain Exchange 354, 372
Womans' Christian Temperance Union
   (WCTU) 92, 157
Women's issues 30, 80, 90, 92-3, 129,
   131, 154, 157-9, 161, 164, 208, 213,
   248-9, 256-7, 282, 331, 350, 379; and
   education 283; and prohibition 90,
   92, 154, 157, 159; and social
   services 92; suffrage 30, 90, 92-3,
   131, 154, 157-9, 161, 208, 331; war
   effort 154, 157, 350, 379; in
   workforce 80, 92, 154, 158-9, 164,
   213, 248-9, 256-7, 379
Wood, Elizabeth Wyn 291
Wood, Henry Wise 135-6
Woods, H.O. 382
Woodsworth, J.S. 2-3, 14-17, 21, 89,
   105, 165, 204, 206, 227, 280, 318
Woodward's 74
Woolworth 75
Wordsworth, William 281
Workers' Unity League. See Labour
Workmen's Compensation 75

World Bank 394
'World in Action' (NFB series) 384
World War I 110, 119-23, 126-7,
   139-45, 150-1, 153, 169, 172, 188,
   194, 200, 202, 212, 223, 230, 262,
   300-2, 317, 335, 339, 351, 362-3, 370,
   375, 380, 384; casualties 150-1,
   230-1, 350
World War II 169, 180-1, 246, 274-5,
   315-19, 322, 326, 332-3, 335, 337-48,
   351, 363, 375, 379-80, 384;
   casualties 332, 341, 344-5, 347, 350
Wright, Orville and Wilbur 23
Wrong, Hume 296-7, 301, 311

YMCA 299
Ypres 140, 143, 147, 154